Taste of Home's
Holiday
Get-Togethers

Taste of Home.

A TASTE OF HOME/READER'S DIGEST BOOK

Editor: Heidi Reuter Lloyd
Senior Art Director: Sandra Ploy
Proofreader: Jean Steiner
Editorial Assistant: Barb Czysz
Food Editor: Janaan Cunningham
Senior Recipe Editor: Sue A. Jurack
Food Photography: Reiman Photo Studio

Senior Editor/Retail Books: Jennifer Olski
Executive Editor/Books: Heidi Reuter Lloyd
Creative Director: Ardyth Cope
Senior Vice President/Editor in Chief: Catherine Cassidy
President: Barbara Newton
Founder: Roy Reiman

Pictured on front cover:
Turkey with Sausage-Pecan Stuffing (pg. 150), Broccoli with Cheese Sauce (pg. 57),
Cherry Cream Torte (pg. 194) and Italian Horn Cookies (pg. 273).
Cover photo by: Dan Roberts

International Standard Book Number (10): 0-89821-495-5
International Standard Book Number (13): 978-0-89821-495-6
Library of Congress Control Number: 2006925159

For other Taste of Home books and products, visit www.tasteofhome.com.
For more Reader's Digest products and information, visit
www.rd.com (in the United States)
www.rd.ca (in Canada)

Printed in China.
3 5 7 9 10 8 6 4 2

Taste of Home's
Holiday
Get-Togethers

549 Delicious Recipes for a Festive Holiday Season!

The holidays bring together family, friends, food and fun. This cookbook contains 549 recipes to help you share the joy of the season with those close to you. Whether you're planning a casual get-together or a sit-down dinner for Thanksgiving, Christmas, New Year's Day or another special occasion, you can plan the perfect menu.

Taste of Home's Holiday Get-Togethers is packed with more than 500 festive recipes that taste delicious and look great. You'll find holiday favorites from families just like yours. Plus, new ideas allow you to experiment using tried-and-true family recipes from fellow cooks.

This collection has some of the best, most-requested recipes published by *Taste of Home* and its sister publications. If you're not familiar with *Taste of Home*, it's the most popular cooking magazine in the world.

Each recipe we print comes from great cooks across the country who've been serving their specialties to appreciative loved ones for years. After these home cooks share their favorites, the home economists in our Taste of Home Test Kitchen prepare and try every dish.

Many of the recipes have gorgeous, full-color photos, so you can see how they look before you make them. We know from our own experience that makes it easier on the cook.

We hope you'll enjoy *Taste of Home's Holiday Get-Togethers* and the dishes it contains. All of us here at *Taste of Home* wish you and yours a happy holiday season!

Breakfast & Brunch

Morning Mix-Up, page 19

Tomato Quiche

(Pictured above)

I first tried this recipe at a family gathering and loved it! It is a great meatless brunch dish, served hot or cold. This is my most-requested dish for parties and a fairly simple one to make. Enjoy! —Heidi Anne Quinn
West Kingston, Rhode Island

- 1 cup chopped onion
- 2 tablespoons butter
- 4 large tomatoes, peeled, chopped, seeded and drained
- 1 teaspoon salt
- 1/4 teaspoon pepper
- 1/4 teaspoon dried thyme
- 2 cups (8 ounces) shredded Monterey Jack cheese, *divided*
- 1 unbaked pastry shell (10 inches)
- 4 eggs
- 1-1/2 cups half-and-half cream

In a skillet, saute onion in butter until tender. Add tomatoes, salt, pepper and thyme. Cook over medium-high heat until liquid is almost evaporated, about 10-15 minutes. Remove from heat.

Sprinkle 1 cup cheese into pastry shell. Cover with tomato mixture; sprinkle with remaining cheese. In a mixing bowl, beat eggs until foamy. Stir in half-and-half cream; mix well. Pour into pastry shell.

Bake at 425° for 10 minutes. Reduce heat to 325°; bake 40 minutes more or until top begins to brown and a knife inserted near the center comes out clean. Let stand 10 minutes before cutting. **Yield:** 6-8 servings.

Cranberry Kuchen

This German coffee cake has been served at family breakfasts for more than five generations. There is no recipe requested more by our large family.
—Linda Bright, Wichita, Kansas

- 2 packages (1/4 ounce *each*) active dry yeast
- 1/4 cup warm water (110° to 115°)
- 1 cup warm milk (110° to 115°)
- 1/4 cup butter, softened
- 1/4 cup sugar
- 1 teaspoon salt
- 1 egg
- 3-1/2 to 4 cups all-purpose flour

CRANBERRY SAUCE:
- 2 cups water
- 1-1/2 cups sugar
- 4 cups fresh *or* frozen cranberries

EGG MIXTURE:
- 8 eggs
- 3/4 cup evaporated milk
- 3/4 cup sugar

TOPPING:
- 2 cups all-purpose flour
- 2 cups sugar
- 1 cup cold butter

In a mixing bowl, dissolve yeast in warm water. Add milk, butter, sugar, salt, egg and 2 cups flour. Beat until smooth. Stir in enough remaining flour to form a soft dough. Do not knead. Cover; let rise in a warm place until doubled, about 1 hour.

Meanwhile, in a saucepan, bring water and sugar to a boil. Add cranberries. Reduce heat; cover and simmer for 10 minutes. Remove from the heat; set aside.

In a bowl, combine the eggs, evaporated milk and sugar; beat well. Divide half of the egg mixture between two greased 13-in. x 9-in. x 2-in. baking pans; set remaining egg mixture aside.

Punch dough down. Divide in half. Pat each portion over egg mixture in pans. Spoon cranberry sauce over dough. Drizzle with remaining egg mixture.

For topping, combine flour and sugar in a bowl. Cut in butter until crumbly; sprinkle over the top. Bake at 350° for 25-30 minutes or until lightly browned. **Yield:** 2 kuchens.

Stuffed Apricot French Toast

(Pictured below)

In our family, this special recipe is often served for our Christmas Day brunch. I was always looking for something unique to serve, and this rich, colorful dish certainly fills the bill. It tastes so good! —Deb Leland
Three Rivers, Michigan

1	package (8 ounces) cream cheese, softened
1-1/2	teaspoons vanilla extract, *divided*
1/2	cup finely chopped walnuts
1	loaf (1-1/2 pounds) French bread
4	eggs
1	cup heavy whipping cream
1/2	teaspoon ground nutmeg
1	jar (12 ounces) apricot preserves
1/2	cup orange juice

In a mixing bowl, beat cream cheese and 1 teaspoon vanilla until fluffy. Stir in nuts; set aside.

Cut bread into 1-1/2-in. slices; cut a pocket in the top of each slice. Fill each pocket with about 2 tablespoons of cream cheese mixture.

In another bowl, beat eggs, cream, nutmeg and remaining vanilla. Dip both sides of bread into egg mixture, being careful not to squeeze out the filling. Cook on a lightly greased griddle until golden brown on both sides. Place on an ungreased baking sheet; bake at 300° for 20 minutes.

Meanwhile, combine preserves and orange juice in a small saucepan; heat through. Drizzle over hot French toast. **Yield:** about 8 servings.

Bacon and Eggs Casserole

(Pictured above)

Because it requires so little time to prepare and is such a great hit with family and friends alike, this is a favorite of mine to make for brunches. Served with a fruit salad, hot muffins and croissants, it's excellent for an after-church brunch. —Deanna Durward-Orr
Windsor, Ontario

4	bacon strips
18	eggs
1	cup milk
1	cup (4 ounces) shredded cheddar cheese
1	cup (8 ounces) sour cream
1/4	cup sliced green onions
1	to 1-1/2 teaspoons salt
1/2	teaspoon pepper

In a skillet over medium heat, cook bacon until crisp; drain. In a large bowl, beat eggs. Add milk, cheese, sour cream, onions, salt and pepper. Pour into a greased 3-qt. baking dish. Crumble bacon and sprinkle on top.

Bake, uncovered, at 325° for 40-45 minutes or until a knife inserted near the center comes out clean. Let stand for 5 minutes. **Yield:** 8-10 servings.

Top to bottom: Apple Streusel Muffins,
Aunt Betty's Blueberry Muffins and
Lemon Raspberry Jumbo Muffins

Lemon Raspberry Jumbo Muffins

(Pictured at left)

These are my favorite muffins because they can be made with blueberries instead of raspberries with the same delicious results. —Carol Thoreson, Rockford, Illinois

> 2 cups all-purpose flour
> 1 cup sugar
> 3 teaspoons baking powder
> 1/2 teaspoon salt
> 2 eggs
> 1 cup half-and-half cream
> 1/2 cup vegetable oil
> 1 teaspoon lemon extract
> 1 cup fresh *or* frozen unsweetened raspberries

In a large bowl, combine the flour, sugar, baking powder and salt. In another bowl, combine the eggs, cream, oil and extract. Stir into the dry ingredients just until moistened. Fold in the raspberries.

Fill greased jumbo muffin cups two-thirds full. Bake at 400° for 22-25 minutes or until a toothpick comes out clean. Cool for 5 minutes before removing from pan to a wire rack. Serve warm. **Yield:** 8 jumbo muffins.

Editor's Note: If using frozen raspberries, do not thaw before adding to the batter. Sixteen regular-size muffin cups may be used; bake for 18-20 minutes.

Aunt Betty's Blueberry Muffins

(Pictured at left)

My Aunt Betty bakes many items each Christmas, but I look forward to these mouth-watering muffins the most. —Sheila Raleigh, Kechi, Kansas

> 1/2 cup old-fashioned oats
> 1/2 cup orange juice
> 1 egg
> 1/2 cup vegetable oil
> 1/2 cup sugar
> 1-1/2 cups all-purpose flour
> 1-1/4 teaspoons baking powder
> 1/2 teaspoon salt
> 1/4 teaspoon baking soda

> 1 cup fresh *or* frozen blueberries
> TOPPING:
> 2 tablespoons sugar
> 1/2 teaspoon ground cinnamon

In a large bowl, combine oats and orange juice; let stand for 5 minutes. Beat in the egg, oil and sugar until blended. Combine the flour, baking powder, salt and baking soda; stir into oat mixture just until moistened. Fold in blueberries.

Fill greased or paper-lined muffin cups two-thirds full. Combine topping ingredients; sprinkle over batter. Bake at 400° for 20-25 minutes or until a toothpick comes out clean. Cool for 5 minutes before removing from pan to a wire rack. **Yield:** about 1 dozen.

Editor's Note: If using frozen blueberries, do not thaw before adding to the batter.

Apple Streusel Muffins

(Pictured at left)

Pieces of tender apples appear in every bite of these pretty muffins. —Michele Olsen
Wessington Springs, South Dakota

> 2 cups all-purpose flour
> 1 cup sugar
> 3 teaspoons baking powder
> 1-1/4 teaspoons ground cinnamon
> 1/2 teaspoon baking soda
> 1/2 teaspoon salt
> 2 eggs
> 1 cup (8 ounces) sour cream
> 1/4 cup butter, melted
> 1-1/2 cups chopped peeled tart apples
> TOPPING:
> 1/4 cup sugar
> 3 tablespoons all-purpose flour
> 1/4 teaspoon ground cinnamon
> 2 tablespoons cold butter

In a large bowl, combine dry ingredients. In another bowl, beat the eggs, sour cream and butter. Stir into dry ingredients just until moistened. Fold in apples. Fill greased or paper-lined muffin cups two-thirds full.

For topping, combine sugar, flour and cinnamon. Cut in butter until mixture resembles coarse crumbs. Sprinkle a rounded teaspoonful over each muffin. Bake at 400° for 18-20 minutes or until a toothpick comes out clean. Cool for 5 minutes before removing from pans to wire racks. Serve warm. **Yield:** 16 muffins.

Farmer's Strata

(Pictured above)

For an inexpensive and easy-to-prepare dish, try this hearty casserole. You can assemble it ahead and bake it just before folks arrive for your holiday brunch. It includes tasty basic ingredients like bacon, cheese and potatoes.   —Pat Kuether, Westminster, Colorado

  1 **pound sliced bacon, diced**
  2 **cups chopped fully cooked ham**
  1 **small onion, chopped**
 10 **slices bread, cubed**
  1 **cup cubed cooked potatoes**
  3 **cups (12 ounces) shredded cheddar cheese**
  8 **eggs**
  3 **cups milk**
  1 **tablespoon Worcestershire sauce**
  1 **teaspoon ground mustard**
Pinch salt and pepper

In a skillet, cook bacon until crisp; add ham and onion. Cook and stir until onion is tender; drain.

In a greased 13-in. x 9-in. x 2-in. baking dish, layer half the bread cubes, potatoes and cheese. Top with all of the bacon mixture. Repeat layers of bread, potatoes and cheese.

In a bowl, beat the eggs; add milk, Worcestershire sauce, mustard, salt and pepper. Pour over all. Cover and refrigerate overnight. Remove from refrigerator 30 minutes before baking. Bake, uncovered, at 325° for 65-70 minutes or until a knife inserted near the center comes out clean. **Yield:** 12-16 servings.

Rhubarb Coffee Cake

(Pictured below)

My daughter gave me the recipe for this moist coffee cake. It mixes up quickly and is ideal for a weekend breakfast.   —Page Alexander, Baldwin City, Kansas

  1/2 **cup butter, softened**
  1/2 **cup packed brown sugar**
  1/4 **cup sugar**
    1 **egg**
    1 **teaspoon vanilla extract**
1-1/4 **cups all-purpose flour**
  3/4 **cup whole wheat flour**
    1 **teaspoon baking powder**
  1/2 **teaspoon baking soda**
  1/4 **teaspoon salt**
  1/4 **teaspoon ground cinnamon**
    1 **cup buttermilk**
    2 **cups diced fresh *or* frozen rhubarb**
TOPPING:
  1/4 **cup packed brown sugar**
1-1/2 **teaspoons ground cinnamon**
  1/2 **cup chopped walnuts**

In a mixing bowl, cream butter and sugars. Add egg and vanilla; beat until fluffy. Combine flours, baking powder, baking soda, salt and cinnamon; add to creamed mixture alternately with buttermilk, mixing well after each addition. Stir in rhubarb. Pour into a greased 13-in. x 9-in. x 2-in. baking dish.

Combine the topping ingredients; sprinkle evenly over batter. Bake at 350° for 35 minutes or until a toothpick inserted near the center comes out clean. Serve warm or at room temperature. **Yield:** 12-16 servings.

Editor's Note: If using frozen rhubarb, measure rhubarb while still frozen, then thaw completely. Drain in colander, but do not press liquid out.

Almond Croissants

These tender croissants are a little lighter than others I've tried. A close friend of mine serves these every Christmas and Easter.   *—Patricia Glass*
East Wenatchee, Washington

    1 **package (1/4 ounce) active dry yeast**
1/4 **cup warm water (110° to 115°)**
    4 **cups all-purpose flour**
1/4 **cup sugar**
    1 **teaspoon salt**
    1 **cup cold butter**
3/4 **cup warm milk (110° to 115°)**
    3 **egg yolks**
FILLING:
1/2 **cup almond paste**
    1 **egg white**
1/4 **cup confectioners' sugar**
EGG WASH:
    1 **egg white**
    1 **tablespoon water**
1/4 **cup sliced almonds**

In a bowl, dissolve yeast in warm water. In a large bowl, combine the flour, sugar and salt. Cut in butter until crumbly. Add milk and egg yolks to yeast mixture; mix well. Stir into flour mixture; mix well. Do not knead. Cover and refrigerate overnight. In a mixing bowl, beat filling ingredients until smooth.

Turn dough onto a lightly floured surface; divide in half. Roll each into a 12-in. circle; cut into eight wedges. Spread filling over wedges. Roll up from wide end and place with pointed end down 3 in. apart on ungreased baking sheets. Curve ends to form a crescent shape.

Cover and let rise in a warm place for 1 hour (dough will not double). Beat egg white and water; brush over croissants. Sprinkle with almonds. Bake at 350° for 15-20 minutes. Remove from pans to wire racks to cool. **Yield:** 16 rolls.

Brunch Time-Savers

Speed up breakfast or brunch preparations without getting up at the crack of dawn by gathering recipe ingredients together the night before.

For instance, combine biscuit or muffin ingredients (keeping dry ingredients separate from moist ingredients), and grease muffin tins so they're ready to go. Or chop vegetables and shred cheeses for omelets or scrambles; combine the egg mixture and refrigerate overnight.

Cranberry Muffins

(Pictured above)

This recipe is one of my most favorite ways to use cranberries. I've often given these fresh-baked muffins as a gift to friends, and they're always well received.
—Ronni Dufour, Lebanon, Connecticut

    2 **cups all-purpose flour**
    1 **cup sugar**
1-1/2 **teaspoons baking powder**
    1 **teaspoon ground nutmeg**
    1 **teaspoon ground cinnamon**
1/2 **teaspoon baking soda**
1/2 **teaspoon ground ginger**
1/2 **teaspoon salt**
    2 **teaspoons grated orange peel**
1/2 **cup shortening**
3/4 **cup orange juice**
    2 **eggs, beaten**
    1 **tablespoon vanilla extract**
1-1/2 **cups coarsely chopped cranberries**
1-1/2 **cups chopped pecans**

In a large bowl, combine the first nine ingredients. Cut in shortening until crumbly. Stir in orange juice, eggs and vanilla just until moistened. Fold in cranberries and pecans.

Fill greased or paper-lined muffin cups two-thirds full. Bake at 375° for 18-20 minutes or until a toothpick comes out clean. Cool in pans for 10 minutes before removing to wire racks. **Yield:** 1-1/2 dozen.

Left to right: Cranberry Cinnamon Christmas Tree Rolls and Lemon Candy Canes

Cranberry Cinnamon Christmas Tree Rolls

(Pictured at left)

These festive rolls are sure to spark lively conversations at your holiday brunch. Colorful cranberries make an appetizing addition to ordinary cinnamon rolls.
—*Margery Richmond, Lacombe, Alberta*

- 1 tablespoon active dry yeast
- 1/2 cup warm water (110° to 115°)
- 1/2 cup sour cream
- 1/4 cup butter
- 1/4 cup sugar
- 1 teaspoon salt
- 2 eggs
- 3-3/4 to 4-1/4 cups all-purpose flour

FILLING:
- 2 cups fresh *or* frozen cranberries
- 1/2 cup water
- 1-1/2 cups packed brown sugar, *divided*
- 1 cup chopped pecans
- 1/3 cup butter, softened
- 1 tablespoon ground cinnamon
- 1/4 cup butter, melted

TOPPING:
- 1/4 cup corn syrup
- 3/4 cup confectioners' sugar
- 1 tablespoon milk

Cranberries and red and green candied cherries, halved

In a mixing bowl, dissolve yeast in warm water. In a small saucepan, heat sour cream and butter to 110°-115°. Add the sour cream mixture, sugar, salt, eggs and 1-1/2 cups flour to yeast mixture. Beat on medium speed for 2 minutes. Stir in enough remaining flour to form a soft dough. Turn onto a floured surface; knead until smooth and elastic, about 6-8 minutes. Place in a greased bowl, turning once to grease top. Cover and let rise in a warm place until doubled, about 1-1/2 hours.

Meanwhile, in a saucepan, bring cranberries and water to a boil. Cover and boil gently for 5 minutes. Stir in 1/2 cup brown sugar. Reduce heat; simmer, uncovered, for 5 minutes or until thickened, stirring occasionally. Cool. Combine the pecans, softened butter, cinnamon and remaining brown sugar; set aside.

Punch dough down. Turn onto a lightly floured surface; divide in half. Roll each into a 14-in. x 12-in. rectangle. Brush each with 1 tablespoon melted butter. Spread half of the filling to within 1/2 in. of edges. Sprinkle with half of the pecan mixture. Roll up, jelly-roll style, starting with a long side;

pinch seam to seal. Brush with remaining melted butter.

To form a tree from each log, cut a 2-in. piece from one end for a tree trunk; set aside. Then cut each log into 15 slices. Cover two baking sheets with foil and grease well. Center one slice near the top of each prepared baking sheet. Arrange slice with sides touching in four more rows, adding one slice for each row, forming a tree. Center the reserved slice lengthwise below the tree for trunk. Cover and let rise until doubled, about 45 minutes.

Bake at 350° for 25-30 minutes or until golden. In a saucepan, heat corn syrup over low heat. Transfer foil with trees onto wire racks; brush with corn syrup. Cool for 20 minutes.

Combine confectioners' sugar and milk. Fill a small pastry or plastic bag; cut a small hole in corner of bag. Pipe on trees for garlands. Garnish with cranberries and candied cherries. **Yield:** 2 trees (16 rolls each).

Lemon Candy Canes

(Pictured at left)

We enjoy looking at these cute candy cane rolls as much as we love eating them! For even more festive fun, I sometimes decorate them with sliced candied cherries.
—*Marie Frangpane, Eugene, Oregon*

- 1 package (1/4 ounce) active dry yeast
- 1/2 cup warm water (110° to 115°)
- 1/3 cup sour cream
- 1 egg
- 3 tablespoons butter, softened
- 3 tablespoons sugar
- 1 teaspoon salt
- 2-3/4 to 3 cups all-purpose flour

FILLING:
- 1/2 cup finely chopped walnuts *or* pecans
- 1/3 cup sugar
- 3 tablespoons butter, melted
- 1 tablespoon grated lemon peel

LEMON ICING:
- 1 cup confectioners' sugar
- 1 tablespoon lemon juice
- 1 tablespoon water
- 1/4 teaspoon vanilla extract

In a mixing bowl, dissolve yeast in warm water. Add the sour cream, egg, butter, sugar, salt and 1-1/4 cups flour. Beat un-

Lemon Candy Canes continued on page 14 ➲

↩ *Lemon Candy Canes* continued from page 13

til smooth. Stir in enough remaining flour to form a soft dough. Turn onto a floured surface; knead until smooth and elastic, about 6-8 minutes. Place in a greased bowl, turning once to grease top. Cover and let rise in a warm place until doubled, about 1 hour.

Punch dough down. Turn onto a lightly floured surface; divide in half. Let rest for 10 minutes. Roll each into a 12-in. x 8-in. rectangle. In a bowl, combine filling ingredients; mix well. Spread half of filling over dough to within 1/2 in. of edges. Fold in half lengthwise; pinch seam to seal. Cut into 12 strips. Holding both ends of strip, twist each strip three or four times. Place 2 in. apart on greased baking sheets. Curve one end to form a cane. Cover and let rise until doubled, about 30 minutes.

Bake at 375° for 12-14 minutes or until golden brown. Remove from pans to wire racks to cool. Combine icing ingredients; drizzle over rolls. **Yield:** 2 dozen.

Fruity Breakfast Sauce

(Pictured below)

This is our family's favorite breakfast topping. Sometimes I'll substitute cherry pie filling for the blueberry pie filling—it's tasty, too!
—Rita Wagenmann
Grangeville, Idaho

6 cups finely chopped rhubarb
4 cups sugar
1 can (21 ounces) blueberry pie filling
1 package (3 ounces) raspberry gelatin

In a saucepan, bring rhubarb and sugar to a boil. Boil for 10 minutes. Remove from the heat; add pie filling and mix well. Bring to a boil. Remove from the heat and stir in gelatin. Store the sauce in jars or freezer containers. Refrigerate or freeze until serving. Serve with pancakes, waffles, toast or English muffins. **Yield:** 7 cups.

Quiche Lorraine

(Pictured above)

Ideal for a brunch or luncheon, this classic recipe highlights a delicious meal. Try serving a wedge with fresh fruit of the season and homemade muffins for a plate that will look as good as the food tastes!
—Marcy Cella, L'Anse, Michigan

CRUST:
2 cups all-purpose flour
1/2 teaspoon salt
3/4 cup butter-flavored shortening
3 to 4 tablespoons cold water
FILLING:
12 bacon strips, cooked and crumbled

4 **eggs**
2 **cups half-and-half cream**
1/4 **teaspoon salt**
1/8 **teaspoon ground nutmeg**
1-1/4 **cups shredded Swiss cheese**

Combine flour and salt in a bowl. Cut in shortening until crumbly. Gradually add water, tossing with a fork until dough forms a ball. Divide dough in half. On a lightly floured surface, roll half of dough to fit a 9-in. pie plate; transfer to pie plate. Trim and flute edges. Chill. Wrap remaining dough; chill or freeze for another use.

For filling, sprinkle crumbled bacon in the chilled pie crust. In a bowl, beat eggs, cream, salt and nutmeg. Stir in cheese. Pour into crust. Bake at 425° for 15 minutes. Reduce temperature to 325°; bake 30-40 minutes longer or until a knife inserted near the center comes out clean. Let stand 10 minutes before cutting. **Yield:** 6 servings.

Chocolate Cinnamon Doughnuts

(Pictured above right)

These doughnuts are a favorite of our three grown children. Make them up at night. Then the next morning, it's quick and easy to roll them out and fry them when everyone else is getting ready for the day.
—*Judi Eake, Chaffee, Missouri*

2 **eggs**
1-1/4 **cups sugar**
1/4 **cup vegetable oil**
1 **teaspoon vanilla extract**
4 **cups all-purpose flour**
1/3 **cup unsweetened cocoa**
4 **teaspoons baking powder**
1 **teaspoon ground cinnamon**
3/4 **teaspoon salt**
1/4 **teaspoon baking soda**
3/4 **cup buttermilk**
Oil for deep-fat frying
GLAZE:
4 **cups sifted confectioners' sugar**
1 **teaspoon vanilla extract**
1/2 **teaspoon ground cinnamon**
6 **tablespoons milk**

In a mixing bowl, beat eggs and sugar until mixture is thick and lemon-colored. Stir in oil and vanilla. In another bowl, combine flour, cocoa, baking powder, cinnamon, salt and baking soda. Stir into egg mixture alternately with buttermilk. Chill.

Divide dough in half and put half in the refrigerator. On a lightly floured surface, roll to 1/2-in. thickness. Cut with a 2-1/2-in. floured doughnut cutter. Repeat with remaining dough.

Heat oil in an electric skillet or deep-fat fryer to 375°; fry doughnuts until golden. Drain on paper towels. Combine glaze ingredients and dip tops of warm doughnuts. **Yield:** 2 dozen.

Doughnut Do's and Don'ts

- Doughnut shapes can be made with a doughnut cutter or with two biscuit cutters, one large and one small (for the hole).
- Chilling any doughnut dough before frying reduces the amount of oil absorbed during frying.
- Don't fill the pot more than halfway with oil to allow for bubbling and splattering.
- Fry only a few doughnuts at a time; crowding the pan will lower the oil's temperature and create greasier doughnuts.
- Cool warm doughnuts on a rack at least 10 minutes before serving.
- Unglazed doughnuts may be frozen in a plastic bag for up to 6 months.
- To reheat frozen doughnuts, place them (still frozen) on an ungreased baking sheet, lightly cover with foil and heat at 350° for 10-15 minutes.

Lemon Cheese Braid

(Pictured at left)

This recipe came from my mom, who is an excellent cook. It always gets rave reviews. Although fairly simple to make, when you finish you'll feel a sense of accomplishment because it tastes delicious and looks so impressive. —Grace Dickey, Vernonia, Oregon

    1 package (1/4 ounce) active dry yeast
    3 tablespoons warm water (110° to 115°)
1/4 cup sugar
1/3 cup milk
1/4 cup butter, melted
    2 eggs
1/2 teaspoon salt
    3 to 3-1/2 cups all-purpose flour
FILLING:
    2 packages (one 8 ounces, one 3 ounces) cream cheese, softened
1/2 cup sugar
    1 egg
    1 teaspoon grated lemon peel
ICING:
1/2 cup confectioners' sugar
    2 to 3 teaspoons milk
1/4 teaspoon vanilla extract

In a mixing bowl, dissolve yeast in warm water; let stand for 5 minutes. Add sugar, milk, butter, eggs, salt and 2 cups flour; beat on low speed for 3 minutes. Stir in enough of the remaining flour to form a soft dough. Knead on a floured surface until smooth and elastic, about 6-8 minutes. Place in a greased bowl, turning once to grease top. Cover and let rise in a warm place until doubled, about 1 hour. Meanwhile, beat filling ingredients in a mixing bowl until fluffy; set aside.

Punch dough down. On a floured surface, roll into a 14-in. x 12-in. rectangle. Place on a greased baking sheet. Spread filling down center third of rectangle. On each long side, cut 1-in.-wide strips, 3 in. into center. Starting at one end, fold alternating strips at an angle across filling. Seal end. Cover and let rise for 30 minutes.

Bake at 375° for 25-30 minutes or until golden brown. Cool. Combine icing ingredients; drizzle over bread. **Yield:** 12-14 servings.

Hash Brown Quiche

(Pictured at left)

We love to have guests stay with us, and this is a great dish to serve for breakfast. To save time in the morning, I sometimes make the hash brown crust and chop the ham, cheese and peppers the night before. —Jan Peters, Chandler, Minnesota

    3 cups frozen loose-pack shredded hash browns, thawed
1/3 cup butter, melted
    1 cup diced fully cooked ham
    1 cup (4 ounces) shredded cheddar cheese
1/4 cup diced green pepper
    2 eggs
1/2 cup milk
1/2 teaspoon salt
1/4 teaspoon pepper

Press hash browns between paper towel to remove excess moisture. Press into the bottom and up the sides of an ungreased 9-in. pie plate. Drizzle with butter. Bake at 425° for 25 minutes. Combine the ham, cheese and green pepper; spoon over the crust.

In a small bowl, beat eggs, milk, salt and pepper. Pour over all. Reduce heat to 350°; bake for 25-30 minutes or until a knife inserted near the center comes out clean. Allow to stand for 10 minutes before cutting. **Yield:** 6 servings.

Say 'Cheese'

- There are two broad categories of natural cheese: ripened (such as cheddar and Swiss) and fresh (such as cottage cheese and cream cheese).
- Cheese yields: four ounces (1/4 pound) firm, semifirm or semisoft cheese = about 1 cup grated cheese.
- Cheeses like cheddar, Swiss and Monterey Jack are easier to grate if they're cold. Hard cheeses like Parmesan and Romano are easier to handle at room temperature.
- Make food processor cleanup easier by spraying the metal blade or grating disk with nonstick cooking spray before you begin grating cheese.
- Store sweet breads, desserts and other treats containing cream cheese in the refrigerator.

Beef and Cheddar Quiche

(Pictured above)

This recipe is easy to prepare and perfect for a busy schedule. I've also made this recipe with salmon by substituting two cans for the ground beef and adding 1 tablespoon of fresh lemon juice. —*Jeanne Lee Terrace Park, Ohio*

3/4 **pound ground beef**
1 **unbaked pastry shell (9 inches)**
3 **eggs, beaten**
1/2 **cup mayonnaise**
1/2 **cup milk**
1/2 **cup chopped onion**
4 **teaspoons cornstarch**
1 **teaspoon salt**
1/2 **teaspoon pepper**
2 **cups (8 ounces) shredded cheddar cheese,** *divided*

In a skillet over medium heat, cook the beef until no longer pink. Meanwhile, line unpricked pastry shell with a double thickness of heavy-duty foil. Bake at 450° for 5 minutes. Remove foil; bake for 5 minutes more. Set aside.

Drain beef; place in a large bowl. Add the eggs, mayonnaise, milk, onion, cornstarch, salt, pepper and 1 cup cheese. Pour into crust. Bake at 350° for 35-40 minutes or until a knife inserted near the center comes out clean. If necessary, cover the edges of crust with foil to prevent overbrowning. Sprinkle with remaining cheese. Let stand 5-10 minutes before cutting. **Yield:** 6-8 servings.

Editor's Note: Reduced-fat or fat-free mayonnaise is not recomended for this recipe.

Banana Brunch Punch

(Pictured below)

A cold glass of refreshing punch really brightens a brunch. It's nice to serve a crisp beverage like this that's more special than plain juice. With bananas, orange juice and lemonade, it can add tropical flair to a winter day. —*Mary Anne McWhirter, Pearland, Texas*

6 **medium ripe bananas**
1 **can (12 ounces) frozen orange juice concentrate, thawed**
1 **can (6 ounces) frozen lemonade concentrate, thawed**
3 **cups warm water,** *divided*
2 **cups sugar,** *divided*
1 **can (46 ounces) pineapple juice**
3 **bottles (2 liters** *each***) lemon-lime soda**
Orange slices, optional

In a blender or food processor, blend bananas and concentrate until smooth. Remove half of the mixture and set aside. Add 1-1/2 cups of water and 1 cup sugar to mixture in blender; blend until smooth. Place in a large freezer container. Repeat

Potluck Eggs Benedict

(Pictured below)

This hearty breakfast dish is super served over warm fluffy biscuits. Folks can't wait to dig in to the combination of eggs, ham, cheese and asparagus.
— *Pauline van Breemen, Franklin, Indiana*

    1   pound fresh asparagus, trimmed
  3/4   cup butter
  3/4   cup all-purpose flour
    4   cups milk
    1   can (14-1/2 ounces) chicken broth
    1   pound cubed fully cooked ham
    1   cup (4 ounces) shredded cheddar cheese
    8   hard-cooked eggs, quartered
  1/2   teaspoon salt
  1/8   teaspoon cayenne pepper
   10   to 12 biscuits, warmed

Cut asparagus into 1/2-in. pieces, using only tender parts of spears. Cook in a small amount of boiling water until tender, about 5 minutes; drain. Set aside to cool.

Melt butter in a saucepan; stir in flour until smooth. Add milk and broth; bring to a boil. Cook and stir for 2 minutes. Add ham and cheese; stir until the cheese melts. Add eggs, salt, cayenne and asparagus; heat though. Serve over biscuits. **Yield:** 10-12 servings.

with remaining banana mixture, water and sugar; add to container. Cover and freeze until solid.

One hour before serving, take punch base out of freezer. Just before serving, place in a large punch bowl. Add pineapple juice and soda; stir until well blended. Garnish with orange slices if desired. **Yield:** 60-70 servings (10 quarts).

Morning Mix-Up

(Pictured above and on page 5)

This filling dish is super to serve for breakfast or supper. It's one of my family's favorites—even our daughter eats a hearty helping. Eggs, cheese, hash browns and ham go well together. — *Kim Scholting*
Springfield, Nebraska

    2   cups frozen hash browns
    1   cup chopped fully cooked ham
  1/2   cup chopped onion
    2   tablespoons vegetable oil
    6   eggs
Salt and pepper to taste
    1   cup (4 ounces) shredded cheddar cheese
Minced chives

In a large skillet, saute potatoes, ham and onion in oil for 10 minutes or until potatoes are tender. In a small bowl, beat eggs, salt and pepper. Add to the skillet; cook, stirring occasionally, until eggs are set. Remove from the heat and gently stir in cheese. Spoon onto a serving platter; sprinkle with chives. **Yield:** 4 servings.

Clockwise from left: Mary's Baked Fruit, Peach Breakfast Slush and Spiced Pears

Mary's Baked Fruit

(Pictured at left)

My family first sampled baked fruit years ago while dining out. They liked it so much I decided to create my own version. I like mine even better!
—*Mary Neville, Fredericktown, Missouri*

- 1 can (16 ounces) apricot halves, drained
- 1 can (16 ounces) pear halves, drained
- 1 can (30 ounces) whole plums, drained, halved and pitted
- 1 can (29 ounces) peach halves, drained
- 1 can (8 ounces) pineapple slices, undrained
- 1/3 cup packed brown sugar
- 1 tablespoon butter
- 1/2 teaspoon ground cinnamon
- 1/4 teaspoon ground cloves

In a greased 13-in. x 9-in. x 2-in. baking dish, starting at a 9-in. end, arrange rows of fruit in the following order: half of the apricots, pears and plums, all of the peaches, then remaining apricots, pears and plums. Drain pineapple, reserving 1/2 cup of juice. Lay pineapple over fruit in pan.

In a saucepan, combine the pineapple juice, brown sugar, butter, cinnamon and cloves. Cook and stir until sugar is dissolved and butter is melted. Pour over the fruit. Bake, uncovered, at 350° for 20-25 minutes or until mixture is heated through. **Yield:** 12-16 servings.

Breakfast Cookies

I like to give my family a hearty start in the morning, especially when they have to eat in a hurry. These easy-to-make "cookies" are perfect for breakfast on the run and really appeal to the kid in all of us.
—*Wanda Cox, Roscommon, Michigan*

- 2/3 cup butter, softened
- 2/3 cup sugar
- 1 egg, lightly beaten
- 1 teaspoon vanilla extract
- 3/4 cup all-purpose flour
- 1/2 teaspoon baking soda
- 1/2 teaspoon salt
- 1-1/2 cups old-fashioned oats
- 1/2 cup wheat germ
- 1 cup (4 ounces) shredded cheddar cheese
- 6 bacon strips, cooked and crumbled

In a mixing bowl, cream butter and sugar. Add egg and vanilla; mix well. Combine flour, baking soda and salt; add to creamed mixture and mix well. Stir in oats and wheat germ. Fold in cheese and bacon.

Drop by rounded teaspoonsful 2 in. apart onto ungreased baking sheets. Bake at 350° for 15-17 minutes or until light brown. **Yield:** about 3 dozen.

Peach Breakfast Slush

(Pictured at left)

This refreshing beverage is a favorite of mine to serve at our many brunch get-togethers. Because it's made ahead of time, I can avoid the last-minute rush before my guests arrive.
—*Karen Hamilton*
Ludington, Michigan

- 1 can (16 ounces) sliced peaches, drained
- 1 can (6 ounces) frozen orange juice concentrate, thawed
- 1-1/2 cups apricot nectar
- 2 cups chilled lemon-lime soda

In a blender, combine peaches, orange juice and nectar; blend until smooth. Pour into a freezer container; cover and freeze until firm. To serve, scoop 2/3 cup frozen mixture into a glass; add 1/3 cup soda. **Yield:** 6 servings.

Spiced Pears

(Pictured at left)

I try to serve a fruit dish with every breakfast to get some extra vitamins in our diet. Not only are these pears quick and easy to prepare, they're delicious!
—*Sue Fisher, Northfield Falls, Vermont*

- 1 can (16 ounces) pear halves
- 1/3 cup packed brown sugar
- 3/4 teaspoon ground nutmeg
- 3/4 teaspoon ground cinnamon

Drain the pears, reserving syrup; set the pears aside. Place the syrup, brown sugar, nutmeg and cinnamon in a saucepan. Bring to a boil.

Reduce the heat and simmer, uncovered, for 5 minutes, stirring frequently. Add the pears and simmer about 5 minutes more or until heated through. **Yield:** 4 servings.

Apricot Cheese Danish

(Pictured above)

My family thinks this delicious danish is a real treat. It's a treat to make, too, since you mix it up at night, then just roll it out and bake the next morning.
—*Florence Schafer, Jackson, Minnesota*

    1 package (1/4 ounce) active dry yeast
  1/4 cup warm water (110° to 115°)
    2 eggs
  1/2 cup butter, softened
  1/2 cup sour cream
    3 tablespoons sugar
    3 cups all-purpose flour
  1/4 teaspoon salt
FILLING:
    2 packages (8 ounces *each*) cream cheese,
       softened
  1/2 cup sugar
    2 egg yolks
    2 teaspoons vanilla extract
  1/4 cup apricot preserves
Confectioners' sugar

In a large mixing bowl, dissolve yeast in water. Add eggs, butter, sour cream and sugar. Gradually add 2 cups flour and salt; beat until smooth. Stir in remaining flour (dough will be soft and sticky). Place in a greased bowl. Cover; refrigerate overnight.

For filling, beat cream cheese, sugar, egg yolks and vanilla in a mixing bowl until smooth. Turn dough onto a floured surface; knead two to three times. Divide in half. Roll each half in-

to a 16-in. x 10-in. oval and place on greased baking sheets. Spread 1-1/4 cups filling over each oval to within 1 in. of edges. Fold longest side over filling; pinch edges to seal. Cover and let rise in a warm place until doubled, about 1 hour.

Bake at 375° for 20-22 minutes or until golden brown. Cool on a wire rack. Spread preserves on top. Dust with confectioners' sugar. Store in the refrigerator. **Yield:** 2 loaves.

Sheepherder's Breakfast

(Pictured below)

My sister-in-law always made this delicious breakfast dish when we were camping. It's a sure hit with the breakfast crowd! —*Pauletta Bushnell, Albany, Oregon*

    1 pound sliced bacon, diced
    1 medium onion, chopped
    2 packages (16 ounces *each*) frozen shredded hash
       brown potatoes, thawed
    7 to 10 eggs
Salt and pepper to taste
    2 cups (8 ounces) shredded cheddar cheese,
       optional
Minced fresh parsley

In a large skillet, cook bacon and onion until bacon is crisp. Remove mixture and set aside. Reserve 1/2 cup of drippings. Add hash browns to drippings; mix well. Cook over medium heat for 10 minutes, turning when browned. Stir in reserved bacon mixture.

Using a spoon, make 7 to 10 wells in hash browns. Break an egg into each well. Sprinkle with salt, pepper and cheese if desired. Cover and cook over low heat for about 10 minutes or until eggs are completely set. Garnish with parsley; serve immediately. **Yield:** 7-10 servings.

Buttermilk Pecan Waffles

(Pictured at right)

I like cooking with buttermilk. These nutty, golden waffles are my husband's favorite breakfast, so we enjoy them often. They're as easy to prepare as regular waffles, but their unique taste makes them exceptional.
—Edna Hoffman, Hebron, Indiana

- **2 cups all-purpose flour**
- **1 tablespoon baking powder**
- **1 teaspoon baking soda**
- **1/2 teaspoon salt**
- **4 eggs**
- **2 cups buttermilk**
- **1/2 cup butter, melted**
- **3 tablespoons chopped pecans**

Combine the flour, baking powder, baking soda and salt; set aside. In a mixing bowl, beat eggs until light. Add buttermilk; mix well. Add dry ingredients and beat until batter is smooth. Stir in butter.

Pour about 3/4 cup batter onto a lightly greased preheated waffle iron. Sprinkle with a few pecans. Bake according to manufacturer's directions until golden brown. **Yield:** 7 waffles (about 8 inches each).

Farm-Style Sausage Bake

This dish is a hearty meal all by itself. My family thinks it's fantastic. I hope that yours will enjoy it, too.
—Catherine O'Hara, Bridgeton, New Jersey

- **6 medium potatoes (about 2 pounds), peeled and cubed**
- **3 to 4 green onions, sliced**
- **2 garlic cloves, minced**

- **3/4 cup milk**
- **2 tablespoons butter**
- **2 egg yolks**
- **Dash *each* pepper and ground nutmeg**
- **1 pound smoked sausage links, sliced**
- **1/2 cup diced mozzarella cheese**
- **2 tablespoons grated Parmesan cheese**
- **2 tablespoons dried parsley flakes**
- **1 teaspoon dried thyme *or* sage**

Cook potatoes in boiling salted water until tender. Drain and transfer to a mixing bowl; mash potatoes. Add the onions, garlic, milk, butter, egg yolks, pepper and nutmeg; beat until light and fluffy. Stir in the sausage, cheeses and parsley.

Spoon into a greased 2-qt. baking dish. Sprinkle with thyme or sage. Bake, uncovered, at 400° for 30 minutes or until lightly browned and heated through. **Yield:** 6 servings.

Bubbling Basics

For success with baked goods, make sure your baking powder and/or baking soda is fresh. The shelf life for these products is about 6 months. After you check the expiration date, here's another way to determine freshness:

- Place 1 teaspoon baking powder in a cup and add 1/3 cup hot tap water.
- Place 1/4 teaspoon baking soda in a cup and add 2 teaspoons vinegar.

If active bubbling occurs, the products are fine to use. If not, they should be replaced.

*Top to bottom: Special Long Johns,
Bacon Potato Omelet and
Christmas Breakfast Casserole*

Bacon Potato Omelet

(Pictured at left)

For a fun way to present basic breakfast ingredients, try this family favorite. I inherited the recipe from my mother-in-law. —Nancy Meeks, Verona, Virginia

> 3 **bacon strips, diced**
> 2 **cups diced peeled potatoes**
> 1 **medium onion, chopped**
> 3 **eggs, lightly beaten**
> **Salt and pepper to taste**
> 1/2 **cup shredded cheddar cheese**

In a 9-in. nonstick skillet, cook bacon until crisp. Drain, reserving drippings. Set bacon aside. Cook potatoes and onion in drippings until tender, stirring occasionally. Add eggs, salt and pepper; mix gently. Cover and cook over medium heat until eggs are completely set. Sprinkle with cheese. Remove from heat; cover and let stand until cheese is melted. Sprinkle with bacon. Carefully run a knife around edge of skillet to loosen; transfer to a serving plate. Cut into wedges. **Yield:** 3 servings.

Christmas Breakfast Casserole

(Pictured at left)

Spicy sausage, herbs and vegetables fill this egg casserole with hearty flavor. I like to make it for Christmas breakfast. —Debbie Carter, O'Fallon, Illinois

> 1 **pound bulk Italian sausage**
> 1 **cup chopped onion**
> 1 **jar (7 ounces) roasted red peppers, drained and chopped, *divided***
> 1 **package (10 ounces) frozen chopped spinach, thawed and well drained**
> 1 **cup all-purpose flour**
> 1/4 **cup grated Parmesan cheese**
> 1 **teaspoon dried basil**
> 1/2 **teaspoon salt**
> 8 **eggs**
> 2 **cups milk**
> 1 **cup (4 ounces) shredded provolone cheese**
> **Fresh rosemary sprigs, optional**

In a skillet, cook sausage and onion over medium heat until sausage is no longer pink; drain. Transfer to a greased 3-qt. baking dish. Sprinkle with half of the red peppers and all of the spinach. In a mixing bowl, combine flour, Parmesan cheese, basil and salt. Combine eggs and milk; add to dry ingredients and mix well. Pour over spinach.

Bake at 425° for 20-25 minutes or until a knife inserted near the center comes out clean. Sprinkle with provolone cheese and remaining red peppers. Bake 2 minutes longer or until cheese is melted. Let stand 5 minutes before cutting. Garnish with rosemary if desired. **Yield:** 10-12 servings.

Special Long Johns

(Pictured at left)

My husband and I have been making these doughnuts regularly for years. He does the frying, and I whip up the frosting. —Beverly Curp, Festus, Missouri

> 3 **packages (1/4 ounce *each*) active dry yeast**
> 1/2 **cup warm water (110° to 115°)**
> 1/2 **cup shortening**
> 1 **cup boiling water**
> 1 **cup evaporated milk**
> 1/4 **teaspoon lemon extract**
> 2 **eggs**
> 1/2 **cup sugar**
> 2 **teaspoons salt**
> 1/2 **teaspoon ground nutmeg**
> 8-1/2 **to 9 cups all-purpose flour**
> **Oil for deep-fat frying**
> **FROSTING:**
> 3/4 **cup packed brown sugar**
> 6 **tablespoons butter**
> 1/3 **cup half-and-half cream**
> 3 **cups confectioners' sugar**
> 1 **teaspoon vanilla extract**

In a mixing bowl, dissolve yeast in warm water. In a small bowl, combine shortening and boiling water. Stir in milk and extract; cool to 110°-115°. Add to yeast mixture. Beat in eggs, sugar, salt and nutmeg. Add enough flour to form a soft dough. Turn onto a floured surface; knead until smooth and elastic, about 5 minutes. Cover; let rest for 10 minutes. On a floured surface, roll out dough to an 18-in. x 12-in. rectangle. Cut into 6-in. x 1-in. strips. Cover; let rise in a warm place until doubled, about 1 hour.

Heat oil in an electric skillet or deep-fat fryer to 375°. Fry dough strips in oil for 2 minutes or until golden brown, turning once. Drain on paper towels. For frosting, combine brown sugar, butter and cream in a saucepan. Bring to a boil; boil and stir for 2 minutes. Remove from the heat. Stir in confectioners' sugar and vanilla; beat with a portable mixer until creamy. Frost the long johns. **Yield:** 3 dozen.

Caramel Pecan Rolls

(Pictured above)

These rolls rise nice and high and hold their shape. And the gooey caramel sauce is scrumptious.
—Carolyn Buschkamp, Emmetsburg, Iowa

- 2 **cups milk**
- 1/2 **cup water**
- 1/2 **cup sugar**
- 1/2 **cup butter**
- 1/3 **cup cornmeal**
- 2 **teaspoons salt**
- 7 **to 7-1/2 cups all-purpose flour,** *divided*
- 2 **packages (1/4 ounce** *each***) active dry yeast**
- 2 **eggs**

TOPPING:
- 2 **cups packed brown sugar**
- 1/2 **cup butter**
- 1/2 **cup milk**
- 1/2 **to 1 cup chopped pecans**

FILLING:
- 1/4 **cup butter, softened**
- 1/2 **cup sugar**
- 2 **teaspoons ground cinnamon**

In a saucepan, combine the first six ingredients; bring to a boil, stirring frequently. Set aside to cool to 120°-130°. In a mixing bowl, combine 2 cups flour and yeast. Add cooled cornmeal mixture; beat on low until smooth. Add eggs and 1 cup of flour; mix for 1 minute. Stir in enough remaining flour to form a soft dough. Turn onto a floured surface; knead until smooth and elastic, about 6-8 minutes. Place in a greased bowl, turning once to grease top. Cover and let rise in a warm place until doubled, about 1 hour.

Combine the first three topping ingredients in a saucepan; bring to a boil, stirring occasionally. Pour into two greased 13-in. x 9-in. x 2-in. baking pans. Sprinkle with pecans; set aside. Punch dough down; divide in half. Roll each into a 15-in. x 12-in. rectangle; spread with butter.

Combine sugar and cinnamon; sprinkle over butter. Roll up dough starting with a long side; pinch seams and ends to seal. Cut each roll into 12 slices. Place 12 slices, cut side down, in each baking pan. Cover and let rise in a warm place until nearly doubled, about 30 minutes. Bake at 375° for 20-25 minutes or until golden brown. Let cool 1 minute; invert onto serving platters. **Yield:** 2 dozen.

Scrambled Egg Casserole

(Pictured below)

There's nothing nicer than a delicious egg dish you can prepare the night before so you're not "scrambling" when guests arrive. With satisfying ingredients like ham and a creamy cheese sauce, this dish is really special. *—Mary Anne McWhirter, Pearland, Texas*

8 tablespoons butter, *divided*
2 tablespoons all-purpose flour
1/2 teaspoon salt
1/8 teaspoon pepper
2 cups milk
1 cup (4 ounces) process cheese (Velveeta), shredded
1 cup cubed fully cooked ham
1/4 cup sliced green onions
12 eggs, beaten
1 can (4 ounces) mushroom stems and pieces, drained
1-1/2 cups soft bread crumbs
Additional sliced green onions, optional

In a medium saucepan, melt 2 tablespoons butter. Add flour, salt and pepper; cook and stir until mixture begins to bubble. Gradually stir in milk; cook until thickened and bubbly, stirring constantly. Remove from the heat. Add the cheese; mix well and set aside.

In a large skillet, saute ham and onions in 3 tablespoons butter until onions are tender. Add eggs; cook and stir until they begin to set. Add the mushrooms and cheese sauce; mix well. Pour into a greased 11-in. x 7-in. x 2-in. baking dish. Melt remaining butter; toss with bread crumbs. Sprinkle over top of casserole. Cover and refrigerate for 2-3 hours or overnight. Remove from refrigerator 30 minutes before baking.

Bake, uncovered, at 350° for 25-30 minutes or until top is golden. Sprinkle with onions if desired. **Yield:** 6-8 servings.

Breakfast Ham Ring

This recipe is a dandy one to have on hand! You can make it ahead and freeze it. It can also bake while you're attending church, then be ready for a brunch with friends afterward.
—Betty Becker
Columbus, Wisconsin

10 eggs
1 pound ground fully cooked ham
1 pound bulk pork sausage
1-1/2 cups soft bread crumbs
1/2 cup milk
2 tablespoons dried parsley flakes
1 tablespoon prepared horseradish

In a large bowl, lightly beat 2 eggs. Add the ham, sausage, bread crumbs, milk, parsley and horseradish; mix well. Press into a greased 6-cup ring mold.

Bake at 350° for 1-1/4 hours. Toward the end of the bak-

ing time, cook and scramble remaining eggs, seasoning as desired. Remove ring from oven and drain juices; unmold onto a serving platter. Fill the center with cooked scrambled eggs. Serve immediately. **Yield:** 8 servings.

Cranberry Nut Muffins

(Pictured above)

These are delicious, beautiful muffins. I serve them during the holidays or any time cranberries are available. The leftovers always make good breakfast treats.
—Flo Burtnett, Gage, Oklahoma

2 cups all-purpose flour
3/4 cup packed brown sugar
2 teaspoons baking powder
2 eggs
2/3 cup orange juice
1/3 cup vegetable oil
1 cup fresh *or* frozen cranberries, coarsely chopped
1 cup chopped pecans

In a large bowl, combine flour, brown sugar and baking powder. In another bowl, beat eggs. Add orange juice and oil; stir into dry ingredients just until moistened. Fold in cranberries and pecans.

Spoon into 12 greased or paper-lined muffin cups (cups will be almost full). Bake at 375° for 20 minutes or until golden brown. Remove from pan to cool on a wire rack. **Yield:** 1 dozen.

Editor's Note: Freeze muffins in freezer bags and thaw as needed.

Delicious Potato Doughnuts

(Pictured below)

I first tried these tasty treats at my sister's house and thought they were the best I've ever had. They're easy to make, and the fudge frosting tops them off well.
—*Pat Davis, Beulah, Michigan*

        2 **cups hot mashed potatoes (mashed with milk and butter)**
    2-1/2 **cups sugar**
        2 **cups buttermilk**
        2 **eggs, lightly beaten**
        2 **tablespoons butter, melted**
        2 **teaspoons baking soda**
        2 **teaspoons baking powder**
        1 **teaspoon ground nutmeg**
      1/2 **teaspoon salt**
    6-1/2 **to 7 cups all-purpose flour**
Oil for deep-fat frying
FAST FUDGE FROSTING:
        4 **cups (1 pound) confectioners' sugar**
      1/2 **cup baking cocoa**
      1/4 **teaspoon salt**
      1/3 **cup boiling water**
      1/3 **cup butter, melted**
        1 **teaspoon vanilla extract**

In a large bowl, combine potatoes, sugar, buttermilk and eggs. Stir in butter, baking soda, baking powder, nutmeg, salt and enough of the flour to form a soft dough. Turn onto a lightly floured surface; pat to 3/4-in. thickness. Cut with a 2-

1/2-in. floured doughnut cutter. In an electric skillet, heat 1 in. of oil to 375°. Fry the doughnuts for 2 minutes per side or until browned. Drain on paper towels. For frosting, sift sugar, cocoa and salt into a large bowl. Stir in water, butter and vanilla. Dip tops of warm doughnuts in frosting. **Yield:** 4 dozen.

Breakfast Sausage Bread

(Pictured above)

Any time we take this savory, satisfying bread to a potluck, it goes over very well. We never bring any home. —*Shirley Caldwell, Northwood, Ohio*

        2 **loaves (1 pound *each*) frozen white bread dough, thawed**
      1/2 **pound mild pork sausage**
      1/2 **pound hot pork sausage**
    1-1/2 **cups diced fresh mushrooms**
      1/2 **cup chopped onion**
        3 **eggs**
    2-1/2 **cups (10 ounces) shredded mozzarella cheese**
        1 **teaspoon dried basil**
        1 **teaspoon dried parsley flakes**
        1 **teaspoon dried rosemary, crushed**
        1 **teaspoon garlic powder**

Allow dough to rise until nearly doubled. Meanwhile, in a skillet over medium heat, cook and crumble sausage. Add mushrooms and onion. Cook and stir until the sausage is no longer pink and vegetables are tender; drain. Cool. Beat 1 egg; set aside.

To sausage mixture, add 2 eggs, cheese and seasonings; mix well. Roll each loaf of dough into a 16-in. x 12-in. rectangle. Spread half the sausage mixture on each loaf to within 1 in. of edges. Roll up jelly-roll style, starting at a narrow end; seal edges. Place on a greased baking sheet.

Bake at 350° for 25 minutes; brush with beaten egg. Bake 5-10 minutes more or until golden brown. Serve warm. **Yield:** 2 loaves.

Feather-Light Muffins

Your family will likely gobble up these airy muffins, which won me a blue ribbon at our county fair. Pretty as well as tasty, their hint of spice will brighten any breakfast. —Sonja Blow, Groveland, California

    1/3 cup shortening
    1/2 cup sugar
      1 egg
  1-1/2 cups cake flour
  1-1/2 teaspoons baking powder
    1/2 teaspoon salt
    1/4 teaspoon ground nutmeg
    1/2 cup milk
TOPPING:
    1/2 cup sugar
      1 teaspoon ground cinnamon
    1/2 cup butter, melted

In a mixing bowl, cream shortening, sugar and egg. Combine dry ingredients; add to creamed mixture alternately with milk. Fill greased muffin tins two-thirds full.

Bake at 325° for 20-25 minutes or until golden. Let cool for 3-4 minutes. Meanwhile, combine sugar and cinnamon in a small bowl. Roll warm muffins in melted butter, then in sugar mixture. Serve warm. **Yield:** 8-10 muffins.

Cranberry Crumble Coffee Cake

(Pictured at right)

This delicious coffee cake doesn't last long! People are delighted to find the ruby cranberry sauce swirled inside. —Jeani Robinson, Weirton, West Virginia

    1/4 cup chopped almonds
    1/2 cup butter, softened
      1 cup sugar
      1 teaspoon vanilla extract
      2 eggs
      2 cups all-purpose flour
  1-1/4 teaspoons baking powder
    1/2 teaspoon baking soda
    1/4 teaspoon salt
      1 cup (8 ounces) sour cream
      1 cup whole-berry cranberry sauce
TOPPING:
    1/4 cup all-purpose flour
    1/4 cup sugar
    1/4 cup chopped almonds
    1/4 teaspoon vanilla extract
      2 tablespoons cold butter

Sprinkle almonds over the bottom of a greased 9-in. springform pan; set aside. In a mixing bowl, cream the butter, sugar and vanilla; beat on medium for 1-2 minutes. Add eggs, one at a time, beating well after each addition.

Combine dry ingredients; add alternately with sour cream to creamed mixture. Mix well. Spread 3 cups over almonds. Spoon cranberry sauce over batter. Top with remaining batter. For topping, combine flour, sugar, almonds and vanilla; cut in butter until crumbly. Sprinkle over batter.

Bake at 350° for 70-75 minutes or until a toothpick inserted near the center comes out clean. Cool in pan on a wire rack for 15 minutes; remove sides of pan. Serve warm. **Yield:** 12 servings.

utes or until well blended. Cool to room temperature.

In a mixing bowl, dissolve yeast in water. Add sour cream mixture and eggs; mix well. Gradually stir in flour. (Dough will be very soft.) Cover and refrigerate overnight. For filling, combine ingredients in a mixing bowl until well blended.

Turn dough onto a floured surface; knead 5-6 times. Divide into four portions. Roll each portion into a 12-in. x 8-in. rectangle. Spread 1/4 of the filling on each to within 1 in. of edges. Roll up, jelly-roll style, starting with a long side; pinch seams and ends to seal.

Place, seam side down, on greased baking sheets. Cut six X's on top of loaves. Cover and let rise until nearly doubled, about 1 hour.

Bake at 375° for 20-25 minutes or until golden brown. Cool on wire racks. Combine the first three glaze ingredients; drizzle over loaves. Sprinkle with almonds if desired. Store in the refrigerator. **Yield:** 4 loaves.

Cream Cheese Coffee Cake

(Pictured above)

You can't just eat one slice of this treat with its rich filling peeking out of sweet yeast bread. Once you savor a piece, you'll know the extra work is worth it.
—Mary Anne McWhirter, Pearland, Texas

    1 cup (8 ounces) sour cream
  1/2 cup sugar
  1/2 cup butter
    1 teaspoon salt
    2 packages (1/4 ounce *each*) active dry yeast
  1/2 cup warm water (110° to 115°)
    2 eggs, beaten
    4 cups all-purpose flour
FILLING:
    2 packages (8 ounces *each*) cream cheese,
       softened
  3/4 cup sugar
    1 egg, beaten
    2 teaspoons vanilla extract
  1/8 teaspoon salt
GLAZE:
 2-1/2 cups confectioners' sugar
  1/4 cup milk
    1 teaspoon vanilla extract
Toasted sliced almonds, optional

In a saucepan, combine sour cream, sugar, butter and salt. Cook over medium-low heat, stirring constantly, for 5-10 min-

Ham and Potato Frittata

(Pictured below)

Easy and delicious, this hearty dish's been appreciated whenever I've served it...breakfast, lunch or dinner. Reheated or cold, the leftovers are also great!
—Katie Dreibelbis, State College, Pennsylvania

    3 tablespoons butter, *divided*
    1 pound red potatoes, cooked and sliced

1-1/2 cups thinly sliced fresh mushrooms
1 cup thinly sliced onion
1 sweet red pepper, cut into thin strips
2 cups diced fully cooked ham
2 teaspoons minced fresh garlic
1 tablespoon olive oil
1/2 cup minced fresh parsley *or* basil
8 eggs
Salt and pepper to taste
1-1/2 cups (6 ounces) shredded cheddar *or* Swiss cheese

In a 10-in. cast-iron or other ovenproof skillet, melt 2 tablespoons butter. Brown potatoes over medium-high heat. Remove and set aside. In the same skillet, melt the remaining butter; saute the mushrooms, onion, red pepper, ham and garlic over medium-high heat until vegetables are tender. Remove and set aside.

In the same skillet, heat oil over medium-low. Add potatoes, ham/vegetable mixture and parsley. In a bowl, beat eggs, salt and pepper. Pour into skillet; cover and cook for 10-15 minutes or until eggs are nearly set.

Preheat broiler; place uncovered skillet 6 in. from the heat for 2 minutes or until eggs are set. Sprinkle with cheese and broil until melted. Cut into wedges. **Yield:** 6 servings.

Sweet Pineapple Muffins

The sweetness of pineapple shines through in these tasty muffins. They're sure to be gobbled up in no time! —Tina Hanson, Portage, Wisconsin

2 cups all-purpose flour
2 cups sugar
1 teaspoon baking soda
1 teaspoon baking powder
2 cans (8 ounces *each*) crushed pineapple, undrained
2 eggs
1/2 cup vegetable oil

In a large bowl, combine flour, sugar, baking soda and baking powder. In another bowl, mix pineapple, eggs and oil; stir into the dry ingredients just until moistened. Fill greased or paper-lined muffin cups two-thirds full.

Bake at 350° for 20-25 minutes or until a toothpick comes out clean. Cool in pan for 10 minutes before removing to a wire rack. **Yield:** about 20 muffins.

Drop Doughnuts

(Pictured above)

For over 35 years, I've been using leftover mashed potatoes to make these light and fluffy doughnuts. The recipe was originally created by my neighbor's mother-in-law. The doughnuts are great for breakfast or as a snack anytime. —Marilyn Kleinfall Elk Grove Village, Illinois

1/2 cup mashed potatoes (prepared with milk and butter)
1/4 cup sugar
1 egg, beaten
1/2 cup sour cream
1/2 teaspoon vanilla extract
1-1/2 cups all-purpose flour
1/2 teaspoon baking soda
1/4 teaspoon baking powder
Oil for deep-fat frying
Additional sugar *or* confectioners' sugar, optional

In a bowl, combine potatoes, sugar, egg, sour cream and vanilla. Combine the flour, baking soda and baking powder; stir into potato mixture.

Heat oil in an electric skillet or deep-fat fryer to 375°. Drop dough by teaspoonfuls, 5 to 6 at a time, into hot oil. Fry for 1 minute on each side or until golden brown. Drain on paper towels. Roll in sugar if desired. Serve immediately. **Yield:** 3 to 3-1/2 dozen.

Egg and Sausage Strata

(Pictured above)

I especially like to make this breakfast dish when we have weekend guests. I fix it the night before, and the next morning I can sit, eat and enjoy their company.
—Gail Carney, Arlington, Texas

- 12 slices white bread, crusts removed, cubed
- 1-1/2 pounds bulk pork sausage
- 1/3 cup chopped onion
- 1/4 cup chopped green pepper
- 1 jar (2 ounces) chopped pimientos, drained
- 6 eggs
- 3 cups milk
- 2 teaspoons Worcestershire sauce
- 1 teaspoon ground mustard
- 1/2 teaspoon salt
- 1/4 teaspoon pepper
- 1/4 teaspoon dried oregano

Line a greased 13-in. x 9-in. x 2-in. pan with bread cubes; set aside. In a skillet, cook sausage with the onion and green pepper over medium heat until meat is no longer pink; drain. Stir in pimientos; sprinkle over bread. In a bowl, beat eggs, milk, Worcestershire sauce, mustard, salt, pepper and oregano. Pour over sausage mixture.

Cover and refrigerate overnight. Cover and bake at 325° for 1 hour and 20 minutes. Uncover and bake 10 minutes longer or until a knife inserted near the center comes out clean. Let stand 10 minutes before serving. **Yield:** 12-15 servings.

Berry Cream Coffee Cake

Raspberry preserves are in the fruity filling for this delightful coffee cake. —Marjorie Miller, Haven, Kansas

- 1 package (3 ounces) cream cheese
- 1/4 cup cold butter
- 2 cups biscuit/baking mix
- 1/3 cup milk
- 1/2 cup raspberry preserves

GLAZE:
- 1 cup confectioners' sugar
- 1 to 2 tablespoons milk
- 1/2 teaspoon vanilla extract

With a pastry blender, cut cream cheese and butter into biscuit mix until mixture resembles coarse crumbs. Stir in milk just until moistened. Turn onto a floured surface; knead 8-10 times or until dough is smooth.

On waxed paper, roll dough into a 12-in. x 8-in. rectangle. Turn onto a greased 15-in. x 10-in. x 1-in. baking pan. Spread preserves down center third of rectangle. On each long side, cut 1-in.-wide strips about 2-1/2 in. into center.

Starting at one end, fold alternating strips at an angle across preserves. Seal end. Bake at 425° for 12-15 minutes. Combine glaze ingredients and drizzle over top. **Yield:** 8-10 servings.

Hot Fruit Compote

This simple-to-prepare compote is a tasty way to get fruit into your meal when fresh fruit is not plentiful. Perfect with ham, pork, chicken or turkey, this dish can also help to stretch a meal when guests pop in.
—Judy Kimball, Haverhill, Massachusetts

- 1 can (12 ounces) frozen orange juice concentrate, thawed
- 2 tablespoons cornstarch
- 2 pounds apples, peeled, cored and sliced
- 1 can (15 ounces) pitted dark sweet cherries, drained
- 1-1/2 cups fresh *or* frozen cranberries
- 1 can (8 ounces) pineapple chunks, drained
- 1 package (6 ounces) dried apricots, cooked and drained
- 1/4 cup apple juice, optional

In a large bowl, combine orange juice concentrate and corn-starch; stir until smooth. Add fruit; stir to coat. Pour into a buttered 3-qt. casserole. If desired, pour apple juice over all. Cover and bake at 350° for 50-60 minutes or until hot and bubbly. **Yield:** 12 servings.

Cherry Cream Scones

(Pictured below)

These scones freeze well. When you're ready to serve them, all you need to do is simply thaw and heat them up. —Carrie Sherril, Forestville, Wisconsin

      3/4 **cup dried cherries**
        1 **cup boiling water**
        3 **cups all-purpose flour**
        3 **tablespoons sugar**
        1 **tablespoon baking powder**
      1/2 **teaspoon salt**
      1/2 **teaspoon cream of tartar**
      1/2 **cup cold butter**
        1 **egg,** *separated*
      1/2 **cup sour cream**
      3/4 **cup half-and-half cream**
    1-1/2 **teaspoons almond extract**
Additional sugar

Soak cherries in water for 10 minutes. Drain and set aside. In a large mixing bowl, combine flour, sugar, baking powder, salt and cream of tartar. Cut in butter until crumbly. Set aside. In a small bowl, combine egg yolk, sour cream, cream and al-mond extract. Add to flour mixture; stir until a soft dough forms. Turn out onto a lightly floured surface; knead gently six to eight times. Knead in cherries.

Divide dough in half and shape into balls. Roll each ball into a 6-in. circle. Cut each into six wedges. Place on a lightly greased baking sheet. Beat egg white until foamy; brush tops of scones and sprinkle with sugar. Bake at 400° for 15-20 min-utes. Serve warm. **Yield:** 1 dozen.

Tacoed Eggs

(Pictured above)

One morning, I was searching the kitchen for a way to jazz up scrambled eggs. When I couldn't find any bacon bits, I used leftover taco filling from the night before. —Mary Smith, Huntington, Indiana

        8 **eggs, beaten**
      1/2 **cup shredded cheddar cheese**
        2 **tablespoons finely chopped onion**
        2 **tablespoons finely chopped green pepper**
        1 **to 4 drops hot pepper sauce**
      1/2 **cup cooked taco-seasoned ground beef**
Flour tortillas, warmed, optional
Salsa, optional

In a bowl, combine eggs, cheese, onion, green pepper and hot pepper sauce. Cook and stir in a nonstick skillet until eggs begin to set. Add taco meat; cook until eggs are complete-ly set. If desired, spoon onto a warmed tortilla and roll up; top with salsa. **Yield:** 4 servings.

Puffy Apple Omelet

(Pictured below)

With all the eggs our chickens produce, I could make this omelet every day! I guess I consider it to be mostly a festive dish, but you could fix it anytime...including for a light supper.
—Melissa Davenport
Campbell, Minnesota

    3 tablespoons all-purpose flour
  1/4 teaspoon baking powder
  1/8 teaspoon salt, optional
    2 eggs, *separated*
    3 tablespoons milk
    3 tablespoons sugar
    1 tablespoon lemon juice
TOPPING:
    1 large apple, thinly sliced
    1 teaspoon sugar
  1/4 teaspoon ground cinnamon

In a small bowl, combine flour, baking powder and salt if desired; mix well. Add the egg yolks and milk; mix well and set aside.

In a small mixing bowl, beat egg whites until foamy. Gradually add sugar, beating until stiff peaks form. Fold in yolk mixture and lemon juice.

Pour into a greased 1-1/2-qt. shallow baking dish. Arrange the apple slices on top. Combine the sugar and cinnamon; sprinkle over all.

Bake, uncovered, at 375° for 18-20 minutes or until a knife inserted near the center comes out clean. Serve immediately. **Yield:** 2 servings.

Cream Cheese Puffs

These puffs make a great addition to my family's breakfast buffet. Since they start with refrigerated biscuits, they're a breeze to make!
—Diane Xavier
Hilmar, California

  1/2 cup sugar
    1 teaspoon ground cinnamon
  1/4 cup butter, melted
  1/2 teaspoon vanilla extract
    1 tube (10 ounces) refrigerated biscuits
    1 package (3 ounces) cream cheese, cut into 10 cubes

In a small bowl, combine the sugar and cinnamon. In another bowl, combine the butter and vanilla. Separate dough into 10 biscuits; press each into a 3-in. circle.

Dip cream cheese cubes in butter and then in cinnamon-sugar. Place one in the center of each biscuit. Fold dough over cube; seal and shape into balls.

Dip balls in butter and then in cinnamon-sugar. Place seam side down in greased muffin cups. Bake at 375° for 14-18 minutes or until golden brown. Serve warm. **Yield:** 10 muffins.

Honey Raisin Muffins

The sweetness of honey brings out the flavor of the raisins in these muffins. My family can't get enough of them, so I make them often for everyone to enjoy.
—Joyce Reece, Mena, Arkansas

  1-1/4 cups all-purpose flour
      1 tablespoon baking powder
    1/4 teaspoon salt
      2 cups Raisin Bran cereal
      1 cup milk
    1/4 cup honey
      1 egg, lightly beaten
      3 tablespoons vegetable oil

Combine flour, baking powder and salt; set aside. In a large bowl, combine cereal, milk and honey; let stand until softened, about 2 minutes. Stir in egg and oil; mix well. Add dry ingredients; stir just until moistened. Fill greased or paper-lined muffin cups two-thirds full.

Bake at 400° for 18-20 minutes or until a toothpick comes out clean. Cool in pan 10 minutes before removing to a wire rack. **Yield:** about 10 muffins.

Feather-Light Doughnuts

(Pictured below)

When I was growing up, we always had an abundance of leftover mashed potatoes and often used them in these fluffy doughnuts. —Darlene Alexander, Nekoosa, Wisconsin

> 2 packages (1/4 ounce *each*) active dry yeast
> 1-1/2 cups warm milk (110° to 115°)
> 1 cup cold mashed potatoes
> 1-1/2 cups sugar, *divided*
> 1/2 cup vegetable oil
> 2 teaspoons salt
> 2 teaspoons vanilla extract
> 1/2 teaspoon baking soda
> 1/2 teaspoon baking powder
> 2 eggs
> 5-1/2 to 6 cups all-purpose flour
> 1/2 teaspoon ground cinnamon

Oil for deep-fat frying

In a large mixing bowl, dissolve yeast in warm milk. Add potatoes, 1/2 cup sugar, oil, salt, vanilla, baking soda, baking powder and eggs; mix well. Add enough flour to form a soft dough (do not knead).

Place in a greased bowl, turning once to grease top. Cover and let rise in a warm place until doubled, about 1 hour. Punch dough down; roll out on a floured surface to 1/2-in. thickness. Cut with a 3-in. doughnut cutter. Place on greased baking sheets; cover and let rise until almost doubled, about 45 minutes.

Meanwhile, combine the cinnamon and remaining sugar; set aside. Heat oil in an electric skillet or deep-fat fryer to 375°; fry doughnuts until golden on both sides. Drain on paper towels; roll in cinnamon-sugar while still warm. **Yield:** about 2-1/2 dozen.

Maple Toast and Eggs

(Pictured above)

My home's in the country, right next door to my sister and brother-in-law's. They and their two children all love this dish each time I serve it as a special evening meal. But it can also be made for breakfast or lunch. —Susan Buttel, Plattsburgh, New York

> 12 bacon strips, diced
> 1/2 cup maple syrup
> 1/4 cup butter
> 12 slices white bread
> 12 eggs

Salt and pepper to taste

In a large skillet, cook bacon until crisp; remove to paper towels to drain. In a small saucepan, heat syrup and butter until butter is melted; set aside.

Trim crusts from bread; flatten slices with a rolling pin. Brush one side generously with syrup mixture; press each slice into an ungreased muffin cup with syrup side down. Divide bacon among muffin cups. Carefully break one egg into each cup. Sprinkle with salt and pepper. Cover with foil.

Bake at 400° for 18-20 minutes or until the eggs are set. Serve immediately. **Yield:** 12 servings.

Peanut Butter Muffins

*A hint of nuts gives these muffins a unique flavor that's
just right for breakfast!* —*Caroline Sanders*
Kansas City, Missouri

      2 **eggs**
  1/3 **cup sugar**
      1 **cup milk**
  1/4 **cup peanut butter**
      2 **cups biscuit/baking mix**
      3 **tablespoons jam**

In a mixing bowl, beat eggs, sugar, milk and peanut butter until smooth. Stir in baking mix. Fill greased or paper-lined muffin cups two-thirds full. Top each with 1/2 teaspoon jam.
    Bake at 375° for 15-20 minutes or until a toothpick insert-
ed in the cupcake comes out clean. Cool in pan 10 minutes
before removing to a wire rack. **Yield:** about 12 muffins.

Caramel Apple Coffee Cake

*When friends or relatives visit, I'm sure to have the cof-
fee brewing and to serve this scrumptious cake!*
—*Ruth Turner, Marinette, Wisconsin*

      3 **eggs**
      2 **cups sugar**
  1-1/2 **cups vegetable oil**
      2 **teaspoons vanilla extract**
      3 **cups all-purpose flour**
      1 **teaspoon salt**
      1 **teaspoon baking soda**
      3 **cups chopped peeled apples**
      1 **cup coarsely chopped pecans**
TOPPING:
      1 **cup packed brown sugar**
  1/2 **cup butter**
  1/4 **cup milk**
Pinch salt

In a mixing bowl, beat eggs until foamy; gradually add sugar.
Blend in the vegetable oil and vanilla. Combine flour, salt and
baking soda; add to egg mixture. Stir in apples and pecans.
    Pour into a greased 10-in. tube pan; bake at 350° for 1
hour and 15 minutes or until a toothpick inserted near center
comes out clean. Cool in pan for 10 minutes. Remove cake to
a serving platter.

For topping, combine all ingredients in a saucepan; boil 3
minutes, stirring constantly. Slowly pour over warm cake (some
topping will run down onto the serving plate). **Yield:** 12-16
servings.

Grandma's Orange Rolls

*Our two children and grandchildren love these fine-
textured sweet rolls. We have our own orange, lime and
grapefruit trees, and it's such a pleasure to go out and
pick fruit right off the tree.* —*Norma Poole*
Auburndale, Florida

      1 **package (1/4 ounce) active dry yeast**
  1/4 **cup warm water (110° to 115°)**
      1 **cup warm milk (110° to 115°)**
  1/4 **cup shortening**
  1/4 **cup sugar**
      1 **teaspoon salt**
      1 **egg, lightly beaten**
  3-1/2 to 3-3/4 **cups all-purpose flour**
FILLING:
      1 **cup sugar**
  1/2 **cup butter, softened**
      2 **tablespoons grated orange peel**
GLAZE:
      1 **cup confectioners' sugar**
      4 **teaspoons butter, softened**
      4 to 5 **teaspoons milk**
  1/2 **teaspoon lemon extract**

In a small bowl, dissolve yeast in water. In a large mixing
bowl, mix milk, shortening, sugar, salt and egg. Add yeast mixture and blend. Stir in enough flour to form a soft dough.
    Knead on a lightly floured surface until smooth and elas-
tic, about 6-8 minutes. Place in a greased bowl, turning once
to grease top. Cover and let rise in a warm place until doubled,
about 1 hour. Punch dough down; divide in half. Roll each
half into a 15-in. x 10-in. rectangle.
    Mix filling ingredients until smooth. Spread half the filling on
each rectangle. Roll up, jelly-roll style, starting with a long end.
Cut each into 15 rolls. Place in two greased 11-in. x 7-in. x 2-
in. baking pans. Cover and let rise until doubled, about 45
minutes.
    Bake at 375° for 20-25 minutes or until lightly browned.
Mix together all of the glaze ingredients; spread over warm rolls.
Yield: 30 rolls.

Appetizers & Beverages

Bread Pot Fondue, page 51

Clockwise from top right: Ruby-Red Pretzel Dip, Southwestern Star Dip and Christmas Cheese Ball

Southwestern Star Dip

(Pictured at left)

I enjoyed this sensational dip at a holiday party and begged for the recipe. —Joan Hallford
North Richland Hills, Texas

- 2 cups (8 ounces) shredded sharp cheddar cheese
- 1 cup mayonnaise
- 1 can (4-1/2 ounces) chopped ripe olives, drained, *divided*
- 1 can (4 ounces) chopped green chilies, undrained
- 1/4 teaspoon garlic powder
- 1/8 teaspoon hot pepper sauce
- 1 medium tomato, chopped
- 1/4 cup chopped green onions

Tortilla chips

In a bowl, combine cheese, mayonnaise, 1/3 cup olives, chilies, garlic powder and hot pepper sauce. Transfer to an ungreased 9-in. pie plate.

Bake, uncovered, at 350° for 20 minutes or until hot and bubbly. Sprinkle tomato on top in the shape of a star; outline with remaining olives. Sprinkle onions around the star. Serve with tortilla chips. **Yield:** 2-2/3 cups.

Editor's Note: Reduced-fat or fat-free mayonnaise is not recommended for this recipe.

Ruby-Red Pretzel Dip

(Pictured at left)

Plain pretzels get a pretty coating and tangy taste from this thick, festive blend. —Grace Yaskovic
Branchville, New Jersey

- 1 can (16 ounces) jellied cranberry sauce
- 3/4 cup sugar
- 1/4 cup vinegar
- 1 teaspoon ground ginger
- 1 teaspoon ground mustard
- 1/4 teaspoon ground cinnamon
- 1/8 teaspoon pepper
- 1 tablespoon all-purpose flour
- 1 tablespoon cold water

Red food coloring, optional
Pretzels

In a saucepan, combine the cranberry sauce, sugar, vinegar, ginger, mustard, cinnamon and pepper; whisk over medium heat until smooth. Combine flour and cold water until smooth; add to cranberry mixture. Bring to a boil; cook and stir for 2 minutes.

Transfer to a bowl; stir in food coloring if desired. Cover and chill overnight. Serve with pretzels. **Yield:** 2 cups.

Christmas Cheese Ball

(Pictured at left)

This rich cheese spread is delicious and wonderfully attractive. —Esther Shank, Harrisonville, Virginia

- 2 packages (8 ounces *each*) cream cheese, softened
- 2 cups (8 ounces) shredded sharp cheddar cheese
- 1 tablespoon finely chopped onion
- 1 tablespoon diced pimientos
- 1 tablespoon diced green pepper
- 2 teaspoons Worcestershire sauce
- 1 teaspoon lemon juice

Chopped pecans, toasted
Assorted crackers

In a mixing bowl, combine cream cheese, cheddar cheese, onion, pimientos, green pepper, Worcestershire sauce and lemon juice; mix well.

Shape into two balls; roll in pecans. Cover and chill. Remove from the refrigerator 15 minutes before serving. Serve with crackers. **Yield:** 2 cheese balls (1-1/2 cups each).

'Spice' to Know

- Ground spices quickly lose their aroma and flavor, so buy them in small quantities.
- Store spices in airtight containers in a cool, dark place for no more than 6 months. Do not store them over a stovetop or other hot location.
- Note your date of purchase on the spice bottle to keep track of how old it is.
- Make finding spices easier by alphabetizing them.
- Whole spices (such as allspice, cloves and nutmeg) can be ground fresh, but they'll have more punch than preground spices.

Creamy Caramel Dip

(Pictured above)

Because I feed three hungry "men" (my husband, a member of the Royal Canadian Mounted Police, and our two boys), I love satisfying snacks that are easy to make like this dip. I modified a friend's recipe. We sure appreciate this cool, light treat. —Karen Laubman
Spruce Grove, Alberta

1 package (8 ounces) cream cheese, softened
3/4 cup packed brown sugar
1 cup (8 ounces) sour cream
2 teaspoons vanilla extract
2 teaspoons lemon juice
1 cup cold milk
1 package (3.4 ounces) instant vanilla pudding mix
Assorted fresh fruit

In a mixing bowl, beat cream cheese and brown sugar until smooth. Add the sour cream, vanilla, lemon juice, milk and pudding mix, beating well after each addition. Cover and chill for at least 1 hour. Serve with fruit. Refrigerate leftovers. **Yield:** 3-1/2 cups.

Layered Shrimp Dip

(Pictured at right)

People's eyes light up when I set this special snack on the table. It has a terrific combination of flavors and looks so pretty. —Sue Broyles, Cherokee, Texas

1 package (3 ounces) cream cheese, softened
6 tablespoons salsa, *divided*
1/2 cup seafood sauce
3 cans (6 ounces *each*) small shrimp, rinsed and drained
1 can (2-1/4 ounces) sliced ripe olives, drained
1 cup (4 ounces) shredded cheddar cheese
1 cup (4 ounces) shredded Monterey Jack cheese
Sliced green onions
Tortilla chips

Combine cream cheese and 3 tablespoons salsa; spread into an ungreased 9-in. pie plate. Combine seafood sauce and remaining salsa; spread over cream cheese. Place shrimp evenly over top. Sprinkle with olives. Combine cheeses; sprinkle over olives. Top with onions. Chill. Serve with tortilla chips. Refrigerate leftovers. **Yield:** 12-16 servings.

Microwave Snack Mix

I zap this fun snack in my microwave. The peanuts and pretzels come out so crisp you'd think they were baked. —Priscilla Weaver, Hagerstown, Maryland

      1/2 cup butter
        2 teaspoons chili powder
        1 teaspoon ground cumin
      1/2 teaspoon garlic powder
        5 cups oyster crackers
        3 cups miniature pretzels
    2-1/2 cups salted peanuts
        2 tablespoons Parmesan cheese

In a small microwave-safe bowl, combine butter, chili powder, cumin and garlic powder. Cover and microwave on high for 45-60 seconds or until butter is melted.

In a 3-qt. microwave-safe dish, combine crackers, pretzels and peanuts. Add butter mixture and mix lightly. Sprinkle with Parmesan cheese and toss to coat. Microwave, uncovered, on high for 7-8 minutes or until mixture begins to toast, carefully stirring every 2 minutes. Cool completely. Store in an airtight container. **Yield:** 10 cups.

Editor's Note: This recipe was tested in a 700-watt microwave.

Ham 'n' Cheese Tortillas

(Pictured above)

My family eats these tasty tortillas as fast as I can make them. Good thing they can be made in a hurry! They're a new and flavorful way to serve ham and cheese.
—Jamie Whitaker, Aurora, Missouri

Vegetable oil for frying
        6 flour tortillas (10 inches), quartered
        3 packages (6 ounces *each*) boiled ham (24 slices)
    4-1/2 cups shredded cheddar cheese
        1 cup picante sauce *or* salsa
Garlic salt
Sour cream and minced chives, optional

In an electric skillet, heat 2 in. of oil to 375°. Fry tortilla wedges, a few at a time, until lightly browned and crispy. Drain on paper towels. Place wedges in a single layer on baking sheets.

Top each with a folded ham slice, 3 tablespoons cheese and 2 teaspoons picante sauce. Sprinkle with garlic salt. Broil 4-6 in. from the heat until cheese is melted, about 2 minutes. Serve warm. If desired, top with a dollop of sour cream and sprinkle with chives. **Yield:** 2 dozen.

Baked Tortilla Chips

You can also brush tortillas with olive oil, season to taste with salt and pepper and cut into wedges. Arrange wedges in a single layer on lightly greased baking sheets. Bake at 350° for 5-10 minutes or until crisp. Cool on paper towels.

Cranberry Apple Cider

(Pictured above)

I love to start this soothing cider in the slow cooker on nights before my husband goes hunting. Then he can fill his thermos and take it with him out into the cold. The cider has a terrific fruit flavor we both enjoy.
—*Jennifer Naboka, North Plainfield, New Jersey*

    4 cups water
    4 cups apple juice
    1 can (12 ounces) frozen apple juice concentrate, thawed
    1 medium apple, peeled and sliced
    1 cup fresh *or* frozen cranberries
    1 medium orange, peeled and sectioned
    1 cinnamon stick

In a slow cooker, combine all ingredients; mix well. Cover and cook on low for 2 hours or until cider reaches desired temperature. Discard cinnamon stick. If desired, remove fruit with a slotted spoon before serving. **Yield:** 10 servings (about 2-1/2 quarts).

Creamy
Horseradish Dip

In this simple-to-prepare vegetable dip, horseradish shines through without being too overpowering.
—*Barbara Coleman, Dunbar, West Virginia*

    1 cup mayonnaise
    2 tablespoons prepared horseradish
    1 teaspoon white wine vinegar
    1/2 teaspoon curry powder
    1/2 teaspoon garlic salt *or* 1/4 teaspoon garlic powder
    1/2 teaspoon ground mustard
Assorted fresh vegetables

In a bowl, combine the mayonnaise, horseradish, vinegar, curry, garlic salt and mustard. Cover and chill for at least 1 hour. Serve with vegetables. Refrigerate leftovers. **Yield:** about 1 cup.

Christmas Party
Pinwheels

(Pictured below)

These festive appetizers look so special and pretty that folks can't resist them! The refreshing flavor of ranch dressing and crisp colorful vegetables make these pinwheels a pleasure to serve to holiday guests.
—*Janis Plourde, Smooth Rock Falls, Ontario*

    2 packages (8 ounces *each*) cream cheese, softened
    1 envelope ranch salad dressing mix
    1/2 cup minced sweet red pepper
    1/2 cup minced celery
    1/4 cup sliced green onions
    1/4 cup sliced stuffed olives
    3 to 4 flour tortillas (10 inches)

In a mixing bowl, beat cream cheese and salad dressing mix until smooth. Add red pepper, celery, onions and olives; mix well. Spread about 3/4 cup on each tortilla. Roll up tightly; wrap in plastic wrap. Refrigerate for at least 2 hours. Slice into 1/2-in. pieces. **Yield:** 15-20 servings.

Spinach Deviled Eggs

(Pictured above)

Spinach adds unexpected color and flavor to this tasty variation on deviled eggs. They're easy to make with leftover eggs and an attractive addition to a party spread. —Dorothy Sander, Evansville, Indiana

> 12 **hard-cooked eggs**
> 1/4 **cup mayonnaise**
> 2 **tablespoons vinegar**
> 2 **tablespoons butter, softened**
> 1 **tablespoon sugar**
> 1/2 **teaspoon pepper**
> 1/4 **teaspoon salt**
> 1/2 **cup frozen chopped spinach, thawed and squeezed dry**
> 4 **bacon strips, cooked and crumbled**

Slice eggs in half lengthwise; remove yolks and set whites aside. In a small bowl, mash yolks with a fork. Stir in the mayonnaise, vinegar, butter, sugar, pepper and salt. Add spinach and mix well. Stir in the bacon; spoon into egg whites. Serve immediately. **Yield:** 2 dozen.

Homemade Eggnog

(Pictured below)

After just one taste, folks will know this holiday treat is homemade, not a store-bought variety.
—Pat Waymire, Yellow Springs, Ohio

> 12 **eggs**
> 1-1/2 **cups sugar**
> 1/2 **teaspoon salt**
> 2 **quarts milk, *divided***
> 2 **tablespoons vanilla extract**
> 1 **teaspoon ground nutmeg**
> 2 **cups heavy whipping cream**
> **Additional nutmeg, optional**

In a heavy 4-qt. saucepan, whisk together eggs, sugar and salt. Gradually add 1 qt. of milk. Cook and stir over low heat until a thermometer reads 160°-170°, about 30-35 minutes. Pour into a large heatproof bowl; stir in vanilla, nutmeg and remaining milk. Place bowl in an ice-water bath, stirring frequently until mixture is cool. If mixture separates, process in a blender until smooth. Cover and refrigerate for at least 3 hours.

When ready to serve, beat the cream in a mixing bowl on high until soft peaks form; whisk gently into cooled milk mixture. Pour into a chilled 5-qt. punch bowl. Sprinkle with nutmeg if desired. **Yield:** 3-1/2 quarts.

Editor's Note: Eggnog may be stored, covered, in the refrigerator for several days. Whisk gently before serving.

Top to bottom:
Hot Apple Punch,
Pinecone-Shaped Spread,
Artichoke Dip and
Bacon Rounds

Pinecone-Shaped Spread

(Pictured at left)

Spreading Christmas cheer is deliciously simple with this holiday novelty. Originally my mother's recipe, it always gets raves. —Lisa Pointer, Leadore, Idaho

 1 package (8 ounces) cream cheese, softened
 1/2 cup mayonnaise
 5 bacon strips, cooked and crumbled
 1 tablespoon finely chopped green onion
 1/2 teaspoon dill weed
 1/8 teaspoon pepper
 1-1/4 cups whole unblanched almonds, toasted
Fresh rosemary sprigs, optional
Assorted crackers *or* raw vegetables

In a bowl, combine the first six ingredients. Chill. Form into two pinecone shapes on a serving platter. Beginning at the narrow end of each shape, arrange almonds in overlapping rows. Garnish with rosemary if desired. Serve with crackers or vegetables. **Yield:** 1-1/2 cups.

Bacon Rounds

(Pictured at left)

On my family's list of favorite nibbles, this appetizer is tops. I've served the satisfying canapes at showers and brunches. —Edie Despain, Logan, Utah

 1 cup mayonnaise
 1 tablespoon grated Parmesan cheese
 2 teaspoons Worcestershire sauce
 1/4 teaspoon paprika
 1/8 teaspoon celery seed
 1/8 teaspoon garlic powder
 1/8 teaspoon pepper
 2 cups (8 ounces) shredded cheddar cheese
 8 bacon strips, cooked and crumbled
 1/3 cup chopped salted peanuts
 4 green onions, thinly sliced
 24 small French bread slices *or* 12 slices white bread
Additional sliced green onions, optional

In a bowl, combine the first seven ingredients; mix well. Stir in cheese, bacon, peanuts and onions; mix well. Spread over bread. Sprinkle with additional onions if desired. Place on un-greased baking sheets. Bake at 400° for 8-10 minutes or until lightly browned. If using white bread, cut into quarters. **Yield:** 4 dozen.

 Editor's Note: Rounds may be frozen before baking. Bake at 400° for 10-12 minutes or until lightly browned (they do not need to be thawed first).

Hot Apple Punch

(Pictured at left)

With its soothing cinnamon seasoning, this fresh and flavorful apple punch is a must for Christmastime. —Dawn Supina, Edmonton, Alberta

 2 cinnamon sticks (about 3 inches *each*), broken
 10 whole cloves
 6 whole allspice *or* 2 whole nutmeg
 2 quarts apple juice
Additional cinnamon sticks, optional

Place the cinnamon sticks, cloves and allspice on a double thickness of cheesecloth; bring up the corners and tie with string to form a bag. Place in a large saucepan with apple juice (or place loose spices in pan and strain before serving).

 Bring to a boil. Reduce heat; cover and simmer for 30 minutes. Remove spice bag. Serve punch hot in mugs. Garnish with cinnamon sticks if desired. **Yield:** 2 quarts.

Artichoke Dip

(Pictured at left)

Crackers make great dippers for this creamy appetizer (chips and breadsticks work well, too). It's become the traditional introduction to our family's Christmas Eve dinner. —Mrs. William Garner, Austin, Texas

 1 can (14 ounces) artichoke hearts, drained and chopped
 1 cup mayonnaise
 1/3 to 1/2 cup grated Parmesan cheese
 1 garlic clove, minced
Dash hot pepper sauce
Paprika, optional
Assorted crackers

In a bowl, combine the first five ingredients. Transfer to a greased 1-qt. baking dish. Sprinkle with paprika if desired. Bake, uncovered, at 300° for 30 minutes. Serve warm with assorted crackers. **Yield:** 2 cups.

Tangy Meatballs

(Pictured above)

These hearty meatballs are a family favorite and a big hit wherever they go! In their delicious barbecue sauce, they're a perfect dish to pass and also work well as hors d'oeuvres. —Jane Barta, St. Thomas, North Dakota

    2 eggs
    2 cups quick-cooking *or* old-fashioned oats
    1 can (12 ounces) evaporated milk
    1 cup chopped onion
    2 teaspoons salt
  1/2 teaspoon pepper
  1/2 teaspoon garlic powder
    3 pounds ground beef
SAUCE:
    2 cups ketchup
1-1/2 cups packed brown sugar
  1/2 cup chopped onion
    1 to 2 teaspoons Liquid Smoke, optional
  1/2 teaspoon garlic powder

In a large bowl, beat eggs. Add oats, milk, onion, salt, pepper and garlic powder. Crumble beef over mixture and mix well. Shape into 1-1/2-in. balls. Place in two 13-in. x 9-in. x 2-in. baking pans. Bake, uncovered, at 375° for 30 minutes or until juices run clear. Remove from the oven and drain. Place all of the meatballs in one of the pans.

In a saucepan, bring all sauce ingredients to a boil. Pour over meatballs. Return to the oven and bake, uncovered, for 20 minutes. **Yield:** 4 dozen.

Mustard Egg Dip

When I tried this recipe, my family discovered that the flavor of deviled eggs makes a surprisingly good dip for fresh vegetables. —Janie Carr, Fort Davis, Texas

    6 hard-cooked eggs, finely chopped
  1/3 cup mayonnaise
    1 tablespoon butter, softened
    2 teaspoons lemon juice
    1 teaspoon prepared mustard
    1 teaspoon Worcestershire sauce
  1/2 teaspoon salt
  1/4 teaspoon pepper
Hot pepper sauce to taste
  3/4 teaspoon Liquid Smoke, optional
Green *or* sweet red peppers and other raw vegetables for dipping

In a bowl, combine the hard-cooked eggs, mayonnaise, butter, lemon juice, mustard, Worcestershire sauce, salt, pepper and hot pepper sauce; add Liquid Smoke if desired.

Mix until smooth. Serve with sliced peppers and other vegetables, or, if desired, cut peppers in half lengthwise and fill with dip. **Yield:** 1-3/4 cups.

Spicy Cranberry Warmer

(Pictured below left)

My husband and I operate a small bed-and-breakfast inn. I like serving this drink to winter guests as they warm up in front of the fireplace. It's a favorite with everyone for its heavenly scent. —Marlene Cartwright
Sierra City, California

- 3 **whole cloves**
- 2 **cinnamon sticks**
- 2 **whole allspice**
- 4 **cups apple cider**
- 1/3 **cup packed brown sugar**
- 4 **cups cranberry juice**

Additional cinnamon sticks, optional

Place first three ingredients in a double thickness of cheesecloth. Bring up corners of cloth and tie with a string to form a bag. Place with cider in a large saucepan. (Or place loose spices in saucepan and strain before serving.)

Simmer, covered, for 5 minutes. Stir in sugar and simmer for 5 minutes. Add cranberry juice and heat to simmering temperature. Serve hot in mugs. Garnish with cinnamon sticks if desired. **Yield:** 8-10 servings.

Hot Buttered Lemonade

Since my husband had fond childhood memories of this winter warmer-upper, I simmered up a batch. It's delicious, simple to prepare for drop-in guests and sets a soothing holiday mood. —Jennifer Jones
Springfield, Missouri

- 3 **cups water**
- 3/4 **cup lemon juice**
- 2/3 **cup sugar**
- 1-1/2 **teaspoons grated lemon peel**
- 1 **tablespoon butter**
- 4 **cinnamon sticks (4 inches *each*), optional**

In a saucepan over medium heat, simmer water, lemon juice, sugar and lemon peel until sugar is dissolved. Pour into mugs; dot each with butter. Serve with a cinnamon stick if desired. **Yield:** 4 servings (about 1 cup each).

Three-in-One Cheese Ball

(Pictured above)

Every Christmas, I make these cheese balls for many get-togethers. They aren't only for the holidays, however. You'll find they freeze well and last for a week in the refrigerator. —Mary Anne Marston
Almonte, Ontario

- 1 **package (8 ounces) cream cheese, softened**
- 4 **cups (16 ounces) shredded cheddar cheese, room temperature**
- 2 **tablespoons milk**
- 2 **tablespoons dried minced onion**
- 2 **tablespoons Worcestershire sauce**

Coarsely cracked black pepper
- 1/2 **cup (2 ounces) crumbled blue cheese**

Minced fresh parsley
- 1/4 **teaspoon garlic powder**

Finely chopped pecans
Assorted crackers *or* pretzels

In a mixing bowl, beat the first five ingredients until fluffy. Divide into thirds (about 1 cup each). Shape first portion into a ball; roll in cracked pepper. Add the blue cheese to the second portion; mix well. Shape into a ball; roll in parsley. Add garlic powder to the remaining portion; mix well. Shape into a ball; roll in nuts. Cover and refrigerate. Remove from refrigerator 15 minutes before serving. Serve with crackers or pretzels. **Yield:** 3 cheese balls.

Ham 'n' Cheese Quiches

(Pictured below)

When I need a festive finger food, this recipe's the one I reach for. With cheese in both the crust and the filling, eating one quiche naturally leads to another.
—*Virginia Abraham, Vicksburg, Mississippi*

- 1/2 cup cold butter
- 1 jar (5 ounces) process sharp cheddar cheese spread
- 1 cup all-purpose flour
- 2 tablespoons cold water

FILLING:
- 1 egg
- 1/2 cup milk
- 1/4 teaspoon salt
- 1/2 cup finely chopped fully cooked ham
- 1/2 cup shredded Monterey Jack cheese
- 1 tablespoon minced fresh parsley, optional

In a bowl, cut butter and cheese spread into flour until well blended. Add water and toss with a fork until a ball forms. Refrigerate for 1 hour. Press tablespoonfuls onto the bottom and up the sides of greased miniature muffin cups.

In a bowl, beat the egg, milk and salt. Stir in the ham, cheese and parsley if desired. Spoon a rounded teaspoonful into each shell. Bake at 350° for 28-32 minutes or until golden brown. Let stand 5 minutes before serving. **Yield:** 2 dozen.

Banana Milk Drink

(Pictured above)

There's no better way to start the day than with this breakfast drink. If you like bananas, you'll love this beverage! —*Jeanne Brown, Buffalo, New York*

- 1 large ripe banana
- 1 cup milk
- 1-1/2 to 2 teaspoons sugar
- 1/2 teaspoon vanilla extract

Dash ground cinnamon, optional

Place the first four ingredients in a blender; cover and process until smooth. Pour into glasses; sprinkle with cinnamon if desired. Serve immediately. **Yield:** 2 servings.

Hot Mustard Popcorn

When friends pop in at Yuletide, I like to dish up yummy munchies like this one. —*Diane Hixon Niceville, Florida*

- 1 teaspoon ground mustard
- 1/2 teaspoon dried thyme
- 1/2 teaspoon salt
- 1/4 teaspoon pepper

Dash cayenne pepper
- 3 quarts freshly popped popcorn

Combine the ground mustard, thyme, salt, pepper and cayenne. Place popcorn in a large bowl; add the seasonings and toss. **Yield:** 3 quarts.

Breakfast Wassail

(Pictured below)

This fruity beverage is great all year-round and tasty hot or chilled. I got the recipe from a co-worker and made it one Christmas for a family gathering. Now whenever we get together for the holidays, I'm always the designated wassail-maker. —Amy Holtsclaw Carbondale, Illinois

> 1 **bottle (64 ounces) cranberry juice**
> 1 **bottle (32 ounces) apple juice**
> 1 **can (12 ounces) frozen pineapple juice concentrate, undiluted**
> 1 **can (12 ounces) frozen lemonade concentrate, undiluted**
> 3 **to 4 cinnamon sticks**
> 1 **quart water, optional**

Additional cinnamon sticks, optional

In a large saucepan or Dutch oven, combine the first five ingredients. Bring to a boil. Reduce heat; cover and simmer for 1 hour. Remove cinnamon sticks. Add water if desired. Serve hot or cold. Garnish with cinnamon stick stirrers if desired. **Yield:** about 4 quarts.

Bread Pot Fondue

(Pictured above and on page 37)

Bring this fun fondue to a buffet or potluck and you'll be the toast of the gathering. Folks always ask for the recipe. —Terry Christensen, Roy, Utah

> 2 **cups (8 ounces) shredded cheddar cheese**
> 1-1/2 **cups (12 ounces) sour cream**
> 2 **packages (3 ounces *each*) cream cheese, softened**
> 1/4 **pound chopped fully cooked ham**
> 1/2 **cup finely chopped green onions**
> 1 **can (4 ounces) chopped green chilies**
> 1 **teaspoon Worcestershire sauce**
> 1 **round loaf (1 to 1-1/2 pounds) Italian bread**

Assorted fresh vegetables

In a mixing bowl, combine the first three ingredients. Stir in ham, onions, chilies and Worcestershire sauce; set aside. Cut top fourth off loaf of bread; carefully hollow out top and bottom, leaving a 1/2-in. shell. Cube the removed bread; set aside.

Spoon the ham mixture into the bottom shell, mounding slightly. Replace top; wrap tightly with a double layer of heavy-duty foil. Bake at 350° for 1 to 1-1/2 hours. Stir before serving. Serve with reserved bread cubes and vegetables. **Yield:** 4 cups.

Clockwise from top: Elegant Cheese Torte, Pizza Poppers, Sausage-Filled Stars and Smoked Almonds (recipe on page 54)

Pizza Poppers

(Pictured at left)

Both my husband and I are big pizza fans, so we created these pizza rolls. I think they'd be fun to set out for Santa to enjoy.—Denise Sargent, Pittsfield, New Hampshire

      4 to 4-1/2 cups all-purpose flour
    1/3 cup sugar
      1 package (1/4 ounce) active dry yeast
      1 teaspoon dried oregano
    1/2 teaspoon salt
      1 cup water
      1 tablespoon shortening
      1 egg
      3 cups (12 ounces) shredded mozzarella cheese
  1-1/3 cups minced pepperoni (about 5 ounces)
      2 cups pizza sauce, warmed

In a mixing bowl, combine 2 cups of flour, sugar, yeast, oregano and salt. Heat water and shortening to 120°-130°; add to flour mixture along with the egg. Beat on medium speed for 1 minute. Stir in cheese and pepperoni; mix well. Add enough remaining flour to form a soft dough.

Turn onto a floured surface; knead until smooth and elastic, about 6-8 minutes. Place in a greased bowl, turning once to grease top. Cover and let rise in a warm place until doubled, about 1 hour. Punch dough down; divide into four portions.

Cut each portion into eight pieces; roll each piece into a 12-in. rope. Tie into a loose knot, leaving two long ends. Fold top end under roll; bring bottom end up and press into center of the roll.

Place on greased baking sheets. Cover and let rise until doubled, about 30 minutes. Bake at 375° for 10-12 minutes or until golden brown. Serve warm with pizza sauce. **Yield:** 32 appetizers.

Sausage-Filled Stars

(Pictured at left)

*My family loves these snacks with a savory sausage-cheese filling. The star shape is perfect for Christmas.
—Minnie Bell Millsaps, McCaysville, Georgia*

      1 pound bulk sausage
  1-1/2 cups (6 ounces) shredded cheddar cheese
  1-1/2 cups (6 ounces) shredded Monterey Jack cheese
      1 medium sweet red pepper, diced

      1 medium green pepper, diced
      1 can (4 ounces) chopped green chilies, drained
      1 can (4-1/2 ounces) chopped ripe olives, drained
      1 envelope ranch salad dressing mix
     48 wonton wrappers
Vegetable oil

In a skillet, cook sausage over medium heat until no longer pink; drain. Add cheeses, peppers, chilies, olives and dressing mix; mix well. Set aside. Brush both sides of wrappers with oil; press onto bottom and up sides of greased muffin cups.

Bake at 350° for 5 minutes or until golden brown. Transfer to a baking sheet. Fill each with about 2 tablespoons of the sausage mixture. Bake for 5 minutes or until heated through. Serve warm. **Yield:** 4 dozen.

Elegant Cheese Torte

(Pictured at left)

Rich and creamy, this eye-catching torte makes quite an impression. Every time I take it to a party, it receives rave reviews!   —Donna Cline, Pensacola, Florida

      4 packages (8 ounces *each*) cream cheese, softened
      1 cup butter, softened
      2 teaspoons coarsely ground pepper
      1 jar (5-3/4 ounces) stuffed olives, drained and chopped
      8 cups (32 ounces) shredded sharp cheddar cheese, room temperature
    3/4 cup apple cider, room temperature
  2-1/4 teaspoons paprika
      1 cup chopped pecans, toasted
Grapes and assorted crackers

In a mixing bowl, beat the cream cheese and butter until smooth. Remove 3-1/2 cups to a small bowl; stir in pepper and set aside. Fold olives into the remaining cream cheese mixture. Spread evenly over the bottom of a 9-in. springform pan; set aside.

In a mixing bowl, beat cheddar cheese, cider and paprika on low speed for 1 minute. Beat on high until almost smooth. Spread half over olive layer. Top with peppered cheese mixture. Top with remaining cheddar mixture. Cover with plastic wrap; refrigerate for 6 hours or until firm. Place on serving plate and remove sides of pan. Press pecans into top; garnish with grapes. Serve with crackers. **Yield:** 24-30 servings.

Smoked Almonds

(Pictured on page 52)

We like to take the flavorful nuts to all sorts of gatherings, from fancy holiday affairs to casual luncheons.
—*Sheila Flodin, Farmington, Minnesota*

> 1 egg white
> 2 teaspoons garlic powder
> 2 teaspoons celery salt
> 1/4 teaspoon salt
> 1/2 teaspoon Liquid Smoke, optional
> 3 cups whole unblanched almonds, toasted and cooled

In a bowl, whisk egg white until foamy. Add garlic powder, celery salt, salt and Liquid Smoke if desired; stir until blended. Add almonds; stir until well coated. Evenly spread almonds in a 15-in. x 10-in. x 1-in. baking pan coated with nonstick cooking spray. Bake at 300° for 30 minutes, stirring every 10 minutes. Cool. Store in an airtight container. **Yield:** 3 cups.

Crunchy Cheese Dip

(Pictured above)

The combination of flavors makes this dip very interesting as well as delicious. It's a challenge to not eat a lot while you're making it. I'm usually anxious for my guests to arrive so I can serve it and dig in!
—*Deborah Hill, Coffeyville, Kansas*

> 1 can (8 ounces) pineapple tidbits
> 2 packages (8 ounces *each*) cream cheese, softened
> 1 can (8 ounces) water chestnuts, drained and chopped
> 3 tablespoons minced chives
> 1 teaspoon seasoned salt
> 1/4 teaspoon pepper
> 1 cup chopped pecans

Fresh chopped parsley
Assorted crackers

Drain pineapple, reserving 1 tablespoon juice. In a small bowl, combine pineapple, cream cheese, water chestnuts, chives, salt, pepper and pecans. Stir in reserved juice; mix well. Garnish with parsley. Cover and chill. Serve with crackers. **Yield:** about 3-1/2 cups.

Fruity Milkshakes

(Pictured below)

Shake up your breakfast and surprise the family by pouring tall glasses of this tasty blend instead of plain fruit juice or milk.
—*Renae Moncur, Burley, Idaho*

> 1 can (6 ounces) frozen apple juice concentrate, thawed
> 1 carton (8 ounces) vanilla yogurt

1   medium ripe banana, sliced
1/2   cup instant nonfat dry milk powder
1/4   teaspoon coconut extract
1   to 3 teaspoons honey
12   ice cubes

In a blender, combine the first five ingredients. Cover and blend until well mixed. Add honey and ice; cover and process on high until the ice is crushed and mixture is foamy. Pour into glasses. **Yield:** about 4 cups.

Continental Cheese Spread

Just the right combination of cheeses, parsley, onion garlic and thyme make this dip irresistible. One taste and I think you'll agree!   —Mrs. Thomas Wigglesworth
Absecon, New Jersey

1   package (8 ounces) cream cheese, softened
1   tablespoon milk
3   tablespoons grated Parmesan cheese
1   tablespoon minced fresh parsley
1   tablespoon minced green onion
1   garlic clove, minced
1/2   teaspoon dried thyme
1/8   teaspoon pepper

In a bowl, beat cream cheese and milk until fluffy. Add Parmesan cheese, parsley, onion, garlic, thyme and pepper. Mix until well blended. Cover and refrigerate for at least 1 hour. Store leftovers in refrigerator. **Yield:** 1 cup.

White Hot Chocolate

This is a favorite at my house. The creamy drink is smooth and soothing with a hint of spice.
—Debbi Smith, Crossett, Arkansas

3   cups half-and-half cream, *divided*
2/3   cup vanilla *or* white chips
1   cinnamon stick (3 inches)
1/8   teaspoon ground nutmeg
1   teaspoon vanilla extract
1/4   teaspoon almond extract
Ground cinnamon, optional

In a saucepan, combine 1/4 cup cream, chips, cinnamon stick and nutmeg. Stir over low heat until chips are melted; discard cinnamon stick. Add remaining cream; stir until heated through. Remove from the heat; add extracts. Sprinkle each serving with ground cinnamon if desired. **Yield:** 4 servings.

Salmon Appetizers

(Pictured above)

I often rely on these pretty pinwheels when entertaining. They're easy to prepare, and they prove to be popular at parties and other get-togethers.
—Evelyn Gebhardt, Kasilof, Alaska

1   can (14-3/4 ounces) salmon, drained, bones and skin removed
1   package (8 ounces) cream cheese, softened
4   tablespoons salsa
2   tablespoons chopped fresh parsley
1   teaspoon dried cilantro
1/4   teaspoon ground cumin, optional
8   flour tortillas (8 inches)

In a small bowl, combine salmon, cream cheese, salsa, parsley, cilantro and cumin if desired. Spread about 2 tablespoons of the salmon mixture over each tortilla. Roll each tortilla up tightly and wrap individually with plastic wrap. Refrigerate 2-3 hours. Slice each tortilla into bite-size pieces. **Yield:** about 48 appetizers.

Salmon Canapes

(Pictured at right)

This appealing appetizer, with its delicate smoked salmon taste and dash of holiday color, is simply irresistible!
—Dorothy Anderson, Ottawa, Kansas

1 can (7-1/2 ounces) red salmon, drained, skin and bones removed
2 tablespoons minced celery
2 tablespoons minced green onions with tops
3 tablespoons mayonnaise
1/2 teaspoon lemon juice
1/4 teaspoon salt
1/8 teaspoon pepper
1/8 teaspoon Liquid Smoke, optional
1 small cucumber, thinly sliced
Snack rye bread, toast *or* crackers
Fresh dill *or* parsley sprigs *and/or* sliced pimientos

In a bowl, combine salmon, celery and onions. Add mayonnaise, lemon juice, salt, pepper and Liquid Smoke if desired; mix well. Cover and chill at least 1 hour. Just before serving, place cucumber slices on bread or crackers and top with salmon mixture. Garnish with dill, parsley and/or pimientos. **Yield:** 1 cup spread.

Crab-Stuffed Cherry Tomatoes

(Pictured at right)

For a little something special, I include these petite pleasers on the menu of our holiday parties.
—Marcia Keckhaver, Burlington, Wisconsin

1 pint cherry tomatoes
1 can (6 ounces) crabmeat, drained, flaked and cartilage removed
1/2 cup diced green pepper
2 green onions, diced
2 tablespoons Italian-seasoned bread crumbs
1 teaspoon white wine vinegar
1/2 teaspoon dried parsley flakes
1/4 teaspoon dill weed
1/8 teaspoon salt, optional

Cut a thin slice off tops of tomatoes and carefully scoop out insides; invert on paper towels to drain. In a small bowl, combine remaining ingredients; mix well. Stuff the tomatoes; place in an ungreased 13-in. x 9-in. x 2-in. baking dish. Bake, uncovered, at 350° for 8-10 minutes or until heated through. Serve warm. **Yield:** about 1-1/2 dozen.

Holiday Eggnog

(Pictured at right)

This classic Christmas beverage gets a new twist with the addition of rich coffee flavor.
—Lisa Reuter, Hilliard, Ohio

12 eggs
1-1/2 cups sugar
1/2 teaspoon salt
2 quarts milk, *divided*
3 tablespoons instant coffee granules
2 tablespoons vanilla extract
1 teaspoon ground nutmeg
2 cups heavy whipping cream
Additional whipped cream and nutmeg, optional

In a heavy 4-qt. saucepan, whisk together eggs, sugar and salt. Gradually add 1 qt. of milk and instant coffee granules. Cook over low heat, stirring constantly, until a thermometer reads 160°, about 25 minutes. Pour into a large bowl; stir in vanilla, nutmeg and remaining milk. Place bowl in an ice-water bath; stir frequently until mixture is cool. If mixture separates, process in a blender until smooth. Cover and refrigerate for at least 3 hours.

When ready to serve, beat cream in a mixing bowl on high until soft peaks form; whisk gently into cooled mixture. Pour into a chilled 5-qt. punch bowl. If desired, top with dollops of whipped cream and sprinkle with nutmeg. **Yield:** 18 servings (about 3/4 cup each).

Strawberry Dip

(Pictured at right)

Fresh and fruity, this versatile dip lends a hint of summertime to Yuletide. It's light in taste and pretty in holiday pink.
—Doris Soliwoda, La Mesa, California

1 package (8 ounces) cream cheese, softened
1/2 cup sour cream
1 carton (6 ounces) lemon yogurt
1/4 cup mashed strawberries
3 tablespoons honey
1 tablespoon maple syrup
Fresh fruit

In a mixing bowl, beat cream cheese and sour cream until smooth. Add yogurt, strawberries, honey and syrup; mix well. Refrigerate for at least 4 hours. Stir before serving. Use fresh fruit for dipping. **Yield:** about 2 cups dip.

Clockwise from top right: Chicken Wings with
Spicy Apricot Sauce (recipe on page 58),
Crab-Stuffed Cherry Tomatoes, Salmon Canapes,
Strawberry Dip and Holiday Eggnog

Chicken Wings with Spicy Apricot Sauce

(Pictured on page 57)

Everyone gobbles these up at Christmas potlucks! My mother gave me the recipe for this anytime appetizer with a flavorful sweet-and-sour sauce.
—Shirley Eckert, Crestline, Ohio

        3 dozen whole chicken wings
1-1/2 cups cornstarch
        1 tablespoon baking powder
1-1/2 teaspoons salt
        1/2 teaspoon pepper
        1/2 teaspoon sugar
        3 eggs, beaten
Oil for deep-fat frying
SAUCE:
        1 cup (3 ounces) dried apricots
1-1/4 cups water
        2 tablespoons sugar
        2 tablespoons cider vinegar
        2 tablespoons honey
        1/8 to 1/4 teaspoon cayenne pepper

Cut chicken wings into three sections; discard wing tip section. In a shallow bowl or large resealable plastic bag, combine cornstarch, baking powder, salt, pepper and sugar. Dip chicken pieces in eggs, then coat generously with cornstarch mixture. In an electric skillet or deep-fat fryer, heat oil to 350°. Fry chicken wings, a few at a time, for about 9 minutes or until juices run clear. Drain on paper towels. Keep warm.

Meanwhile, combine the apricots and water in a saucepan; bring to a boil. Reduce heat; cover and simmer until apricots are tender. Transfer to a blender or food processor. Add sugar, vinegar, honey and cayenne; puree until smooth. Cool slightly. Serve with chicken wings. **Yield:** 6 dozen.

Dilly Shrimp

A good friend shared the recipe for these delicious hors d'oeuvres. The zesty sauce complements the shrimp nicely and guarantees they'll prove popular.
—Diana Holmes, Hubertus, Wisconsin

1-1/2 cups mayonnaise
        1/2 cup sour cream
        1/3 cup lemon juice
        1/4 cup sugar
        1 large red onion, thinly sliced
        2 tablespoons dill weed
        1/4 teaspoon salt
        32 medium cooked shrimp (about 2 pounds), peeled and deveined

In a bowl, combine mayonnaise, sour cream, lemon juice and sugar. Stir in onion, dill, salt and shrimp. Cover and refrigerate for 8 hours or overnight. Serve with toothpicks. **Yield:** 10 servings.

Sausage-Stuffed Mushrooms

(Pictured below left)

Pennsylvania is often referred to as the "Mushroom Capital of the World." This recipe, which puts fresh mushrooms to mouth-watering use, is a delicious appetizer and is always the hit of the party. —Beatrice Vetrano, Landenberg, Pennsylvania

        12 to 15 large fresh mushrooms
        2 tablespoons butter, *divided*
        2 tablespoons chopped onion
        1 tablespoon lemon juice
        1/4 teaspoon dried basil
Salt and pepper to taste
        4 ounces bulk Italian sausage
        1 tablespoon chopped fresh parsley
        2 tablespoons dried bread crumbs
        2 tablespoons grated Parmesan cheese

Remove stems from the mushrooms. Chop stems finely; reserve caps. Place stems in paper towel and squeeze to remove any liquid.

In a medium skillet, heat 1-1/2 tablespoons butter. Cook the stems and onion in hot butter until tender. Add the lemon juice, basil, salt and pepper; cook until almost all of the liquid has evaporated. Cool mixture.

Combine mushroom mixture with sausage and parsley. Stuff into the mushroom caps. Combine bread crumbs and cheese;

Sweet Potato Cheese Ball

(Pictured below)

My husband and I farm 300 acres of sweet potatoes. I promote our product at fairs, ag expos and school functions. I pass out recipes, and this distinctive cheese ball is one of the favorites. —Edwina Harper
Bastrop, Louisiana

    1 package (8 ounces) cream cheese, softened
    2 cups cold mashed sweet potatoes
1/4 cup finely chopped onion
    2 tablespoons finely chopped jalapeno pepper
    1 teaspoon seasoned salt
    1 teaspoon Worcestershire sauce
    1 teaspoon Louisiana hot sauce
1/2 to 1 teaspoon hot pepper sauce
1/4 cup chopped pecans
Assorted crackers, breadsticks *or* raw vegetables

In a mixing bowl, beat cream cheese and sweet potatoes until smooth. Add the next seven ingredients; mix well. Cover and refrigerate for 4 hours or until easy to handle. Shape into a ball; cover and refrigerate for 4 hours or until firm. Serve with crackers, breadsticks or vegetables. **Yield:** about 3 cups.

    Editor's Note: When cutting or seeding hot peppers, use rubber or plastic gloves to protect your hands. Avoid touching your face.

sprinkle over stuffed mushrooms. Dot each with remaining butter. Place in a greased baking pan and bake at 400° for 20 minutes. Baste occasionally with pan juices. Serve hot. **Yield:** 12-15 servings.

Two-Fruit Frosty

(Pictured above)

This is a refreshing and colorful drink to serve for brunch. The cinnamon and nutmeg give it the right amount of zing. —Angie Hansen, Gildford, Montana

1-1/2 cups fresh *or* frozen blueberries *or* huckleberries
    1 cup frozen unsweetened sliced peaches, thawed
    1 cup milk
    1 cup (8 ounces) vanilla yogurt
1/4 to 1/3 cup honey
1/2 teaspoon ground cinnamon
1/2 teaspoon ground nutmeg
Cinnamon sticks, optional

Combine blueberries, peaches and milk in a blender; cover and process on high. Add yogurt, honey, cinnamon and nutmeg; blend well. Pour into glasses. Garnish with cinnamon sticks if desired. Serve immediately. **Yield:** 4 (1-cup) servings.

Fiesta Pinwheels

Whenever I serve these make-ahead appetizers, they disappear fast. When a friend at the office shared them with me, I knew in one bite I'd be bringing her recipe home for the holidays. —Diane Martin
Brown Deer, Wisconsin

    1 package (8 ounces) cream cheese, softened
    1/2 cup sour cream
    1/4 cup picante sauce
    2 tablespoons taco seasoning mix
Dash garlic powder
    1 can (4-1/2 ounces) chopped ripe olives, drained
    1 can (4 ounces) chopped green chilies
    1 cup (4 ounces) finely shredded cheddar cheese
    1/2 cup thinly sliced green onions
    8 flour tortillas (10 inches)
Salsa

In a small mixing bowl, beat cream cheese, sour cream, picante sauce, taco seasoning and garlic powder until smooth. Stir in olives, chilies, cheese and onions. Spread about 1/2 cup on each tortilla. Roll up jelly-roll style; wrap in plastic wrap. Refrigerate for 2 hours or overnight. Slice into 1-in. pieces. Serve with salsa. **Yield:** about 5 dozen.

    Editor's Note: Pinwheels may be prepared ahead and frozen. Thaw in the refrigerator.

Morning Orange Drink

(Pictured above)

Although it requires only a few basic ingredients and little preparation, this drink always draws raves from overnight guests about its "wake-up" taste.
—Joyce Mummau, Mt. Airy, Maryland

    1 can (6 ounces) frozen orange juice concentrate
    1 cup cold water
    1 cup milk
  1/3 cup sugar
    1 teaspoon vanilla extract
   10 ice cubes

Combine the first five ingredients in a blender; process at high speed. Add ice cubes, a few at a time, blending until smooth. Serve immediately. **Yield:** 4-6 servings.

Nutty O's

Almonds add a nice nutty flavor to this tasty snack. It's perfect for potlucks and not too sweet. Served in a decorative dish, basket or tin, it has a golden festive look.
—Karen Buchholz, Sitka, Alaska

    1 cup packed brown sugar
    1 cup dark corn syrup
  1/2 cup butter
   12 cups Cheerios
    2 cups pecan halves
    1 cup whole almonds

In a large saucepan, heat brown sugar, corn syrup and butter until sugar is dissolved. Stir in cereal and nuts; mix well. Sread onto greased 15-in. x 10-in. x 1-in. baking pans. Bake at 325° for 15 minutes. Cool for 10 minutes; stir to loosen from pan. Cool completely. Store in an airtight container. **Yield:** 16 cups.

Curried Chicken Triangles

Plain refrigerated crescent rolls shape up festively into these time-saving treats. Serve the savory triangles warm, then stand back and watch them vanish.
—*Anne Marie Cardilino, Kettering, Ohio*

2 tubes (8 ounces *each*) refrigerated crescent rolls
1 can (5 ounces) chunk white chicken, undrained
1 can (8 ounces) sliced water chestnuts, drained and chopped
1 cup (4 ounces) shredded Swiss cheese
1/2 cup chopped green onions
1/3 cup mayonnaise
1 teaspoon lemon juice
1/2 teaspoon curry powder
1/2 teaspoon garlic salt
Paprika, optional

Separate crescent dough; cut each piece into four triangles. Place on greased baking sheets. In a bowl, break up chicken. Add the water chestnuts, cheese, onions, mayonnaise, lemon juice, curry powder and garlic salt; mix well.

Drop by rounded teaspoonfuls onto triangles. Sprinkle with paprika if desired. Bake at 350° for 12-15 minutes or until edges are lightly browned. Serve warm. **Yield:** about 5-1/2 dozen.

Hot Broccoli Dip

So many friends ask about the special flavor of this dip. The mystery is rosemary! I especially like to serve this hot dip during the holidays, but my family loves it all year-round. —*Betty Reinholt, Culver, Indiana*

1/2 cup finely chopped onion
1/2 cup finely chopped celery
2 tablespoons butter
1 package (16 ounces) process American cheese, cut into cubes
2 cups chopped fresh broccoli, blanched
1/2 teaspoon dried rosemary, crushed
1 loaf (1 pound) round bread
Assorted fresh vegetables, optional

In a small saucepan, saute onion and celery in butter until tender. Add cheese and cook over low heat until melted. Stir in broccoli and rosemary.

Cut top off bread; scoop out center. Cut center piece into cubes. Pour dip into center of bread. Serve with bread cubes and/or raw vegetables if desired. **Yield:** 10-12 appetizer servings (3 cups).

Apricot Wraps

(Pictured below)

I accumulated a large recipe collection from around the world while my husband served in the Air Force for 25 years. This mouth-watering appetizer is one of our favorites, and we enjoy sharing it with friends.
—*Jane Ashworth, Beavercreek, Ohio*

1 package (14 ounces) dried apricots
1/2 cup whole almonds
1 pound sliced bacon
1/4 cup plum *or* apple jelly
2 tablespoons soy sauce

Fold each apricot around an almond. Cut bacon strips into thirds; wrap a strip around each apricot and secure with a toothpick. Place on two ungreased 15-in. x 10-in. x 1-in. baking pans. Bake, uncovered, at 375° for 25 minutes or until bacon is crisp, turning once.

In a small saucepan, combine jelly and soy sauce; cook and stir over low heat for 5 minutes or until warmed and smooth. Remove apricots to paper towels to drain. Serve with sauce. **Yield:** about 4-1/2 dozen.

Festive Apple-Cheese Log

With apples, pecans and cinnamon, this fun spread tastes almost like dessert. —Anna Mayer
Fort Branch, Indiana

1 package (8 ounces) cream cheese, softened
1/2 cup finely chopped tart apple
1/4 cup chopped pecans
1/4 teaspoon ground cinnamon
Additional chopped pecans, toasted
Vanilla wafers, sugar cookies *or* assorted crackers

In a bowl, combine cream cheese, apple, pecans and cinnamon. Shape into a log; roll in toasted pecans. Cover and refrigerate. Remove from the refrigerator 20 minutes before serving. Serve with vanilla wafers, cookies or crackers. **Yield:** 1 cheese log.

Fiesta Crab Dip

This mild, fresh-tasting crab dip tempts taste buds with a hint of picante. —Patricia Walls, Aurora, Minnesota

1 package (8 ounces) cream cheese, softened
1 cup picante sauce
1 package (8 ounces) imitation crabmeat, chopped
1 cup (4 ounces) shredded cheddar cheese
1/3 cup thinly sliced green onions
2 tablespoons sliced ripe olives
2 tablespoons diced fresh tomato
2 tablespoons minced fresh cilantro
Tortilla chips, assorted crackers *or* fresh vegetables

In a mixing bowl, combine the cream cheese and picante sauce. Add crab, cheese and onions; mix well. Cover and refrigerate. Transfer to a serving bowl. Sprinkle with olives, tomato and cilantro. Serve with chips, crackers or vegetables. **Yield:** 3 cups.

Victorian Iced Tea

Pretty and refreshing, this flavored iced tea is well-received at any special gathering. —Robin Fuhrman
Fond du Lac, Wisconsin

4 individual tea bags
4 cups boiling water

1 can (11-1/2 ounces) frozen cranberry-raspberry juice concentrate, thawed
4 cups cold water
Ice cubes and fresh mint

Place tea bags in a teapot; add boiling water. Cover and steep for 5 minutes. Remove and discard tea bags. Refrigerate tea in a covered container.

Just before serving, combine cranberry-raspberry concentrate and cold water in a 2-1/2-qt. pitcher; stir in tea. Serve on ice. Garnish with mint. **Yield:** 10 (1-cup) servings.

Four-Cheese Pate

This impressive and festive-looking cheese spread is simple to put together and never fails to get raves at parties. —Jeanne Messina, Darien, Connecticut

3 packages (8 ounces *each*) cream cheese, softened, *divided*
2 tablespoons milk
2 tablespoons sour cream
3/4 cup chopped pecans
4 ounces Brie *or* Camembert, rind removed, softened
1 cup (4 ounces) shredded Swiss cheese
4 ounces crumbled blue cheese
1/2 cup pecan halves
Red and green apple slices *or* crackers

In a mixing bowl, beat one package of cream cheese with milk and sour cream until smooth. Spread into a 9-in. pie plate lined with plastic wrap. Sprinkle with chopped pecans.

In a mixing bowl, beat Brie, Swiss, blue cheese and remaining cream cheese until thoroughly combined. Gently spread over chopped pecans, smoothing the top to form a flat surface. Cover and chill overnight or up to 3-4 days.

Before serving, invert onto a plate and remove plastic wrap. Arrange pecan halves on top. Serve with apples or crackers. **Yield:** 16-20 servings.

Hard-Cooking Eggs

To cook eggs in their shells, place them in a single layer in a saucepan and cover with at least 1 in. of water. Cover and bring to a boil; remove from heat and let stand in the water for 15-17 minutes. Drain off hot water and immediately cover with cold water until completely cooled.

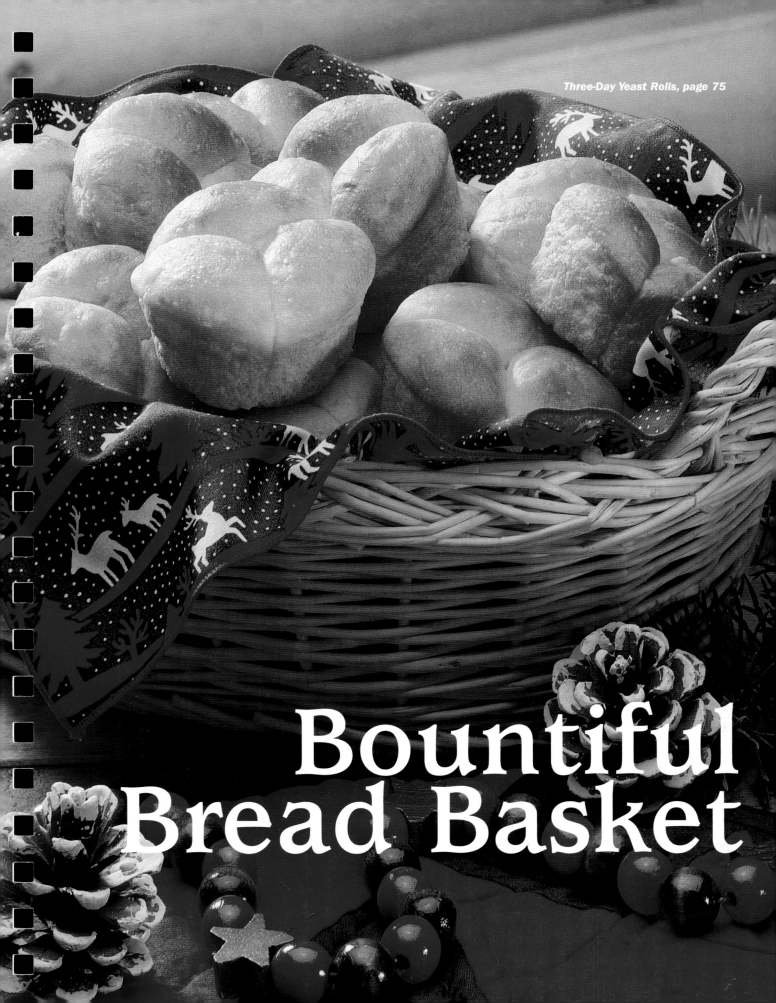

Three-Day Yeast Rolls, page 75

Bountiful Bread Basket

Top to bottom: Onion French Bread and Cherry Lattice Coffee Cake

Onion French Bread

(Pictured at left)

Holiday meals are even more memorable with this chewy onion bread. —Sandi Pichon, Slidell, Louisiana

- **5** **to 5-1/2 cups all-purpose flour**
- **1** **envelope onion soup mix**
- **2** **packages (1/4 ounce *each*) active dry yeast**
- **3** **tablespoons sugar**
- **2** **teaspoons salt**
- **2** **cups warm water (120° to 130°)**
- **2** **tablespoons shortening**
- **1** **egg white**
- **1** **tablespoon water**

In a mixing bowl, combine 2 cups flour, soup mix, yeast, sugar and salt; add warm water and shortening. Beat on medium speed for 3 minutes. Add enough remaining flour to form a soft dough. Turn onto a floured surface; knead until smooth and elastic, about 3 minutes. Place in a greased bowl, turning once to grease top.

Cover and let rise in a warm place until doubled, about 1 hour. Punch dough down; knead 4-5 times. Divide in half. Roll each portion into a 14-in. x 6-in. rectangle. Roll up, jelly-roll style, starting with a long side; pinch edges and ends to seal. Place seam side down on a greased baking sheet.

Beat egg white and water; brush over loaves. Cover with plastic wrap that has been sprayed with nonstick cooking spray; let rise until doubled, about 30-40 minutes. With a sharp knife, make four shallow diagonal cuts across the top. Bake at 375° for 30-35 minutes or until golden brown. Cool on a wire rack. **Yield:** 2 loaves.

Cherry Lattice Coffee Cake

(Pictured at left)

This coffee cake is an all-time favorite with my seven grandchildren. —Mrs. Otto Stank, Pound, Wisconsin

- **1** **package (1/4 ounce) active dry yeast**
- **1/4** **cup warm water (110° to 115°)**
- **1** **cup (8 ounces) sour cream**
- **1** **egg**
- **3** **tablespoons sugar**
- **2** **tablespoons butter, softened**
- **1** **teaspoon salt**
- **3** **cups all-purpose flour**

FILLING:
- **2-1/2** **cups fresh *or* frozen pitted tart cherries, thawed, rinsed and drained**
- **1/2** **to 3/4 cup sugar**
- **1/2** **cup chopped almonds, toasted**
- **2** **tablespoons all-purpose flour**

Dash salt

In a mixing bowl, dissolve yeast in water; let stand for 5 minutes. Add sour cream, egg, sugar, butter, salt and 2 cups flour; beat until smooth. Add enough remaining flour to form a soft dough. Turn onto a floured surface; knead until smooth and elastic, about 6-8 minutes. Place in a greased bowl, turning once to grease top.

Cover and let rise in a warm place until doubled, about 1 hour. Punch dough down. Reserve 1 cup dough. Divide remaining dough in half. Roll each portion into a 9-in. circle; place in greased 9-in. round baking pans.

Combine filling ingredients; spread over dough to within 1/2 in. of edge. Roll out reserved dough to 1/4-in. thickness; cut into 1/2-in. strips. Make a lattice top over filling. Cover and let rise until doubled, about 45 minutes. Bake at 375° for 15 minutes. Cover top with foil; bake 20 minutes longer or until browned. **Yield:** 2 coffee cakes.

Easy Batter Rolls

The first thing my guests ask when they come for dinner is if I'm serving these dinner rolls. They are all smiles when I assure them the answer is yes.
—Thomasina Brunner, Gloversville, New York

- **3** **cups all-purpose flour**
- **2** **tablespoons sugar**
- **1** **package (1/4 ounce) active dry yeast**
- **1** **teaspoon salt**
- **1** **cup water**
- **2** **tablespoons butter**
- **1** **egg**

Melted butter

In a mixing bowl, combine 2 cups flour, sugar, yeast and salt. In a saucepan, heat water and butter to 120°-130°. Add to dry ingredients; beat until blended. Add egg; beat on low for 30 seconds, then on high for 3 minutes. Stir in remaining flour (batter will be stiff). Do not knead. Cover; let rise in a warm place until doubled, about 30 minutes. Stir dough down. Fill greased muffin cups half full. Cover, let rise until doubled, about 40 minutes.

Bake at 350° for 15-20 minutes or until golden brown. Cool for 1 minute before removing from pan to a wire rack. Brush tops with melted butter. **Yield:** 1 dozen.

Italian Cheese Twists

(Pictured above)

My family loves breadsticks, and this recipe was an immediate success. The breadsticks look delicate and fancy, but they aren't tricky to make using prepared bread dough. We love the herb flavor. —Marna Heitz
Farley, Iowa

- 1 **loaf (1 pound) frozen bread dough, thawed**
- 1/4 **cup butter, softened**
- 1/4 **teaspoon garlic powder**
- 1/4 **teaspoon *each* dried basil, oregano and marjoram**
- 3/4 **cup shredded mozzarella cheese**
- 1 **egg**
- 1 **tablespoon water**
- 2 **tablespoons sesame seeds *and/or* grated Parmesan cheese**

On a lightly floured surface, roll dough into a 12-in. square. Combine butter and seasonings; spread over dough. Sprinkle with mozzarella cheese.

Fold dough into thirds. Cut crosswise into 24 strips, 1/2 in. each. Twist each strip twice; pinch ends to seal. Place the strips 2 in. apart on a greased baking sheet. Cover and let rise in a warm place until almost doubled, about 30 minutes.

In a small bowl, beat egg and water; brush over the twists.

Sprinkle with sesame seeds and/or Parmesan cheese. Bake at 375° for 10-12 minutes or until light golden brown. **Yield:** 2 dozen.

Mom's Buttermilk Biscuits

(Pictured below)

These fluffy biscuits are so tasty served warm, slathered with butter or used to mop every last drop of gravy off your plate. I can still see Mom pulling these tender biscuits out of the oven. —Vera Reid
Laramie, Wyoming

- 2 **cups all-purpose flour**
- 2 **teaspoons baking powder**
- 1/2 **teaspoon baking soda**
- 1/2 **teaspoon salt**
- 1/4 **cup shortening**
- 3/4 **cup buttermilk**

In a bowl, combine the flour, baking powder, baking soda and salt; cut in shortening until the mixture resembles coarse crumbs. Stir in buttermilk; knead dough gently.

Roll out to 1/2-in. thickness. Cut with a 2-1/2-in. biscuit cutter and place on a lightly greased baking sheet. Bake at 450° for 10-15 minutes or until the biscuits are golden brown. **Yield:** 10 biscuits.

Honey Wheat Bread

(Pictured below)

This recipe produces two beautiful, high loaves that have wonderful texture and slice well. The tempting aroma of this bread baking can cut the chill from a cold winter day. —Dorothy Anderson, Ottawa, Kansas

  2-1/2 to 3 cups all-purpose flour
  3-1/2 cups whole wheat flour, *divided*
      2 packages (1/4 ounce *each*) active dry yeast
      1 cup milk
  1-1/4 cups water
    1/4 cup honey
      3 tablespoons butter
      1 tablespoon salt

In a large mixing bowl, combine 2 cups all-purpose flour, 2 cups whole wheat flour and yeast. In a saucepan, heat milk, water, honey, butter and salt to 120°-130°; add to flour mixture. Blend on low speed until moistened; beat on medium for 3 minutes. Gradually stir in remaining whole wheat flour and enough of the remaining all-purpose flour to form a soft dough.

Turn onto a floured surface; knead until smooth and elastic, about 6-8 minutes. Place in a greased bowl, turning once to grease top. Cover and let rise in a warm place until doubled, about 1 hour. Punch dough down.

Shape into two loaves; place in greased 8-in. x 4-in. x 2-in. loaf pans. Cover and let rise until doubled, about 1 hour. Bake at 375° for 40-45 minutes. Remove from pans to cool on wire racks. **Yield:** 2 loaves.

Easy Potato Rolls

(Pictured above)

After I discovered this recipe, it became a mainstay for me. I make the dough ahead of time when company is coming, and I try to keep some in the refrigerator to make for "hay hands" on our cattle ranch.
—Jeanette McKinney, Belleview, Missouri

    2/3 cup sugar
    2/3 cup shortening
      1 cup mashed potatoes
  2-1/2 teaspoons salt
      2 eggs
      2 packages (1/4 ounce *each*) active dry yeast
  1-1/3 cups warm water (110° to 115°), *divided*
      6 to 6-1/2 cups all-purpose flour

In a large mixing bowl, cream sugar and shortening. Add potatoes, salt and eggs. In a small bowl, dissolve yeast in 2/3 cup of warm water; add to creamed mixture. Beat in 2 cups flour and remaining water. Add enough remaining flour to form a soft dough.

Shape into a ball; do not knead. Place in a greased bowl, turning once to grease top. Cover and let rise in a warm place until doubled, about 1 hour. Punch dough down; divide into thirds. Shape each portion into 15 balls and arrange in three greased 9-in. round baking pans. Cover and let rise until doubled, about 30 minutes. Bake at 375° for 20-25 minutes. Remove from pans to cool on wire racks. **Yield:** 45 rolls.

Top to bottom: Cloverleaf Rolls and
Crispy Almond Strips

Cloverleaf Rolls

(Pictured at left)

Tender and tasty, these rolls have been a favorite among our friends and family for many years. I'm the official holiday baker for our clan, so I bake dozens of these come Christmas. —Pam Hays
Little Rock, Arkansas

 2 **packages (1/4 ounce *each*) active dry yeast**
 1/2 **cup warm water (110° to 115°)**
 1-1/2 **cups warm milk (110° to 115°)**
 1/2 **cup sugar**
 1 **egg**
 1/4 **cup shortening**
 2 **teaspoons salt**
 5-1/2 **to 6 cups all-purpose flour**

In a mixing bowl, dissolve yeast in water. Beat in milk, sugar, egg, shortening and salt and 2 cups of flour until smooth. Stir in enough of the remaining flour to form a soft dough.

Turn onto a floured surface; knead until smooth and elastic, about 6-8 minutes. Place in a greased bowl, turning once to grease top. Cover and let rise in a warm place until doubled, about 1 hour. Punch dough down.

Roll into 90 balls; place three balls each in greased muffin cups. Cover and let rise until doubled, about 45 minutes. Bake at 375° for 12-14 minutes or until golden brown. Cool on wire racks. **Yield:** 2-1/2 dozen.

Crispy Almond Strips

(Pictured at left)

Remember sprinkling cinnamon and sugar on pieces of pastry dough and popping them in the oven along with the pie you just helped make? That's just what these crisp strips taste like. —Darlene Markel
Roseburg, Oregon

 1 **cup cold butter**
 2 **cups all-purpose flour**
 1/2 **cup sour cream**
 2/3 **cup sugar, *divided***
 1 **cup ground almonds**
 1 **teaspoon ground cinnamon**

In a bowl, cut butter into flour until mixture resembles coarse crumbs. With a fork, stir in sour cream until blended. Divide in half; shape each half into a ball and flatten. Wrap tightly and freeze for 20 minutes.

Sprinkle 1/3 cup sugar on a lightly floured surface; roll each portion of dough into a 12-in. square. Combine the ground almonds, cinnamon and remaining sugar; sprinkle over the dough.

Using a rolling pin, press the nut mixture into the dough. Cut into 1-in. strips; cut each strip widthwise into thirds. Place the strips 1 in. apart on greased baking sheets. Bake at 400° for 12-14 minutes or until golden brown. **Yield:** 6 dozen.

Squash Braid

My friend gave me this recipe when I first started making bread. It's golden on the outside and the in-side—beautiful and colorful besides being so deli-cious. I love to bake it in the fall and winter. —Amy Martin, Waddell, Arizona

 1 **package (1/4 ounce) active dry yeast**
 2 **tablespoons warm water (110° to 115°)**
 1 **cup mashed cooked butternut squash**
 1/3 **cup warm milk (110° to 115°)**
 1/4 **cup butter, softened**
 1 **egg**
 3 **tablespoons brown sugar**
 1/4 **teaspoon salt**
 3 **to 3-1/2 cups all-purpose flour**
GLAZE:
 1 **egg, beaten**
 1 **tablespoon water**

In a small bowl, dissolve the yeast in warm water. In a mixing bowl, combine the squash, milk, butter, egg, brown sugar and salt; mix well. Add the yeast mixture and 1-1/2 cups all-pur-pose flour; mix well. Add enough of the remaining flour to form a soft dough.

Turn onto a floured surface; knead until smooth and elastic, about 6-8 minutes. Place in a greased bowl, turning once to grease top. Cover and let rise in a warm place until doubled, about 1 hour. Punch dough down.

Divide the dough into thirds; roll each third into an 18-in. rope. Place on a greased baking sheet. Braid ropes together; pinch ends. Cover and let the dough rise until nearly doubled, about 30 minutes. Combine glaze ingredients; brush over braid.

Bake at 350° for 20-25 minutes or until golden brown. Remove from pan and cool on a wire rack. **Yield:** 1 loaf.

Cinnamon Twists

(Pictured below)

These delightful golden twists are perfect as part of a holiday meal. The brown sugar and cinnamon give them a delicate spicy flavor. It's a good thing the recipe makes a big batch because people can rarely eat just one.
—Janet Mooberry, Peoria, Illinois

- 1 package (1/4 ounce) active dry yeast
- 3/4 cup warm water (110° to 115°), *divided*
- 4 to 4-1/2 cups all-purpose flour
- 1/4 cup sugar
- 1-1/2 teaspoons salt
- 1/2 cup warm milk (110° to 115°)
- 1/4 cup butter, softened
- 1 egg

FILLING:
- 1/4 cup butter, melted
- 1/2 cup packed brown sugar
- 4 teaspoons ground cinnamon

In a large mixing bowl, dissolve yeast in 1/4 cup warm water. Add 2 cups of flour, sugar, salt, milk, butter, egg and remaining water; beat on medium speed for 2 minutes. Stir in enough remaining flour to form a soft dough.

Turn onto a floured surface; knead until smooth and elastic, about 6-8 minutes. Place in a greased bowl, turning once to grease top. Cover and let rise in a warm place until doubled, about 1 hour. Punch down. Roll into a 16-in. x 12-in. rectangle. Brush with butter.

Combine brown sugar and cinnamon; sprinkle over butter. Let dough rest for 6 minutes. Cut lengthwise into three 16-in. x 4-in. strips. Cut each strip into sixteen 4-in. x 1-in. pieces. Twist and place on greased baking sheets. Cover and let rise until doubled, about 30 minutes. Bake at 350° for 15 minutes or until golden. **Yield:** 4 dozen.

Cherry Apricot Tea Bread

(Pictured above)

This recipe makes three loaves of bread. My family eats up one loaf, then I give one loaf as a gift and freeze the other.
—Patty Bourne, Owings, Maryland

FILLING:
- 1 package (8 ounces) dried apricots, chopped
- 2 cups boiling water
- 1 jar (16 ounces) maraschino cherries, drained and chopped

BREAD:
- 2 packages (1/4 ounce *each*) active dry yeast
- 1/2 cup warm water (110° to 115°)
- 2 cups (16 ounces) sour cream
- 1/3 cup sugar
- 1/4 cup butter, melted
- 1-1/2 teaspoons salt

         2 **eggs**
6-1/2 **to 7 cups all-purpose flour**
GLAZE:
         1 **cup confectioners' sugar**
         1 **tablespoon milk**
**Additional maraschino cherries and dried apricots,
   optional**

In a small bowl, combine apricots and water; let stand for 1 hour. Drain. Add cherries; set aside. In a mixing bowl, dissolve yeast in water; let stand for 5 minutes. Add sour cream, sugar, butter, salt, eggs and 2 cups flour; beat until smooth. Stir in enough remaining flour to form a soft dough.

Turn onto a floured surface; knead until smooth and elastic, about 6-8 minutes. Place in a greased bowl, turning once to grease top. Cover and let rise in a warm place until doubled, about 1 hour. Punch dough down; divide into thirds. On a floured surface, roll each third into a 15-in. x 6-in. rectangle.

Place each on a greased baking sheet. Spoon a third of the filling down the center of each rectangle. On each long side, cut 1-in.-wide strips 2 in. into the center. Starting at one end, fold alternating strips at an angle across filling. Seal end. Cover and let rise until almost doubled, about 30 minutes.

Bake at 375° for 15-20 minutes or until golden brown. Cover with foil if browning too fast. Cool. Combine sugar and milk; drizzle over bread. Garnish with cherries and apricots if desired. **Yield:** 3 loaves.

Cornmeal Muffins

Corn bread is very popular in this part of the country as a complement to soup. These muffins are easy to make.
                      —Amelia Moody, Pasadena, Texas

      1 **cup all-purpose flour**
      1 **cup yellow cornmeal**
1/3 **cup sugar**
      1 **tablespoon baking powder**
      1 **teaspoon salt**
      2 **tablespoons finely chopped onion**
      1 **cup cream-style corn**
1/2 **cup mayonnaise**
      3 **tablespoons vegetable oil**
      1 **egg**

In a large mixing bowl, combine flour, cornmeal, sugar, baking powder and salt. Add onion, corn, mayonnaise, oil and egg; stir just until dry ingredients are moistened. Fill greased or paper-lined muffin cups two-thirds full. Bake at 400° for 20 minutes. **Yield:** 12 muffins.

Skillet Herb Bread

(Pictured below)

My grandmother, aunts and mom were all good cooks, and each had her own specialty when it came to bread. But Mom's was my favorite.   *—Shirley Smith*
                                              Yorba Linda, California

1-1/2 **cups all-purpose flour**
         2 **tablespoons sugar**
         4 **teaspoons baking powder**
1-1/2 **teaspoons salt**
         1 **teaspoon rubbed sage**
         1 **teaspoon dried thyme**
1-1/2 **cups yellow cornmeal**
1-1/2 **cups chopped celery**
         1 **cup chopped onion**
         1 **jar (2 ounces) chopped pimientos, drained**
         3 **eggs, beaten**
1-1/2 **cups milk**
1/3 **cup vegetable oil**

In a large bowl, combine the flour, sugar, baking powder, salt, sage and thyme. Combine cornmeal, celery, onion and pimientos; add to dry ingredients and mix well. Add eggs, milk and oil; stir just until moistened.

Pour into a greased 10- or 11-in. ovenproof skillet. Bake at 400° for 35-45 minutes or until a toothpick comes out clean. Serve warm. **Yield:** 10 servings.

Whole Wheat Refrigerator Rolls

(Pictured above)

This roll recipe is easy and versatile. I like to mix up the dough beforehand and let it rise in the refrigerator.
—Sharon Mensing, Greenfield, Iowa

  2 **packages (1/4 ounce *each*) active dry yeast**
  2 **cups warm water (110° to 115°)**
1/2 **cup sugar**
  2 **teaspoons salt**
4-1/2 to 5 **cups all-purpose flour**
  1 **egg**
1/4 **cup vegetable oil**
  2 **cups whole wheat flour**

In a mixing bowl, dissolve yeast in water. Let stand 5 minutes. Blend in sugar, salt and 3 cups all-purpose flour at low speed until moistened; beat 2 minutes at medium speed. Beat in egg and oil.

By hand, gradually stir in whole wheat flour and enough remaining all-purpose flour to form a soft dough. Turn onto a lightly floured surface. Knead until smooth and elastic, about 6-8 minutes. Place in a greased bowl, turning once to grease top. Cover and let rise until doubled or cover and refrigerate. Punch dough down and form into dinner rolls.

Place on greased baking sheets for plain rolls, or in greased muffin tins for cloverleaf rolls. Cover and let rise until doubled, about 1 hour for dough prepared the same day or 1-2 hours for refrigerated dough. Bake at 375° for 10-12 minutes or until light golden brown. Serve warm. **Yield:** 2 dozen.

Editor's Note: Dough may be kept up to 3 days in the refrigerator. Punch down daily.

Cranberry Fruit Bread

(Pictured below)

My family looks forward to this flavorful combination of cranberry bread and fruitcake for the holidays. This bread also freezes well. *—Ellen Puotinen*
Tower, Minnesota

  1 **package (12 ounces) fresh *or* frozen cranberries, halved**
  2 **cups pecan halves**
  1 **cup chopped mixed candied fruit**
  1 **cup chopped dates**
  1 **cup golden raisins**
  1 **tablespoon grated orange peel**
  4 **cups all-purpose flour, *divided***
  2 **cups sugar**
  1 **tablespoon baking powder**
  1 **teaspoon baking soda**
1/4 **teaspoon salt**
  2 **eggs**
  1 **cup orange juice**
1/4 **cup shortening, melted**
1/4 **cup warm water**

Combine the first six ingredients with 1/4 cup flour; set aside. In another bowl, combine sugar, baking powder, baking soda, salt and remaining flour; set aside.

In a large mixing bowl, beat eggs. Add orange juice, shortening and water. Add flour mixture; stir just until combined. Fold in cranberry mixture. Spoon into three greased and waxed paper-lined 8-1/2-in. x 4-1/2-in. x 2-1/2-in. loaf pans.

Bake at 350° for 60-65 minutes or until a toothpick comes out clean. Cool 10 minutes in the pans. Remove to a wire rack. Remove waxed paper and continue to cool on the rack. **Yield:** 3 loaves.

Three-Day Yeast Rolls

(Pictured on page 63)

These rolls are excellent for Thanksgiving, Christmas or most any time you have company or a special occasion to celebrate. I especially like them because I can get the time-consuming steps out of the way days before I serve them. —Kelly Hardgrave, Hartman, Arkansas

> 2 packages (1/4 ounce *each*) active dry yeast
> 2 cups warm water (110° to 115°), *divided*
> 1 cup butter, softened
> 3/4 cup sugar
> 2 eggs
> 2 teaspoons salt
> 7-1/2 to 8 cups all-purpose flour
> Additional butter, melted, optional

In a mixing bowl, dissolve yeast in 1/4 cup water. Add butter, sugar, eggs, salt and remaining water; mix well. Add 2 cups flour; beat until smooth. Gradually stir in enough remaining flour to form a soft dough (do not knead).

Place in a greased bowl, turning once to grease top. Cover and refrigerate for up to 3 days. Punch dough down each day. When ready to use, turn out onto a floured surface; knead until smooth and elastic, about 6-8 minutes. Shape into rolls as desired.

Place in greased muffin cups or on baking sheets. Cover and let rise until nearly doubled, about 1 hour. Bake at 375° for 10-15 minutes or until golden brown. Brush with butter if desired. Immediately remove to wire racks to cool. **Yield:** 3-4 dozen.

Apple Ladder Loaf

(Pictured above right)

I first served my family this rich bread with its spicy apple filling years ago. From the first bite, it was a hit with everyone. —Norma Foster, Compton, Illinois

> 2 packages (1/4 ounce *each*) active dry yeast
> 1/4 cup warm water (110° to 115°)
> 1/2 cup warm milk (110° to 115°)
> 1/2 cup butter, softened
> 1/3 cup sugar
> 4 eggs
> 1 teaspoon salt
> 4-1/2 to 4-3/4 cups all-purpose flour
> FILLING:
> 1/3 cup packed brown sugar

> 2 tablespoons all-purpose flour
> 1-1/4 teaspoons ground cinnamon
> 1/2 teaspoon ground nutmeg
> 1/8 teaspoon ground allspice
> 4 cups thinly sliced peeled tart apples
> 1/4 cup butter, softened
> ICING:
> 1 cup confectioners' sugar
> 1 to 2 tablespoons orange juice
> 1/4 teaspoon vanilla extract

In a mixing bowl, dissolve yeast in water. Add milk, butter, sugar, eggs, salt and 2 cups flour. Beat on low speed for 3 minutes. Stir in enough remaining flour to form a soft dough. Turn onto a floured surface; knead until smooth and elastic, about 6-8 minutes. Place in a greased bowl, turning once to grease top. Cover and refrigerate overnight; punch down after 1-2 hours.

For filling, combine brown sugar, flour, cinnamon, nutmeg and allspice in a small bowl. Add apples; toss to coat. Set aside. Punch dough down; divide in half. Roll each half into a 12-in. x 9-in. rectangle. Place each rectangle on a greased baking sheet. Spread with butter. Spread filling down center third of each rectangle.

On each long side, cut 1-in.-wide strips 3 in. into center. Starting at one end, fold alternating strips at an angle across filling; seal ends. Cover and let rise for 45-60 minutes or until nearly doubled. Bake at 350° for 30-40 minutes or until golden brown. Combine icing ingredients until smooth; drizzle over warm loaves. **Yield:** 2 loaves.

Orange Date Nut Bread

(Pictured below)

Pecans are very plentiful in the South, and this is one of my favorite ways to use them. No other date nut bread I've tried is anywhere near as flavorful as this one. —Joan Huggins, Waynesboro, Mississippi

- 2 **eggs**
- 2 **tablespoons butter**
- 3/4 **cup sugar**
- 1 **small unpeeled orange, cut into pieces and seeded**
- 1 **cup pitted chopped dates**
- 1-3/4 **cups all-purpose flour**
- 1 **teaspoon baking soda**
- 1 **teaspoon salt**
- 1 **cup chopped pecans**

SAUCE:
- 1/2 **cup orange juice**
- 1/2 **cup sugar**

Place eggs, butter, sugar, orange pieces and dates in a blender or food processor. Cover and process until finely chopped. Transfer to a large mixing bowl. In a separate bowl, combine flour, baking soda and salt; add to orange mixture and mix well.

Stir in the pecans. Pour into a greased 9-in. x 5-in. x 3-in. baking pan.

Bake at 325° for 1 hour or until a toothpick inserted near center comes out clean. If bread begins to darken, cover with foil during last few minutes of baking.

Meanwhile, for sauce, heat orange juice and sugar until sugar is dissolved. Prick bread with a toothpick; pour hot sauce over top. Cool in pan 15 minutes before removing to a wire rack to cool completely. **Yield:** 1 loaf.

Yogurt Yeast Rolls

(Pictured above)

People tend to snap up these fluffy, golden rolls in a hurry whenever I take them to a potluck. It's a nice contribution since rolls are easy to transport and one batch goes a long way. —Carol Forcum, Marion, Illinois

- 1-1/2 **cups whole wheat flour**
- 3-1/4 **cups all-purpose flour, *divided***
- 2 **packages (1/4 ounce *each*) active dry yeast**
- 2 **teaspoons salt**
- 1/2 **teaspoon baking soda**
- 1-1/2 **cups (12 ounces) plain yogurt**
- 1/2 **cup water**
- 3 **tablespoons butter**
- 2 **tablespoons honey**

In a mixing bowl, combine whole wheat flour, 1/2 cup all-purpose flour, yeast, salt and baking soda. In a saucepan over low heat, heat yogurt, water, butter and honey to 120°-130°. Pour

over dry ingredients; blend well. Beat on medium speed for 3 minutes. Add enough remaining all-purpose flour to form a soft dough.

Turn onto a floured surface; knead until smooth and elastic, about 6-8 minutes. Place in a greased bowl, turning once to grease top. Cover and let rise in a warm place until doubled, about 1 hour. Punch dough down; divide into 24 pieces.

Roll each piece into a 9-in. rope. To form S-shaped rolls, coil each end of rope toward center in opposite directions. Place 3 in. apart on greased baking sheets. Cover and let rise until doubled, about 30 minutes.

Bake at 400° for 15 minutes or until golden brown. Spray tops with nonstick cooking spray while warm. Cool on wire racks. **Yield:** 2 dozen.

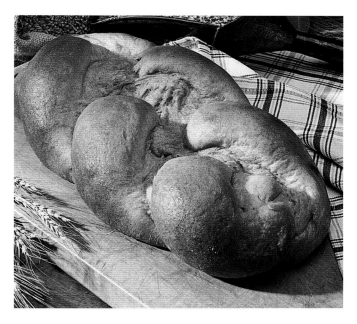

Cheese Twists

(Pictured above right)

These impressive loaves take a little time to prepare, but they're well worth the effort. I've used the recipe for several years. I love making bread—there's no better way to work out life's little frustrations and with such yummy results! —Michelle Beran, Claflin, Kansas

- **3-1/4 cups all-purpose flour**
- **2 packages (1/4 ounce *each*) active dry yeast**
- **1-1/2 cups buttermilk**
- **3/4 cup butter**
- **1/2 cup sugar**
- **1/2 teaspoon salt**
- **5 eggs**
- **3-1/2 to 4 cups whole wheat flour, *divided***
- **2 cups (8 ounces) shredded cheddar cheese**

In a large mixing bowl, combine all-purpose flour and yeast. In a saucepan, heat buttermilk, butter, sugar and salt to 120°-130°; add to flour mixture. Blend on low speed until moistened. Add eggs; beat on low for 30 seconds. Beat on high for 3 minutes. Stir in enough whole wheat flour to make a soft dough.

Turn onto a floured surface; knead until smooth and elastic, about 6-8 minutes. Place in a greased bowl, turning once to grease top. Cover and let rise in a warm place until nearly doubled, about 1 hour. Punch dough down; divide in half.

On a lightly floured surface, roll each into a 12-in. x 9-in. rectangle. Cut each into three 12-in. x 3-in. strips. Combine cheese with 2 tablespoons of the remaining whole wheat flour; sprinkle 1/3 cup down center of each strip. Bring long edges together over cheese and pinch to seal.

Place three strips seam side down on greased baking sheets. Braid strips together; secure ends. Cover and let rise until doubled, about 45 minutes. Bake at 375° for 20-25 minutes or until golden. Immediately remove to wire racks; cool. **Yield:** 2 loaves.

No-Knead Whole Wheat Bread

This simple recipe requires no kneading, so you can mix this up with less fuss. It still has that great fresh-from-the-oven flavor your family is sure to appreciate! —Barbara Ann Gross, APO, New York

- **1 package (1/4 ounce) active dry yeast**
- **1-1/4 cups warm water (110°-115°)**
- **2 tablespoons honey**
- **2 tablespoons butter**
- **1 teaspoon salt**
- **1-1/2 cup whole wheat flour**
- **1-1/2 cups all-purpose flour**

In a large mixing bowl, dissolve yeast in warm water. Stir in honey; add butter, salt and whole wheat flour. Beat on low speed until well-blended. Stir in all-purpose flour. Cover and let rise in a warm place until doubled, about 30 minutes.

Stir 30 strokes with a spoon; pour batter into a greased 8-1/2-in. x 4-1/2-in. bread pan. cover and let rise in a warm place until batter reaches edge of pan, about 30 minutes. Bake at 375° for 30-40 minutes. Cool on wire rack. **Yield:** 1 loaf.

Sally Lunn
Batter Bread

(Pictured below)

The tantalizing aroma of this golden loaf baking always draws people into my mother's kitchen. With its circular shape, it's a pretty bread, too. I've never seen it last more than 2 hours once it's out of the oven!
—Jeanne Voss, Anaheim Hills, California

    1 package (1/4 ounce) active dry yeast
1/2 cup warm water (110° to 115°)
    1 cup warm milk (110° to 115°)
1/2 cup butter, softened
1/4 cup sugar
    2 teaspoons salt
    3 eggs
5-1/2 to 6 cups all-purpose flour
HONEY BUTTER:
1/2 cup butter, softened
1/2 cup honey

In a mixing bowl, dissolve yeast in warm water. Add the milk, butter, sugar, salt, eggs and 3 cups flour. Beat until smooth. Stir in enough remaining flour to form a soft dough (do not knead). Cover and let rise in a warm place until doubled, about 1 hour.

Stir the dough down. Spoon into a greased and floured 10-in. tube pan. Cover and let rise until doubled, about 1 hour. Bake at 400° for 25-30 minutes or until golden brown. Remove from pan to a wire rack.

Combine the honey butter ingredients until smooth. Serve with bread. **Yield:** 12-16 servings.

Blue-Ribbon
Herb Rolls

(Pictured above)

I developed these rolls by using several ideas and techniques while learning the art of bread making. It won a blue ribbon at our county fair.   —Mary Ann Evans
Tarpon Springs, Florida

    2 packages (1/4 ounce *each*) active dry yeast
2-3/4 cups warm water (110° to 115°), *divided*
    1 egg, beaten
1/3 cup vegetable oil
1/4 cup honey *or* molasses
    1 tablespoon salt
    2 teaspoons dill weed
    2 teaspoons dried thyme
    2 teaspoons dried basil
    1 teaspoon onion powder
    4 cups whole wheat flour
    4 to 4-1/2 cups all-purpose flour

In a mixing bowl, dissolve yeast in 1/2 cup warm water. Add the next nine ingredients and remaining water; beat until smooth. Gradually add enough all-purpose flour to form a soft dough. Turn onto a floured surface; knead until smooth and elastic, about 6-8 minutes.

Place in a greased bowl, turning once to grease top. Cover and let rise in a warm place until doubled, about 1 hour. Punch dough down. Shape into 1-in. balls. Place three balls each in greased muffin cups. Cover and let rise until doubled, about 20-25 minutes.

Bake at 375° for 12-15 minutes or until golden brown. Remove from pan to a wire rack. **Yield:** 4 dozen.

Sweet 'n' Savory Date Loaves

My family and I were thrilled when this won "best of show" for quick breads at the state fair. I sometimes substitute peach nectar for the apricot nectar with terrific results. —Diane Card, Hilliard, Ohio

1-1/2	cups apricot nectar
1-1/2	cups chopped dates
1/2	cup chopped dried apricots
1	tablespoon grated orange peel
1-1/4	teaspoons dried rosemary, crushed
1/2	cup butter, softened
1	cup sugar
1	egg
1/3	cup evaporated milk
2-1/4	cups all-purpose flour
1-1/2	teaspoons baking soda

In a saucepan, bring the apricot nectar, dates and apricots to a boil. Reduce heat; cover and simmer for 5 minutes. Remove from the heat; add orange peel and rosemary. Cool for 10 minutes.

In a mixing bowl, cream butter and sugar. Beat in egg and milk. Combine flour and baking soda; add to creamed mixture alternately with date mixture. Pour into three greased 5-3/4-in. x 3-in. x 2-in. loaf pans.

Bake at 375° for 30-35 minutes or until a toothpick comes out clean. Cool for 10 minutes before removing from pans to wire racks. **Yield:** 3 mini loaves.

Pull-Apart Bacon Bread

(Pictured above right)

I stumbled across this recipe while looking for something different to take to a brunch. Boy, am I glad I did! Everyone asked for the recipe and could not believe it only called for five ingredients. It's the perfect item to bake for an informal get-together or event.
—Traci Collins, Cheyenne, Wyoming

12	bacon strips, diced
1	loaf (1 pound) frozen bread dough, thawed
2	tablespoons olive oil, *divided*

1	cup (4 ounces) shredded mozzarella cheese
1	envelope ranch salad dressing mix

In a skillet, cook bacon over medium heat for 5 minutes or until partially cooked; drain on paper towels. Roll out dough to 1/2-in. thickness; brush with 1 tablespoon of oil. Cut into 1-in. pieces; place in a large bowl. Add the bacon, cheese, salad dressing mix and remaining oil; toss to coat.

Arrange pieces in a 9-in. x 5-in. oval on a greased baking sheet, layering as needed. Cover and let rise in a warm place for 30 minutes or until doubled.

Bake at 350° for 15 minutes. Cover with foil; bake 5-10 minutes longer or until golden brown. **Yield:** 1 loaf.

Bread Basics

- Many yeast bread recipes give a range of flour amounts. Begin by adding the lower amount, using only enough to keep the dough from becoming too sticky to work with.
- When kneading bread, place a damp dish towel under the floured surface you're working on to keep it from moving around on the countertop.

kin, molasses, egg, butter and milk. Beat on low speed for 30 seconds, then on high for 2 minutes. Add the remaining flour; beat on high for 2 minutes.

Pour into two greased 4-1/2-in. x 2-1/2-in. x 1-1/2-in. loaf pans. (There will be a small amount of batter in each pan.) Combine topping ingredients; sprinkle over batter.

Bake at 350° for 35-40 minutes or until a toothpick inserted near the center comes out clean. Cool for 10 minutes before removing to wire racks to cool completely. **Yield:** 2 mini loaves.

Parker House Rolls

(Pictured below)

My mom is especially well-known for the delectable things she bakes, like these moist, golden rolls. When that basket comes around the table, we all automatically take two because one is just never enough.
— *Sandra Melnychenko, Grandview, Manitoba*

    1 **package (1/4 ounce) active dry yeast**
    1 **teaspoon plus 6 tablespoons sugar,** *divided*
    1 **cup warm water (110° to 115°),** *divided*

Pumpkin Gingerbread

(Pictured above)

Pumpkin and ginger are so compatible that to use them in one recipe makes this quick bread doubly delicious. This is my favorite bread during the holiday season because these old-fashioned flavors evoke warm memories of times past.
— *Mrs. Edwin Hill*
Santa Barbara, California

    1 **cup all-purpose flour,** *divided*
  1/4 **cup packed brown sugar**
    1 **teaspoon baking powder**
  1/2 **teaspoon ground cinnamon**
  1/2 **teaspoon ground ginger**
  1/4 **teaspoon baking soda**
  1/4 **cup canned pumpkin**
  1/4 **cup molasses**
    1 **egg**
2-1/2 **tablespoons butter, softened**
    2 **tablespoons milk**
TOPPING:
  1/3 **cup chopped walnuts**
    1 **tablespoon sugar**

In a small mixing bowl, combine 1/2 cup flour, brown sugar, baking powder, cinnamon, ginger and baking soda. Add pump-

1 cup warm milk (110° to 115°)
1 tablespoon salt
5-1/2 to 6 cups all-purpose flour
1 egg
2 tablespoons plus 2 teaspoons vegetable oil
3 tablespoons butter, melted, optional

In a mixing bowl, dissolve yeast and 1 teaspoon sugar in 1/2 cup water; let stand for 10 minutes. Add milk, salt and remaining sugar and water. Gradually add 2 cups flour; beat until smooth. Beat in egg and oil. Stir in enough remaining flour to make a soft dough.

Turn onto a floured surface; knead until smooth and elastic, about 6-8 minutes. Place in a greased bowl, turning once to grease top. Cover and let rise in a warm place until doubled, about 1 hour. Punch dough down. Divide in half; roll each half on a floured surface to 1/3- or 1/2-in. thickness.

Cut with a floured 2-1/2-in. round cutter. Brush with butter if desired. Using the dull edge of a table knife, make an off-center crease in each roll. Fold along crease so the large half is on top. Press along folded edge.

Place 2-3 in. apart on greased baking sheets. Cover and let rise until doubled, about 30 minutes. Bake at 375° for 15-20 minutes or until golden brown. Remove from pans and cool on wire racks. **Yield:** 2-1/2 dozen.

Sour Cream Twists

(Pictured above right)

The recipe for these tasty twists has been in my family for generations. I like to give them a festive look for the holidays by adding red or green colored sugar.
—Kathy Floyd, Greenville, Florida

1 package (1/4 ounce) active dry yeast
1/4 cup warm water (110° to 115°)

Better Butter

Stir things up by making your own flavored butter! You can add minced herbs, grated cheeses, ground and toasted sesame seeds, spices, mustards, syrups, liquors or juices. Begin with softened butter and blend or beat in your favorite ingredient. When adding a liquid (honey, maple syrup, orange juice, etc.), add it gradually and beat constantly to prevent the mixture from separating.

4 cups all-purpose flour
3/4 teaspoon salt
1/2 cup cold butter
1/2 cup shortening
2 eggs, lightly beaten
1/2 cup sour cream
3 teaspoons vanilla extract, *divided*
1-1/2 cups sugar
Red *or* green colored sugar

In a small bowl, dissolve yeast in water. In a mixing bowl, combine flour and salt. Cut in butter and shortening until mixture resembles coarse crumb. Stir in eggs, sour cream, 1 teaspoon vanilla and the yeast mixture. Mix thoroughly (dough will be stiff and resemble pie pastry).

Combine white sugar and remaining vanilla; lightly sprinkle 1/2 cup over a pastry cloth. Roll out half of the dough into a rectangle. Sprinkle with about 1 tablespoon of the sugar mixture plus some red or green colored sugar.

Fold rectangle into thirds (fold one end of dough over center and fold other end over to make three layers). Give dough a quarter turn and repeat rolling, sugaring and folding two more times. Roll out into a 16-in. x 9-in. rectangle. Cut into 3-in. x 1-in. strips. Twist each strip two or three times.

Place on chilled ungreased baking sheets. Repeat with remaining dough, sugar mixture and colored sugar. Bake at 375° for 15-20 minutes or until light golden brown. Cool on wire racks. **Yield:** 8 dozen.

Top to bottom: Christmas Stollen (recipe on page 84), Cranberry Christmas Canes and Butter Rings

Butter Rings

(Pictured at left)

Mother used to make this coffee cake for special occasions. She clipped the recipe from a newspaper more than 55 years ago; it's still a treasured favorite.
—*Florence McBride, Harvard, Illinois*

- 1 package (1/4 ounce) active dry yeast
- 3 tablespoons sugar, *divided*
- 1/4 cup warm milk (110° to 115°)
- 4 cups all-purpose flour
- 1 teaspoon salt
- 1/2 cup cold butter
- 3 egg yolks
- 1 cup half-and-half cream, heated to lukewarm

Chopped nuts for garnish

ICING:
- 1 cup confectioners' sugar
- 1 tablespoon milk
- 1/4 teaspoon vanilla extract

Dissolve yeast and 2 teaspoons sugar in milk; set aside. Combine flour, salt and remaining sugar. Cut in butter until crumbly. Beat the egg yolks into the cream; add to the flour mixture along with the yeast mixture. Blend well and form into a ball. Place dough in a greased bowl; cover and refrigerate overnight.

Punch dough down; place on a lightly floured surface and divide into six balls. Roll each ball into a 24-in. rope. On a greased baking sheet, twist two ropes together, then shape into a 6- to 8-in. ring. Pinch ends together and sprinkle with nuts. Repeat with remaining two rings.

Cover and allow to rise until almost doubled, about 30-45 minutes. Bake at 350° for about 25 minutes or until golden brown. Place on wire racks. Combine icing ingredients; drizzle over warm rings. **Yield:** 3 coffee cakes.

Cranberry Christmas Canes

(Pictured at left)

I received this recipe from my county home economist. See if it becomes a Christmas-morning tradition at your house like it has at ours!
—*Jan Malone*
Arapaho, Oklahoma

FILLING:
- 1-1/2 cups finely chopped fresh *or* frozen cranberries
- 1/2 cup sugar
- 1/2 cup raisins
- 1/3 cup chopped pecans
- 1/3 cup honey
- 1-1/2 teaspoons grated orange peel

DOUGH:
- 1 cup milk
- 1 package (1/4 ounce) active dry yeast
- 1/4 cup warm water (110° to 115°)
- 4 cups all-purpose flour
- 1/4 cup sugar
- 1 teaspoon salt
- 1 teaspoon grated lemon peel
- 1 cup cold butter
- 2 eggs, beaten

Confectioners' sugar icing, optional

In a saucepan, combine all filling ingredients. Bring to a boil; reduce heat and cook 5 minutes. Cool to room temperature.

Meanwhile, in a small saucepan, heat milk over medium heat until bubbles form around sides of pan; cool to lukewarm. Dissolve yeast in water; set aside. In a large mixing bowl, combine flour, sugar, salt and lemon peel. Cut in butter until the mixture resembles coarse crumbs. Add milk, yeast mixture and eggs. Combine to form a soft dough.

Place dough in a greased bowl. Cover tightly with plastic wrap; refrigerate for at least 2 hours. Divide dough in half. On a well-floured surface, roll out each half of the dough into an 18-in. x 15-in. rectangle.

Divide the filling and spread on each rectangle. Fold each rectangle into thirds, starting with the 15-in. side. Cut each piece into 15 short strips. Twist each strip and shape into a candy cane.

Place on greased baking sheets. Bake at 375° for 15-18 minutes or until golden brown. Cool on wire racks. Frost with confectioners' sugar icing if desired. **Yield:** 30 sweet rolls.

Freezing Holiday Breads

- Before cutting or storing your homemade breads, make sure they have cooled completely, sitting right side up on a rack.
- To freeze bread, double wrap it to make sure it is airtight. You can freeze yeast breads for up to 3 months; quick breads for up to 6 months. Wait to frost, glaze or ice the breads until they are thawed and ready to serve.

Christmas Stollen

(Pictured on page 82)

This is my favorite bread during the holidays. I've made it many times to give as Christmas gifts, and I always receive compliments on it. —Jenny Nichols
Arlington, Texas

1-1/2 **cups warm milk** *or* **water (110° to 115°)**
2 **packages (1/4 ounce** *each***) active dry yeast**
6-1/2 **to 7-1/2 cups all-purpose flour,** *divided*
1-1/2 **cups butter, softened**
3/4 **cup sugar**
3 **eggs**
3/4 **teaspoon salt**
3/4 **teaspoon grated lemon peel**
1/2 **pound raisins**
1/2 **pound chopped blanched almonds**
1/2 **cup chopped candied fruit**
3 **tablespoons butter, melted**
LEMON GLAZE:
1-1/4 **cups confectioners' sugar**
1/4 **cup lemon juice**
1 **teaspoon vanilla extract**

Combine milk and yeast. Let stand 3-5 minutes. Add 1 cup flour; mix well. Cover and let rest in a warm place until light and foamy, about 1 hour.

In a large mixing bowl, cream softened butter and sugar. Beat in eggs, one at a time. Add salt and lemon peel. Stir in

the yeast mixture and enough remaining flour to form a soft dough. Turn onto a floured surface; knead until smooth and elastic, about 6-8 minutes. Place in a greased bowl, turning once to grease top. Cover and let rise in a warm place until doubled, about 1 hour.

Punch dough down; knead in raisins, nuts and fruit. Divide into two parts; roll each into a 15-in. x 8-in. oval. Fold each in half lengthwise and place on a greased baking sheet. Brush with melted butter.

Cover and let rise until almost doubled, about 45 minutes. Bake at 350° for 30-40 minutes or until golden brown. Cool on wire racks.

Combine all glaze ingredients; brush over tops of cooled loaves. **Yield:** 2 loaves.

Orange Date Bread

(Pictured below left)

I loved visiting my aunt—she was an excellent baker, and her kitchen always smelled great. With her inspiration, I now bake this moist, yummy bread every holiday season. Christmas wouldn't be the same without it.
—Joann Wolfe, Sunland, California

1 **cup butter, softened**
2 **cups sugar**
3 **eggs**
4 **cups all-purpose flour**
1 **teaspoon baking soda**
1 **teaspoon salt**
1-1/3 **cups buttermilk**
1 **cup chopped walnuts**
1 **cup chopped dates**
1 **tablespoon grated orange peel**
GLAZE:
1/2 **cup sugar**
1/4 **cup orange juice**
2 **tablespoons grated orange peel**

In a mixing bowl, cream butter and sugar. Add eggs; mix well. Combine flour, baking soda and salt; add to creamed mixture alternately with buttermilk. Fold in walnuts, dates and orange peel. Pour into two greased and floured 8-1/2-in. x 4-1/2-in. x 2-1/2-in. loaf pans.

Bake at 350° for 60-65 minutes or until a toothpick comes out clean. Combine glaze ingredients; spoon half over hot bread. Cool for 10 minutes. Remove from pans; spoon remaining glaze over bread. **Yield:** 2 loaves.

Pumpkin Chocolate Chip Bread

(Pictured above)

I've enhanced and revised this recipe many times over the years. Adults and children alike love it!
—Sheri Barber, East Aurora, New York

1/2	cup butter, softened
1	cup sugar
1-1/4	cups canned pumpkin
2	eggs
2	cups all-purpose flour
1	teaspoon baking soda
1	teaspoon ground cinnamon
1/2	teaspoon ground nutmeg
1/2	teaspoon pumpkin pie spice
1/4	teaspoon ground cloves
1/4	teaspoon ground ginger
1/4	cup semisweet chocolate chips
1/4	cup chopped walnuts

GLAZE:

1/2	cup confectioners' sugar
1	tablespoon heavy whipping cream

In a mixing bowl, cream butter and sugar. Beat in pumpkin and eggs. Combine next seven ingredients; stir into creamed mixture and blend well. Stir in chocolate chips and nuts.

Pour into a greased and floured 9-in. x 5-in. x 3-in. loaf pan. Bake at 350° for 45-50 minutes or until a toothpick comes out clean. Cool on a wire rack. Combine glaze ingredients; drizzle over bread. **Yield:** 1 loaf.

Mincemeat Coffee Cake

(Pictured below)

For years my grandmother and I would have a contest to see whose mincemeat coffee cake was the best (our families voted). After years of losses, I modified my original recipe and finally won. I share my winning recipe with you. —Ed Layton, Absecon, New Jersey

2	packages (1/4 ounce *each*) active dry yeast
1-1/4	cups warm milk (110° to 115°), *divided*
1/2	cup sugar
1/2	cup butter, softened
2	eggs
2	teaspoons salt
1	teaspoon ground cinnamon
1/8	teaspoon *each* ground allspice, cloves and mace
5	to 5-1/2 cups all-purpose flour
1-1/2	cups prepared mincemeat

Confectioners' sugar

In a large bowl, dissolve yeast in 1/2 cup milk. Add sugar, butter, eggs, salt, cinnamon, allspice, cloves, mace, 2-1/2 cups flour and the remaining milk; beat until smooth. Stir in enough remaining flour to form a soft dough. Turn onto a floured surface; knead until smooth and elastic, about 6-8 minutes. Place in a greased bowl, turning once to grease top. Cover and let rise in a warm place until doubled, about 1 hour. Punch dough down; let rest 10 minutes.

Turn onto a lightly floured surface. Roll into a 16-in. x 12-in. rectangle. Spread mincemeat to within 1 in. of edges. Roll up from one long side. Pinch seams; join and seal ends to form a circle. Place in a greased 10-in. fluted tube pan. Cover and let rise until nearly doubled, about 30 minutes.

Bake at 375° for 40-45 minutes or until golden. Cool 10 minutes in pan before removing to a wire rack. Just before serving, dust with confectioners' sugar. **Yield:** 12-16 servings.

Braided Cardamom Rings

(Pictured above)

Most Christmases, I'll take one of my rings to my husband's family and one to my family. Of course, I make sure to keep enough at home, too. They look so festive with the colorful cherries. —Jo Learman, Caro, Michigan

 1 package (1/4 ounce) active dry yeast
 1/4 cup warm water (110° to 115°)
 2-1/2 cups warm milk (110° to 115°)
 3/4 cup butter, softened
 1 egg, beaten
 1 cup sugar
 1-1/2 teaspoons ground cardamom
 1/2 teaspoon salt
 8-3/4 to 9-1/4 cups all-purpose flour
LEMON ICING:
 2 cups confectioners' sugar
 3 to 4 tablespoons milk
 1/4 teaspoon lemon extract
Red and green candied cherries, halved, optional

In a mixing bowl, dissolve yeast in water. Add milk, butter, egg, sugar, cardamom and salt; mix well. Add 6 cups of flour; beat until smooth. Stir in enough of the remaining flour to form a soft dough. Turn onto a floured surface; knead until smooth and elastic, about 6-8 minutes. Place in a greased bowl, turning once to grease top.

Cover and let rise in a warm place until doubled, about 1-1/2 to 2 hours.

Punch dough down and divide in half. Divide each half into three portions. Shape each portion into a 24-in.-long rope. Place three ropes on a greased baking sheet; braid. Form into a ring; pinch edges tightly together. Repeat with remaining dough. Cover and let rise until doubled, about 40 minutes. Bake at 350° for 30-35 minutes or until golden brown. Cool on wire racks.

For icing, combine confectioners' sugar, milk and extract; spoon over rings, allowing icing to drizzle down the sides. Decorate with cherries if desired. **Yield:** 2 coffee cakes.

Editor's Note: Rings may be iced and served warm if desired.

Lemon Poppy Seed Bread

The days that I have time for baking are few and far between. That's why this extra-quick bread is perfect. You and your family will love the ease of preparation and the delicious flavor. —Karen Dougherty
Freeport, Illinois

 1 package (18-1/4 ounces) white cake mix without pudding
 1 package (3.4 ounces) instant lemon pudding mix
 4 eggs
 1 cup warm water
 1/2 cup vegetable oil
 4 teaspoons poppy seeds

In a mixing bowl, combine the cake and pudding mixes, eggs, water and oil; beat until well mixed. Fold in poppy seeds. Pour into two greased 9-in. x 5-in. x 3-in. loaf pans. Bake at 350° for 35-40 minutes or until a toothpick comes out clean. Cool in pans for 10 minutes before removing to a wire rack. **Yield:** 2 loaves.

Poppy Seed Trivia

There are about 900,000 tiny poppy seeds found in a pound. You can store poppy seeds up to six months when stored in an airtight container in the refrigerator.

Apricot Cheese Crescents

(Pictured below)

Traditionally, I bake these for Christmas. A cross between sweet breads and cookies, they're also something that I have been asked to make for weddings.
—Ruth Gilhousen, Knoxdale, Pennsylvania

      2 cups all-purpose flour
   1/2 teaspoon salt
      1 cup cold butter
      1 cup (8 ounces) small-curd cottage cheese
FILLING:
      1 package (6 ounces) dried apricots
   1/2 cup water
   1/2 cup sugar
TOPPING:
   3/4 cup finely chopped almonds
   1/2 cup sugar
      1 egg white, lightly beaten

In a large bowl, combine flour and salt; cut in butter until crumbly. Add cottage cheese; mix well. Shape into 1-in. balls. Cover and refrigerate several hours or overnight.

For the filling, combine apricots and water in a saucepan. Cover and simmer for 20 minutes. Cool for 10 minutes. Pour into a blender; cover and process on high speed until smooth. Transfer to a bowl; stir in sugar. Cover and chill.

For topping, combine almonds and sugar; set aside. On a floured surface, roll the balls into 2-1/2-in. circles. Spoon about 1 teaspoon of filling onto each. Fold dough over filling

and pinch edges to seal. Place on greased baking sheets. Brush tops with egg white; sprinkle with almond mixture. Bake at 375° for 12-15 minutes or until lightly browned. **Yield:** 4-1/2 dozen.

Best Ever Banana Bread

(Pictured above)

Whenever I pass a display of bananas in the grocery store, I can almost smell the wonderful aroma of this bread. It really is good!
—Gert Kaiser
Kenosha, Wisconsin

   1-3/4 cups all-purpose flour
   1-1/2 cups sugar
        1 teaspoon baking soda
     1/2 teaspoon salt
        2 eggs
        2 medium ripe bananas, mashed (1 cup)
     1/2 cup vegetable oil
     1/4 cup plus 1 tablespoon buttermilk
        1 teaspoon vanilla extract
        1 cup chopped walnuts

In a large bowl, combine flour, sugar, baking soda and salt. In another mixing bowl, combine eggs, bananas, oil, buttermilk and vanilla; add to dry ingredients, stirring just until combined. Fold in nuts. Pour into a greased 9-in. x 5-in. x 3-in. baking pan.

Bake at 325° for 1 hour and 20 minutes or until a toothpick inserted near the center comes out clean. Cool for 10 minutes; remove from pan to a wire rack. **Yield:** 1 loaf.

Top to bottom: Holiday Sour
Cream Rings, Cranberry Orange
Loaf (recipe on page 90)
and Swiss Butterhorns

Holiday Sour Cream Rings

(Pictured at left)

These delicious sour cream rings have become part of our traditional Christmas breakfast. But my family and friends love the sweet flavor so much, I find myself making them throughout the year as well.
—Lois McAtee, Oceanside, California

- 2 packages (1/4 ounce *each*) active dry yeast
- 1/4 cup warm water (110° to 115°)
- 2 eggs, lightly beaten
- 2 cups (16 ounces) sour cream
- 2/3 cup sugar
- 1/3 cup butter, melted
- 1-1/2 teaspoons salt
- 1 teaspoon ground mace
- 1 teaspoon ground cardamom
- 5-3/4 to 6-1/2 cups all-purpose flour
- 1/2 cup *each* raisins, chopped candied pineapple and chopped candied cherries
- 1 tablespoon brandy *or* orange juice
- 1-1/3 cups confectioners' sugar
- 4 to 6 teaspoons orange juice

Whole candied cherries

In a large mixing bowl, dissolve yeast in warm water. Add eggs, sour cream, sugar, butter, salt, mace, cardamom and 3 cups flour; beat until smooth. Add enough remaining flour to form a soft dough. Turn onto a floured surface; knead until smooth and elastic, about 6-8 minutes. Place in a greased bowl, turning once to grease top. Cover and let rise in a warm place until doubled, about 1 hour.

Meanwhile, combine raisins, pineapple, cherries and brandy or orange juice; mix well and set aside. Punch dough down. Pat into a 16-in. x 12-in. rectangle. Sprinkle with fruit. Fold over and knead lightly to distribute fruit. Divide dough into sixths. Roll each portion into a 16-in. rope. Place two ropes on a greased baking sheet. Intertwine them seven to eight times, joining ends to form a ring. Repeat with remaining dough.

Cover and let rise until nearly doubled, about 45 minutes. Bake at 350° for 30-35 minutes or until golden. Cool 15 minutes. Combine confectioners' sugar and orange juice; spread over rings. Decorate with candied cherries. **Yield:** 3 loaves.

Swiss Butterhorns

(Pictured at left)

My husband and I like to entertain at breakfast, and we're always looking for new recipes. So I was thrilled when my daughter shared this butterhorn recipe with me. They're so rich, light and easy to make.
—Cheryl Paulsen, Granville, Iowa

DOUGH:
- 2 cups all-purpose flour
- 1/4 teaspoon salt
- 1/2 cup cold margarine
- 1/3 cup cold butter
- 1 egg yolk, lightly beaten
- 3/4 cup sour cream

FILLING:
- 1/2 cup chopped pecans
- 1/2 cup sugar
- 1 teaspoon ground cinnamon

GLAZE (optional):
- 1 cup confectioners' sugar
- 2 tablespoons milk
- 1/4 teaspoon vanilla extract

In a large bowl, combine flour and salt. Cut in margarine and butter until crumbly. Stir in egg yolk and sour cream; shape into a ball. Chill several hours or overnight. Divide dough into thirds.

On a well-floured surface, roll each portion into a 12-in. circle. Combine filling ingredients. Sprinkle a third of the filling over each circle. Cut each circle into 12 wedges. Roll each wedge, starting at the wide end. Place on greased baking sheets with points down. Bake at 350° for 15-18 minutes or until lightly browned. Combine all glaze ingredients and spread on warm rolls if desired. **Yield:** 3 dozen.

Shaping Butterhorns

Roll a portion of the dough into a 12-in. circle. Cut into wedges, sprinkle with filling if desired and roll up, beginning at the wide end. Repeat with remaining dough.

Cranberry Orange Loaf

(Pictured on page 88)

I'm a true morning person who loves entertaining at breakfast. It's so much fun to get up early, set a pretty table and share a delicious breakfast with friends.
—Peggy Frazier, Indianapolis, Indiana

        2 cups all-purpose flour
        1 cup sugar
    1-1/2 teaspoons baking powder
        1 teaspoon baking soda
      1/2 teaspoon salt
        1 egg
      1/2 cup orange juice
Grated peel of 1 orange
        2 tablespoons butter, melted
        2 tablespoons hot water
        1 cup fresh *or* frozen cranberries
        1 cup chopped walnuts

In a large mixing bowl, combine the flour, sugar, baking powder, baking soda and salt. In a small bowl, beat the egg; add the orange juice, peel, butter and water. Stir into dry ingredients just until moistened. Fold in the cranberries and nuts. Spoon into a greased 9-in. x 5-in. x 3-in. loaf pan or two 5-in. x 2-1/2-in. x 2-in. mini-loaf pans.

Bake at 325° for 1 hour or until a toothpick inserted in the center comes out clean. Cool in pan for 10 minutes before removing to a wire rack. **Yield:** 1 loaf or 2 mini loaves.

Pumpkin Bread

A friend graciously shared her "secret recipe" with me. It's such a favorite that I'm not allowed to enter my family's get-togethers without this bread in hand!
—Shirley Sober, Granada Hills, California

        1 cup butter, softened
        3 cups sugar
        3 eggs
        3 cups all-purpose flour
        1 tablespoon baking powder
    1-1/2 teaspoons baking soda
    1-1/2 teaspoons ground cinnamon
    1-1/2 teaspoons ground cloves
    1-1/2 teaspoons ground nutmeg
        1 can (16 ounces) solid-pack pumpkin

In a mixing bowl, cream butter and sugar. Add eggs; mix well. Combine dry ingredients; stir into creamed mixture just until moistened. Stir in pumpkin. Pour into two greased 9-in. x 5-in. x 3-in. loaf pans. Bake at 350° for 1 hour or until a toothpick inserted near the center comes out clean. Cool in pans for 10 minutes before removing to wire racks. **Yield:** 2 loaves.

Potato Pan Rolls

(Pictured at left)

My family loves these rolls, which is why they're requested often. They don't take long to make because quick-rise yeast is used.
—Connie Storckman Evanston, Wyoming

  4-1/2 to 5 cups all-purpose flour
        3 tablespoons sugar
        2 packages (1/4 ounce *each*) quick-rise yeast
    1-1/2 teaspoons salt
    1-1/4 cups water
        3 tablespoons butter
      1/2 cup mashed potatoes (prepared without milk *or* butter)
Additional all-purpose flour

In a mixing bowl, combine 2 cups flour, sugar, yeast and salt. In a saucepan, heat water and butter to 120°-130°. Add to dry ingredients; beat until smooth. Stir in mashed potatoes and enough remaining flour to form a soft dough. Turn onto a floured surface; knead until smooth and elastic, about 6-8 minutes. Cover and let rest for 10 minutes.

In a mixing bowl, dissolve yeast in 1/4 cup water. Add sugar, molasses, shortening, salt and remaining water; stir well. Add rye flour; beat until smooth. Add enough all-purpose flour to form a soft dough. Turn onto a floured surface; knead until smooth and elastic, about 6-8 minutes. Place in a greased bowl, turning once to grease top. Cover and let rise in a warm place until doubled, about 1-1/2 hours.

Punch dough down. Shape into four round loaves. Place on greased baking sheets. Cover and let rise until doubled, about 45-60 minutes. Bake at 350° for 30-35 minutes or until golden brown. Brush with butter. **Yield:** 4 loaves.

Cinnamon Raisin Bread

Slices of warm cinnamon bread and a cup of hot tea work wonders for holiday visitors to our home. My mother received this recipe from a friend in West Virginia. —Joan Ort, Milford, New Jersey

> 2 **packages (1/4 ounce *each*) active dry yeast**
> 2 **cups warm water (110° to 115°)**
> 1 **cup sugar, *divided***
> 1/4 **cup vegetable oil**
> 1 **tablespoon salt**
> 2 **eggs**
> 6 **to 6-1/2 cups all-purpose flour**
> 1 **cup raisins**
> **Additional vegetable oil**
> 1 **tablespoon ground cinnamon**

In a mixing bowl, dissolve yeast in warm water. Add 1/2 cup sugar, oil, salt, eggs and 4 cups flour. Beat until smooth. Stir in enough remaining flour to form a soft dough. Turn onto a floured surface; knead until smooth and elastic, about 6-8 minutes.

Place in a greased bowl, turning once to grease top. Cover and let rise in a warm place until doubled, about 1 hour. Punch dough down.

Turn onto a lightly floured surface; divide in half. Knead 1/2 cup raisins into each portion; roll into a 15-in. x 9-in. rectangle. Brush with additional oil.

Combine cinnamon and remaining sugar; sprinkle to within 1/2 in. of edges. Tightly roll up, jelly-roll style, starting with a short side; pinch seam to seal.

Place, seam side down, in two greased 9-in. x 5-in. x 3-in. loaf pans. Cover and let rise until doubled, about 30 minutes. Brush with oil. Bake at 375° for 45-50 minutes or until golden brown. Remove from pans to wire racks to cool. **Yield:** 2 loaves.

Divide into 16 pieces. Shape each into a ball. Place in two greased 8-in. or 9-in. round baking pans. Cover and let rise in a warm place until doubled, about 30 minutes. Sprinkle with additional flour. Bake at 400° for 18-22 minutes or until golden brown. Remove from pans to wire racks to cool. **Yield:** 16 rolls.

Swedish Rye Bread

(Pictured above)

This recipe came from my mother, and it's long been a family favorite. You can make a meal of it with soup and a salad. —Mary Ann Ross, Crown Point, Indiana

> 1 **package (1/4 ounce) active dry yeast**
> 1-3/4 **cups warm water (110° to 115°), *divided***
> 1/4 **cup packed brown sugar**
> 1/4 **cup molasses**
> 2 **tablespoons shortening**
> 2 **teaspoons salt**
> 2-1/2 **cups rye flour**
> 3-3/4 **to 4-1/4 cups all-purpose flour**
> 2 **tablespoons butter, melted**

Cheesy Round Bread

This bread, which looks similar to focaccia, has a light olive and garlic flavor. We enjoy generous slices with soup. —*Ruthe Krohne, Fort Wayne, Indiana*

      1 **package (16 ounces) hot roll mix**
    3/4 **cup warm water (120° to 130°)**
      1 **egg**
      1 **tablespoon butter, softened**
  1-1/2 **teaspoons garlic salt**
    1/2 **teaspoon dried oregano**
    1/2 **teaspoon paprika**
    3/4 **cup shredded cheddar cheese**
    1/2 **cup chopped ripe olives, well drained**
      1 **egg white, beaten**

In a mixing bowl, combine contents of roll mix and yeast packet. Add warm water; mix well. Add the egg, butter and seasonings. Turn onto a floured surface. Knead in cheese and olives. Place in a greased bowl, turning once to grease top. Cover and let rise in a warm place until doubled, about 1 hour.

Punch dough down. Press into a 12-in. pizza pan. Cover and let rise in a warm place until doubled, about 30 minutes. With a sharp knife, make three or four slashes across top of loaf. Brush with egg white. Bake at 325° for 40-45 minutes or until golden brown. Cool for 5 minutes before removing from pan to a wire rack. **Yield:** 1 loaf.

Garlic Potato Biscuits

We grow our own potatoes and garlic, so these delectable biscuits are on our table often. I make biscuits a lot because they're quicker and easier than rolls. —*Diane Hixon, Niceville, Florida*

    1/2 **pound diced peeled potatoes (about 1 large)**
      3 **to 4 garlic cloves, peeled**
    1/3 **cup butter, softened**
      1 **teaspoon salt**
    1/4 **teaspoon pepper**
      2 **cups all-purpose flour**
      1 **tablespoon baking powder**
    1/3 **cup milk**

Place potatoes and garlic cloves in a saucepan. Add enough water to cover. Bring to a boil. Reduce heat; cover and simmer until tender. Drain well.

Mash potatoes and garlic with butter, salt and pepper. In a bowl, combine flour and baking powder; stir in potato mixture until mixture resembles coarse crumbs. Add milk and stir well.

Turn onto a lightly floured surface. Roll to 1/2-in. thickness; cut with a floured 2-in. biscuit cutter. Place 1 in. apart on an ungreased baking sheet. Bake at 450° for 10-12 minutes or until golden brown. Serve warm. **Yield:** 15 biscuits.

Sweet Sesame Bread

Aniseed gives this festive Greek bread its unusual yet pleasing flavor. Everyone in the family runs to the kitchen for a fresh-from-the-oven slice. It also stars on the table for special occasions. —*Kristi Parker, Merrimack, New Hampshire*

      1 **tablespoon active dry yeast**
    1/2 **cup warm water (110° to 115°)**
    1/4 **cup butter, softened**
    1/4 **cup sugar**
      3 **tablespoons instant nonfat dry milk powder**
    1/2 **teaspoon salt**
    1/2 **teaspoon crushed aniseed**
      2 **eggs**
  2-1/2 **to 3 cups all-purpose flour**
TOPPING:
      1 **egg**
      1 **tablespoon milk**
      2 **tablespoons sesame seeds**
      2 **tablespoons chopped almonds**
      2 **tablespoons sugar**

In a mixing bowl, dissolve yeast in warm water. Add the butter, sugar, milk powder, salt, aniseed, eggs and 2 cups flour. Beat on low speed for 3 minutes. Stir in enough remaining flour to form a soft dough. Turn onto a floured surface; knead until smooth and elastic, about 6-8 minutes. Place in a greased bowl, turning once to grease top. Cover and let rise in a warm place until doubled, about 1 hour. Punch dough down. Turn onto a lightly floured surface; divide into thirds.

Shape each into a 15-in. rope. Place ropes on a greased baking sheet; braid. Pinch ends to seal and tuck under. Cover and let rise until doubled, about 45 minutes. Beat egg and milk; brush over braid. Sprinkle with sesame seeds, almonds and sugar. Bake at 350° for 25-30 minutes or until golden brown. Remove from pan to a wire rack to cool. Serve warm or at room temperature. **Yield:** 1 loaf.

Winter Cabbage Salad, page 122

Soups, Salads & Sandwiches

Seafood Salad Sandwiches

I've enjoyed cooking for many years...luckily my husband and two sons were always ready to try new recipes. Now I have three grandsons who love to come and eat at Grandma's house. —Saundra Woods
Woodbury, Tennessee

      8 ounces cooked salad shrimp *or* flaked cooked
         crab
    3/4 cup chopped celery
    2/3 cup mayonnaise
      1 teaspoon dried minced onion
    1/2 teaspoon dried tarragon, crushed
    1/2 teaspoon hot pepper sauce
      4 sandwich buns, split
Fresh spinach leaves

In a medium bowl, combine the first six ingredients; mix well. Chill for at least 1 hour. Spoon 1/2 cup onto each bun; top with spinach leaves. **Yield:** 4 servings.

Apricot Gelatin Salad

(Pictured below)

A family who usually passes up molded salads will hunt for this fruity version at our covered dish buffet. Not only is it delicious, it adds color to any meal.
—Neva Jane Upp, Hutchinson, Kansas

      2 cans (16 ounces *each*) apricot halves
Pinch salt
      2 packages (3 ounces *each*) orange gelatin
      1 can (6 ounces) frozen orange juice concentrate,
         thawed
      1 tablespoon lemon juice
      1 cup lemon-lime soda

Drain apricots, reserving 1-1/2 cups juice; set apricots aside. In a small saucepan over medium heat, bring apricot juice and salt to a boil. Remove from the heat; add gelatin and stir until dissolved.

In a blender, process apricots, orange juice concentrate and lemon juice until smooth. Add to gelatin mixture along with soda; mix well.

Pour into a 6-cup mold that has been sprayed with nonstick cooking spray. Chill until firm. **Yield:** 10 servings.

Green Salad with Poppy Seed Dressing

(Pictured above)

Colorful and refreshing, this green salad is a delightful addition to any menu! The dressing's an easy one to make, and it provides a tangy blend of sweet and sour.
—Toni Garman, Spokane, Washington

1　head lettuce, torn into bite-size pieces
1　small cucumber, sliced
1/4　medium red onion, sliced
DRESSING:
1　cup honey
1　cup vinegar
1　cup vegetable oil
1　tablespoon poppy seeds
2　slices red onion, finely diced

In a large salad bowl, toss together lettuce, cucumber and red onion; set aside. In a glass jar with a tight-fitting lid, combine all dressing ingredients; shake until well blended. Just before serving, pour about 1/2 cup dressing over salad; toss lightly. Cover and refrigerate remaining dressing for up to 1 week. **Yield:** 3 cups dressing.

Golden Autumn Soup

(Pictured below)

Here's a great way to use the freshest produce harvested in fall. It's a hot and hearty soup that I like to make for everyday dinners and special-occasion suppers.
—Janet Willick, St. Michael, Alberta

5　medium parsnips, peeled and chopped
5　medium carrots, sliced
2　medium onions, chopped

1　medium sweet potato, peeled and chopped
1　medium turnip, peeled and chopped
2　celery ribs, sliced
2　bay leaves
3　cans (14-1/2 ounces *each*) chicken broth
2　cups half-and-half cream *or* evaporated fat-free milk
1　teaspoon dried tarragon
1/4　teaspoon pepper

In a Dutch oven or soup kettle, combine the first eight ingredients; simmer for 30 minutes or until vegetables are tender. Remove bay leaves. Let cool for 20 minutes. Puree in small batches in a blender; return to kettle. Add cream, tarragon and pepper; heat through. **Yield:** 12 servings (3 quarts).

Pork Salad Rolls

Our sons request these sandwiches so much I often prepare extra pork roast with this recipe in mind. They especially like them served on tortillas.
—Katie Koziolek, Hartland, Minnesota

1/2　cup mayonnaise
1　teaspoon Dijon mustard
1/2　teaspoon lemon juice
1/2　teaspoon seasoned salt
1/4　teaspoon pepper
3　cups shredded cooked pork
1/2　cup thinly sliced celery
1/2　cup halved seedless green grapes
6　flour tortillas (6-1/2 inches) *or* rolls
Lettuce leaves, optional

In a medium bowl, combine the mayonnaise, mustard, lemon juice, seasoned salt and pepper. Add pork, celery and grapes; mix well. Refrigerate for at least 1 hour. Spoon 1/2 cup onto each tortilla; add lettuce if desired. Roll up. **Yield:** 6 servings.

Soup's On

Soups make an elegant first course for a special meal. When selecting a soup for dinner, choose something that complements the flavors of the other dishes. A creamy bisque goes well with grilled meats and sauteed vegetables, but would be too much with a rich entree like stroganoff.

Four-Fruit Compote

(Pictured at right)

A beautiful side dish, this compote spotlights winter fruit like bananas, apples, oranges and pineapple. Of course, it can be made anytime of year. I'm sure you'll get as many smiles as I do when I bring out this refreshing salad. —Donna Long, Searcy, Arkansas

    1 can (20 ounces) pineapple chunks, undrained
  1/2 cup sugar
    2 tablespoons cornstarch
  1/3 cup orange juice
    1 tablespoon lemon juice
    1 can (11 ounces) mandarin oranges, drained
    3 to 4 unpeeled apples, chopped
    2 to 3 firm bananas, sliced

Drain pineapple, reserving 3/4 cup juice. In a saucepan, combine sugar and cornstarch. Add pineapple juice, orange juice and lemon juice. Cook and stir over medium heat for 2 minutes or until thickened and bubbly. Remove from the heat; set aside.

In a bowl, combine pineapple chunks, oranges, apples and bananas. Pour warm sauce over the fruit; stir gently to coat. Cover and refrigerate. **Yield:** 12-16 servings.

Matzo Ball Soup

My mother is of Russian descent and would make this for Friday night dinner while I was growing up. It's a very comforting soup that brings back many happy memories. —Bernice Polak, New Smyrna Beach, Florida

    1 broiler-fryer chicken (3-1/2 to 4 pounds), cut up
    2 quarts water
    6 carrots, cut in half lengthwise, then into 2-inch pieces
    1 large onion, peeled
    2 celery ribs, cut in half
    2 sprigs fresh dill (3 inches)
    1 can (49 ounces) chicken broth
    2 teaspoons salt
  1/2 teaspoon pepper
    2 cups cooked noodles
MATZO BALLS:
    2 eggs

    1 cup matzo meal
    2 tablespoons shortening
    2 tablespoons minced fresh parsley
    2 teaspoons salt
Dash pepper
  1/2 to 1 cup cold water

Place chicken and water in an 8-qt. soup kettle. Cover and bring to a boil; skim fat. Add carrots, onion and celery. Fold dill in half and wrap many times with kitchen string; add to soup. Bring to a boil. Reduce heat to medium-low; cover but keep lid ajar and simmer for 2-1/2 hours.

Meanwhile, combine first six matzo ball ingredients in a medium bowl. Add enough water to make a thick pancake-like batter. Refrigerate for 2 hours (mixture thickens as it stands).

Remove and discard onion, celery and dill from broth. Remove chicken and allow to cool; debone and cut into chunks. Skim fat from broth. Return chicken to kettle. Add canned broth, salt and pepper; bring to a boil. Reduce heat; cover and simmer.

To complete matzo balls, bring 4 qts. water to a boil in a 5-qt. Dutch oven. With very wet hands, form heaping teaspoonfuls of batter into balls. If mixture is too thin, stir in 1-2 tablespoons of matzo meal. Drop balls into boiling water. (They will sink when dropped but will rise in a few minutes.) Cook for 10 minutes. Remove with slotted spoon and add to simmering soup. Add noodles; heat through. **Yield:** 18 servings (4-1/2 quarts).

Lime Gelatin Salad

(Pictured below)

I've made this refreshing recipe hundreds of times! It can be a salad or dessert. When I take it to a potluck, it's always one of the first things to disappear.
—Louise Harding, Newburgh, New York

- 1 package (6 ounces) lime gelatin
- 1 cup boiling water
- 1 package (8 ounces) cream cheese, softened
- 1/2 teaspoon vanilla extract
- 1 can (15 ounces) mandarin oranges, drained
- 1 can (8 ounces) crushed pineapple, drained
- 1 cup lemon-lime soda
- 1/2 cup chopped pecans
- 1 carton (8 ounces) frozen whipped topping, thawed, *divided*

Dissolve gelatin in water. In a mixing bowl, beat cream cheese until fluffy. Stir in gelatin mixture and beat until smooth. Stir in vanilla, oranges, pineapple, soda and pecans. Chill until mixture mounds slightly when dropped from a spoon. Fold in three-fourths of the whipped topping.

Pour into a 13-in. x 9-in. x 2-in. dish. Refrigerate for 3-4 hours or until firm. Cut into squares; garnish with the remaining whipped topping. **Yield:** 16-20 servings.

Ruby Apple Salad

(Pictured above)

This is a pretty salad and tastes good, too. Years ago, there used to be local apple contests that my two children and I would enter. One year we made a clean sweep of the awards and I believe this recipe was one of the winners! —Priscilla Weaver, Hagerstown, Maryland

- 1 package (3 ounces) cherry gelatin
- 2 tablespoons red-hot candies
- 1-3/4 cups boiling water
- 1-1/2 to 2 cups chopped apples
- 1/2 cup chopped celery
- 1/2 cup chopped walnuts

In a bowl, stir gelatin and candies in boiling water until dissolved. Chill until partially set. Fold in apples, celery and walnuts. Pour into a 1-qt. serving bowl. Refrigerate until firm, at least 4 hours. **Yield:** 6-8 servings.

Pineapple Pointer

An enzyme in pineapple (also in figs, guava, kiwifruit and papaya) can prevent gelatin from setting properly. Heat destroys the enzyme, so cooked or canned pineapple can be used in gelatin mixtures.

Taco Soup

Taco Soup

(Pictured at left)

This is a fun dish to serve when entertaining. Folks can fill their bowls with whatever garnish ingredients they like and then top it with the soup. It's like a taco in a bowl! —Tammie Lightner, Bynum, Montana

      2 **cans (28 ounces *each*) diced tomatoes, undrained**
      1 **quart water**
      1 **tablespoon chicken bouillon granules**
  1-1/2 **teaspoons chili powder**
    1/2 **teaspoon ground cumin**
      8 **ounces Monterey Jack *or* cheddar cheese, cubed**
      1 **medium tomato, chopped**
      1 **medium avocado, chopped**
      1 **can (2-1/4 ounces) sliced ripe olives, drained**
    1/4 **cup sliced green onions**
      3 **cups tortilla chips**

In a blender or food processor, puree tomatoes until smooth; pour into a 3-qt. saucepan. Add the water, bouillon, chili powder and cumin; bring to a boil. Reduce heat; cover and simmer for 20 minutes.

In soup bowls, layer cheese, tomato, avocado, olives, onions and chips. Top with hot soup and serve immediately. **Yield:** 8 servings (2 quarts).

Turkey Mornay

This recipe proves that leftover holiday turkey doesn't have to be lifeless! Liven up your extra turkey by serving it with a creamy Swiss cheese sauce and tender asparagus over toasted bread. —Shirley Nowicki Temperance, Michigan

      3 **tablespoons butter**
      3 **tablespoons all-purpose flour**
    1/2 **teaspoon salt**
    1/8 **teaspoon pepper**
      2 **cups milk**
    3/4 **cup shredded Swiss cheese**
      4 **slices white bread, toasted**
      4 **slices cooked turkey breast**
      1 **can (15 ounces) asparagus spears, drained**
      2 **tablespoons shredded Parmesan cheese**

In a saucepan over medium heat, cook butter, flour, salt and pepper until smooth. Gradually add milk. Bring to a boil; cook

and stir for 2 minutes or until thickened. Add Swiss cheese; stir until melted.

Place bread in a shallow baking pan; top with turkey, asparagus and 1/2 cup sauce. Sprinkle with Parmesan cheese. Broil 5 in. from the heat for 4-6 minutes or until browned and bubbly. **Yield:** 4 servings.

Swedish Potato Dumpling Soup

Family and friends gather around our table throughout the year to enjoy good company and great food. As part of our traditional Christmas Eve meal, I serve this hearty soup. —Margaret Peterson, Genoa, Nebraska

      1 **broiler-fryer chicken (3-1/2 to 4 pounds), cut up**
  6-1/2 **cups water**
      2 **teaspoons salt, optional**
      2 **celery ribs, quartered**
      1 **medium carrot, quartered**
      1 **small onion, peeled**
      4 **whole peppercorns**
      2 **whole cloves**
      2 **whole allspice**
      2 **chicken bouillon cubes**
      1 **package (10 ounces) frozen green beans**
      1 **package (12 ounces) frozen noodles**
DUMPLINGS:
      2 **medium potatoes, cooked and mashed (without added milk *or* butter)**
      1 **egg, beaten**
      2 **tablespoons half-and-half cream**
      1 **teaspoon sugar**
    1/4 **teaspoon salt, optional**
    1/2 **cup all-purpose flour**

In a 5-qt. soup kettle, combine the first 10 ingredients. Cover and bring to a boil. Reduce heat; simmer for 3 hours. Remove chicken; allow to cool.

Strain broth, discarding vegetables and seasonings. Add enough water to make 8 cups; return to kettle. Debone chicken and cut into chunks; add to kettle with beans and noodles. Bring to a boil; cook for 20 minutes.

For dumplings, mix potatoes, egg, cream, sugar and salt if desired in a medium bowl. Gradually add flour to make a stiff batter (it should form a peak when spoon is lifted). Drop by teaspoons into boiling soup. Cover and simmer for 3 minutes. **Yield:** 12 servings (3 quarts).

Cranberry Mousse

(Pictured above)

This is a delicious and pretty salad for the holidays, but it's so good that I serve it other times, too. I got the recipe from a neighbor who had served it with a traditional turkey dinner. —Helen Clement, Hemet, California

    1 package (6 ounces) strawberry gelatin
    1 cup boiling water
    1 can (20 ounces) crushed pineapple, undrained
    1 can (16 ounces) whole-berry cranberry sauce
    3 tablespoons lemon juice
    1 teaspoon grated lemon peel
  1/2 teaspoon ground nutmeg
    2 cups (16 ounces) sour cream
  1/2 cup chopped pecans

In a large bowl, dissolve gelatin in boiling water. Drain pineapple, reserving the juice. Set pineapple aside. Add juice to gelatin. Stir in cranberry sauce, lemon juice, peel and nutmeg. Chill until mixture begins to thicken. Fold in sour cream, pineapple and pecans.

Pour into a glass serving bowl or a 9-cup mold that has been coated with nonstick cooking spray. Chill for 2 hours or until set. **Yield:** 16-20 servings.

Herbed Chicken Soup

I love cooking and turning a recipe into my own personal creation. This soup is one I developed gradually over the years. —Myrna Huebert, Tofield, Alberta

    1 broiler-fryer chicken (3 to 3-1/2 pounds), cut up
2-1/2 quarts water
    4 medium carrots, cut into 1/2-inch pieces
    1 medium onion, chopped
  1/2 cup chopped celery
    5 chicken bouillon cubes
    2 tablespoons dried parsley flakes
    1 tablespoon dried thyme
    1 teaspoon *each* dried sage and poultry seasoning
    1 teaspoon salt, optional
  1/2 teaspoon pepper
    1 large bay leaf
    1 package (12 ounces) frozen noodles *or* 2 cups cooked noodles

In a Dutch oven or soup kettle, place the first 12 ingredients. Cover and bring to a boil; skim fat. Reduce heat; cover and and simmer for 1-1/2 hours or until chicken is tender.

Remove chicken; allow to cool. Debone and cut into chunks. Skim fat from broth; bring to a boil. Return chicken to kettle. Add frozen noodles and cook for 20 minutes or until tender, or add cooked noodles and heat through. Remove bay leaf. **Yield:** 16 servings (4 quarts).

Meatless Minestrone

This recipe for traditional Italian soup may have quite a few ingredients, but it couldn't be easier to prepare. Plus it's packed with flavor and nutrition. —Margaret Shauers, Great Bend, Kansas

    1 medium onion, chopped
  3/4 cup sliced celery
    2 medium carrots, sliced
    3 tablespoons butter
    2 cans (14-1/2 ounces *each*) stewed tomatoes
    2 cans (14-1/2 ounces *each*) chicken broth
    2 cups water
    4 cups shredded cabbage
    1 medium potato, peeled and diced
    2 garlic cloves, minced
    1 tablespoon dried basil
2-1/4 teaspoons dried oregano
    2 teaspoons dried parsley flakes
  1/2 teaspoon pepper
Pinch cayenne pepper
    1 can (16 ounces) kidney beans, rinsed and drained
  1/2 cup cooked rice

In a Dutch oven or soup kettle, saute onion, celery and carrots in butter until vegetables are tender. Add tomatoes, broth, water, cabbage, potato and seasonings; bring to a boil. Reduce heat; cover and simmer for 1 hour. Stir in beans and rice; heat through. **Yield:** 9 servings (2-1/4 quarts).

Festive Fruit Salad

(Pictured below)

This fruit salad disappears fast down to the last spoonful. The light dressing doesn't hide the refreshing flavors of the fruit. Pecans add crunch and the rich flavor of the harvest season. —Julianne Johnson
Grove City, Minnesota

  1 can (20 ounces) pineapple chunks
1/2 cup sugar
  3 tablespoons all-purpose flour
  1 egg, lightly beaten
  2 cans (11 ounces *each*) mandarin oranges, drained
  1 can (20 ounces) pears, drained and chopped
  3 kiwifruit, peeled and sliced
  2 large unpeeled apples, chopped
  1 cup pecan halves

Drain pineapple, reserving juice. Set pineapple aside. Pour juice into a small saucepan; add sugar and flour. Bring to a boil. Whisk in egg. Cook and stir over medium heat until thermometer reaches 160° and mixture is thickened. Cool completely. In a large bowl, combine pineapple, oranges, pears, kiwi, apples and pecans. Pour dressing over and blend well. Cover and chill for 1 hour. **Yield:** 12-16 servings.

Chunky Potato Soup

(Pictured above)

This special soup is a true family favorite. I received the recipe from my sister and then passed it on to my daughters. It's perfect served with leftover ham. —Betty Ann Walery, Joplin, Montana

  2 cups water
  2 chicken bouillon cubes
  3 cups cubed peeled potatoes
1/2 cup chopped onion
1/2 cup thinly sliced celery
3/4 teaspoon salt
1/2 teaspoon pepper
  2 cups milk, *divided*
  2 tablespoons all-purpose flour
  1 cup (8 ounces) sour cream
  2 tablespoons chopped fresh parsley
  1 tablespoon chopped chives

In a 3-qt. saucepan over medium heat, combine water, bouillon, potatoes, onion, celery, salt and pepper; bring to a boil. Reduce heat; cover and simmer for 15-20 minutes or until potatoes are tender. Add 1-3/4 cups milk.

Combine flour with remaining milk; stir to form a smooth paste. Add to soup, stirring constantly. Bring to a boil; boil and stir for 2 minutes or until thickened and bubbly. Add a small amount of hot liquid to sour cream; stir to mix. Gradually add to soup, stirring constantly; heat through but do not boil. Add parsley and chives just before serving. **Yield:** 4-6 servings.

Top to bottom: Reuben Deli Sandwiches and French Onion-Beef Strudel

Reuben Deli Sandwiches

(Pictured at left)

Here's a new twist on the classic Reuben sandwich. The filling is easy to prepare and keeps well in the fridge. Add a salad and dessert, and you have a delicious lunch.
—Gigi LaFave Ryan, Longmont, Colorado

- 3/4 cup mayonnaise
- 1 tablespoon chili sauce
- 1-1/2 teaspoons prepared mustard
- 1/4 teaspoon prepared horseradish
- 1 can (14 ounces) sauerkraut, rinsed and well drained
- 3/4 pound finely chopped corned beef (about 3 cups)
- 2 cups (8 ounces) shredded Swiss cheese
- 30 slices rye bread
- 1/2 cup butter, softened

In a large bowl, combine mayonnaise, chili sauce, mustard and horseradish. Stir in sauerkraut, corned beef and Swiss cheese. Spread 1/3 cup on 15 slices of bread; top with remaining bread. Lightly butter the outsides of bread. Toast sandwiches on a hot griddle for 4-5 minutes per side or until golden brown. **Yield:** 15 servings.

French Onion-Beef Strudel

(Pictured at left)

I prepared this flavorful strudel for my craft club meeting, and everyone asked me for the recipe. It makes such a nice presentation, so it's great to serve at gatherings. *—Sherry Keethler, Lake St. Louis, Missouri*

- 1 loaf (1 pound) frozen bread dough, thawed
- 2 cups thinly sliced onion
- 1/4 cup butter
- 6 ounces beef tenderloin *or* sirloin steak (1 inch thick)
- 1 teaspoon all-purpose flour
- 1 teaspoon brown sugar
- 1/2 teaspoon ground cumin

- 1/4 teaspoon salt
- 1/4 teaspoon pepper
- 1/2 cup beef broth
- 3/4 cup shredded Monterey Jack cheese
- 6 tablespoons grated Parmesan cheese, *divided*
- 1 can (10 ounces) beef au jus gravy

Allow dough to rise until nearly doubled. Meanwhile, in a skillet, saute onion in butter over low heat for 15-20 minutes or until golden brown. With a slotted spoon, remove onion from skillet; set aside. Cut beef into 1/8-in. slices; add to skillet. Increase heat to medium; cook and stir for 3 minutes or until browned.

Return onion to skillet. Stir in flour, brown sugar, cumin, salt and pepper. Add broth; cook and stir for 6-8 minutes or until liquid has evaporated. Remove from the heat.

Punch dough down; roll on a floured surface to a 16-in. x 12-in. rectangle. Place on a greased baking sheet. Place beef mixture down the center of the long side of the dough. Sprinkle with Monterey Jack cheese and 4 tablespoons Parmesan cheese.

With a sharp knife, cut dough on each side of beef filling into 1-3/4-in.-wide strips. Fold strips alternately across filling. Sprinkle with remaining Parmesan. Cover and let rise until nearly doubled, about 30 minutes. Bake at 375° for 20-25 minutes or until golden brown. Heat gravy; serve as a dipping sauce. **Yield:** 6 servings.

Cranberry Waldorf Salad

Cranberries grow in the coastal area about 50 miles from our home. When they become available at Thanksgiving, I always make this lovely holiday salad.
—Faye Huff, Longview, Washington

- 1/2 pound fresh *or* frozen cranberries, halved
- 3/4 cup sugar
- 3 cups miniature marshmallows
- 2 cups chopped apples
- 1/2 cup chopped nuts
- 1 can (8 ounces) pineapple tidbits, drained
- 1 cup halved seedless grapes
- 1 cup heavy whipping cream, stiffly beaten

In a large mixing bowl, combine cranberries and sugar; let stand 30 minutes. Add next five ingredients; mix well. Gently fold in whipped cream. Chill until serving. **Yield:** 10-12 servings.

Shaker Bean Soup

(Pictured above)

This soup makes a tasty meal all year long, but it especially hits the spot when the weather is cold. I love cooking (I like to try a new recipe every week), and my family loves soup, so I'm always looking for one more.
—Deborah Amrine, Grand Haven, Michigan

        1 pound dried great northern beans
        1 meaty ham bone *or* 2 smoked ham hocks
        1 large onion, chopped
        3 celery ribs, diced
        2 carrots, shredded
Salt to taste
    1/2 teaspoon pepper
    1/2 teaspoon dried thyme
        1 can (28 ounces) crushed tomatoes in puree
        2 tablespoons brown sugar
1-1/2 cups finely shredded fresh spinach leaves

Place beans in a soup kettle; add water to cover by 2 in. Bring to a boil; boil for 2 minutes. Remove from heat; let stand for 1 hour. Drain beans and discard liquid. In the same kettle, place ham bone or hocks, 3 qts. water and beans.

Bring to a boil; reduce heat. Cover and simmer for 1-1/2 hours or until meat easily falls from the bone. Remove bones from broth and, when cool enough to handle, trim meat. Discard bones. Add ham, onion, celery, carrots, salt, pepper and thyme. Cover and simmer 1 hour or until beans are tender. Add tomatoes and brown sugar. Cook for 10 minutes. Just before serving, add spinach. **Yield:** 5 quarts.

Black Bean and Corn Salad

Even folks who normally don't care for black beans will find this fresh dish delicious. With its contrasting colors and wonderful cumin dressing, this salad is a great addition to any meal.
—Margaret Allen
Abingdon, Virginia

    1/3 cup olive oil
        1 tablespoon red wine vinegar
        1 teaspoon cider vinegar
        1 garlic clove, minced
    1/2 teaspoon ground cumin
    1/2 teaspoon dried oregano
    1/2 teaspoon salt, optional
    1/4 teaspoon sugar
    1/8 teaspoon ground red *or* cayenne pepper
        2 cans (15 ounces *each*) black beans, rinsed
            and drained
        1 can (8 ounces) whole kernel corn, drained
    3/4 cup chopped red onion
    1/2 cup chopped sweet red pepper

In a bowl, whisk the first nine ingredients until well blended. Add the beans, corn, onion and red pepper; toss well. Cover and chill 8 hours or overnight. **Yield:** 12 servings.

Turkey Fruit Salad

This salad is a great way to use leftover turkey. The fruit makes it refreshing, and the apples and toasted nuts give it a nice crunch.
—Mary Anne Mayberry
Fairmont, Minnesota

    1/2 cup mayonnaise
        2 tablespoons honey
    1/8 teaspoon ground ginger
        2 cups cubed cooked turkey
        1 can (11 ounces) mandarin oranges, drained
        1 cup chopped unpeeled apple
        1 cup grape halves
        1 can (8-1/4 ounces) pineapple chunks, drained
    1/2 cup pecan halves, toasted

In a large bowl, combine mayonnaise, honey and ginger. Stir in turkey, oranges, apple, grapes and pineapple. Refrigerate for 1 hour. Sprinkle with toasted pecans just before serving. **Yield:** 8 servings.

Ruby Red Raspberry Salad

(Pictured below)

A refreshing and attractive side dish, this salad adds a festive touch to any table. Children especially like this slightly sweet salad. —Marge Clark
West Lebanon, Indiana

      1 **package (3 ounces) raspberry gelatin**
      2 **cups boiling water, *divided***
      1 **package (10 ounces) frozen raspberries in syrup**
 1-1/2 **cups sour cream**
      1 **package (3 ounces) cherry gelatin**
      1 **can (20 ounces) crushed pineapple, drained**
      1 **can (16 ounces) whole-berry cranberry sauce**
Lettuce leaves
Mayonnaise and mint leaves, optional

Dissolve raspberry gelatin in 1 cup boiling water. Add raspberries and stir until berries are thawed and separated. Pour into a 13-in. x 9-in. x 2-in. pan; chill until set. Carefully spread with sour cream; chill.

Dissolve cherry gelatin in remaining boiling water. Add the pineapple and cranberry sauce and mix well. Allow to thicken slightly. Carefully spoon over sour cream mixture; chill. Cut into squares and serve on lettuce leaves. If desired, top each with a dollop of mayonnaise and garnish with a mint leaf. **Yield:** 12-16 servings.

Green Salad with Onion Dressing

(Pictured above)

This is such an elegant salad, it will dress up any table. The caramelized onion in the dressing tastes fantastic. It's never failed to be a hit whenever I've served it to both friends and family. —Cara Bonnema
Painesville, Ohio

      1 **large onion, peeled and cut into eighths**
      8 **tablespoons olive oil, *divided***
 1-1/2 **teaspoons sugar**
    1/4 **cup chicken broth**
      2 **tablespoons white wine vinegar**
    1/4 **teaspoon salt**
     14 **cups torn salad greens**
      1 **cup chopped walnuts, toasted**
    1/2 **cup thinly sliced red onion**

Place onion in a baking dish. Drizzle with 1 tablespoon oil; sprinkle with sugar. Bake, uncovered, at 400° for 30 minutes. Turn and bake 25-30 minutes longer, stirring several times, until onion is tender and lightly browned. Cool for 30 minutes.

Place onion in a blender or food processor; add broth, vinegar, salt and remaining oil. Cover and process until smooth (mixture will be thick). Chill. Just before serving, toss greens, walnuts, red onion and dressing in a large salad bowl. **Yield:** 12 servings.

Tropical Turkey Salad

(Pictured below)

Forever on the lookout for good simple dishes to prepare, I tried this delicious salad while on a trip. It's lovely with all the colors and textures, and satisfying with a mixture of turkey, fruits and vegetables. The tangy raspberry dressing is irresistible. —Rosalind Canada
White Bluff, Tennessee

>   5 cups torn fresh spinach
>   3 cups torn lettuce
>   2 cups cubed cooked turkey
>   2 slices red onion, separated into rings
>   1/2 cup chopped green pepper
>   1/2 cup mandarin oranges
>   1/2 cup sliced celery
>   1/2 cup pineapple chunks
>   1/3 cup vegetable oil
>   1/4 cup raspberry syrup
>   2 tablespoons red wine vinegar
> 1-1/2 teaspoons honey
>   1/2 teaspoon celery seed
>   1/2 cup sliced almonds, toasted
>   1/4 cup flaked coconut, toasted

Line a large salad bowl with spinach and lettuce. Combine the next six ingredients; spoon into bowl. In a jar with tight-fitting lid, combine oil, raspberry syrup, vinegar, honey and celery seed; shake well. Pour over the salad. Top with almonds and coconut. Serve immediately. **Yield:** 6 servings.

Sausage Broccoli Chowder

(Pictured above)

Our cold New England winters frequently call for a dinner that warms you all over. This chowder does that. —Donald Roberts, Amherst, New Hampshire

>   1 pound bulk Italian sausage
>   1 medium onion, chopped
>   3 garlic cloves, minced
>   1/2 pound fresh mushrooms, sliced
>   2 tablespoons butter
>   2 cups broccoli florets
>   2 to 3 medium carrots, diced
>   2 cans (14-1/2 ounces *each*) chicken broth
>   1 can (10-3/4 ounces) condensed cream of
>   mushroom soup, undiluted
>   9 ounces cheese tortellini, cooked and drained
>   1/2 teaspoon pepper
>   1/2 teaspoon dried basil
>   1/2 teaspoon dried thyme
>   2 quarts half-and-half cream
>   1/2 cup grated Romano cheese

In a skillet, cook sausage over medium heat until no longer pink. Remove to paper towels to drain; set aside. In the same skillet, saute onion, garlic and mushrooms in butter until tender; set aside.

In a Dutch oven, cook the broccoli and carrots in chicken broth until tender. Stir in sausage and the mushroom mixture. Add soup, tortellini, pepper, basil and thyme; heat through. Stir in cream and Romano cheese; heat through. **Yield:** 12-16 servings (4 quarts).

Wild Duck Gumbo

(Pictured below)

Our family and friends just love this delightful, rich gumbo. It's such a unique way to serve this wild bird.
—Doris Heath, Bryson City, North Carolina

    2 wild ducks, cut up
  1/2 cup vegetable oil
  2/3 cup all-purpose flour
    1 pound fully cooked smoked sausage, sliced
    2 cups chopped onion
1-1/2 cups chopped green pepper
1-1/2 cups sliced celery
    2 tablespoons minced fresh parsley
    1 tablespoon minced garlic
    1 can (14-1/2 ounces) stewed tomatoes, undrained
    2 bay leaves
    2 tablespoons Worcestershire sauce
1-1/2 teaspoons pepper
    1 teaspoon salt
    1 teaspoon dried thyme
  1/4 teaspoon cayenne pepper
    2 quarts water
Hot cooked rice

In a Dutch oven over medium heat, brown duck in batches in oil. Remove and set aside. Discard all but 2/3 cup drippings. Add flour to drippings; cook and stir over medium heat until brown, 12-14 minutes. Add sausage, onion, green pepper, celery, parsley and garlic.

Cook for 10 minutes, stirring occasionally. Add next eight ingredients; mix well. Add duck; bring to a boil. Reduce heat; cover and simmer 60-75 minutes or until duck is tender. Remove duck. Cool. Debone and cut into chunks; return to pan. Simmer 5-10 minutes or until heated through. Remove bay leaves. Serve with rice. **Yield:** 16 servings (4 quarts).

◆◆◆

Fluffy Fruit Salad

(Pictured above)

I like to bring my mom's fruit salad to potlucks. Its smooth sauce combined with all the colorful fruit makes it popular.
—Anne Heinonen, Howell, Michigan

    2 cans (20 ounces *each*) crushed pineapple
  2/3 cup sugar
    2 tablespoons all-purpose flour
    2 eggs, lightly beaten
  1/4 cup orange juice
    3 tablespoons lemon juice
    1 tablespoon vegetable oil
    2 cans (17 ounces *each*) fruit cocktail, drained
    2 cans (11 ounces *each*) mandarin oranges, drained
    2 bananas, sliced
    1 cup heavy whipping cream, whipped

Drain pineapple, reserving 1 cup juice in a small saucepan. Set pineapple aside. To saucepan, add sugar, flour, eggs, orange juice, lemon juice and oil. Bring to a boil, stirring constantly. Boil for 1 minute; remove from heat and let cool.

In a large bowl, combine pineapple, fruit cocktail, oranges and bananas. Fold in whipped cream and cooled sauce. Chill for several hours. **Yield:** 12-16 servings.

Harvest Turkey Soup

(Pictured above)

The recipe for this super soup evolved over the years. The herbs and spices make it taste terrific!
—Linda Sand, Winsted, Connecticut

- 1 turkey carcass (from a 12-pound turkey)
- 5 quarts water
- 2 large carrots, shredded
- 1 cup chopped celery
- 1 large onion, chopped
- 4 chicken bouillon cubes
- 1 can (28 ounces) stewed tomatoes
- 3/4 cup fresh *or* frozen peas
- 3/4 cup long grain rice
- 1 package (10 ounces) frozen chopped spinach
- 1 tablespoon salt
- 3/4 teaspoon pepper
- 1/2 teaspoon dried marjoram
- 1/2 teaspoon dried thyme

Place the turkey carcass and water in a Dutch oven or soup kettle; bring to a boil. Reduce heat; cover and simmer for 1-1/2 hours. Remove carcass; allow to cool. Remove turkey from bones and cut into bite-size pieces; set aside. Strain broth. Add carrots, celery, onion and bouillon; bring to a boil. Reduce heat; cover and simmer for 30 minutes.

Add tomatoes, peas, rice, spinach, salt, pepper, marjoram, thyme and reserved turkey. Return to a boil; cook, uncovered, for 20 minutes or until rice is tender. **Yield:** 22 servings (5-1/2 quarts).

German Potato Salad

(Pictured below)

A dear German friend gave me this recipe. I take this satisfying salad to many gatherings. —Donna Cline
Pensacola, Kansas

- 12 medium potatoes
- 12 bacon strips
- 1-1/2 cups chopped onion
- 1/4 cup all-purpose flour
- 1/4 cup sugar
- 1 tablespoon salt
- 1 teaspoon celery seed
- 1 teaspoon ground mustard
- Pinch pepper
- 1-1/2 cups water
- 3/4 cup vinegar
- Chopped fresh parsley

In a saucepan, cook potatoes until just tender; drain. Peel and slice into a large bowl; set aside. In a skillet, cook bacon until crisp. Remove bacon to paper towels; discard all but 1/3 cup of drippings. Saute onion in drippings until tender.

Stir in the next six ingredients. Gradually stir in water and vinegar; bring to a boil, stirring constantly. Cook and stir 2 minutes more. Pour over potatoes. Crumble bacon and gently stir into potatoes. Sprinkle with parsley. **Yield:** 12-14 servings.

Add the cucumbers, green onions, parsley, basil and pepper; mix well. Chill for 2 hours. Fold in pecans just before serving. **Yield:** 16-18 servings.

Winter Vegetable Soup

(Pictured below)

I've enjoyed this soup for years because it tastes so good, is simple to make and doesn't leave a lot of leftovers. —Mavis Diment, Marcus, Iowa

- 1/2 **cup sliced green onions**
- 1 **tablespoon vegetable oil**
- 1 **can (14-1/2 ounces) chicken broth**
- 1 **small potato, peeled and cubed**
- 1 **large carrot, sliced**
- 1/4 **teaspoon dried thyme**
- 1 **cup broccoli florets**
- 1/4 **teaspoon salt**
- 1/8 **teaspoon pepper**

In a medium saucepan, saute onions in oil until tender. Add the next four ingredients; bring to a boil. Reduce heat; simmer, uncovered, for 5 minutes. Add the broccoli, salt and pepper; simmer, uncovered, for 7 minutes or until vegetables are tender. **Yield:** 2 servings.

Lemon Rice Salad

(Pictured above)

This refreshing salad is wonderful served year-round. People seem to enjoy the combination of flavors. I like that it can be prepared ahead. —Margery Richmond Lacombe, Alberta

- 1 **cup olive oil**
- 1/3 **cup white wine vinegar**
- 1 **garlic clove, minced**
- 1 **to 2 teaspoons grated lemon peel**
- 2 **teaspoons sugar**
- 1 **teaspoon Dijon mustard**
- 1/2 **teaspoon salt**
- 6 **cups cooked long grain rice**
- 2 **cups cooked wild rice**
- 2 **cups diced seeded cucumbers**
- 2/3 **cup thinly sliced green onions**
- 1/4 **cup minced fresh parsley**
- 1/4 **cup minced fresh basil *or* 1 tablespoon dried basil**
- 1/2 **teaspoon pepper**
- 1/2 **cup chopped pecans, toasted**

In a jar with a tight-fitting lid, combine the first seven ingredients; shake well. In a large bowl, combine long grain and wild rice; add dressing and toss. Cover; refrigerate overnight.

Top to bottom: Broccoli Turkey Salad and Onion Cheese Soup

Onion Cheese Soup

(Pictured at left)

I made a few adjustments to this savory soup recipe, so now it's rich, buttery and cheesy.
—Janice Pogozelski, Cleveland, Ohio

        1 **large onion, chopped**
        3 **tablespoons butter**
        3 **tablespoons all-purpose flour**
    1/2 **teaspoon salt**
Pepper to taste
        4 **cups milk**
        2 **cups (8 ounces) shredded Colby-Monterey Jack cheese**
Seasoned salad croutons
Grated Parmesan cheese, optional

In a large saucepan, saute the onion in butter. Stir in the flour, salt and pepper until blended. Gradually add milk. Bring to a boil; cook and stir for 2 minutes or until thickened. Stir in Colby-Monterey Jack cheese until melted. Serve with croutons and Parmesan cheese if desired. **Yield:** 6 servings.

Broccoli Turkey Salad

(Pictured at left)

This medley of turkey, broccoli, pineapple and greens is especially good for a holiday meal. —Joyana McShane
El Cajon, California

        1 **can (8 ounces) unsweetened pineapple chunks**
        2 **cups** *each* **torn salad greens and fresh spinach**
        2 **cups broccoli florets**
        1 **green pepper, julienned**
    1/2 **cup thinly sliced red onion**
        2 **cups cubed cooked turkey**
    1/4 **cup olive oil**
        2 **tablespoons balsamic vinegar**
        1 **tablespoon poppy seeds**
        2 **teaspoons sugar**
        2 **teaspoons Dijon mustard**

Drain the pineapple, reserving 2 tablespoons juice; set aside (discard remaining juice or save for another use). In a large bowl, combine the greens, spinach, broccoli, green pepper, onion, turkey and pineapple.

In a small bowl, combine oil, vinegar, poppy seeds, sugar, mustard and reserved pineapple juice; mix well. Pour over salad and toss to coat. Serve immediately. **Yield:** 10 servings.

Fresh Vegetable Salad

It was such a treat to have a crisp, garden-fresh salad back when Mom didn't have much room in our little ice-box to keep produce chilled. —Ruth Seitz
Columbus Junction, Iowa

        2 **cups broccoli florets**
        2 **cups cauliflowerets**
    1/2 **cup chopped celery**
    1/2 **cup chopped green pepper**
    1/2 **cup chopped onion**
    1/4 **cup grated carrot**
        1 **cup mayonnaise**
    1/4 **cup sugar**
        3 **tablespoons grated Parmesan cheese**
        2 **bacon strips, cooked and crumbled**

Toss vegetables in a large salad bowl. In a small bowl, combine mayonnaise, sugar and Parmesan cheese; pour over vegetables and toss to coat. Cover and chill. Sprinkle with bacon just before serving. Refrigerate any leftover salad. **Yield:** 8 servings.

Split Pea Soup

This hearty classic is a great dish for all cooks, whether a beginner or more experienced. Not only is it nourishing and inexpensive, it's simple to make. My family can't get enough of it!
—John Croce
Yarmouthport, Massachusetts

        1 **pound green split peas**
        2 **smoked ham hocks (about 1-1/2 pounds)**
        2 **celery ribs, finely chopped**
        1 **medium onion, finely chopped**
        1 **medium carrot, finely chopped**
        2 **chicken bouillon cubes**
        1 **teaspoon garlic powder**
        1 **teaspoon salt**
    1/2 **teaspoon dried oregano**
    1/4 **teaspoon pepper**
        8 **to 10 cups water**
        1 **bay leaf**

In a large saucepan, combine all of the ingredients; bring to a boil. Reduce the heat; leaving the cover ajar, simmer for 3 hours, stirring occasionally. Remove and discard the bay leaf.

Remove the ham hocks; when cool enough to handle, cut meat into bite-size pieces. Return meat to the soup and heat through. **Yield:** 6-8 servings (2 quarts).

"Bring an Ingredient" Soup

(Pictured below)

Why not try something different for your next party and serve this soup? Your guests will help you prepare it, so that means less fuss for you, and it's fun to get everyone involved. —Mary Anne McWhirter, Pearland, Texas

> 4 cups thinly sliced onions
> 1 garlic clove, minced
> 3 tablespoons butter
> 3 tablespoons all-purpose flour
> 6 cans (14-1/2 ounces *each*) beef broth
> 2 cups tomato puree
> 1 tablespoon red wine vinegar
> 1 tablespoon Worcestershire sauce
> 1 tablespoon sugar
> 1/2 teaspoon *each* dried oregano, tarragon, ground cumin, salt and pepper
> 1/4 to 1/2 teaspoon hot pepper sauce

VEGETABLES (choose two or three):
> 1-1/2 cups *each* diced green pepper, tomato *or* carrots
> 2 cups sliced fresh mushrooms

MEATS (choose two):
> 3 cups cooked mini meatballs
> 3 cups cubed cooked chicken
> 3 cups diced fully cooked ham
> 1 package (10 ounces) smoked kielbasa, sliced and browned

GARNISHES (choose three or four):
Shredded cheddar cheese, garbanzo beans, sour cream, chopped fresh parsley, croutons *or* popcorn

In a large Dutch oven, saute the onions and garlic in butter until tender. Stir in flour and blend well. Add broth, puree, vinegar and seasonings; mix well. Bring to a boil; reduce heat and simmer for 40 minutes.

Add two or three vegetables; simmer for 30 minutes or until tender. Add two meats; heat through. Garnish as desired. **Yield:** 16-18 servings (4-1/2 quarts).

Italian Chicken Soup

Nothing chases the winter chills away like a steaming bowl of this chicken soup. It's a comforting dish.
—John Croce, Yarmouthport, Massachusetts

> 4 chicken breast halves (bone in)
> 1 large onion, halved
> 1 large carrot, quartered
> 3 celery ribs with leaves, chopped
> 2 cans (14-1/2 ounces *each*) chicken broth
> 2 cups water
> 2 chicken bouillon cubes
> 2 bay leaves
> 1 can (14-1/2 ounces) diced tomatoes, undrained
> 6 to 8 green onions, thinly sliced
> 1/2 cup chopped fresh parsley
> 1/4 cup ketchup
> 1 teaspoon salt
> 1 teaspoon dried rosemary, crushed
> 1/2 teaspoon dried basil
> 2 garlic cloves, minced
> 1/2 teaspoon pepper
> 2 cans (15-1/2 ounces *each*) kidney beans, rinsed and drained
> 1/4 cup grated Romano cheese

In a 5-qt. Dutch oven, combine the first eight ingredients; bring to a boil. Reduce heat; leaving cover ajar, simmer for 1-1/2 hours. Remove chicken; strain and reserve broth. Discard vegetables and bay leaves.

Festive Tossed Salad

(Pictured above)

I owe my discovery of this salad to my sister-in-law, a Louisiana native and a fabulous cook. It's always a hit.
—*Ruby Williams, Bogalusa, Louisiana*

    2 tablespoons vegetable oil
    1 tablespoon lemon juice
    1 tablespoon honey
  1/4 teaspoon sugar
  1/4 teaspoon garlic powder
Dash salt
    2 to 3 cups torn salad greens
    1 celery rib, sliced
    1 medium carrot, shredded
    2 green onions, sliced
  1/2 cup mandarin oranges
    1 tablespoon sliced almonds, toasted

In a jar with tight-fitting lid, combine the first six ingredients; shake well. In a salad bowl, toss the greens, celery, carrot, onions and oranges. Add dressing and toss to coat; sprinkle with almonds. Serve immediately. **Yield:** 2 servings.

When the chicken is cool enough to handle, remove skin and bones; discard. Cut chicken into bite-size pieces; set aside. Return broth to kettle; add tomatoes, onions, parsley, ketchup, salt, rosemary, basil, garlic and pepper; bring to a boil. Reduce heat; leaving cover ajar, simmer for 45 minutes. Add beans, cheese and chicken; heat through. **Yield:** 12-14 servings (3-1/2 quarts).

Popover with Hot Turkey Salad

(Pictured below)

I first tasted this tempting hot turkey salad at a club dinner. Now I often serve it at home!
—*Mary Anne Mayberry, Fairmont, Minnesota*

    2 eggs
    1 cup milk
    1 cup all-purpose flour
  1/2 teaspoon salt
    4 cups diced cooked turkey
    2 cups diced celery
    2 cups (8 ounces) shredded cheddar cheese
    1 can (2-1/4 ounces) sliced ripe olives, drained
    1 cup mayonnaise
  1/4 cup milk
  1/8 teaspoon pepper
Pinch onion powder
  1-1/2 cups crushed potato chips
Tomato wedges, optional

In a mixing bowl, beat eggs until lemon-colored and foamy. Add milk, flour and salt; beat just until smooth (do not overbeat). Pour into a greased 10-in. glass pie plate. Bake at 400° for 35-40 minutes or until deep golden brown. Immediately prick with a fork in the center to allow steam to escape.

Combine the next eight ingredients in a saucepan; cook and stir over low heat until heated through. Stir in potato chips. Spoon into popover. Garnish with tomato wedges if desired. Serve immediately. **Yield:** 10-12 servings.

Top to bottom: Macaroni and Cheese Soup, Spinach Cheese Soup and Swiss 'n' Cheddar Broccoli Soup

Spinach Cheese Soup

(Pictured at left)

A friend brought a pot of this steaming soup to our home after our first child was born. Three kids later, I'm still getting requests to make it frequently.
—Susan Bontrager, Middlebury, Indiana

    1 large onion, chopped
    4 garlic cloves, minced
    1 tablespoon olive oil
    6 cups chicken broth
    8 ounces uncooked linguine
    1 package (10 ounces) frozen chopped
        spinach, thawed and well drained
    2 cups cubed cooked chicken
    6 cups milk
    3 cups (12 ounces) shredded Swiss cheese
    3 cups (12 ounces) shredded brick *or*
        Monterey Jack cheese

In a soup kettle or Dutch oven, saute onion and garlic in oil until tender. Add broth; bring to a boil. Add linguine and cook for 8-10 minutes or until tender. Reduce heat. Add spinach and chicken; heat through but do not boil. Stir in milk; heat through. Add cheeses and stir just until melted. Serve immediately. **Yield:** 14-16 servings (4 quarts).

Swiss 'n' Cheddar Broccoli Soup

(Pictured at left)

With two varieties of cheese—Swiss and cheddar—this soup is delicious!   —Ada Lee Cook, Vernon, Texas

    4 cups water, *divided*
    4 teaspoons chicken bouillon granules
    2 packages (10 ounces *each*) frozen chopped
        broccoli
    4 cups milk
    1/2 teaspoon salt
    1/4 teaspoon pepper
    1/8 teaspoon ground nutmeg
    1/2 cup all-purpose flour
1-1/4 cups (5 ounces) shredded Swiss cheese
    3/4 cup shredded cheddar cheese

In a large saucepan, combine 3 cups water and bouillon; heat until bouillon is dissolved. Add broccoli; cover and cook over low heat until tender, about 8 minutes.

Stir in milk, salt, pepper and nutmeg. Combine flour and remaining water; stir into soup. Cook and stir over medium heat for 3 minutes or until thick and bubbly. Remove from the heat. Add cheeses; stir until melted. **Yield:** 8 servings (2 quarts).

Macaroni and Cheese Soup

(Pictured at left)

I've worked in the food service industry for too many years to count and have made this one-of-a-kind soup at many different jobs. It's always been a big hit.
—Emma Head, Sunrise Beach, Missouri

    3 quarts water
    5 teaspoons chicken bouillon granules
1-1/2 cups sliced celery
    2 large carrots, shredded
    1 large onion, chopped
    1 medium green pepper, chopped
2-1/2 cups uncooked elbow macaroni
    1 cup butter
    3/4 cup all-purpose flour
    6 cups milk
    1 pound process American cheese, cubed

In a soup kettle or Dutch oven, bring water and bouillon to a boil. Add celery, carrots, onion and green pepper; cook for 4 minutes or until tender. Add macaroni. Cover and return to a boil; boil for 2 minutes. Remove from the heat; let stand for 8-10 minutes or until macaroni is just tender.

Meanwhile, melt butter in a saucepan. Add flour, stirring until smooth. Gradually add milk, stirring constantly. Bring to a boil; cook and stir for 2 minutes. Stir in cheese until melted; add to undrained macaroni mixture. **Yield:** 20 servings (5 quarts).

Soup Making Tips

Since everyone likes different levels of salt in soup, add only a portion of the salt called for in a recipe at the beginning of the cooking process. When the soup is nearly ready to be served, taste it and adjust the salt—or allow others to salt their own soup bowls.

To speed up soup preparation, chop and measure the vegetables the night before, and store them in resealable plastic bags or covered bowls. The next day, assembling the soup is a breeze!

Surprise Fruit Salad

With only four ingredients—including the "surprise" of candy—this makes a fast and delicious salad as well as a delightful dessert.   —Julie Sterchi, Flora, Illinois

- 1 carton (12 ounces) frozen whipped topping, thawed
- 2 red apples, cubed
- 2 green apples, cubed
- 4 Snickers candy bars (2.07 ounces *each*), cut into 1/2-inch chunks

Combine all ingredients in a large bowl; cover and chill. Store in the refrigerator. **Yield:** 12-14 servings.

Christmas Crunch Salad

(Pictured below)

With its creamy dressing and colorful vegetables, this salad is both lovely and refreshing.
—Mary Anne McWhirter, Pearland, Texas

- 4 cups fresh broccoli florets (about 3/4 pound)
- 4 cups fresh cauliflowerets (about 3/4 pound)
- 1 medium red onion, chopped
- 2 cups cherry tomatoes, halved

DRESSING:
- 1 cup mayonnaise
- 1/2 cup sour cream
- 1 to 2 tablespoons sugar
- 1 tablespoon vinegar

Salt and pepper to taste

In a large salad bowl, combine vegetables. Whisk the dressing ingredients until smooth; pour over vegetables and toss to coat. Cover and chill for at least 2 hours. **Yield:** 16-18 servings.

Cauliflower Wild Rice Soup

This soup is versatile because it makes a fine complement to a main meal, or it can be a meal in itself.
—Judy Schield, Merrill, Wisconsin

- 1 medium onion, chopped
- 1 cup thinly sliced celery
- 1 cup sliced fresh mushrooms
- 1/2 cup butter
- 1/2 cup all-purpose flour
- 1 quart chicken broth
- 2 cups cooked wild rice
- 2 cups cauliflowerets, cooked
- 1 cup half-and-half cream

In a large saucepan, saute onion, celery and mushrooms in butter until tender. Sprinkle with flour; stir to coat well. Gradually add chicken broth. Cook and stir until thickened. Stir in wild rice, cauliflower and cream until well blended. Cook gently until heated through; do not boil. **Yield:** 6-8 servings (about 2 quarts).

Blue Cheese Tomato Soup

This recipe comes in handy when I want to serve a fancier soup without a lot of extra fuss.   —Mary Stiner Fremont, New Hampshire

- 1 bottle (32 ounces) tomato juice, *divided*
- 1 package (3 ounces) cream cheese, softened
- 2 to 4 ounces crumbled blue cheese, *divided*
- 1 small onion, coarsely chopped
- 1 tablespoon Worcestershire sauce
- 1 tablespoon sugar
- 2 teaspoons lemon juice
- 1/2 teaspoon pepper
- 1/4 teaspoon salt

Toasted garlic bread, optional

In a blender or food processor, combine 2 cups tomato juice, cream cheese, half of the blue cheese, onion, Worcestershire sauce, sugar, lemon juice, pepper and salt; process until smooth. Pour into a large bowl; stir in remaining tomato juice. Chill at least 1 hour. Top with garlic bread if desired and remaining blue cheese. **Yield:** 6 servings.

Turkey Wild Rice Soup

(Pictured below)

A dear friend brought me some of this soup when I was ill—it really hit the spot. I asked her for the recipe, and I've made it several times since. Now I like to take it to friends when they're not feeling well. It's filling and really warms you up on a wintry day! —Doris Cox
New Freedom, Pennsylvania

- **1 medium onion, chopped**
- **1 can (4 ounces) mushroom stems and pieces, drained**
- **2 tablespoons butter**
- **3 cups water**
- **2 cups chicken broth**
- **1 package (6 ounces) long grain and wild rice mix**
- **2 cups diced cooked turkey**
- **1 cup heavy whipping cream**
Minced fresh parsley

In a large saucepan, saute onion and mushrooms in butter until onion is tender. Add water, broth and rice mix and contents of seasoning packet; bring to a boil. Reduce heat; simmer for 20-25 minutes or until rice is tender. Stir in turkey and cream and heat through. Sprinkle with parsley. **Yield:** 6 servings.

Swedish Meatball Soup

(Pictured above)

To me, this is a very comforting, filling, homey soup. I especially like cooking it during winter months and serving it with hot rolls, bread or muffins.
—Debora Taylor, Inkom, Idaho

- **1 egg**
- **2 cups half-and-half cream, *divided***
- **1 cup soft bread crumbs**
- **1 small onion, finely chopped**
- **1-3/4 teaspoons salt, *divided***
- **1-1/2 pounds ground beef**
- **1 tablespoon butter**
- **3 tablespoons all-purpose flour**
- **3/4 teaspoon beef bouillon granules**
- **1/2 teaspoon pepper**
- **1/8 to 1/4 teaspoon garlic salt**
- **3 cups water**
- **1 pound red potatoes, cubed**
- **1 package (10 ounces) frozen peas, thawed**

In a bowl, beat egg; add 1/3 cup cream, bread crumbs, onion and 1 teaspoon of salt. Add beef; mix well. Shape into 1/2-in. balls. In a Dutch oven or soup kettle, brown meatballs in butter, half at a time. Remove from the pan; set aside. Drain fat.

To pan, add flour, bouillon, pepper, garlic salt and remaining salt; stir until smooth. Gradually stir in water; bring to a boil, stirring often. Add potatoes and meatballs. Reduce heat; cover and simmer for 25 minutes or until the potatoes are tender. Stir in the peas and remaining cream; heat through. **Yield:** 9 servings (about 2 quarts).

Top to bottom: Three-Ring Mold,
Poppy Seed Dressing and
Special Fruit Salad

Three-Ring Mold

(Pictured at left)

A dear friend shared this recipe with me some 30 years ago. My family never seems to tire of seeing this salad on the table. Not only is it tasty, it's pretty as well.
—Anne Maurer, Chicago, Illinois

FIRST LAYER:
- 2 cans (29 ounces *each*) pear halves
- 1 package (3 ounces) cherry gelatin
- 3/4 cup boiling water

SECOND LAYER:
- 1 package (8 ounces) cream cheese, softened
- 1 package (3 ounces) lemon gelatin
- 3/4 cup boiling water
- 3/4 cup cold water
- 1 cup heavy whipping cream, whipped

THIRD LAYER:
- 1 can (20 ounces) crushed pineapple
- 1 package (3 ounces) lime gelatin
- 3/4 cup boiling water

Drain pears, reserving 3/4 cup juice. Arrange pears in a 4-qt. glass bowl or trifle dish. Dissolve cherry gelatin in boiling water; add reserved juice. Pour over pears. Chill until firm.

For second layer, beat cream cheese in a mixing bowl until smooth and creamy. Dissolve lemon gelatin in boiling water; gradually add to cream cheese. Beat until smooth. Stir in cold water. Add cream and blend until smooth. Pour over first layer. Chill until firm.

For third layer, drain pineapple, reserving 3/4 cup juice. Dissolve lime gelatin in boiling water; add pineapple and reserved juice. Pour over second layer. Chill until firm. **Yield:** 16-18 servings.

Editor's Note: This salad takes time to prepare since each layer must be set before the next layer is added.

Poppy Seed Dressing

(Pictured at left)

I like to serve this tangy dressing over fruit but have found it also adds a subtle sweet flavor to salad greens and chicken. It's very easy to prepare and tastes fresh.
—Elizabeth Hibbs, Brooksville, Florida

- 3/4 cup olive oil
- 1/3 cup honey
- 1/4 cup red wine vinegar
- 2 tablespoons poppy seeds
- 1 tablespoon finely chopped onion
- 1 tablespoon Dijon mustard
- 1/2 teaspoon salt

Combine all ingredients in a blender; process for 30 seconds. Chill. Stir before using. **Yield:** 1-1/3 cups.

Special Fruit Salad

(Pictured at left)

The combination of juices in the dressing brings out the fabulous flavors of all the fruits featured in this salad. It's one of my most requested recipes.
—Alice Orton, Big Bear Lake, California

- 1 can (20 ounces) pineapple chunks
- 2 cups diced red apples
- 2 cups cubed cantaloupe
- 1 cup seedless green grapes, halved
- 1 cup halved fresh strawberries
- 3 ripe kiwifruit, peeled and sliced

DRESSING:
- 1/2 cup mayonnaise
- 1/2 cup sour cream
- 2 tablespoons sugar
- 1 tablespoon orange juice
- 1-1/2 teaspoons lemon juice
- 1/2 teaspoon grated lemon peel
- 1/2 teaspoon grated orange peel

Drain pineapple, reserving 1 tablespoon juice. Combine all fruit in a large bowl; cover and chill. In a small bowl, combine reserved pineapple juice and dressing ingredients; mix well. Cover and chill. Spoon dressing over fruit or toss just before serving. **Yield:** 8-10 servings.

Strawberry Pointers

When picking fresh strawberries, it's best to use small, shallow containers so the fragile berries aren't crushed.

To slice strawberries quickly and evenly, use an egg slicer.

When a recipe calls for mashed berries, use a pastry blender. It's quicker than using a fork.

Savory Cheese Soup

(Pictured above)

This delicious soup recipe was shared by a friend and instantly became a hit with my husband. Its big cheese flavor blends wonderfully with the vegetables. I first served this creamy soup as part of a holiday meal, but now we enjoy it throughout the year. —Dee Falk
Stromsburg, Nebraska

1/4 cup chopped onion
3 tablespoons butter
1/4 cup all-purpose flour
1/4 teaspoon salt
1/8 teaspoon pepper
1/8 teaspoon garlic powder
2 cups milk
1 can (14-1/2 ounces) chicken broth
1/2 cup shredded carrots
1/2 cup finely chopped celery
1-1/2 cups (6 ounces) shredded cheddar cheese
3/4 cup shredded mozzarella cheese
Fresh *or* dried chives, optional

In a large saucepan, saute onion in butter until tender. Add flour, salt, pepper and garlic powder; stir until smooth. Gradually add milk; cook and stir over medium heat until thickened and bubbly.

Meanwhile, bring chicken broth to a boil in a small saucepan. Add carrots and celery; simmer for 5 minutes or until vegetables are tender. Add to milk mixture and stir until blended. Add cheeses. Cook and stir until melted (do not boil). Garnish with chives if desired. **Yield:** about 4 servings.

Tart Cherry Salad

This recipe has been in my family for years; we especially use it during the holiday season. It's pleasantly tart and a perfect complement to any meal.
—Bea Wittman, Ridgway, Pennsylvania

2 cans (16 ounces *each*) tart red cherries
2 cans (8 ounces *each*) crushed pineapple
1 cup sugar
2 packages (6 ounces *each*) cherry gelatin
3 cups ginger ale
3/4 cup flaked coconut
1 cup chopped nuts, optional

Drain cherries and pineapple, reserving juices. Set fruit aside. Add enough water to combined juices to make 3-1/4 cups; pour into a saucepan. Add sugar; bring to a boil. Remove from the heat; stir in gelatin until dissolved. Add the cherries, pineapple and ginger ale.

Chill until partially set. Stir in coconut and nuts if desired. Pour into a 3-qt. mold or 13-in. x 9-in. x 2-in. pan coated with nonstick cooking spray. Chill until firm, about 3 hours. **Yield:** 16-18 servings.

Creamy Pumpkin Soup

A few years ago when our pumpkin harvest was very plentiful, I experimented and came up with this recipe.
—Emmi Schneider, Oak Lake, Manitoba

1 medium onion, chopped
2 tablespoons butter
2 cans (14-1/2 ounces *each*) chicken broth
2 cups sliced peeled potatoes
2 cups canned pumpkin
2 to 2-1/2 cups milk
1/2 teaspoon ground nutmeg
1/2 teaspoon salt
1/4 teaspoon pepper
1 cup (8 ounces) sour cream
1 tablespoon chopped fresh parsley
3 bacon strips, cooked and crumbled

In a large saucepan, saute onion in butter until tender. Add the broth, potatoes and pumpkin; cook until the potatoes are tender, about 15 minutes. Remove from the heat; cool. Puree half of the mixture at a time in a blender or food processor until smooth; return all to the pan.

Add the milk, nutmeg, salt and pepper; heat through. Meanwhile, combine the sour cream and parsley. Spoon soup into bowls; top each with a dollop of sour cream and sprinkle with crumbled bacon. **Yield:** 6 servings (1-1/2 quarts).

Creamy Orange Salad

This cool, light and pretty salad has a refreshing orange taste that complements a big holiday meal. With just five ingredients, it's very simple to prepare. I've served it for my family and shared it at potlucks.
—Priscilla Weaver, Hagerstown, Maryland

- 1 package (6 ounces) orange gelatin
- 2 cups boiling water
- 2 packages (3 ounces *each*) cream cheese, softened
- 1 can (14 ounces) sweetened condensed milk
- 1 carton (8 ounces) frozen whipped topping, thawed
- Maraschino cherry, fresh mint stem and mandarin oranges, optional

In a bowl, dissolve gelatin in water. In a mixing bowl, beat cream cheese until fluffy. Gradually blend in the hot gelatin mixture, beating on low speed until smooth. Stir in the milk; fold in whipped topping. Transfer to a 2-1/2-qt. serving bowl. Refrigerate for 4 hours or until firm. If desired, garnish with a flower made of cherry, mint and oranges. **Yield:** 10-12 servings.

Pecan-Pear Tossed Salad

(Pictured below left)

To save time, I prepare the ingredients and dressing the day before, then combine them just before serving. This salad has become a star at family gatherings.
—Marjean Claassen, Sedgwick, Kansas

- 2 tablespoons fresh raspberries
- 3/4 cup olive oil
- 3 tablespoons cider vinegar
- 2 tablespoons plus 1 teaspoon sugar
- 1/4 to 1/2 teaspoon pepper

SALAD:
- 4 medium ripe pears, thinly sliced
- 2 teaspoons lemon juice
- 8 cups torn salad greens
- 2/3 cup pecan halves, toasted
- 1/2 cup fresh raspberries
- 1/3 cup (2 ounces) crumbled feta cheese

Press raspberries through a sieve, reserving juice. Discard seeds. In a jar with a tight-fitting lid, combine oil, vinegar, sugar, pepper and reserved raspberry juice; shake well. Toss pear slices with lemon juice; drain. In a salad bowl, combine the salad greens, pears, pecans and raspberries. Sprinkle with cheese. Drizzle with dressing. **Yield:** 8 servings.

Cream of Mushroom Soup

My daughter-in-law, who is a gourmet cook, served this soup as the first course for Thanksgiving dinner. She'd gotten the recipe from her mom and graciously shared it with me. —Anne Kulick, Phillipsburg, New Jersey

- 1/4 cup chopped onion
- 2 tablespoons butter
- 3 cups sliced fresh mushrooms
- 6 tablespoons all-purpose flour
- 2 cans (14-1/2 ounces *each*) chicken broth
- 1 cup half-and-half cream
- 1/2 teaspoon salt
- 1/8 teaspoon pepper

In a large saucepan, saute onion in butter until tender. Add mushrooms and saute until tender. Combine flour and broth until smooth; stir into the mushroom mixture. Bring to a boil; cook and stir for 2 minutes or until thickened. Reduce heat. Stir in the cream, salt and pepper. Simmer, uncovered, for 15 minutes, stirring often. **Yield:** 4-6 servings.

Winter Cabbage Salad

(Pictured on page 93)

My mother made this recipe for as long as I can remember. She'd serve it as a vegetable, salad or garnish at family meals, ladies' church luncheons and potluck parties. —Eleanor Shuknecht, Elba, New York

    2 cups cider vinegar
    1 cup sugar
    2 tablespoons salt
    1 tablespoon mustard seed
  3/4 teaspoon celery seed
  1/2 teaspoon ground turmeric
   10 cups thinly sliced cabbage (about 2-1/4 pounds)
    3 medium onions, thinly sliced
    2 medium sweet red peppers, thinly sliced
    1 medium green pepper, thinly sliced

In a saucepan, bring the first six ingredients to a boil. Reduce heat; simmer, uncovered, for 5 minutes. Remove from the heat and allow to cool. In a large bowl, combine cabbage, onions and peppers. Pour vinegar mixture over vegetables and stir to coat. Cover and refrigerate overnight. **Yield:** 16-20 servings.

Italian Submarine Sandwich

I first sampled this at a dinner where it was served as an appetizer, and I almost didn't have room for the main course! Since then, it's become one of our family's standard sandwiches. —Susan Brown Richland, Washington

    2 jars (2 ounces *each*) diced pimientos, drained
    1 can (4-1/4 ounces) chopped ripe olives
  2/3 cup chopped stuffed olives
  1/2 cup olive oil
  1/2 cup minced fresh parsley
    3 garlic cloves, minced
    1 teaspoon dried oregano
  1/4 teaspoon pepper
    1 loaf (1 pound) Italian bread
  1/3 pound thinly sliced fully cooked ham
  1/3 pound thinly sliced Genoa salami
  1/3 pound thinly sliced provolone *or* mozzarella cheese

In a jar with a tight-fitting lid, combine the pimientos, olives, oil, parsley, garlic, oregano and pepper. Refrigerate for at least 12 hours. Cut bread in half lengthwise; hollow out top and bottom, leaving a 1-in. shell. (Discard removed bread or save for another use.)

Drain 2 tablespoons liquid from olive mixture; spread on the inside of bread top. Spoon 1 cup olive mixture evenly into bottom of bread shell.

Layer with ham, salami and cheese; spread with remaining olive mixture. Replace bread top. Slice into serving-size pieces. **Yield:** 4-6 servings.

Texas Turkey Soup

I'm not really fond of soup, so I was a little hesitant to try this recipe. But after some adjustments over the years, I've come to love this one-of-a-kind turkey soup. It really warms you on a chilly day. —Betty Bakas Lakehills, Texas

    2 quarts turkey broth
    4 cups cubed cooked turkey
    2 large white onions, halved
    2 celery ribs, sliced
    3 medium carrots, sliced
    1 cup *each* frozen corn, cut green beans and peas
    2 bay leaves
  1/2 to 1 teaspoon dried tarragon
  3/4 teaspoon garlic powder
  1/4 to 1/2 teaspoon hot pepper sauce
Salt and pepper to taste
  1-1/2 cups uncooked noodles
    1 tablespoon cornstarch
    1 tablespoon water

In a Dutch oven or soup kettle, combine broth, turkey, onions, celery, carrots, corn, beans, peas, bay leaves, tarragon, garlic powder, pepper sauce, salt and pepper. Bring to a boil. Reduce heat; cover and simmer for 20-30 minutes or until vegetables are tender. Return to a boil; add noodles.

Reduce heat; cover and simmer for 15-20 minutes or until noodles are tender. Combine cornstarch and water until smooth; add to soup. Bring to a boil; boil for 2 minutes, stirring constantly. Remove bay leaves. **Yield:** 10-12 servings (3 quarts).

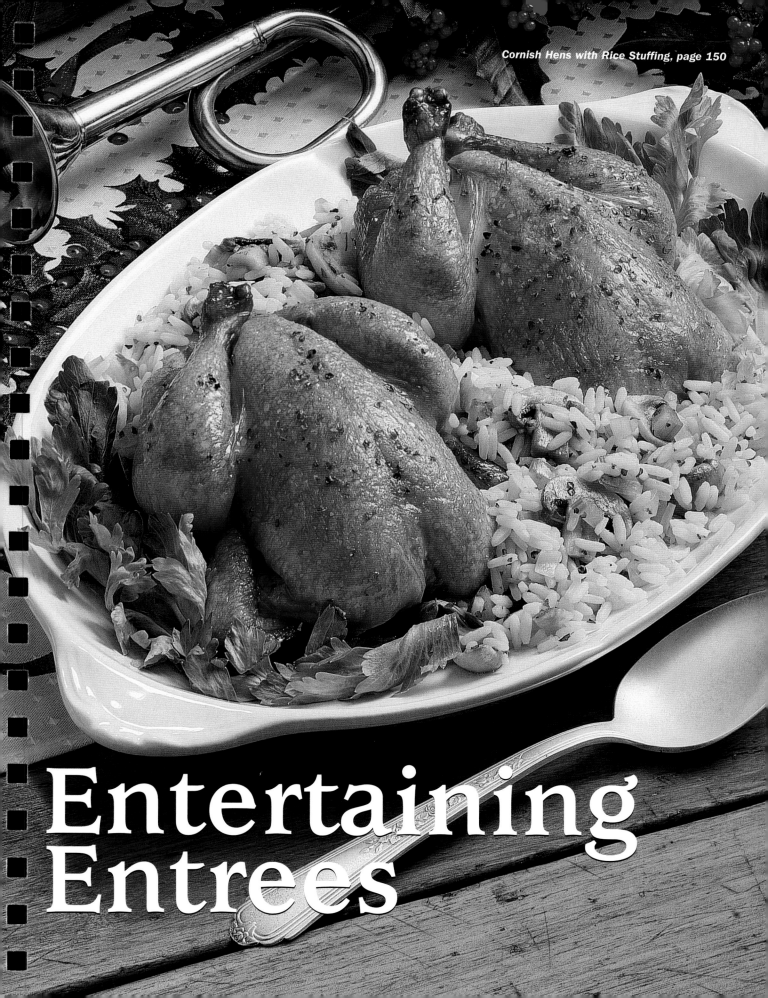

Cornish Hens with Rice Stuffing, page 150

Entertaining Entrees

sauce and ginger. Add to the skillet; cook and stir until thickened and bubbly. Return turkey to skillet with pea pods; cook and stir until heated through. If desired, serve over rice and top with cashews. **Yield:** 6 servings.

Beef Enchiladas

(Pictured below)

Warm up a cold winter night with a hearty serving of Tex-Mex food. This easy one-dish meal gives me more time to spend with guests. —Mary Anne McWhirter Pearland, Texas

       1 **pound ground beef**
       1 **cup cottage cheese**
       1 **can (4-1/4 ounces) chopped ripe olives, drained**
       2 **tablespoons minced fresh parsley**
     1/2 **teaspoon garlic powder**
     1/2 **teaspoon salt**
     1/4 **teaspoon pepper**
       8 **flour tortillas (7 inches)**
SAUCE:
       1 **medium onion, chopped**
     1/2 **medium green pepper, chopped**
       1 **tablespoon vegetable oil**
       1 **can (15 ounces) tomato sauce**
       1 **can (4 ounces) chopped green chilies**

Turkey Stir-Fry

(Pictured above)

Here's a tasty way to prepare turkey any time of year. My family loves the tender turkey strips, colorful vegetables and crunchy cashews. You don't always have to fix the whole bird to enjoy the wonderful taste of turkey.
—Julianne Johnson, Grove City, Minnesota

   1-1/2 **pounds uncooked boneless skinless turkey
            breast, cut into strips**
       1 **tablespoon vegetable oil**
       1 **small onion, chopped**
       1 **carrot, julienned**
     1/2 **medium green pepper, sliced**
       2 **cups fresh mushrooms, sliced**
       1 **cup chicken broth**
       3 **tablespoons cornstarch**
       3 **tablespoons soy sauce**
     1/2 **teaspoon ground ginger**
       2 **cups pea pods, trimmed**
Cooked rice, optional
     1/3 **cup cashews, optional**

In a large skillet or wok, stir-fry turkey in oil over medium-high heat until no longer pink, about 5-6 minutes. Remove turkey and keep warm. Stir-fry the onion, carrot, green pepper and mushrooms until crisp-tender, about 5 minutes.

In a small bowl, combine chicken broth, cornstarch, soy

2 **teaspoons chili powder**
1 **teaspoon sugar**
1/2 **teaspoon garlic powder**
1 **cup (4 ounces) shredded cheddar cheese**

In a skillet, cook beef over medium heat until no longer pink. Drain. Combine with cottage cheese, olives, parsley, garlic powder, salt and pepper. Place about 1/3 cup filling on each tortilla; roll up. Place tortillas, seam side down, in an ungreased 13-in. x 9-in. x 2-in. baking dish.

For sauce, saute the onion and green pepper in oil until tender. Add tomato sauce, green chilies, chili powder, sugar and garlic powder. Pour over tortillas. Cover and bake at 350° for 30 minutes. Sprinkle with cheese and return to the oven for 5 minutes or until cheese is melted. **Yield:** 4 servings.

Pumpkin Stew

(Pictured at right)

This deliciously different stew is cooked and served right in the pumpkin shell. It makes a pretty presentation at a potluck. —Donna Mosher, Augusta, Montana

2 **pounds beef stew meat, cut into 1-inch cubes**
3 **tablespoons vegetable oil, *divided***
1 **cup water**
3 **large potatoes, peeled and cut into 1-inch cubes**
4 **medium carrots, sliced**
1 **large green pepper, cut into 1/2-inch pieces**
4 **garlic cloves, minced**
1 **medium onion, chopped**
2 **teaspoons salt**
1/2 **teaspoon pepper**
2 **tablespoons instant beef bouillon granules**
1 **can (14-1/2 ounces) diced tomatoes, undrained**
1 **pumpkin (10 to 12 pounds)**

In a Dutch oven, brown meat in 2 tablespoons oil. Add the water, potatoes, carrots, green pepper, garlic, onion, salt and pepper. Cover and simmer for 2 hours. Stir in the bouillon and tomatoes.

Wash pumpkin; cut a 6- to 8-in. circle around top stem. Remove top and set aside; discard seeds and loose fibers from inside. Place pumpkin in a shallow sturdy baking pan. Spoon stew into pumpkin and replace the top. Brush outside of pumpkin with remaining oil.

Bake at 325° for 2 hours or just until the pumpkin is tender (do not overbake). Serve stew from pumpkin, scooping out some pumpkin with each serving. **Yield:** 8-10 servings.

Spiced Ham with Apple Relish

If you think Thanksgiving turkey tastes good as a leftover, try this. The ham's wonderful served cold on a bun with hot or cold relish spooned on the top. The meat can be sliced and cooked up in a soup as well.
—Vicki Tasker, Oakland, Maryland

1 **teaspoon ground cloves**
1 **teaspoon ground allspice**
1 **boneless fully cooked ham (3 to 4 pounds)**
APPLE RELISH:
4 **medium tart apples, peeled and chopped**
2 **cups sugar**
1 **cup chopped dried apricots**
1 **cup golden raisins**
1/4 **cup vinegar**
2 **tablespoons grated orange peel**
1/2 **cup slivered almonds, toasted**

Combine cloves and allspice; rub over ham. Wrap tightly in foil and place in a shallow baking pan. Bake at 325° for 1 to 1-1/2 hours or until a meat thermometer reads 140° and ham is heated through.

In a large saucepan, combine the first six relish ingredients. Bring to a boil, stirring constantly. Reduce heat; simmer for 25-30 minutes or until thickened. Stir in almonds. Slice ham; serve with the relish. **Yield:** 8-10 servings (4 cups relish).

Top to bottom: Roast Pork with Raspberry Sauce, Italian Beef Sandwiches (recipe on page 129) and Slow-Cooked Rump Roast

Slow-Cooked Rump Roast

(Pictured at left)

I enjoy a good pot roast, but I was tired of the same old thing…so I started experimenting. Cooking the beef in horseradish sauce gives it a tangy flavor.
—Mimi Walker, Palmyra, Pennsylvania

- 1 boneless beef rump roast (3 to 3-1/2 pounds)
- 2 tablespoons vegetable oil
- 4 medium carrots, halved lengthwise and cut into 2-inch pieces
- 3 medium potatoes, peeled and cut into chunks
- 2 small onions, sliced
- 1/2 cup water
- 6 to 8 tablespoons horseradish sauce
- 1/4 cup red wine vinegar
- 1/4 cup Worcestershire sauce
- 2 garlic cloves, minced
- 1-1/2 to 2 teaspoons celery salt
- 3 tablespoons cornstarch
- 1/3 cup cold water

Cut roast in half. In a large skillet, brown meat on all sides in oil over medium-high heat; drain. Place carrots and potatoes in a 5-qt. slow cooker. Top with meat and onions. Combine the water, horseradish sauce, vinegar, Worcestershire sauce, garlic and celery salt. Pour over meat. Cover and cook on low for 10-11 hours or until meat and vegetables are tender.

Combine cornstarch and cold water until smooth; stir into slow cooker. Cover and cook on high for 30 minutes or until gravy is thickened. **Yield:** 6-8 servings.

Roast Pork with Raspberry Sauce

(Pictured at left)

Want to treat your guests to a spectacular meal? Plan this pork as the centerpiece of your menu. The fruity sauce enhances the meat's flavor and looks so pretty!
—Carolyn Zimmerman, Fairbury, Illinois

- 1 teaspoon salt
- 1 teaspoon rubbed sage
- 1 teaspoon pepper
- 1 boneless pork loin roast (3-1/2 to 4 pounds)

SAUCE:
- 1 package (10 ounces) frozen sweetened raspberries, thawed
- 1-1/2 cups sugar
- 1/4 cup white vinegar
- 1/4 teaspoon *each* ground ginger, nutmeg and cloves
- 1/4 cup cornstarch
- 1 tablespoon butter, melted
- 1 tablespoon lemon juice
- 3 to 4 drops red food coloring, optional

Combine the salt, sage and pepper; rub over entire roast. Place roast fat side up on a rack in a shallow roasting pan. Bake, uncovered, at 350° for 70-80 minutes or until a meat thermometer reads 160°.

For the sauce, drain raspberries, reserving liquid. Set berries aside. Add enough water to juice to measure 3/4 cup. In a saucepan, combine the sugar, vinegar, spices and 1/2 cup raspberry juice. Bring to a boil. Reduce heat; simmer, uncovered, for 10 minutes.

Combine cornstarch and remaining raspberry juice until smooth; stir into the saucepan. Bring to a boil; cook and stir for 2 minutes or until thickened. Remove from the heat. Stir in the butter, lemon juice, food coloring if desired and reserved raspberries.

Let roast stand for 10-15 minutes before slicing. Serve with raspberry sauce. **Yield:** 8-10 servings.

Holiday Ham

Ham makes appearances at all of our holiday dinners. I also like to use whole pineapple rings and maraschino cherries. —Betty Butler, Union Bridge, Maryland

- 1 can (8 ounces) crushed pineapple, undrained
- 1/2 spiral-sliced fully cooked bone-in ham (8 to 10 pounds)
- 1-1/2 cups packed brown sugar
- 1/2 teaspoon seasoned salt

Drain pineapple, reserving juice. Place ham on a rack in a shallow roasting pan. Combine brown sugar and seasoned salt; rub over ham. Spoon crushed pineapple over ham; gently pour reserved pineapple juice over top.

Bake, uncovered, at 325° for 1-1/2 to 2 hours or until a meat thermometer reads 140° and ham is heated through. Baste frequently with brown sugar mixture. **Yield:** about 18-20 servings.

Turkey Dressing Pie

(Pictured above)

I fix turkey all year long, and I purposely make too much just so we can have this later on. It's a nice way to use up leftover turkey, especially around the holidays.
—De De Boekelheide, Northville, South Dakota

3-1/2 **to 4 cups cooked turkey dressing**
1/2 **cup turkey *or* chicken broth**
2 **tablespoons butter, melted**
1 **egg, beaten**
1/2 **cup chopped onion**
1 **tablespoon vegetable oil**
3 **cups diced cooked turkey**
1 **cup turkey gravy**
1 **cup frozen peas, optional**
2 **tablespoons dried parsley flakes**
2 **tablespoons diced pimientos**
1 **teaspoon Worcestershire sauce**
1/2 **teaspoon dried thyme**
4 **slices process American cheese, optional**

In a large bowl, combine dressing, broth, butter and egg; mix well. Press onto the bottom and up the sides of an ungreased 10-in. pie plate; set aside.

In a large skillet, saute onion in oil until tender. Stir in turkey, gravy, peas if desired, parsley, pimientos, Worcestershire sauce and thyme; heat through. Pour into crust.

Bake at 375° for 20 minutes or until golden. If desired, arrange cheese slices on top of pie and bake 5 minutes longer or until cheese is melted. **Yield:** 6 servings.

Pork and Winter Squash Stew

(Pictured below)

Here in the high desert area of California, we do get snow. So this stew's especially popular in winter.
—Evelyn Plyler, Apple Valley, California

2 **pounds lean boneless pork, cut into 1-inch cubes**
2 **tablespoons vegetable oil, *divided***
2 **cups chopped onion**
2 **garlic cloves, minced**
3 **cups sliced fresh mushrooms**
2-1/2 **cups sliced carrots**
2 **cans (14-1/2 ounces *each*) Italian stewed tomatoes**
2 **teaspoons dried thyme**
1-1/2 **teaspoons salt**
1/2 **teaspoon pepper**
4 **cups cubed peeled butternut squash**
Hot cooked noodles, optional

In a 5-qt. Dutch oven, brown pork in 1 tablespoon of oil. Remove from pan; drain and set aside. Heat remaining oil in the same pan over medium heat. Saute the onion and garlic for 3 minutes.

Return pork to pan. Add the mushrooms, carrots, tomatoes, thyme, salt and pepper; bring to a boil. Reduce heat; cover and simmer for 1 hour.

Add squash; simmer, uncovered, for 30 minutes or until meat and vegetables are tender. Serve over noodles if desired. **Yield:** 8 servings.

Italian Beef Sandwiches

(Pictured on page 126)

I'm a paramedic/firefighter, and slow-cooked recipes like this one suit my unpredictable schedule. My husband, children and the hungry bunch at the firehouse love these robust sandwiches. —Kristen Swihart
Perrysburg, Ohio

  1 jar (11-1/2 ounces) pepperoncinis
  1 boneless beef chuck roast (3-1/2 to 4 pounds)
1/4 cup water
1-3/4 teaspoons dried basil
1-1/2 teaspoons garlic powder
1-1/2 teaspoons dried oregano
1-1/4 teaspoons salt
1/4 teaspoon pepper
  1 large onion, sliced and quartered
 10 to 12 hard rolls, split

Drain pepperoncinis, reserving liquid. Remove and discard stems of peppers; set peppers aside. Cut roast into large chunks; place a third of the meat in a 5-qt. slow cooker. Add the water.

In a small bowl, combine the basil, garlic powder, oregano, salt and pepper; sprinkle half over beef. Layer with half of the remaining meat, then onion, reserved peppers and liquid. Top with remaining meat and herb mixture.

Cover and cook on low for 8-9 hours or until meat is tender. Shred beef with two forks. Using a slotted spoon, serve beef and peppers on rolls. **Yield:** 10-12 servings.

    Editor's Note: Look for pepperoncinis (pickled peppers) in the pickle and olive section of your grocery store.

Orange-Glazed Chicken with Rice

(Pictured above right)

I've enjoyed cooking ever since I was a child. I can remember standing on a stool and watching Mother make bread on the old Hoosier cupboard. I have made this recipe often. —Irlene Schauer, Rochester, Minnesota

1/2 cup currant jelly
1/2 cup water, *divided*
1/4 cup orange juice concentrate
  2 tablespoons cornstarch
  1 teaspoon ground mustard
Dash hot pepper sauce
1/2 cup all-purpose flour
1/4 teaspoon salt
  1 broiler/fryer chicken (3-1/2 to 4 pounds), cut up
  2 tablespoons vegetable oil
RICE:
  1 cup diced celery
1/4 cup chopped onion
  2 tablespoons butter
1-1/3 cups water
1-1/3 cups uncooked instant rice
  2 tablespoons orange juice concentrate
1/2 teaspoon salt

In a saucepan, combine jelly, 1/4 cup water and concentrate. Cook and stir on low until jelly is melted. Combine cornstarch and remaining water until smooth; gradually stir into jelly mixture along with mustard and hot pepper sauce. Bring to a boil, stirring constantly. Cook about 2 minutes more; remove from heat and set aside. Combine flour and salt; dredge chicken.

In a skillet over medium heat, brown chicken in oil. Place in a greased 13-in. x 9-in. x 2-in. baking dish. Pour sauce over chicken. Cover and bake at 350° for 20 minutes. Baste with sauce. Bake, uncovered, 45 minutes longer or until juices run clear.

Meanwhile, in a saucepan, saute celery and onion in butter until crisp-tender. Add water; bring to a boil. Stir in rice, concentrate and salt. Cover and remove from heat; let stand 5-7 minutes or until water is absorbed. Serve chicken over rice. **Yield:** 4-6 servings.

Creamy Sausage Stew

(Pictured below)

Depending on the time of year, I serve my stew with bread or sweet corn muffins and fresh butter, and with salad or fruit. Then, since it tastes even better the next day, we have it for lunch on the rare occasions there are leftovers! —Rosemary Jesse, Cabool, Missouri

- 8 to 10 medium red potatoes, cut into 1-1/2-inch pieces
- 2 large white onions, quartered
- 1 large green pepper, cut into 1-inch pieces
- 1 large sweet red pepper, cut into 1-inch pieces
- 2 pounds smoked Polish sausage, cut into 1-inch slices
- 1/3 cup vegetable oil
- 1 tablespoon dried basil
- 2 teaspoons salt
- 1 teaspoon pepper
- 1 pint heavy whipping cream
- 3 tablespoons cornstarch
- 3 tablespoons cold water

Place potatoes in a 5-qt. roasting pan. Add onions, peppers and sausage; toss gently. Combine oil, basil, salt and pepper. Pour over the meat and vegetables; toss well. Cover and bake at 350° for 45 minutes; stir. Add the cream; cover and bake 30-40 minutes longer or until potatoes are tender.

Combine cornstarch and water; stir into stew. Place on stovetop and bring to a boil, stirring constantly until thickened. **Yield:** 10-12 servings.

Turkey Tetrazzini

(Pictured above)

This recipe comes from a cookbook our church compiled. It's convenient because it can be made ahead and frozen. After the holidays, we use leftover turkey to prepare a meal for university students. They clean their plates! —Gladys Waldrop, Calvert City, Kentucky

- 1 package (7 ounces) spaghetti, broken into 2-inch pieces
- 2 cups cubed cooked turkey
- 1 cup (4 ounces) shredded cheddar cheese
- 1 can (10-3/4 ounces) condensed cream of mushroom soup, undiluted
- 1 medium onion, chopped
- 2 cans (4 ounces *each*) sliced mushrooms, drained
- 1/3 cup milk
- 1/4 cup chopped green pepper
- 1 jar (2 ounces) chopped pimientos, drained
- 1/4 teaspoon salt
- 1/8 teaspoon pepper

Additional shredded cheddar cheese, optional

Cook spaghetti according to package directions; drain. Transfer to a large bowl; add the next 10 ingredients and mix well. Spoon into a greased 2-1/2-qt. casserole; sprinkle with cheese if desired. Bake, uncovered, at 375° for 40-45 minutes or until heated through. **Yield:** 6-8 servings.

Roasted Chicken And Potatoes

(Pictured below)

My mom's tender roasted chicken with potatoes and sage dressing is even more delicious than its aroma while baking. —Sandra Melnychenko
Grandview, Manitoba

    1 **cup chopped celery**
    1 **medium onion, chopped**
 1/2 **cup butter**
    2 **tablespoons poultry seasoning**
 1/2 **teaspoon rubbed sage**
    8 **cups cubed day-old white bread**
 1/2 **cup chicken broth**
    1 **roasting chicken (5 to 6 pounds)**
 1/2 **teaspoon paprika**
 1/4 **teaspoon salt**
Pinch pepper
    6 **medium baking potatoes, peeled and quartered**
    1 **teaspoon chopped fresh parsley**

In a skillet, saute celery and onion in butter until tender, about 5 minutes. Add poultry seasoning and sage. Place bread cubes in a large bowl. Stir in celery mixture and broth; mix lightly. Just before baking, stuff the chicken. Place on a rack in a roasting pan; tie the drumsticks together. Combine paprika, salt and pepper; rub over chicken.

Bake, uncovered, at 350° for 1-1/2 hours, basting every 30 minutes. Arrange the potatoes around chicken; cover and bake 1 hour longer or until potatoes are tender and a meat thermometer reads 180°. Sprinkle with parsley. Cover; let stand for

10 minutes before removing stuffing and carving. Reserve pan drippings; thicken for gravy if desired. **Yield:** 4-6 servings.

Hoosier Pork Chop Supper

(Pictured above)

Indiana is one of the leading hog-producing states, so this recipe reflects our region. This one-dish meal is quite easy to make. —Frances Cory, Rockville, Indiana

    1 **medium onion, sliced**
    3 **tablespoons vegetable oil**
    3 **tablespoons all-purpose flour**
    1 **teaspoon salt**
 1/2 **teaspoon pepper**
    4 **pork chops (1-1/2 inches thick)**
    2 **large potatoes, peeled and sliced**
    1 **large carrot, sliced**
    1 **can (16 ounces) diced tomatoes, undrained**
    1 **cup frozen peas**

In a large skillet, saute onion in oil until tender. Remove with a slotted spoon and set aside; reserve drippings in pan. Combine the flour, salt and pepper; coat the pork chops. Brown on both sides in the drippings. Add potatoes, carrot, tomatoes and onion; bring to a boil.

Reduce heat; cover and simmer for 1-1/2 hours, adding the peas during the last 10 minutes. **Yield:** 4 servings.

Swiss Steak

(Pictured above)

This is one of my family's favorite recipes. I sometimes serve it with white or wild rice. You can also substitute venison for the beef if you like.
—Linda Stiles, Baltimore, Ohio

  2 **pounds beef round steak (1 inch thick)**
  3 **tablespoons all-purpose flour**
1/2 **teaspoon salt**
1/4 **teaspoon pepper**
  2 **tablespoons vegetable oil**
  2 **medium onions, sliced**
  2 **celery ribs, chopped**
  1 **can (14-1/2 ounces) diced tomatoes, undrained with liquid, cut up**
  2 **tablespoons Worcestershire sauce**
1/4 **teaspoon dried oregano**
Hot cooked noodles, optional

Cut meat into serving-size pieces and dredge in flour. Sprinkle with salt and pepper. In a skillet or Dutch oven, brown meat on both sides in oil. Top with the onions and celery.

In a medium bowl, combine tomatoes, Worcestershire sauce and oregano; spoon over vegetables. Cover and simmer for 1-1/2 to 2 hours or until meat is tender. Serve over noodles if desired. **Yield:** 6 servings.

Irish Lamb Stew

With our busy schedule, I cook lots of stews. This one is nice because you can prepare it on the weekend and reheat it during the week. It's a great full-course meal to serve family and friends. —Jeanne Dahling
Elgin, Minnesota

  6 **tablespoons all-purpose flour, *divided***
  1 **teaspoon salt**
1/8 **teaspoon pepper**
1-1/2 **pounds lamb stew meat, cut into 1-inch cubes**
  2 **tablespoons vegetable oil**
1/2 **teaspoon dill weed**
  3 **cups water**
  8 **pearl onions**
  3 **medium carrots, cut into 1-inch pieces**
  2 **large potatoes, peeled and cubed**
1/2 **cup half-and-half cream**

Combine 4 tablespoons flour, salt and pepper in a large resealable plastic bag. Add lamb; shake to coat. In a 4-qt. Dutch oven, heat oil; brown lamb on all sides. Add dill and water; bring to a boil.

Reduce heat; cover and simmer for 1-1/2 hours or until meat is almost tender. Add onions, carrots and potatoes. Cover and simmer for 30 minutes or until the meat and vegetables are tender.

Combine cream and remaining flour; stir into stew. Cook and stir until boiling and slightly thickened. **Yield:** 6 servings.

Apple-Stuffed Chicken

(Pictured at right)

A friend served this chicken when we were over for dinner, and we enjoyed it so much I asked for the recipe.
—Joan Wrigley, Lynden, Washington

  1 **package (6 ounces) chicken-flavored stuffing mix**
  1 **broiler/fryer chicken (about 3-1/2 pounds)**
1/2 **teaspoon salt**
1/4 **teaspoon pepper**
  1 **tablespoon vegetable oil**
  1 **cup chopped peeled apple**
1/4 **cup chopped celery**
1/4 **cup chopped walnuts**
1/4 **cup raisins**
1/2 **teaspoon grated lemon peel**

GLAZE:
1/2 cup apple jelly
1 tablespoon lemon juice
1/2 teaspoon ground cinnamon

Prepare stuffing according to package directions. Meanwhile, sprinkle inside of chicken with salt and pepper; rub outside with the oil.

In a large bowl, mix stuffing with apple, celery, nuts, raisins and lemon peel. Stuff chicken. Place with breast side up on a rack in a shallow roasting pan. Bake, uncovered, at 350° for 1 hour.

In a saucepan, combine glaze ingredients; simmer for 3 minutes. Brush over chicken. Bake 20-30 minutes longer or until chicken juices run clear and a meat thermometer reads 180° for the chicken and 165° for the stuffing, brushing occasionally with glaze. Cover and let stand 10 minutes before removing stuffing and carving. **Yield:** 4-6 servings.

Chicken Cannelloni

(Pictured above right)

I entered this recipe in a contest sponsored by a local radio station years ago, and it won Grand Prize! It's a unique takeoff on cannelloni because you are stuffing chicken breasts instead of the usual pasta tubes. I reach for this recipe often. —Barbara Nowakowski
North Tonawanda, New York

1 small onion, sliced
1 garlic clove, minced
3/4 cup thinly sliced carrots
1/2 cup thinly sliced celery
1/2 cup sliced mushrooms
1 tablespoon vegetable oil
1 can (6 ounces) tomato paste
1 can (8 ounces) diced tomatoes, undrained
1-1/2 teaspoons Italian seasoning, *divided*
1 teaspoon sugar
6 boneless skinless chicken breast halves
1/2 cup ricotta cheese
1/4 cup sliced green onions
3 tablespoons grated Parmesan cheese
Dash pepper
1/2 cup mozzarella cheese
Cooked pasta, optional

In a large saucepan, saute onion, garlic, carrots, celery and mushrooms in oil until onion is tender. Add tomato paste, tomatoes, 1 teaspoon Italian seasoning and sugar; bring to a boil. Reduce heat and simmer, uncovered, for 10 minutes.

Meanwhile, pound chicken to 1/4-in. thickness. Combine ricotta cheese, green onions, Parmesan cheese, pepper and remaining Italian seasoning; divide evenly and spoon on top of chicken.

Roll up; place seam side down in an 8-in. square baking dish. Spoon sauce over chicken. Bake, uncovered, at 375° for 25-30 minutes or until the chicken is tender. Sprinkle with mozzarella cheese; let stand for 5 minutes. Serve with pasta if desired. **Yield:** 4-6 servings.

Herbed Pork Roast

(Pictured above)

I received this recipe when we moved to Oklahoma. A going-away party was held for us, and the guests were asked to bring their favorite recipe as a remembrance.
—Elizabeth Area, Stillwater, Oklahoma

1 cup soy sauce
2 tablespoons lemon juice
2 garlic cloves, minced
2 teaspoons dried tarragon
2 teaspoons dried basil
1 teaspoon chives
1 teaspoon rubbed sage
1 teaspoon pepper
1 boneless pork loin roast (3-1/2 to 4 pounds)

In a large resealable plastic bag, combine the first eight ingredients. Add roast; seal and turn to coat. Refrigerate overnight, turning bag several times. Remove roast from bag and place in the roasting pan; pour marinade over roast. Cover the pan and bake at 325° for 2 to 2-1/2 hours or until a thermometer reads 160°. Let stand 15 minutes before slicing. **Yield:** 6-8 servings.

Editor's Note: If using a plastic oven bag, add 1 tablespoon flour to bag and shake to coat. Add marinade and roast.

Place in a shallow roasting pan; refrigerate. Before roasting, make several 1/2-in. slits in top of bag. Bake, uncovered, at 325° for 2 to 2-1/2 hours.

Standing Rib Roast

(Pictured below)

Treat your family to tender slices of standing rib roast or use the seasoning blend on a different beef roast for a hearty, delicious main dish. I love to prepare this recipe for special occasions.
—Lucy Meyring
Walden, Colorado

1 tablespoon lemon-pepper seasoning
1 tablespoon paprika
1-1/2 teaspoons garlic salt
1 teaspoon dried rosemary, crushed
1/2 teaspoon cayenne pepper
1 standing beef rib roast (6 to 7 pounds)
2 cups boiling water
1 teaspoon instant beef bouillon granules

Combine lemon-pepper, paprika, garlic salt, rosemary and cayenne pepper; rub over roast. Place roast with fat side up in a large roasting pan. Bake, uncovered, at 325° until roast reaches desired doneness. Allow 25-27 minutes per pound for medium rare (145° on a meat thermometer), 27-30 minutes for medium (160°) and 32-35 minutes for well-done (170°).
Remove to serving platter and keep warm. Let stand

15 minutes before carving. Pour meat juices from roasting pan into a glass measuring cup; skim off fat. Add boiling water and bouillon to roasting pan and stir to loosen browned bits from pan. Stir in meat juices. Serve with the roast. **Yield:** 10-12 servings.

Roasted Chicken With Rosemary

(Pictured above)

This is a lot like pot roast, only it uses chicken instead of beef. The rosemary gives it a sweet taste and blends well with the garlic, butter and parsley.
—Isabel Zienkosky, Salt Lake City, Utah

- 1/2 **cup butter**
- 2 **tablespoons dried rosemary**
- 2 **tablespoons chopped fresh parsley**
- 3 **garlic cloves, minced**
- 1 **teaspoon salt**
- 1/2 **teaspoon pepper**
- 1 **whole roasting chicken (5 to 6 pounds)**
- 8 **small red potatoes, halved**
- 6 **carrots, cut into 2-inch pieces and halved lengthwise**
- 2 **medium onions, quartered**

In a small saucepan, melt butter. Add rosemary, parsley, garlic, salt and pepper. Place chicken on a rack in a roasting pan; tie drumsticks together. Spoon half of the butter mixture over chicken. Place the potatoes, carrots and onions around chicken. Drizzle remaining butter mixture over vegetables. Cover and bake at 350° for 1-1/2 hours, basting every 30 minutes. Uncover; bake 1 hour longer or until juices run clear, basting occasionally. **Yield:** 6 servings.

Turkey in a Hurry

(Pictured below)

This dish is easy to prepare and really brings some variety to mealtime. It's a delicious way to fix turkey, which cooks up moist and tasty. My husband, our two daughters and I all enjoy it. —Denise Goedeken
Platte Center, Nebraska

- 2 **turkey tenderloins (1-1/2 pounds)**
- 1/4 **cup butter**
- 3/4 **teaspoon dried thyme**
- 1/2 **teaspoon dried rosemary, crushed**
- 1/4 **teaspoon paprika**
- 1/8 **teaspoon garlic powder**

Cut tenderloins in half lengthwise, then into serving-size pieces. Place on rack of broiler pan. In a small saucepan, heat remaining ingredients until butter is melted. Broil turkey until lightly browned on one side. Brush with the herb butter; turn and brown the other side. Brush with butter. Cook 6-8 minutes longer or until turkey juices run clear, basting often with butter. **Yield:** 6 servings.

Top to bottom: Vegetable Pork Chop Dinner, Tangy Glazed Ham and Stuffed Pork Chops

Stuffed Pork Chops

(Pictured at left)

My version of stuffed chops stems from a recipe for stuffed mushrooms. —Sheri Smith
Bethlehem, Pennsylvania

- 1-1/2 cups chopped fresh mushrooms
- 4 green onions, finely chopped
- 1/3 cup finely chopped celery
- 1 tablespoon butter
- 1 small tomato, chopped
- 1/4 to 1/2 teaspoon dried marjoram
- 1/8 to 1/4 teaspoon garlic salt
- 1/8 teaspoon pepper
- 2 slices day-old white bread, cut into 1/4-inch cubes
- 4 pork chops (1 to 1-1/2 inches thick)

In a skillet over medium heat, saute mushrooms, onions and celery in butter until tender. Add the tomato, marjoram, garlic salt and pepper; cook and stir for 5 minutes. Remove from the heat and stir in bread cubes.

Cut a large pocket in the side of each chop. Stuff mushroom mixture into pockets. Place chops in an ungreased shallow baking pan. Bake, uncovered, at 350° for 1 hour or until juices run clear. **Yield:** 4 servings.

Vegetable Pork Chop Dinner

(Pictured at left)

My family loves these savory chops served with mashed potatoes and salad. This meal is perfect for cold winter evenings. —MaryAnn Stoppini, Elmhurst, Pennsylvania

- 1 pound carrots, julienned
- 1 medium onion, sliced
- 1/2 cup raisins
- 3 tablespoons olive oil
- 8 pork chops (3/4 inch thick)
- 1/4 teaspoon salt
- 1/4 teaspoon pepper
- 1/8 teaspoon paprika

Layer carrots, onion and raisins in a 13-in. x 9-in. x 2-in. baking dish; drizzle with oil. Cover; bake at 325° for 15 minutes. Sprinkle pork chops with salt, pepper and paprika; place over vegetables. Cover; bake for 30 minutes. Uncover; bake 20 minutes longer or until pork juices run clear. **Yield:** 8 servings.

Tangy Glazed Ham

(Pictured at left)

After unsuccessfully looking for a satisfying glaze recipe, my daughter and I came up with this version. It's a simple way to dress up any ham you prepare.
—Florence McCray, Johnson City, Tennessee

- 1 boneless fully cooked ham (3 pounds)
- 1/2 cup sweet-and-sour sauce
- 1/4 cup light corn syrup
- 3 tablespoons zesty Italian salad dressing

Place ham in an 11-in. x 7-in. x 2-in. baking pan. Pour remaining ingredients over ham in the order listed. Bake, uncovered, at 325°, basting occasionally, for 1-1/4 to 1-1/2 hours or until a meat thermometer reads 140°. **Yield:** 12 servings.

Sicilian Meat Roll

The addition of ham and mozzarella is a colorful surprise and adds terrific flavor to this meat.
—Mrs. W.G. Dougherty, Crawfordsville, Indiana

- 2 eggs
- 1/2 cup tomato juice
- 3/4 teaspoon dried oregano
- 2 garlic cloves, minced
- 1/4 teaspoon salt
- 1/4 teaspoon pepper
- 2 pounds ground beef
- 3/4 cup soft bread crumbs
- 2 tablespoons minced fresh parsley
- 8 thin slices fully cooked ham
- 1-1/2 cups (6 ounces) shredded mozzarella cheese
- 3 thin slices mozzarella cheese

In a large bowl, combine eggs, tomato juice, oregano, garlic, salt and pepper. Add beef, bread crumbs and parsley; mix well. On a piece of heavy-duty foil, pat meat mixture into a 12-in. x 10-in. rectangle.

Place the ham and shredded cheese on loaf to within 1/2 in. of edges. Roll up, jelly-roll style, beginning with short end; peel foil away while rolling. Place on a greased baking pan with seam side down; seal ends.

Bake, uncovered, at 350° for 70 minutes or until beef is no longer pink. Top with sliced cheese; bake 5 minutes longer or until cheese is melted. **Yield:** 8 servings.

Wild Rice Harvest Casserole

(Pictured below)

Winter is the ideal time to enjoy a big helping of this hearty casserole, packed with wild rice and chicken and topped with cashews. —*Julianne Johnson Grove City, Minnesota*

4 to 5 cups diced cooked chicken
1 cup chopped celery
2 tablespoons butter
2 cans (10-3/4 ounces *each*) condensed cream of mushroom soup, undiluted
2 cups chicken broth
1 jar (4-1/2 ounces) sliced mushrooms, drained
1 small onion, chopped
1 cup uncooked wild rice, rinsed and drained
1/4 teaspoon poultry seasoning
3/4 cup cashew pieces
Chopped fresh parsley

In a skillet, brown chicken and celery in butter. In a large bowl, combine soup and broth until smooth. Add the mushrooms, onion, rice, poultry seasoning and chicken mixture.

Pour into a greased 13-in. x 9-in. x 2-in. baking dish. Cover and bake at 350° for 1 hour. Uncover and bake for 30 minutes. Stir; sprinkle with cashews. Bake 15 minutes longer or until the rice is tender. Garnish with parsley. **Yield:** 10-12 servings.

Turkey Drumstick Dinner

(Pictured above)

I discovered this recipe a long time ago and love it since it uses tasty turkey drumsticks. Our family and friends enjoy this savory meat and potatoes meal. —*Alice Balliet, Kane, Pennsylvania*

4 uncooked turkey drumsticks (about 3 pounds)
2 tablespoons vegetable oil
1 tablespoon butter
1 medium onion, sliced
1 can (14-1/2 ounces) stewed tomatoes
3 chicken bouillon cubes
1 teaspoon garlic salt
1/2 teaspoon dried oregano
1/2 teaspoon dried basil
4 large potatoes, peeled, cooked and quartered
2 medium zucchini, cut into 3/4-inch slices
2 tablespoons cornstarch
2 tablespoons water
Snipped fresh parsley

In a large skillet, brown drumsticks in oil and butter. Place in a 3-qt. Dutch oven. Top with onion slices. In the same skillet, heat tomatoes, bouillon and seasonings until bouillon is dissolved. Pour over the drumsticks. Cover and bake at 325° for 2 hours, basting once or twice.

Add potatoes and zucchini. Cover and bake for 20 minutes. Remove drumsticks and vegetables to a serving dish and keep warm. Combine the cornstarch and water until smooth; stir into tomato mixture. Return to the oven, uncovered, for 10-15 minutes or until slightly thickened. Pour over drumsticks and vegetables. Sprinkle with parsley. **Yield:** 4 servings.

Herb-Crusted Chuck Roast

(Pictured below)

This recipe turns an inexpensive cut of beef into a delicious main dish. —Rita Drewes, Craig, Missouri

- 1/4 **cup dry bread crumbs**
- 2 **tablespoons olive oil**
- 1 **garlic clove, minced**
- 1 **teaspoon ground mustard**
- 1 **teaspoon dried savory**
- 1 **teaspoon pepper**
- 1/2 **teaspoon dried rosemary, crushed**
- 1 **boneless chuck eye *or* top blade roast (about 3 pounds)**

SAUCE:
- 1 **cup (8 ounces) sour cream**
- 3 **tablespoons prepared horseradish**
- 1 **teaspoon lemon juice**
- 1/4 **teaspoon salt**

In a bowl, combine the first seven ingredients. Rub over entire roast. Place on a rack in a shallow roasting pan. Bake, uncovered, at 325° for 1-1/2 to 2 hours or until meat is tender and reaches desired doneness (for medium-rare, a meat thermometer should read 145°; medium, 160°; well-done, 170°). Let stand 10 minutes before carving. Meanwhile, in a bowl, combine the sauce ingredients. Serve with the roast. **Yield:** 8 servings.

Deviled Crab Casserole

(Pictured above)

After creating this recipe, I later pared it down to serve two. I serve this entree often, since it's so easy to assemble. Along with a green salad, dessert and coffee, this casserole makes a delicious lunch or dinner. —Helen Bachman, Champaign, Illinois

- 1 **can (6 ounces) crabmeat, drained, flaked and cartilage removed**
- 1 **cup dry bread crumbs, *divided***
- 3/4 **cup milk**
- 1/4 **cup chopped green onions**
- 2 **hard-cooked eggs, chopped**
- 1/2 **teaspoon salt**
- 1/4 **teaspoon Worcestershire sauce**
- 1/8 **teaspoon ground mustard**
- 1/8 **teaspoon pepper**
- 6 **tablespoons butter, melted, *divided***

Paprika

In a bowl, combine crab, 3/4 cup of bread crumbs, milk, onions, eggs, salt, Worcestershire sauce, mustard and pepper. Add 4 tablespoons of butter; mix well.

Spoon into a greased 1-qt. baking dish. Combine remaining bread crumbs and butter; sprinkle over casserole. Sprinkle with paprika. Bake, uncovered, at 425° for 16-18 minutes or until golden brown and edges are bubbly. **Yield:** 2 servings.

Top to bottom: Fruit-Glazed Roast
Chicken and Chicken and Asparagus

Chicken and Asparagus

(Pictured at left)

Fancy foods don't necessarily mean a lot of fuss. These "bundles" are prepared in no time.
—Janet Hill, Sacramento, California

>   4 **boneless skinless chicken breast halves**
>   24 **fresh asparagus spears, trimmed**
>   1/3 **cup Italian salad dressing**
>   2 **teaspoons soy sauce**
>   1/2 **teaspoon ground ginger**
>   1/2 **teaspoon salt**
>   1/8 **teaspoon pepper**
>   2 **tablespoons sesame seeds**
> **Hot cooked white and wild rice blend, optional**

Cut each chicken breast half into 1/2-in.-wide strips. Wrap two or three strips around three asparagus spears. Repeat with the remaining chicken and asparagus. Arrange in a greased 13-in. x 9-in. x 2-in. baking dish.

Combine salad dressing, soy sauce, ginger, salt and pepper. Pour over the chicken bundles. Cover and bake at 350° for 25 minutes. Uncover; sprinkle with sesame seeds and bake 15 minutes longer or until chicken juices run clear. Serve over rice if desired. **Yield:** 4 servings.

Garlic Pork Roast

Mom cooked for 11 children, so her menus usually featured basic, simple foods. But on New Year's Day, she always treated us to this special pork roast.
—Ruby Williams, Bogalusa, Louisiana

>   1 **pork loin roast, backbone loosened (about 5 pounds)**
>   1/2 **medium green pepper, finely chopped**
>   1/2 **cup thinly sliced green onions**
>   1/2 **cup chopped celery**
>   8 **garlic cloves, minced**
>   1 **teaspoon salt**
>   1/4 **teaspoon cayenne pepper**

With a sharp knife, cut a deep pocket between each rib on meaty side of roast. Combine green pepper, green onions, celery and garlic; stuff deeply into pockets. Season roast with salt and cayenne pepper. Place roast, rib side down, in a shallow roasting pan. Bake, uncovered, at 325° for 2-3 hours or until a meat thermometer reads 170°. Let stand for 15 minutes before carving. **Yield:** 6-8 servings.

Fruit-Glazed Roast Chicken

(Pictured at left)

Whenever I want to serve a special meal with a little flair, this is the recipe I reach for. —Lynn Stromquist
Fridley, Minnesota

>   2 **lemons, quartered**
>   2 **broiler-fryer chickens (3 to 3-1/2 pounds *each*)**
>   3/4 **cup dried apricots**
>   1/3 **cup chicken broth**
>   3 **tablespoons cider vinegar**
>   3 **tablespoons brown sugar**
>   2 **tablespoons lemon juice**
>   2 **tablespoons golden raisins**
>   1/4 **teaspoon ground ginger**
>   1/4 **teaspoon salt**
>   1/2 **cup sugar**
>   1/2 **cup water**
>   2 **cans (16 ounces *each*) pear halves, drained**
>   1 **can (16 ounces) peach halves, drained**
>   1 **can (16 ounces) apricot halves, drained**
>   1 **cup pitted prunes**
> **Lemon leaves, optional**

Place four lemon quarters in body cavity of each chicken; close cavities with skewers or string. Place chickens, breast side up, on a rack in a large roasting pan; bake at 375° for 1-1/2 hours.

Meanwhile, in a food processor or blender, combine dried apricots, broth, vinegar, brown sugar, lemon juice, raisins, ginger and salt. Process until smooth; set aside.

In a small saucepan, bring sugar and water to a boil over medium-high heat. Reduce heat to medium; cook, uncovered, for 7 minutes. In a large bowl, combine pears, peaches, apricots and prunes; pour hot syrup over fruit. Let stand 10 minutes; drain and set aside.

Remove chickens from oven; spread thickly with pureed apricot mixture. Return to oven for 10-15 minutes or until chicken juices run clear. Remove from oven and let stand 10 minutes. Prepare gravy from pan drippings if desired. Place chickens on serving platter; spoon fruit mixture around chickens. Garnish with lemon leaves if desired. Serve with gravy if desired. **Yield:** 8 servings.

Roast Pork with Onion Stuffing

I had the luck of finding this recipe neatly written and tucked inside a cookbook I bought at a garage sale. My family especially likes this in fall when the air takes on a chill. —Catherine Lee, San Jose, California

- **1 boneless pork loin roast (3 pounds)**
- **1 tablespoon olive oil**
- **2 teaspoons salt**
- **1 teaspoon dried thyme**
- **1/2 teaspoon pepper**
- **STUFFING:**
- **4 large onions, chopped**
- **1/4 cup butter**
- **1/4 cup all-purpose flour**
- **1 tablespoon lemon juice**
- **1 teaspoon chicken bouillon granules**
- **1 teaspoon salt**
- **1/4 teaspoon ground nutmeg**
- **1/4 teaspoon pepper**
- **1 cup water**

Rub roast with oil. Combine salt, thyme and pepper; sprinkle over roast. Place roast in a shallow baking pan. Bake, uncovered, at 325° for 2 to 2-1/2 hours or until a meat thermometer reads 160°-170°.

Meanwhile, in a skillet, saute onions in butter for 8-10 minutes or until tender. Stir in flour, lemon juice, bouillon, salt, nutmeg and pepper; add water. Cook over medium heat for 2 minutes, stirring constantly.

Cut roast almost all the way through into 3/8-in. slices. Spoon 1 tablespoon of stuffing between each slice. Spoon remaining stuffing over roast. Bake, uncovered, at 325° for 30 minutes. If desired, thicken pan juices to make gravy. **Yield:** 10 servings.

Baked Ham with Cumberland Sauce

(Pictured at right)

The centerpiece of a beautiful holiday family dinner, this golden ham with tangy jewel-toned sauce is impressive to serve. —Eunice Stoen, Decorah, Iowa

- **1/2 fully cooked bone-in ham (4 to 5 pounds)**
- **1/2 cup packed brown sugar**
- **1 teaspoon ground mustard**

Whole cloves
CUMBERLAND SAUCE:
- **1 cup red currant *or* apple jelly**
- **1/4 cup orange juice**
- **1/4 cup lemon juice**
- **1/4 cup red wine *or* apple juice**
- **2 tablespoons honey**
- **1 tablespoon cornstarch**

Remove skin from ham; score the surface with shallow diagonal cuts, making diamond shapes. Combine brown sugar and mustard; rub into fat of ham. Insert a whole clove in center of each diamond. Place ham on a rack in a shallow roasting pan. Bake, uncovered, at 325° for 1-1/4 to 1-1/2 hours or until a meat thermometer reads 140° and ham is heated through.

Combine all of the sauce ingredients in a saucepan. Cook over medium heat until thickened, stirring often. Serve sauce over the sliced ham. (Sauce recipe can be doubled if desired.) **Yield:** about 16 servings (1-3/4 cups sauce).

Turkey Apple Potpie

(Pictured above right)

Years ago, a neighbor and I collaborated and submitted this recipe for an apple contest. We won first prize! —Phyllis Atherton, South Burlington, Vermont

- **1/4 cup chopped onion**
- **1 tablespoon butter**

2 cans (10-3/4 ounces *each*) condensed cream of chicken soup, undiluted
3 cups cubed cooked turkey
1 large tart apple, cubed
1/3 cup raisins
1 teaspoon lemon juice
1/4 teaspoon ground nutmeg
Pastry for single-crust pie (9 inches)

In a saucepan, saute onion in butter until tender. Add the soup, turkey, apple, raisins, lemon juice and nutmeg; mix well. Spoon into an ungreased 11-in. x 7-in. x 2-in. baking dish.

On a floured surface, roll pastry to fit top of dish. Cut vents in pastry, using a small apple cookie cutter if desired. Place over filling; flute edges. Bake at 425° for 25-30 minutes or until crust is golden brown and filling is bubbly. **Yield:** 6 servings.

Crab-Stuffed Chicken Breasts

(Pictured at right)

I prepare this elegant dish for special occasions. The sauce is so versatile, though, I've used it on pork chops and baked potatoes. —Therese Bechtel
Montgomery Village, Maryland

4 tablespoons butter, *divided*
1/4 cup all-purpose flour
1 cup chicken broth
3/4 cup milk
1/4 cup chopped onion
1 can (6 ounces) crabmeat, drained, flaked and cartilage removed
1 can (4 ounces) mushroom stems and pieces, drained
1/3 cup crushed saltines
2 tablespoons minced fresh parsley
1/2 teaspoon salt
Dash pepper
4 boneless skinless chicken breast halves (about 1 pound)
1 cup (4 ounces) shredded Swiss cheese
1/2 teaspoon paprika

In a saucepan, melt 3 tablespoons butter. Stir in flour until smooth. Gradually stir in broth and milk. Bring to a boil; boil and stir for 2 minutes. Remove from the heat; set aside. In a skillet, saute onion in remaining butter until tender. Add the crab, mushrooms, cracker crumbs, parsley, salt, pepper and 2 tablespoons of the white sauce; heat through.

Flatten chicken to 1/4-in. thickness. Spoon about 1/2 cup of the crab mixture on each chicken breast. Roll up and secure with a toothpick. Place in a greased 9-in. square baking dish. Top with remaining white sauce. Cover and bake at 350° for 30 minutes or until chicken juices run clear. Sprinkle with cheese and paprika. Bake, uncovered, 5 minutes longer or until cheese is melted. Remove toothpicks. **Yield:** 4 servings.

Roasted Duck with Apple-Raisin Stuffing

(Pictured above)

As a boy growing up on the farm, my husband had duck every Sunday. I tried to maintain that tradition after we married more than 50 years ago!
—*Fran Kirchhoff, Harvard, Illinois*

2 domestic ducklings (4 to 5 pounds *each*)
Salt
DRESSING:
    12 ounces bulk pork sausage
    1/2 cup chopped onion
    1/2 cup chopped celery
    1 cup chopped peeled apple
    1/2 cup water
    1 cup golden raisins
    2 tablespoons minced fresh parsley
1-1/2 teaspoons salt
    1 teaspoon rubbed sage
    1/4 teaspoon pepper
    8 cups cubed crustless day-old bread
    3 eggs, lightly beaten
    1/2 cup chicken broth

Sprinkle the inside of ducklings with salt; prick skin well all over and set aside. In a large skillet, cook sausage with onion and celery until sausage is no longer pink and vegetables are tender. Add apple and simmer for 3 minutes, stirring occasionally; drain. Meanwhile, heat water to boiling; pour over raisins. Let stand for 10 minutes; do not drain.

In a large bowl, combine sausage mixture, parsley, raisins, salt, sage and pepper; mix well. Add the bread cubes, eggs and broth; mix lightly. Divide and spoon into ducklings. Place with breast side up on a rack in a large shallow roasting pan. Bake, uncovered, at 350° for 1-3/4 to 2-1/4 hours or until a meat thermometer reads 180° for the duck and 165° for the stuffing. Drain fat from pan as it accumulates. Remove all dressing. **Yield:** 4 servings.

◆◆◆

Braised Lamb Shanks

(Pictured below)

A friend shared this recipe with me many years ago. These lamb shanks make a hearty meal alongside baked potatoes, a hot vegetable and fresh fruit salad. Of course, I include mint jelly on the side.
—*Jeanne McNamara, Camillus, New York*

    2 lamb shanks (about 3 pounds)
    1 cup beef broth
1/4 cup soy sauce
    2 tablespoons brown sugar
    1 garlic clove, minced
    2 teaspoons prepared mustard

Place lamb in a greased 2-1/2-qt. baking dish. Combine broth, soy sauce, brown sugar, garlic and mustard; pour over meat. Cover and bake at 325° for 1-1/2 to 2 hours or until the meat is tender. **Yield:** 2 servings.

Holiday Ham Ring

I always seem to have one of these ham rings in the freezer to share with neighbors during difficult times. Its country-style taste reminds folks of Grandma's kitchen.
—Virginia Alverson, Milroy, Indiana

1-1/2 pounds fully cooked ham, ground
1/2 pound ground pork
3/4 cup graham cracker crumbs
3/4 cup milk
1 egg
1/4 teaspoon ground allspice
1/4 teaspoon pepper
1/2 cup condensed cream of tomato soup, undiluted
1/4 cup vinegar
1/4 cup packed brown sugar
1/2 teaspoon prepared mustard

Combine the first seven ingredients; mix well. On a 15-in. x 10-in. x 1-in. baking pan, shape meat mixture into a 9-1/2-in.-diameter ring. Combine soup, vinegar, brown sugar and mustard; pour half over ham ring. Bake, uncovered, at 350° for 30 minutes. Pour remaining soup mixture over the top; bake 30 minutes longer or until a meat thermometer reads 160°-170°. **Yield:** 8 servings.

Raspberry Basil Chicken

This recipe turns ordinary raspberry jam into a sweet, succulent glaze. With its attractive color and delicious flavor, this chicken is great to serve family and friends.
—Isabelle Pederson, Valley City, North Dakota

1 broiler-fryer chicken (3-1/2 to 4 pounds),
   cut up
1 teaspoon dried basil
1 teaspoon salt
1/2 teaspoon pepper
1 medium onion, thinly sliced
1 cup seedless raspberry jam

Place chicken in a greased 13-in. x 9-in. x 2-in. baking dish. Sprinkle with basil, salt and pepper. Top with onion. Cover and bake at 375° for 30 minutes. Drain pan juices and reserve 1/2 cup (add water to make 1/2 cup if necessary). Add jam; pour over chicken. Bake, uncovered, basting occasionally, for 25 minutes or until chicken juices run clear. **Yield:** 4-6 servings.

Cranberry-Glazed Pork Roast

(Pictured above)

Many pork recipes were too spicy for me, so I decided to try this sweeter alternative. It's become a family favorite during the holidays and year-round.
—Madeline Strauss, Clinton Township, Michigan

1 teaspoon salt
1/2 teaspoon pepper
1 boneless rolled pork loin roast (3 pounds)
1 cup jellied cranberry sauce
1/2 cup orange juice
1/4 cup packed brown sugar

Combine salt and pepper; rub over the roast. Place roast, fat side up, on a rack in a greased roasting pan. Bake, uncovered, at 350° for 1-1/2 hours.

Meanwhile, combine cranberry sauce, orange juice and brown sugar in a saucepan; cook over medium heat until cranberry sauce melts. Brush a fourth over the roast. Bake 30 minutes longer; brush with another fourth of the glaze. Return to the oven for 15 minutes or until a meat thermometer reads 160°-170°. Let stand for 10 minutes before slicing. Warm remaining glaze; serve with roast. **Yield:** 6-8 servings.

Apricot-Filled Pork Tenderloin

This flavorful main course is great for company. The tenderloin tastes wonderful and looks so pretty when it's sliced to reveal a golden apricot center.
—Jo Ann Hettel, Bushnell, Florida

2 pork tenderloins (1 pound *each*)
1 package (6 ounces) dried apricots
MARINADE:
  1/3 cup sweet-and-sour salad dressing
  1/4 cup packed brown sugar
    3 tablespoons teriyaki sauce
    2 tablespoons ketchup
    1 teaspoon Dijon mustard
    1 onion slice, separated into rings
    1 garlic clove, minced
  1/2 teaspoon ground ginger *or* 2 teaspoons minced
    fresh gingerroot
  1/4 teaspoon pepper
  1/8 teaspoon pumpkin pie spice

Make a lengthwise cut three-quarters of the way through each tenderloin; pound with a meat mallet to flatten evenly. Set aside three apricots for marinade. Stuff remaining apricots into tenderloins to within 1/2 in. of ends; secure with toothpicks or kitchen string. Place in a greased 11-in. x 7-in. x 2-in. baking dish.

In a blender, combine the marinade ingredients and reserved apricots. Cover and process until smooth; set aside 1/3 cup. Pour remaining marinade over tenderloins. Cover and refrigerate for at least 2 hours, turning meat often. Drain and discard marinade. Drizzle reserved marinade over meat. Bake, uncovered, at 400° for 30-35 minutes or until a meat thermometer reads 160°-170°. **Yield:** 6 servings.

Stuffed Crown Roast of Pork

(Pictured at right)

I first made this recipe on Christmas...the oohs and aahs from my family were a delight! In addition to the holidays, I sometimes make a crown roast for Sunday dinner—it reminds me of my childhood, when Sunday dinners were always special. —Marianne Severson
West Allis, Wisconsin

1 crown roast of pork (about 8 pounds)
1 pound ground pork
1/2 pound bulk pork sausage
3/4 cup finely chopped onion
    3 tablespoons butter
1/2 cup diced peeled apple
1/4 cup finely chopped celery
1-1/2 cups soft bread crumbs
1/2 cup minced fresh parsley
1-1/2 teaspoons salt
1/2 teaspoon pepper
1/2 teaspoon rubbed sage
Spiced crab apples, optional

Tie roast and place on a rack in a large roasting pan. Cover the bone ends with foil. Insert meat thermometer. Roast at 350° for 2 hours. Meanwhile, in a large skillet, cook the pork and sausage until browned; drain and set aside. In the same skillet, saute onion in butter until tender. Add apple and celery; cook for 5 minutes. Remove from the heat. Add the cooked pork and sausage, crumbs, parsley, salt, pepper and sage; mix well.

Remove roast from oven. Carefully press a double layer of heavy-duty foil into the center of roast to form a base for the stuffing. Spoon stuffing lightly into crown. Return to oven and bake for 1 hour more or until a meat thermometer reads 160°-170°. Transfer to serving platter. Garnish with spiced crab apples if desired. Cut between ribs to serve. **Yield:** 16-20 servings.

Chicken Royale

(Pictured above)

Treat your dinner guests like kings and queens by serving them these individual stuffed chicken breasts.
—Nancy Schubert, Lake Forest, Illinois

    4 whole boneless chicken breasts
    2 cups seasoned bread crumbs
  1/2 cup hot water
   10 tablespoons butter, melted, *divided*
    2 tablespoons finely chopped onion
    1 tablespoon minced fresh parsley
  1/2 teaspoon salt
  1/4 teaspoon poultry seasoning
Pinch pepper
  1/2 cup all-purpose flour
  1/2 teaspoon paprika
SOUR CREAM-MUSHROOM SAUCE:
  1/2 pound fresh mushrooms, sliced
  1/4 cup chopped onion
    2 tablespoons butter
    2 tablespoons all-purpose flour
  1/2 teaspoon salt
  1/2 teaspoon pepper
  1/2 cup heavy whipping cream
  1/2 cup sour cream

Place the chicken breasts with skin side down on a work surface; pound lightly with a meat mallet to an even thickness. For stuffing, combine the bread crumbs, water, 2 tablespoons butter, onion, parsley, salt, poultry seasoning and pepper. Place about 1/3 cup stuffing on each breast; fold in half. Secure with toothpicks. Combine flour and paprika; coat chicken. Place, skewered side down, in a greased 11-in. x 7-in. x 2-in. baking dish. Drizzle with remaining butter.

Bake, uncovered, at 325° for 1-1/4 hours or until tender. Meanwhile, for sauce, saute mushrooms and onion in butter until tender. Stir in flour, salt and pepper. Gradually add whipping cream. Cook and stir until bubbly; cook and stir 1 minute more. Reduce heat; add sour cream. Stir just until heated through; do not boil. Serve over chicken. **Yield:** 4 servings.

Wild Goose with Giblet Stuffing

This recipe is one of our favorite ways to prepare goose, and it's especially nice for the holidays. My husband does a lot of hunting, so I'm always looking for new ways to fix game.
—Louise Laginess
East Jordan, Michigan

    1 dressed wild goose (6 to 8 pounds)
Lemon wedges
Salt
STUFFING:
Goose giblets
    2 cups water
   10 cups crumbled corn bread
    2 large tart apples, chopped
    1 large onion, chopped
  1/3 cup minced fresh parsley
    1 to 2 tablespoons rubbed sage
    1 teaspoon salt
  1/4 teaspoon pepper
  1/4 teaspoon garlic powder
Butter, softened

Rub inside goose cavity with lemon and salt; set aside. In a saucepan, cook giblets in water until tender, about 20-30 minutes. Remove giblets with a slotted spoon and reserve liquid. Chop giblets and place in a large bowl; add corn bread, apples, onion, parsley, sage, salt, pepper and garlic powder. Add enough of the reserved cooking liquid to make a moist stuffing; toss gently.

Stuff the body and neck cavity; truss openings. Place goose, breast side up, on a rack in a shallow roasting pan. Spread with butter. Bake, uncovered, at 325° for 2-1/2 to 3 hours or until fully cooked and tender. If goose is an older bird, add 1 cup of water to pan and cover for the last hour of baking. **Yield:** 6-8 servings.

Apple-Almond Stuffed Turkey

(Pictured above)

I found this terrific recipe a few years back and tried it out on some friends at a dinner party. Everyone enjoyed the combination of flavors and unique ingredients. The currants and apples give the stuffing a nice sweet flavor, and the almonds add crunch. —Laurel McLennan
Medicine Hat, Alberta

    1 loaf (1 pound) sliced bread
    3 medium onions, chopped
    3 medium tart apples, chopped
1-1/2 cups diced fully cooked ham
    1 cup sliced celery
    1 tablespoon dried savory
    2 teaspoons grated lemon peel
1-1/2 teaspoons grated orange peel
    1 teaspoon salt
  1/2 teaspoon pepper
  1/2 teaspoon fennel seed, crushed
  1/2 cup butter
1-1/2 cups slivered almonds, toasted

    1 cup turkey *or* chicken broth
  1/2 cup dried currants
  1/2 cup apple juice
    1 turkey (14 to 16 pounds)

Cut bread into 1/2-in. cubes and place in a single layer on ungreased baking sheets. Bake at 225° for 30-40 minutes, tossing occasionally until partially dried. Meanwhile, in a skillet, saute the next 10 ingredients in butter until onions and apple are tender, about 15 minutes. Transfer to a large bowl. Add the bread cubes, almonds, broth, currants and juice; toss well.

Just before baking, stuff the turkey. Skewer openings; tie drumsticks together. Place on a rack in a roasting pan. Bake, uncovered, at 325° for 4-1/2 to 5 hours or until a meat thermometer reads 185°. When turkey begins to brown, cover lightly with foil and baste if needed. **Yield:** 12 servings (12 cups stuffing).

Editor's Note: Stuffing may be baked separately in a greased 3-qt. baking dish. Cover and bake at 325° for 60 minutes; uncover and bake 10 minutes more.

Special Shrimp Bake

(Pictured below)

My husband and I entertain most weekends, and to me the easiest way of serving a crowd is a buffet. This

dish—a change of pace from turkey during the holidays—can be put together the night before, then baked the following day. —Kathy Houchen
Waldorf, Maryland

    3 quarts water
    1 tablespoon plus 1 teaspoon salt, *divided*
2-1/2 pounds uncooked medium shrimp, peeled and deveined
    2 tablespoons vegetable oil
    1 tablespoon lemon juice
    1/4 cup finely chopped green pepper
    1/4 cup finely chopped onion
    2 tablespoons butter
    1 can (10-3/4 ounces) condensed tomato soup, undiluted
    1 cup heavy whipping cream
2-1/4 cups cooked rice
    1/8 teaspoon *each* ground mace, pepper and cayenne pepper
    1/2 cup slivered almonds, toasted, *divided*

In a Dutch oven, bring water and 1 tablespoon salt to a boil. Add shrimp; cook for 3 minutes or until pink. Drain. Sprinkle shrimp with oil and lemon juice; set aside. In a skillet, saute green pepper and onion in butter for 5 minutes or until tender. Add soup, cream, rice, mace, pepper, cayenne, 1/4 cup of almonds and remaining salt.

Set aside 1 cup of shrimp. Add remaining shrimp to the rice mixture. Transfer to a greased 2-qt. baking dish. Bake, uncovered, at 350° for 30-35 minutes. Top with reserved shrimp and remaining almonds; bake 20 minutes longer or until the shrimp are lightly browned. **Yield:** 8-10 servings.

Norwegian Meatballs

(Pictured above right)

Christmas was the time when our family forgot about the food budget and splurged on one special meal. I can still see Grandmother making dozens of these little meatballs! The hint of spices gives them a savory taste that makes them authentically Norwegian.
—Karen Hoylo, Duluth, Minnesota

    1 egg
  1/2 cup milk
    1 tablespoon cornstarch
    1 medium onion, finely chopped
    1 teaspoon salt

Dash pepper
    1/4 teaspoon ground nutmeg
    1/4 teaspoon ground allspice
    1/4 teaspoon ground ginger
1-1/2 pounds lean ground beef
    3 to 4 tablespoons butter
GRAVY:
    1 tablespoon butter
    2 tablespoons all-purpose flour
    1 cup beef broth
    1/2 cup milk *or* half-and-half cream
Salt and pepper to taste
Minced fresh parsley, optional

In a mixing bowl, beat egg. Add milk, cornstarch, onion, salt, pepper, nutmeg, allspice and ginger. Add beef and mix well. Shape into 1-1/2-in. meatballs. (Mixture will be very soft. For easier shaping, rinse hands in cold water frequently.) In a large skillet over medium heat, brown the meatballs in butter, half at a time, for about 10 minutes or until no pink remains. Turn to brown evenly. Remove meatballs to paper towels to drain, reserving 1 tablespoon drippings in skillet.

For gravy, add butter to the drippings. Stir in flour. Add broth and milk or cream; cook and stir until thickened and bubbly. Cook and stir 1 minute more. Season with salt and pepper. Return meatballs to the skillet; heat through on low heat. Garnish with parsley if desired. **Yield:** 6 servings.

Pork Roast With Fruit Sauce

Savory pork roast gets dressed up for the holidays in this tangy sauce. This is a pretty main dish that always earns me compliments—Dorothy Pritchett, Wills Point, Texas

> 1 pork loin roast with bone (3 to 4 pounds)
> 1 jar (10 ounces) apple jelly
> 1 cup apple juice
> 1/2 teaspoon ground cardamom
> 3/4 cup chopped dried apricots
> 1 tablespoon cornstarch
> 2 tablespoons water

Place roast on a rack in a shallow roasting pan. Bake, uncovered, at 350° for 1-1/2 hours. In a saucepan, combine apple jelly, apple juice and cardamom; cook and stir over medium heat until smooth and heated through. Set aside 1/2 cup. Brush some of the remaining sauce over roast; bake 40-60 minutes longer or until a meat thermometer reads 160°-170°, brushing with sauce every 20 minutes.

Transfer roast to a serving platter and keep warm. Pour pan drippings into a saucepan. Add apricots and reserved fruit sauce; cook over medium heat until softened, about 5 minutes. Combine the cornstarch and water until smooth; add to apricot mixture. Cook and stir until mixture boils, about 2 minutes. Serve with roast. **Yield:** 10-12 servings.

Turkey with Sausage-Pecan Stuffing

The combination of ingredients makes a fabulous stuffed turkey that's become a tradition. My family can't imagine Thanksgiving without this exciting entree.
> *—Keri Scofield Lawson, Fullerton, California*

> 4 medium onions
> 1 pound bulk pork sausage
> 1 package (15 ounces) golden raisins
> 1 cup pecan halves
> 6 celery ribs, diced
> 1/4 teaspoon *each* dried basil, oregano, curry powder, caraway seeds, poultry seasoning, garlic powder, salt and pepper
> 2 packages (6 ounces *each*) stuffing mix

> 2-1/2 cups chicken broth
> 1 turkey (12 to 14 pounds)
> Vegetable oil

Slice two onions; set aside. Chop remaining onions. In a large skillet, cook sausage and chopped onions until meat is no longer pink. Stir in raisins, pecans, celery and seasonings; simmer for 10 minutes. Add stuffing mixes and broth; mix well. Cook and stir for about 5 minutes.

Place reserved onions in turkey cavity. Add 6-7 cups stuffing. (Place remaining stuffing in a greased 1-1/2-qt. baking dish; cover and refrigerate.) Skewer openings and tie drumsticks together. Place on a rack in a roasting pan.

Bake, uncovered, at 325° for 3-1/2 to 4 hours or until a meat thermometer reads 185° for meat and 165° for stuffing, basting occasionally with oil. (Bake reserved stuffing, covered, for 1 hour; uncover and bake 10 minutes more.) When the turkey begins to brown, baste if needed and cover lightly with foil. **Yield:** 12-14 servings (12 cups stuffing).

Cornish Hens with Rice Dressing

(Pictured on page 123)

I found this recipe among my mother's collection. It's a perfect main dish when you're cooking for two. I've even used these hens as a stand-in for turkey on Thanksgiving Day when the group was small.
> *—Geraldine Grisdale, Mt. Pleasant, Michigan*

> 1-1/3 cups chicken broth
> 1/2 cup uncooked long grain rice
> 1/2 cup sliced fresh mushrooms
> 1/4 cup chopped celery
> 2 tablespoons chopped onion
> 1/2 teaspoon dried marjoram, *divided*
> 1/2 teaspoon salt, *divided*
> 2 Cornish hens (1 to 1-1/2 pounds *each*)
> 1 tablespoon vegetable oil
> Pepper to taste

In an ungreased 9-in. square baking dish, combine broth, rice, mushrooms, celery, onion, 1/4 teaspoon of marjoram and 1/4 teaspoon of salt. Place hens on rice mixture and brush with oil. Sprinkle with pepper and remaining marjoram and salt.

Cover and bake at 350° for 1 hour. Uncover and bake 25-35 minutes longer or until juices run clear. **Yield:** 2 servings.

Stuffed Baked Potatoes, page 182

Side Dishes
& Condiments

Sausage-Pecan Turkey Stuffing

(Pictured above)

Since I first tried this, I haven't made another stuffing. The sausage and pecans really give it a different flavor. —Sharon Miller, Millet, Alberta

      9 cups soft bread crumbs
      1 pound bulk pork sausage
      2 cups chopped onion
    1/4 cup butter
      3 unpeeled tart apples, coarsely chopped
      1 cup chopped pecans
    1/2 cup minced fresh parsley
  1-1/2 teaspoons dried thyme
      1 teaspoon rubbed sage
    1/4 teaspoon salt
    1/4 teaspoon pepper
    1/4 cup apple juice
Chicken broth

Place bread crumbs in a large bowl. In a large skillet, cook sausage and onion in butter over medium heat until meat is no longer pink and onion is tender; do not drain. Add to bread crumbs. Stir in apples, pecans, parsley, thyme, sage, salt and pepper; stir in apple juice and enough broth to moisten. Transfer to a greased 3-qt. baking dish. Cover and bake at 325° for 60 minutes. Uncover and bake 10 minutes longer or until lightly browned. **Yield:** 12 cups (enough for one 14- to 16-pound turkey).

Potato Pancakes

(Pictured below)

We grew our own potatoes on the small farm in New Hampshire where I was raised. These pancakes are very good served with any pork dish. —Roseanna Budell
Dunnellon, Florida

      3 cups finely shredded peeled potatoes, well
         drained
      2 eggs, well beaten
  4-1/2 teaspoons all-purpose flour
    1/8 teaspoon baking powder
    1/2 to 1 teaspoon salt
    1/2 teaspoon grated onion
Applesauce *or* maple syrup, optional

In a mixing bowl, gently combine potatoes and eggs. Combine dry ingredients and onion; stir into potato mixture. Drop by tablespoonfuls onto a greased heated skillet. Brown lightly on both sides. Serve with applesauce or syrup if desired. **Yield:** 12 (2-inch) pancakes.

Zesty Carrot Bake

(Pictured below)

For a fun vegetable dish, try these tender carrots in a sauce that gets its zip from horseradish. With a crunchy crumb topping and comforting sauce, it will tempt even those who usually don't care for cooked carrots. —Grace Yaskovic, Branchville, New Jersey

  1 **pound carrots, cut into 1/2-inch slices**
3/4 **cup mayonnaise**
1/3 **cup water**
  2 **tablespoons finely chopped onion**
  1 **tablespoon prepared horseradish**
1/4 **teaspoon pepper**
1/2 **cup dry bread crumbs**
  2 **tablespoons butter, melted**
1/2 **cup shredded sharp cheddar cheese**

Cook carrots until tender. Place in a greased 1-qt. baking dish; set aside. In a small bowl, combine the next five ingredients; mix well. Pour over carrots. Combine bread crumbs and butter; sprinkle on top.

Bake, uncovered, at 350° for 25-30 minutes. Sprinkle with cheese. Bake 2-3 minutes longer or until cheese is melted. **Yield:** 6 servings.

Parmesan Noodles

(Pictured above)

The special blend of flavors in this cheesy side dish makes it companionable to any meal. It's a nice change of pace from regular pasta and cheese dishes.
—Elizabeth Ewan, Parma, Ohio

  2 **packages (3 ounces *each*) cream cheese, softened**
1/2 **cup butter, softened, *divided***
  2 **tablespoons minced fresh parsley**
  1 **teaspoon dried basil**
1/2 **teaspoon lemon-pepper seasoning**
2/3 **cup boiling water**
  1 **garlic clove, minced**
  6 **cups hot cooked thin noodles**
2/3 **cup grated Parmesan cheese, *divided***
Additional parsley, optional

In a small bowl, combine cream cheese, 2 tablespoons butter, parsley, basil and lemon pepper. Stir in water; keep warm. In a saucepan, saute garlic in remaining butter until lightly browned.

Place noodles in a serving bowl; top with garlic mixture. Sprinkle with half of the Parmesan cheese; toss lightly. Spoon cream sauce over noodles and sprinkle with remaining Parmesan. Garnish with parsley if desired. **Yield:** 8 servings.

Sweet Potatoes With Apples

(Pictured below)

This satisfying dish is very welcome at any meal at our house, especially on special occasions. The tart apple slices taste so good baked on top of the mild sweet potatoes. —Jean Winfree, Merrill, Wisconsin

    3   to 3-1/2 pounds sweet potatoes
    2   tart apples, peeled, cored and cut into 1/4-inch
         rings
  1/2   cup orange juice
  1/4   cup packed brown sugar
  1/4   teaspoon ground ginger
  1/4   teaspoon ground cinnamon
    2   tablespoons butter

In a large saucepan, cover sweet potatoes with water; bring to a boil. Reduce heat; cover and simmer for 30 minutes or until tender. Drain and cool slightly. Peel and cut into 1/4-in. slices. Alternate layers of potatoes and apples in a greased 13-in. x 9-in. x 2-in. baking dish. Pour orange juice over top. Mix brown sugar, ginger and cinnamon; sprinkle over potatoes and apples. Dot with butter. Bake, uncovered, at 350° for 35-45 minutes or until apples are tender. **Yield:** 8 servings.

Festive Cauliflower Casserole

(Pictured above)

My family asks for this dish every Christmas. It complements turkey or ham and can be put together the day before the meal. It's a convenience for the cook when the holiday rush is in full swing. —Nancy McDonald Burns, Wyoming

    1   large head cauliflower (2 pounds), cut into
         florets
  1/4   cup diced green pepper
    1   jar (4-1/2 ounces) sliced mushrooms, drained
  1/4   cup butter
  1/3   cup all-purpose flour
  3/4   teaspoon salt
    2   cups milk
    1   jar (2 ounces) diced pimientos, drained
    1   cup (4 ounces) shredded Swiss cheese, *divided*

Cook cauliflower in boiling salted water until crisp-tender; drain. Place in a greased 1-1/2-qt. baking dish. In a saucepan over medium heat, saute green pepper and mushrooms in butter until tender. Add flour and salt; stir until blended. Gradually add milk; bring to a boil, stirring constantly. Cook and stir 2 minutes more or until thickened. Remove from the heat; add pimientos. Stir in 3/4 cup cheese until melted; pour over cauliflower.

Cover and bake at 350° for 20 minutes. Sprinkle with remaining cheese; bake, uncovered, for 10-15 minutes or until cheese is melted. **Yield:** 6-8 servings.

Carrot Souffle

(Pictured below)

This recipe is rooted in my backyard garden. It's an excellent way to dress up veggies. My six grandchildren are happy to eat carrots when they're dished up in this tasty souffle. —Martha Sorrell, Louisville, Kentucky

1-1/2 cups soft bread crumbs
    1 cup milk
    3 eggs, *separated*
    2 cups finely grated carrots
  1/2 cup finely chopped celery
    3 tablespoons minced fresh parsley
    1 tablespoon grated onion
    1 teaspoon salt
  1/4 teaspoon pepper
  1/4 teaspoon cream of tartar

In a bowl, soak bread crumbs in milk. Lightly beat egg yolks; add to crumbs with carrots, celery, parsley, onion, salt and pepper. Mix well. In a mixing bowl, beat egg whites and cream of tartar until stiff peaks form. Gently fold into carrot mixture.

Transfer to a greased 2-qt. baking dish. Bake, uncovered, at 325° for 40-45 minutes or until a knife inserted near the center comes out clean. **Yield:** 6-8 servings.

Apple Cranberry Relish

(Pictured above)

This fresh ruby-colored relish is sweet and tangy, and the apples and celery give it a terrific crunch. At our house, it's a holiday menu mainstay since it's so pleasant with poultry and pork. —Edith McFarland Willits, California

  2 medium navel oranges
  2 packages (12 ounces *each*) fresh *or* frozen cranberries
  2 medium apples, peeled and cut into chunks
  2 celery ribs, cut into chunks
  3 cups sugar

Grate peel of the oranges and set aside. Peel and discard white membrane. Separate orange into sections and place half in a food processor or blender. Add half of the cranberries, apples and celery. Process until coarsely chopped. Transfer to a bowl; repeat with remaining oranges, cranberries, apples and celery. Stir in sugar and reserved orange peel. Cover and refrigerate overnight. **Yield:** 16 servings (8 cups).

1-1/2 pounds ground beef
1/2 cup chopped onion
2 garlic cloves, minced
2 cans (16 ounces *each*) pork and beans
1/3 cup chopped dill pickle
1/3 cup chili sauce
1 teaspoon Worcestershire sauce
1 teaspoon salt
1/2 teaspoon pepper
1/8 teaspoon hot pepper sauce

In a Dutch oven over medium heat, cook beef, onion and garlic until meat is no longer pink; drain. Add remaining ingredients; heat through. **Yield:** 10-12 servings.

Two-Bread Dressing

(Pictured below)

I'm originally from Oregon and was raised on herb stuffing, but my Southern husband would eat only his mother's corn bread stuffing. So I created this recipe as a compromise. —Vanessa Leeson, Bishop, Texas

Parsnip Patties

(Pictured above)

I always grow parsnips in my garden and discovered this quick and delicious way to enjoy them. This recipe is a unique taste-twist on traditional potato pancakes. —A.L. Hensley, Vancouver, Washington

3 cups shredded peeled parsnips (about 1 pound)
1 egg, lightly beaten
1/2 cup all-purpose flour
1/2 teaspoon salt
1/2 cup honey, warmed

In a bowl, combine parsnips, egg, flour and salt. Drop batter by 1/2 cupfuls onto a lightly greased hot griddle. Fry over medium heat for 4-5 minutes per side or until parsnips are tender. Serve with honey. **Yield:** 6 servings.

Western Beans

Start with ground beef and add beans and seasonings. Then you have a great side dish for any meal! —Catherine Skelton, Seligman, Missouri

9 bacon strips, diced
1 cup chopped celery
1/4 cup chopped onion
6 slices bread, toasted and cubed
3 cups coarse corn bread crumbs
1/3 cup minced fresh parsley
1-1/2 teaspoons rubbed sage
1 teaspoon dried thyme
1 teaspoon dried rosemary, crushed
1-1/2 cups chicken broth

In a skillet, cook bacon until crisp. Drain, reserving 2 tablespoons drippings; set bacon aside. Saute celery and onion in drippings until tender. In a large bowl, toss bread, parsley, sage, thyme and rosemary. Add celery, onion, broth and bacon; mix gently. Spoon into a greased 2-qt. baking dish. Bake, uncovered, at 350° for 30-35 minutes or until heated through. **Yield:** 6-8 servings.

Broccoli with Cheese Sauce

(Pictured on front cover)

This creamy cheese sauce is a great way to jazz up veggies like broccoli.

—Sandy Spackman, Trenton, Utah

2 medium bunches broccoli,
  cut into spears
1/4 cup water
2 tablespoons plus 1 teaspoon cornstarch
1/2 teaspoon garlic powder
1/2 teaspoon onion powder
1/8 teaspoon white pepper
1/8 teaspoon ground nutmeg
2 cups milk
2 cups (8 ounces) shredded cheddar cheese
1 teaspoon Worcestershire sauce

Place the broccoli and water in a microwave-safe bowl. Cover and microwave on high for 3-5 minutes or until tender.

Meanwhile, in a small saucepan, whisk the cornstarch, seasonings and milk until smooth. Bring to a boil over medium heat; cook and stir for 1-2 minutes or until thickened. Stir in the cheddar cheese and Worcestershire sauce until cheese is melted. Drain the broccoli; top with cheese sauce. **Yield:** 8 servings.

Editor's Note: This recipe was tested in a 1,100-watt microwave.

Sweet Potato Casserole

(Pictured below)

It wouldn't be Thanksgiving without that versatile root vegetable—the sweet potato. Building on traditional recipes used by my mother and grandmother, I've added maple syrup, brown sugar, dried apricots and more spices to update this holiday casserole.

—Keri Scofield Lawson, Fullerton, California

1 can (2 pounds 8 ounces) cut sweet potatoes,
  drained
1 can (8 ounces) crushed pineapple, drained
1/2 cup maple syrup
1/2 cup pecan halves
1/4 cup sliced dried apricots
1/4 cup packed brown sugar
1 tablespoon butter, melted
1 teaspoon ground cinnamon
1 teaspoon pumpkin pie spice
1/4 teaspoon salt

Place sweet potatoes in an ungreased 1-1/2-qt. baking dish. Combine remaining ingredients; pour over the potatoes. Bake, uncovered, at 350° for 45 minutes or until dish is heated through. **Yield:** 8-10 servings.

Herbed Spinach Bake

(Pictured below)

This is a special side dish my mother liked to serve at church dinners. She was recognized by family and friends as an outstanding cook. It's a pleasure to share her recipe with you.
—Nancy Frank
Lake Ariel, Pennsylvania

- 2 **packages (10 ounces** *each***) frozen chopped spinach**
- 2 **cups cooked rice**
- 2 **cups (8 ounces) shredded cheddar cheese**
- 4 **eggs, beaten**
- 2/3 **cup milk**
- 1/4 **cup butter, softened**
- 1/4 **cup chopped onion**
- 2 **teaspoons salt**
- 1 **teaspoon Worcestershire sauce**
- 1 **teaspoon ground thyme**

Cook spinach according to package directions; drain well, squeezing out excess liquid. In a large bowl, combine spinach with remaining ingredients. Pour into a greased 13-in. x 9-in.

x 2-in. baking dish. Cover and bake at 350° for 20 minutes. Uncover and bake 5 minutes more or until set. **Yield:** 16 servings.

Microwave Brussels Sprouts

(Pictured above)

When your conventional oven is filled with the turkey and side dishes, these dressed-up brussels sprouts can be prepared in the microwave. The cheese topping makes them special enough for a holiday meal.
—Gloria Warczak, Cedarburg, Wisconsin

- 1-1/2 **pounds brussels sprouts**
- 1/4 **cup water**
- 1/4 **teaspoon celery salt**

Pinch pepper

- 1/2 **cup shredded cheddar cheese**
- 1/3 **cup finely crushed cornflakes**
- 1 **tablespoon butter, melted**

Cut an X in the core of each brussels sprout. Place the brussels sprouts in a 1-1/2-qt. microwave-safe dish; add water.

Sprinkle with celery salt and pepper. Cover and microwave on high for 8-10 minutes or until tender, stirring and rotating a quarter turn every 3 minutes. Drain. Sprinkle with cheese; microwave on high for 1-2 minutes or until cheese begins to melt. Combine cornflakes and butter; sprinkle over sprouts. **Yield:** 8 servings.

Editor's Note: This recipe was tested in a 700-watt microwave.

Festive Corn

(Pictured below)

For a deluxe side dish that's easy yet has big impact, I whip up this recipe. It features corn and peppers in a comforting cream cheese sauce. —Joy Beck
Cincinnati, Ohio

    1/4 cup chopped green pepper
    1/4 cup chopped sweet red pepper
      2 green onions, thinly sliced
      2 tablespoons butter
      1 package (8 ounces) cream cheese, cubed
    2/3 cup milk
    3/4 teaspoon salt
    1/8 teaspoon pepper
    1/2 teaspoon dill weed
      1 package (16 ounces) frozen corn, thawed

In a saucepan over medium heat, saute peppers and onions in butter until tender. Add cream cheese, milk, salt, pepper and dill. Cook and stir over low heat until cheese is melted. Add corn; heat through. **Yield:** 6-8 servings.

Turkey Potato Pancakes

(Pictured above)

My husband and our four children like pancakes, and I appreciate quick suppers...so I gave this recipe a try when I saw it. The addition of turkey turns golden potato pancakes into a heartier side dish. —Kathi Duerr
Fulda, Minnesota

      3 eggs
      3 cups shredded peeled potatoes
  1-1/2 cups finely chopped cooked turkey
    1/4 cup sliced green onions with tops
      2 tablespoons all-purpose flour
  1-1/2 teaspoons salt
Vegetable oil
Cranberry sauce, optional

In a bowl, beat the eggs. Add potatoes, turkey, onions, flour and salt; mix well. Heat about 1/4 in. of oil in a large skillet. Pour batter by 1/3 cupfuls into hot oil. Fry 5-6 minutes on each side or until potatoes are tender and pancakes are golden brown. Serve with cranberry sauce if desired. **Yield:** 12 pancakes.

Maple Baked Beans

(Pictured above)

Since my husband raises hogs and my parents produce maple syrup, this recipe's a natural for me!
—*Cindy Huitema, Dunnville, Ontario*

  1 **pound dried navy beans**
  4 **quarts water, *divided***
  6 **slices bacon, cut up *or* 1 cup cubed fully cooked ham**
  1 **medium onion, chopped**
  1 **cup maple syrup**
1/2 **cup ketchup**
1/4 **cup barbecue sauce**
  5 **teaspoons cider vinegar**
  1 **teaspoon prepared mustard**
  1 **teaspoon salt**
1/2 **teaspoon pepper**

Sort and rinse beans; place in a 4-qt. Dutch oven. Cover with 2 qts. cold water. Bring to a boil; reduce heat and simmer for 2 minutes. Remove from the heat. Cover and let stand 1 hour. Drain and rinse beans.

Return beans to Dutch oven; cover with remaining water. Bring to a boil; reduce heat and simmer for 30-40 minutes or until almost tender. Drain and reserve liquid.

In a 2-1/2-qt. casserole or bean pot, combine beans with all remaining ingredients. Cover and bake at 300° for 2-1/2 hours or until tender. Stir occasionally; add reserved bean liquid if necessary. **Yield:** 10-12 servings.

Pear Cranberry Sauce

(Pictured below)

We don't care for regular cranberry sauce, so I usually perk it up with other fruit. This pear version is the one my family requests most often. It's sweet, tangy and a beautiful ruby-red color. Since it keeps well in the refrigerator, I often make it in advance.
—*Joyce Bowman, Lady Lake, Florida*

2-1/2 **cups cubed peeled ripe pears (about 3 medium)**
  1 **cup water**
  1 **to 2 teaspoons minced fresh gingerroot**
  1 **cinnamon stick (3 inches), broken in half**
  1 **package (12 ounces) fresh *or* frozen cranberries**
  1 **to 1-1/4 cups sugar**

In a saucepan, combine the pears, water, ginger and cinnamon. Bring to a boil. Reduce heat; simmer, uncovered, for 5 minutes. Stir in cranberries and sugar. Return to a boil. Reduce heat; simmer, uncovered, for 10-12 minutes or until the cranberries have popped and sauce is slightly thickened, stirring several times. Discard cinnamon sticks. Mash sauce if desired. Cool. Cover and refrigerate. **Yield:** about 2 cups.

No Beans About It

Dried beans can be stored in an airtight container for up to a year in a cool, dry place. Before preparing them, check dried beans thoroughly for tiny pebbles or other debris.

Creole Green Beans

(Pictured above)

Even though our children are grown, my husband and I remain busy. So we rely on speedy recipes that call for everyday ingredients. This peppery treatment really wakes up green beans. —Sue Kuhn, Dublin, Ohio

- 1 package (16 ounces) frozen cut green beans
- 5 bacon strips, diced
- 1 medium onion, chopped
- 1/2 cup chopped green pepper
- 2 tablespoons all-purpose flour
- 2 tablespoons brown sugar
- 1 tablespoon Worcestershire sauce
- 1 teaspoon salt
- 1/2 teaspoon pepper
- 1/2 teaspoon ground mustard
- 1 can (14-1/2 ounces) diced tomatoes, undrained

Cook beans according to package directions. Meanwhile, in a skillet, cook bacon, onion and green pepper over medium heat until bacon is crisp and vegetables are tender. Remove with a slotted spoon.

Stir the flour, brown sugar, Worcestershire sauce, salt, pepper and mustard into the drippings until blended. Stir in tomatoes. Bring to a boil; cook and stir for 2 minutes or until thickened. Drain beans and add to skillet. Stir in bacon mixture. **Yield:** 6 servings.

Mallow-Pecan Acorn Squash

(Pictured below)

Squash has traditionally been a food our family passes up, but this luscious dish is an exception to the rule. You won't find it among our Thanksgiving leftovers—it's one of the first dishes to return empty.
—Kathleen Cox, Wyoming, Michigan

- 2 medium acorn squash, halved and seeded
- 1/3 cup crushed saltines (about 10 crackers)
- 1/4 cup chopped pecans
- 1/4 cup packed brown sugar
- 3 tablespoons butter, melted, divided
- 1/8 teaspoon ground nutmeg
- 1 cup miniature marshmallows

Place squash cut side up in an ungreased 13-in. x 9-in. x 2-in. baking dish. In a bowl, combine the cracker crumbs, pecans, brown sugar, 2 tablespoons butter and nutmeg. Spoon into squash. Brush edges of squash with remaining butter.

Cover and bake at 400° for 55-60 minutes or until squash is tender. Sprinkle with marshmallows. Bake, uncovered, for 3-5 minutes or until golden brown. **Yield:** 4 servings.

Cheddar Potato Strips

(Pictured above)

This easy dish wins compliments every time I serve it to family and guests. Fresh parsley adds flavor and looks nice sprinkled over the melted cheddar cheese.
—Lucinda Walker, Somerset, Pennsylvania

   3 large potatoes, cut into 1/2-inch strips
   1/2 cup milk
   1 tablespoon butter
Salt and pepper to taste
   1/2 cup shredded cheddar cheese
   1 tablespoon minced fresh parsley

In a greased 13-in. x 9-in. x 2-in. baking dish, arrange potatoes in a single layer. Pour milk over potatoes. Dot with butter; sprinkle with salt and pepper.

   Cover and bake at 425° for 30 minutes or until the potatoes are tender. Sprinkle with cheese and parsley. Bake, uncovered, 5 minutes longer or until cheese is melted. **Yield:** 4 servings.

Gingered Lime Carrots

(Pictured at right)

The produce manager at my grocery store suggested this memorable mixture of lightly sweet carrots, zippy ginger and tart lime. It's easy to fall in love with this recipe!
—Dorothy Swanson, St. Louis, Missouri

   1 pound carrots, cut into 1/2-inch slices
   1 tablespoon water
   1 tablespoon lime juice
   1 tablespoon butter
   1 tablespoon honey
   1 teaspoon grated lime peel
   1 teaspoon grated fresh gingerroot
Lime slices

In a 1-1/2-qt. microwave-safe bowl, combine carrots and water. Cover and cook on high for 7-8 minutes or until crisp-tender, stirring once. Let stand for 5 minutes.

   Meanwhile, in a small bowl, combine lime juice, butter, honey, peel and ginger. Cover and microwave on high for 1 minute. Drain carrots; stir in the lime mixture. Cover and cook on high for 1 minute. Garnish with lime. **Yield:** 4 servings.

   Editor's Note: This recipe was tested in an 850-watt microwave.

Orange Rice Medley

(Pictured above right)

My family especially enjoys this lovely, slightly sweet side dish. It looks so pretty with the chopped green and red peppers and orange slices tucked in with the rice. *—Zita Wilensky, North Miami, Florida*

   1/2 cup chopped onion
   1/2 cup chopped green pepper

Cranberry Apple Relish

(Pictured below)

I first made this relish when I was just 14. My mother wasn't able to prepare Thanksgiving dinner that year, so I was the cook for our family of 12! We all liked this dish so much that it became our family's traditional cranberry relish.
—*Bonnie Lee Morris*
Chase, British Columbia

1 navel orange
4 cups fresh *or* frozen cranberries
4 large red apples, peeled and grated
2 cups sugar

Finely grate outer orange peel and set aside. Peel off and discard white membrane. Slice the orange into eight pieces. Place a fourth of cranberries and orange slices in a food processor or blender; process until evenly chopped.

Transfer to a large bowl; repeat until all cranberries and orange slices have been chopped. Stir in the apples, sugar and reserved peel. Cover and refrigerate for at least 4 hours or overnight. **Yield:** 6 cups.

Editor's Note: Relish will keep in an airtight container for 1 week in the refrigerator, or freeze in serving-size portions.

1/2 cup chopped sweet red pepper
2 teaspoons olive oil
1 cup uncooked long grain rice
1-1/2 cups chicken broth
1/2 cup orange juice
1/4 teaspoon salt
Dash pepper
1 can (11 ounces) mandarin oranges, drained and coarsely chopped

In a saucepan over medium heat, saute onion and peppers in oil until tender. Add rice; stir until lightly browned. Add broth, orange juice, salt and pepper; bring to a boil. Reduce heat; cover and simmer for 15-20 minutes or until liquid is absorbed. Stir in the oranges. **Yield:** 6-8 servings.

Veggie Refresher

Limp vegetables like carrots and potatoes can regain their crisp texture if soaked in ice water for at least 1 hour. You can also keep blanched vegetables bright and crisp by draining the hot water, immediately placing the vegetables in ice water until cool and then draining.

Flavorful Rice Dressing

(Pictured above)

My original dressing seems to satisfy people who prefer dressing made with bread and those who prefer a rice variety. It includes both, plus spinach and a hint of orange for unexpected surprises. Leftover dressing (if there is any!) reheats well. —*Gloria Warczak Cedarburg, Wisconsin*

    7 slices day-old bread, torn
    1 cup torn corn bread
  2/3 cup hot water
  1/2 cup thinly sliced celery
  1/2 cup chopped onion
  1/2 cup sliced fresh mushrooms
    1 tablespoon vegetable oil
    1 cup firmly packed sliced fresh spinach
    1 cup cooked long grain rice
  1/2 cup cooked wild rice
  1/2 cup orange juice
    1 egg, beaten
    2 teaspoons rubbed sage
  1/2 teaspoon dried thyme
  1/2 teaspoon salt
  1/4 teaspoon sugar
  1/4 teaspoon pepper

In a large bowl, lightly toss bread and water. In a skillet, saute celery, onion and mushrooms in oil until tender, stirring con-

stantly. Stir into bread mixture. Add remaining ingredients; mix well. Place in a greased 2-qt. baking dish. Cover and bake at 350° for 30 minutes. **Yield:** 8 servings.

Cheesy Turnips And Carrots

(Pictured below)

Mild-tasting turnips and carrots are wonderfully enhanced by ginger, onion and a mouth-watering creamy cheese sauce in this super side dish. The serving bowl is always empty at the end of the meal.
—*Sandra Melnychenko, Grandview, Manitoba*

      3 cups diced peeled turnips
      2 cups sliced carrots
    1/4 teaspoon ground ginger
    3/4 cup water
      1 teaspoon salt, *divided*
    1/2 cup chopped onion
    1/2 cup diced celery
      3 tablespoons butter
      3 tablespoons all-purpose flour
    1/4 teaspoon pepper
  1-1/2 cups milk
      1 cup (4 ounces) shredded cheddar cheese

In a saucepan, combine turnips, carrots, ginger, water and 1/2 teaspoon salt. Cover and cook over medium-high heat for 10-15 minutes or until vegetables are tender; drain and reserve liquid. Set vegetables aside.

In a skillet, saute onion and celery in butter until tender; stir in flour, pepper and remaining salt. Add milk and the vegetable liquid; bring to a boil. Cook and stir until thickened and bubbly. Stir in cheese until melted; stir in the vegetables and heat through. **Yield:** 4-6 servings.

Chili Cheese Grits

(Pictured above)

This zesty dish is a real crowd-pleaser. It's great as a side dish and can also be served as a cold appetizer.
—Martha Lee, Foley, Alabama

        3 cups water
        1 teaspoon salt
        1 garlic clove, minced
        1 cup quick-cooking grits
      1/2 cup butter
    1-1/2 cups (6 ounces) shredded cheddar cheese,
           divided
        3 tablespoons chopped green chilies
        2 eggs
      1/2 cup milk

In a medium saucepan, bring water, salt and garlic to a boil; slowly stir in grits. Reduce heat; cook and stir for 3-5 minutes or until thickened. Remove from the heat. Add butter, 1 cup cheese and chilies; stir until butter is melted. Beat eggs and milk; add to the grits and mix well. Pour into a greased 2-qt. baking dish. Bake, uncovered, at 350° for 45 minutes. Sprinkle with remaining cheese. **Yield:** 6 servings.

Dutch Potato Poultry Stuffing

(Pictured below)

All of my ancestors were Pennsylvania Dutch. Add to that the fact my father was a potato farmer, and you see why we never had a holiday dinner without potato "filling" (Pennsylvania Dutch for stuffing)!
—Sarah Krout, Warrington, Pennsylvania

        5 cups mashed potatoes (without added milk,
           butter *or* seasoning)
        6 cups cubed crustless day-old white bread
    2-1/2 cups chopped onion
        1 cup minced celery leaves
        1 cup minced fresh parsley
        3 tablespoons butter, melted
        1 teaspoon salt
      3/4 teaspoon pepper
        3 eggs
        1 tablespoon all-purpose flour
        1 cup milk

In a large bowl, combine potatoes, bread cubes, onion, celery leaves, parsley, butter, salt and pepper. In a small bowl, beat eggs and flour until smooth; gradually stir in milk. Pour into the potato mixture and mix well. (Add more milk if stuffing seems dry.)

Transfer to a greased 3-qt. baking dish. Cover and bake at 325° for 60 minutes. Uncover and bake 10 minutes longer or until lightly browned. **Yield:** about 10 cups (enough for one 12- to 14-pound turkey).

Creamy Vegetable Casserole

(Pictured below)

I have a fussy eater in my house who absolutely loves this vegetable medley. It can be assembled in a snap, leaving time to fix the main course, set the table or just sit back and relax.
—Tami Kratzer
West Jordan, Utah

1 **package (16 ounces) frozen broccoli, carrots and cauliflower**
1 **can (10-3/4 ounces) condensed cream of mushroom soup, undiluted**
1 **carton (8 ounces) spreadable garden vegetable cream cheese**
1/2 **to 1 cup seasoned croutons**

Prepare the vegetables according to package directions; drain and place in a large bowl. Stir in the soup and cream cheese. Transfer to a greased 1-qt. baking dish. Sprinkle with croutons. Bake, uncovered, at 375° for 25 minutes or until bubbly. **Yield:** 6 servings.

Apricot-Glazed Sweet Potatoes

(Pictured above)

As the wonderful aroma of this dish wafts through the house, I'm always asked, "Is dinner ready yet?" So don't be surprised if your gang comes to the table extra-hungry. —*Joan Huggins, Waynesboro, Mississippi*

3 **pounds sweet potatoes, cooked, peeled and sliced**
1 **cup packed brown sugar**
5 **teaspoons cornstarch**
1/4 **teaspoon salt**
1/8 **teaspoon ground cinnamon**
1 **cup apricot nectar**
1/2 **cup hot water**
2 **teaspoons grated orange peel**
2 **teaspoons butter**
1/2 **cup chopped pecans**

Place sweet potatoes in a greased 13-in. x 9-in. x 2-in. baking dish and set aside. In a saucepan, combine brown sugar, cornstarch, salt and cinnamon; stir in apricot nectar, water and orange peel. Bring to a boil, stirring constantly. Cook and stir for 2 minutes. Remove from heat; stir in butter and pecans. Pour over sweet potatoes. Bake, uncovered, at 350° for 20-25 minutes or until heated through. **Yield:** 8-10 servings.

In a Dutch oven or soup kettle, fry salt pork just until cooked. Drain, reserving 2 tablespoons of drippings. Stir in the remaining ingredients. Bring to a boil. Reduce heat; cover and simmer for 45 minutes or until greens are tender. **Yield:** 8-10 servings.

Editor's Note: Fresh spinach can be substituted for the turnip greens. Reduce the cooking time to 10 minutes or until spinach is tender.

Minty Peas And Onions

(Pictured below)

Mother always relied on peas and onions when she was in a hurry and needed a quick side dish. Besides being easy to prepare, this dish was loved by everyone in our family. It was handed down to my mother by my grandmother. —Santa D'Addario, Brooklyn, New York

> 2 **large onions, cut into 1/2-inch wedges**
> 1/2 **cup chopped sweet red pepper**
> 2 **tablespoons vegetable oil**
> 2 **packages (16 ounces each) frozen peas**
> 2 **tablespoons minced fresh mint or 2 teaspoons dried mint**

In a large skillet, saute onions and red pepper in oil until onions just begin to soften. Add peas. Cook, uncovered, stirring occasionally, for 10 minutes or until heated through. Stir in mint and cook for 1 minute. **Yield:** 8 servings.

Country Turnip Greens

(Pictured above)

This easy recipe results in a delicious dish of cooked greens sure to please any palate. The key is the rich flavor of pork and onion simmered with the fresh greens. —Sandra Pichon, Slidell, Louisiana

> 3/4 **pound lean salt pork or bacon, diced**
> 4-1/2 **pounds fresh turnip greens, trimmed**
> 1-1/2 **cups water**
> 1 **large onion, chopped**
> 1 **teaspoon sugar**
> 1/4 **to 1/2 teaspoon pepper**

Keeping Mint Fresh

Choose mint with evenly colored leaves that don't show any signs of wilting. You can store a bunch of mint in the refrigerator, stems down in a glass of water with a plastic bag over the leaves, for up to 1 week. Change the water every 2 days.

Winter Root Vegetables

(Pictured below)

Christmas dinner wouldn't be the same without this colorful side dish. We love the interesting combination of vegetables including red potatoes, brussels sprouts and parsnips covered with a zippy sauce.
—*Mary Jane Jones, Williamstown, West Virginia*

      2 **pounds small red potatoes, quartered**
      1 **pound brussels sprouts, halved**
    1/2 **pound parsnips, peeled and julienned**
    1/2 **pound carrots, cut into chunks**
    1/2 **pound turnips, peeled and cut into chunks**
    1/2 **cup butter**
      2 **tablespoons prepared horseradish**
      2 **tablespoons cider vinegar**
      2 **tablespoons snipped fresh dill *or* 2 teaspoons dill weed**
    1/2 **teaspoon salt, optional**
    1/4 **teaspoon pepper**

Cook vegetables separately in water until tender; drain. Melt butter; stir in remaining ingredients. Combine the vegetables and butter mixture; toss to coat. **Yield:** 10-12 servings.

Twice-Baked Potato Casserole

(Pictured above)

My daughter gave me this recipe because she knows I love potatoes. The hearty casserole is loaded with a palate-pleasing combination of bacon, cheeses, green onions and sour cream.   —*Betty Miars, Anna, Ohio*

      6 **medium unpeeled potatoes, baked**
    1/4 **teaspoon salt**
    1/4 **teaspoon pepper**
      1 **pound sliced bacon, cooked and crumbled**
      3 **cups (24 ounces) sour cream**
      2 **cups (8 ounces) shredded mozzarella cheese**
      2 **cups (8 ounces) shredded cheddar cheese**
      2 **green onions, chopped**

Cut baked potatoes into 1-in. cubes. Place half in a greased 13-in. x 9-in. x 2-in. baking dish. Sprinkle with half of the salt, pepper and bacon. Top with half of the sour cream and cheeses. Repeat layers. Bake, uncovered, at 350° for 20 minutes or until cheese is melted. Sprinkle with onions. **Yield:** 6-8 servings.

Black-Eyed Peas With Bacon

(Pictured above)

A real Southern favorite, black-eyed peas are traditionally served on New Year's Day to bring good luck. My mother's recipe with bacon, garlic and thyme makes them extra special. —*Ruby Williams*
Bogalusa, Louisiana

- 1 pound black-eyed peas, rinsed and sorted
- 1/2 pound bacon, cooked and crumbled
- 1 large onion, chopped
- 1 garlic clove, minced
- 1 tablespoon butter
- 1/2 teaspoon dried thyme

Salt to taste
Additional crumbled bacon, optional

Place peas, bacon and enough water to cover in a large kettle; bring to a boil. Boil for 2 minutes. Remove from the heat; cover and let stand for 1 hour. Do not drain. In a skillet, saute onion and garlic in butter until tender. Add to the pea mixture with thyme and salt. Return to the heat; cover and simmer for 30 minutes or until peas are soft. Top with crumbled bacon if desired. **Yield:** 6-8 servings.

Cauliflower Au Gratin

(Pictured below)

This dish will make a vegetable lover out of anyone. Whenever I serve it, everyone just raves about it and asks for the recipe. Sometimes I'll substitute broccoli for all or half of the cauliflower, and it tastes just as good!
—*Jacki Ricci, Ely, Nevada*

- 6 tablespoons butter
- 4 ounces fully cooked ham, chopped
- 1 to 2 garlic cloves, minced
- 1 head cauliflower (3 pounds), broken into florets
- 2 tablespoons all-purpose flour
- 1-1/2 cups heavy whipping cream
- 1/4 teaspoon salt

Pepper to taste
Pinch cayenne pepper

- 1-1/2 cups (6 ounces) shredded Swiss cheese
- 2 to 3 tablespoons minced fresh parsley

Melt butter in a large skillet. Saute ham and garlic for 2 minutes. Add cauliflower and cook just until crisp-tender, about 10 minutes. Combine flour and cream until smooth; stir into skillet and blend well. Add salt, pepper and cayenne. Bring to a boil. Reduce heat; cook and stir for 2 minutes.

Transfer to an ungreased 2-qt. baking dish. Sprinkle with cheese. Place under a preheated broiler until lightly browned, about 2-4 minutes. Sprinkle with parsley. Serve immediately. **Yield:** 6-8 servings.

Two-Toned Baked Potatoes

(Pictured below)

I have a reputation for trying out new recipes. Everyone is glad I took a chance on this one.
—Sherree Stahn, Central City, Nebraska

6 medium russet potatoes
6 medium sweet potatoes
2/3 cup sour cream, *divided*
1/3 cup milk
3/4 cup shredded cheddar cheese
4 tablespoons minced chives, *divided*
1-1/2 teaspoons salt, *divided*

Pierce russet and sweet potatoes with a fork. Bake at 400° for 60-70 minutes or until tender. Set sweet potatoes aside. Cut a third off the top of each russet potato; scoop out pulp, leaving skins intact. Place pulp in a bowl; mash with 1/3 cup sour cream, milk, cheese, 2 tablespoons chives and 3/4 teaspoon salt. Set aside.

Cut off the top of each sweet potato; scoop out pulp, leaving skins intact. Mash pulp with remaining sour cream, chives and salt. Stuff mixture into half of each potato skin; spoon russet potato filling into other half. Place on a baking sheet. Bake at 350° for 15-20 minutes or until heated through. **Yield:** 12 servings.

Berry Mallow Yam Bake

(Pictured above)

The blend of cranberries and sweet potatoes in this recipe results in a very pretty appearance—and a unique taste. It's a delicious side dish that I like to prepare for special occasions. —Connie Bolton, San Antonio, Texas

1/2 cup all-purpose flour
1/2 cup packed brown sugar
1/2 cup old-fashioned oats
1/2 teaspoon ground cinnamon
1/3 cup cold butter
2 cups fresh *or* **frozen cranberries**
2 tablespoons sugar
1 can (17 ounces) cut-up yams
Miniature marshmallows, optional

In a small bowl, combine flour, brown sugar, oats and cinnamon. Cut in butter until crumbly; set aside. Sprinkle cranberries with sugar. Drain yams; reserving liquid.

In a greased 2-qt. casserole, layer half the yams, half the cranberries and half the crumb mixture. Repeat the layers, ending with crumbs. Pour reserved yam liquid over all. Bake at 350° for 35 minutes or until heated through. If desired, place several rings of marshmallows around the outer edge of casserole and return to oven just until marshmallows are puffed and lightly browned. **Yield:** 8 servings.

Broccoli Artichoke Casserole

A creamy mellow sauce draped over bold-tasting broccoli and artichokes makes this a great addition to any meal. —Sue Braunschweig, Delafield, Wisconsin

3 packages (10 ounces *each*) frozen broccoli spears, thawed and drained
2 cans (14 ounces *each*) artichoke hearts, drained
1-1/2 cups mayonnaise
1/2 cup butter
1/2 cup grated Parmesan cheese
4 teaspoons lemon juice
1/2 teaspoon celery salt
1/2 cup slivered almonds, optional
2 tablespoons diced pimientos, optional

Arrange broccoli and artichokes in a greased shallow 2-1/2-qt. baking dish; set aside. In a saucepan, combine mayonnaise, butter, cheese, lemon juice and celery salt; cook and stir over low heat until butter is melted and sauce is heated through (do not boil). Pour over broccoli and artichokes. Sprinkle with almonds and pimientos if desired. Bake, uncovered, at 350° for 30-40 minutes or until broccoli is crisp-tender. **Yield:** 8-10 servings.

Holiday Squash

The crunchy topping and touch of sweet maple syrup make this dish our favorite side dish for turkey or ham. —Kay Cripe Wiri, South Auckland, New Zealand

3/4 cup all-purpose flour
3/4 cup packed brown sugar
2 teaspoons ground cinnamon
1 teaspoon ground allspice
1/4 teaspoon salt
1/2 cup butter
1 butternut squash (about 3 pounds)
1 cup chopped pecans
1 cup maple syrup

In a medium bowl, combine flour, brown sugar, cinnamon, allspice and salt; cut in butter until crumbly. Peel squash; cut into 1/2-in. slices, removing seeds when necessary. Put a third of the squash slices in a greased 11-in. x 7-in. x 2-in. baking dish. Sprinkle with 3/4 cup crumb mixture. Layer the remaining squash on top, overlapping when necessary.

Sprinkle remaining crumb mixture over top. Top with pecans. Drizzle with maple syrup. Cover with foil; bake at 350° for 1 hour. Remove foil; bake 10 minutes more or until squash is done. **Yield:** 10-12 servings.

Christmas Cauliflower

(Pictured below)

A Swiss cheese sauce gives this vegetable casserole an extra-special taste. I have served it every Christmas for over 20 years. —Betty Claycomb, Alverton, Pennsylvania

1 large head cauliflower, broken into florets
1/4 cup diced green pepper
1 jar (7.3 ounces) sliced mushrooms, drained
1/4 cup butter
1/3 cup all-purpose flour
2 cups milk
1 cup (4 ounces) shredded Swiss cheese
2 tablespoons diced pimientos
1 teaspoon salt
Paprika, optional

In a large saucepan, cook cauliflower in a small amount of water for 6-7 minutes or until crisp-tender; drain well. In a medium saucepan, saute green pepper and mushrooms in butter for 2 minutes. Add flour; gradually stir in milk. Bring to a boil; boil for 2 minutes, stirring constantly. Remove from the heat; stir in cheese until melted. Add pimientos and salt.

Place half of the cauliflower in a greased 2-qt. baking dish; top with half of the sauce. Repeat layers. Bake, uncovered, at 325° for 25 minutes or until bubbly. Sprinkle with paprika if desired. **Yield:** 8-10 servings.

Creamy Asparagus and Carrots

Asparagus freezes so well I'm able to prepare this casserole year-round, even at the holidays.
—*Darlene Schafer, Corder, Missouri*

  2 medium carrots, cut into 1/4-inch slices
2/3 cup water
  1 pound fresh asparagus, cut into 1-inch pieces
  1 package (3 ounces) cream cheese, softened
  1 teaspoon all-purpose flour
1/4 teaspoon salt
1/8 teaspoon ground nutmeg
Pinch pepper
  1 tablespoon sliced almonds, toasted

In a saucepan, bring carrots and water to a boil; cover and cook for 4 minutes. Add asparagus; cover and cook for 3 minutes or until just tender. Drain, reserving liquid; add enough water to liquid to equal 1/3 cup. Set vegetables aside; return liquid to skillet.

Combine cream cheese, flour, salt, nutmeg and pepper; add to liquid. Cook over low heat, stirring constantly, until cheese melts and sauce is bubbly, about 3 minutes. Stir in vegetables and heat through. Garnish with almonds. **Yield:** 4 servings.

Cauliflower Corn Supreme

My great-aunt gave me this hearty recipe years ago, and I still make it often.
—*Joanie Elbourn*
Gardner, Massachusetts

  3 tablespoons all-purpose flour
  1 teaspoon salt
1/2 teaspoon garlic powder
1/4 teaspoon pepper
  4 cups thinly sliced fresh cauliflower
  1 small sweet onion, chopped
1-1/2 cups fresh corn
  1 small sweet red pepper, chopped
1/2 cup grated Parmesan cheese
  2 tablespoons minced fresh parsley
  2 tablespoons butter
3/4 cup milk
1/4 cup white wine *or* apple juice
  1 cup (4 ounces) shredded mozzarella *or* Swiss cheese

Combine first four ingredients; set aside. In a greased 8-in. square baking dish, layer cauliflower and onion. Sprinkle with flour mixture. Top with corn and red pepper. Sprinkle with Parmesan cheese and parsley; dot with butter. Combine milk and wine or apple juice; pour over vegetables. Sprinkle with cheese. Cover and bake at 350° for 45 minutes. Uncover; bake 15 minutes longer or until vegetables are tender. **Yield:** 6-8 servings.

Potato Stuffing

(*Pictured below*)

This is an old Pennsylvania Dutch recipe. The simple addition of onion and celery gives the potatoes a special flavor, and the parsley adds color.   —*Betty McCloskey*
Pennsauken, New Jersey

  1 large onion, finely chopped
  2 to 3 celery ribs, finely chopped
  6 tablespoons butter
  2 slices white bread, torn
  3 cups mashed potatoes
  2 tablespoons minced fresh parsley

In a large saucepan, saute the onion and celery in butter until tender. Remove from the heat. Add bread, potatoes and parsley; mix well. Spoon into a greased 1-qt. baking dish. Bake, uncovered, at 350° for 45 minutes or until top is lightly browned. **Yield:** 6 servings.

Creamed Celery and Peas

(Pictured above)

This special side dish never fails to have people return-ing for more. The celery and almonds provide a great crunch. It tastes impressive, but it's simple to prepare.
—Dorothy Pritchett, Wills Point, Texas

1/3 cup water
2 cups sliced celery
1 package (10 ounces) frozen peas
1/2 cup sour cream
1/2 teaspoon dried rosemary, crushed
1/4 teaspoon salt
Dash garlic salt
1 tablespoon chopped pimientos, drained
1/4 cup slivered almonds, toasted

In a saucepan over medium heat, bring water to a boil. Add cel-ery; cover and cook for 8 minutes. Add peas; return to a boil. Cover and cook for 2-3 minutes or until vegetables are ten-der; drain.

In a small bowl, combine sour cream, rosemary, salt and gar-lic salt; mix well. Toss vegetables with pimientos; place in a serv-ing bowl. Top with sour cream mixture. Sprinkle with almonds. **Yield:** 6 servings.

Cranberry Baked Beans

(Pictured below)

I knew I'd found a winner when I got the idea to simmer beans in cranberry juice. They're wonderful warm or cold.
—Wendie Osipowicz, New Britain, Connecticut

3 cups dried navy beans
5 cups cranberry juice
1/2 pound lean salt pork, diced
3/4 cup chopped onion
1/2 cup ketchup
1/4 cup molasses
5 teaspoons dark brown sugar
1-1/2 teaspoons ground mustard
1-1/2 teaspoons salt
1/8 teaspoon ground ginger

Place beans in a Dutch oven or soup kettle; add water to cov-er by 2 in. Bring to a boil; boil for 2 minutes. Remove from the heat; cover and let stand for 1 hour. Drain beans and discard liquid. Return beans to Dutch oven. Add cranberry juice; bring to a boil. Reduce heat; cover and simmer for 1 hour or until the beans are almost tender. Drain, reserving cranberry liquid.

Place beans in a 2-1/2-qt. baking dish or bean pot; add remaining ingredients and 1-1/2 cups of cranberry liquid. Cov-er and bake at 350° for 3 hours or until beans are tender and of desired consistency, stirring every 30 minutes. Add re-served cranberry liquid as needed. **Yield:** 10-12 servings.

Herbed Garlic Potatoes

(Pictured at right)

My mom cooks from scratch and rarely uses a recipe. That's how I learned—a pinch of this, a dash of that. But it was actually my dad who invented the basis for this recipe. The potatoes fit any kind of meal—fancy or burgers—and everyone asks me for the recipe.
—*Sherry DesJardin, Fairbanks, Alaska*

   15 small red potatoes (about 2 pounds)
  1/3 cup butter
  1/4 cup minced fresh parsley
    2 tablespoons minced fresh *or* dried chives
1-1/2 teaspoons minced fresh tarragon *or* 1/2 teaspoon dried tarragon
    2 to 3 garlic cloves, minced
    3 bacon strips, cooked and crumbled
  1/2 to 1 teaspoon salt
  1/4 teaspoon pepper

Cut the potatoes in half and place in a saucepan; cover with water. Cover and bring to a boil; cook until tender, about 15 minutes. Drain well. In a large skillet, melt butter. Add the parsley, chives, tarragon and garlic; cook and stir over low heat for 1-2 minutes. Add the potatoes, bacon, salt and pepper; toss to coat. Cook until heated through, about 5 minutes. **Yield:** 6-8 servings.

Church Supper Potatoes

(Pictured at right)

As a pastor's wife, I cook for crowds often. This dish's always a hit. The recipe is very adaptable, and the results disappear. And I've found that everyone likes to see potatoes on a buffet table. —*Michelle Grigsby Beavercreek, Ohio*

    3 pounds russet potatoes (about 9 medium), peeled and cut into 1/2-inch cubes
    2 garlic cloves, peeled
    2 packages (3 ounces *each*) cream cheese, softened
    2 tablespoons butter
  1/2 cup sour cream
    2 cups (8 ounces) shredded cheddar cheese, *divided*
    1 teaspoon garlic salt

    1 teaspoon onion salt
    1 package (10 ounces) frozen chopped spinach, thawed and squeezed dry

Place the potatoes and garlic in a large saucepan; cover with water. Cover and bring to a boil; cook for 20-25 minutes or until very tender. Drain well. In a mixing bowl, mash potatoes and garlic with the cream cheese and butter. Add sour cream, 1 cup of cheddar cheese, garlic salt, onion salt and spinach. Stir just until mixed.

Spread into a greased 2-qt. baking dish. Bake, uncovered, at 350° for 30-35 minutes or until heated through. Top with remaining cheese; bake 5 minutes longer or until the cheese is melted. **Yield:** 10-12 servings.

Cheddar-Mushroom Stuffed Potatoes

(Pictured at right)

To come up with this recipe, I just put together three of my family's favorite ingredients—potatoes, mushrooms and bacon. I prepare it as a quick-and-easy party dish. It's also a natural contribution to a potluck. And I serve it as an entree at times with a side vegetable.
—*Jenean Schuetz, Longmont, Colorado*

    6 large russet potatoes
  2/3 cup heavy whipping cream
    1 cup (4 ounces) shredded cheddar cheese, *divided*
  1/4 cup chopped fresh mushrooms
  1/2 to 1 teaspoon garlic salt
  1/2 teaspoon dried basil
  1/2 teaspoon dried oregano
    4 bacon strips, cooked and crumbled, *divided*

Bake potatoes at 375° for 1 hour or until tender. When cool enough to handle, cut a thin slice off the top of each potato and discard. Scoop out pulp, leaving a 1/4-in. shell; set shells aside.

Place pulp in a mixing bowl; add cream and mash. Blend in 3/4 cup cheese, mushrooms, garlic salt, basil and oregano. Reserve 2 tablespoons bacon; stir the remaining bacon into potato mixture. Spoon into potato shells. Top with remaining cheese and bacon. Microwave on high for 5-8 minutes or bake, uncovered, at 375° for 25-30 minutes or until potatoes are heated through. **Yield:** 6 servings.

Editor's Note: This recipe was tested in an 850-watt microwave.

Clockwise from top: Cheddar-Mushroom Stuffed Potatoes, Golden Mashed Potatoes (recipe on page 176), Herbed Garlic Potatoes and Church Supper Potatoes

Brussels Sprouts Supreme

(Pictured above)

A creamy cheese sauce is the perfect accompaniment for the bold flavor of brussels sprouts. Even those who don't care for this vegetable may enjoy it served this way.
—Edna Hoffman, Hebron, Indiana

    1 pound fresh brussels sprouts, trimmed
    1 cup chopped celery
    2 tablespoons butter
    2 tablespoons all-purpose flour
    1 cup milk
  1/2 cup shredded process American cheese
  1/4 teaspoon salt
Pinch cayenne pepper, optional

Cut an X in the core of each brussels sprout. Place brussels sprouts, celery and a small amount of water in a saucepan; cover and cook for 8 minutes or until crisp-tender.

    Meanwhile, in another saucepan, melt butter. Stir in flour until smooth. Gradually add milk; bring to a boil. Reduce heat; cook and stir for 2 minutes or until thickened. Add cheese, salt and cayenne if desired; stir until cheese is melted. Drain sprouts and celery; top with cheese sauce. **Yield:** 4-6 servings.

Golden Mashed Potatoes

(Pictured on page 175)

When there's no gravy with the meat, this is great to serve in place of regular mashed potatoes. I make it often to take to picnics and church socials. My husband even made it for his family's reunion one year when I couldn't go!　　　—Cindy Stith, Wickliffe, Kentucky

    9 large potatoes (about 4 pounds), peeled and cubed
    1 pound carrots, cut into 1/2-inch chunks
    8 green onions, thinly sliced
  1/2 cup butter
    1 cup (8 ounces) sour cream
1-1/2 teaspoons salt
  1/8 teaspoon pepper
  3/4 cup shredded cheddar cheese

In a soup kettle or Dutch oven, cook the potatoes and carrots in boiling salted water until tender; drain. Place in a mixing bowl; mash and set aside. In a skillet, saute onions in butter until tender. Add to potato mixture. Add sour cream, salt and pepper; mix until blended.

    Transfer to a greased 13-in. x 9-in. x 2-in. baking dish. Sprinkle with cheese. Bake, uncovered, at 350° for 30-40 minutes or until heated through. **Yield:** 10-12 servings.

Barbecued Butter Beans

These are a proven crowd-pleaser. The secret's in the seasoning and in the butter beans you use.
—Mrs. W.L. Doolittle, Crossville, Tennessee

    3 cans (15 ounces *each*) butter beans, rinsed and drained
    1 can (15 ounces) lima beans, rinsed and drained
  1/2 cup ketchup
  1/2 cup beef broth
  1/2 cup packed brown sugar
    3 tablespoons vegetable oil
    2 tablespoons chopped onion
    1 tablespoon dried parsley flakes
Dash Liquid Smoke, optional

Combine all ingredients. Pour into an ungreased 2-qt. baking dish. Bake, uncovered, at 375° for 1 hour or until bubbly. **Yield:** 10 servings.

Merry Christmas Rice

(Pictured below)

Instant rice makes this dish an instant success! It's a recipe I make "by children's demand," and we've found it not only delicious, but a very colorful addition to our Christmas table. —Karen Hoylo, Duluth, Minnesota

  2 cups water, *divided*
1-1/3 cups sugar, *divided*
  2 cups (1/2 pound) fresh *or* **frozen cranberries**
1-1/3 cups quick-cooking rice
  1/4 teaspoon ground cinnamon
  1/8 teaspoon salt
  1 apple, peeled and sliced

In a saucepan, combine 1/2 cup water and 1 cup sugar; bring to a boil. Add the cranberries; return to boiling. Reduce heat; simmer for 10 minutes or until most of the berries pop, stirring occasionally.

Add rice, cinnamon, salt and remaining water and sugar. Bring to a boil. Reduce heat; cover and simmer for 10 minutes. Remove from the heat and stir in apple. Cover and let stand for 10 minutes. **Yield:** 6 servings.

Parmesan Onion Bake

(Pictured above)

Dinner guests in my home know to expect the unexpected! I love experimenting with unusual combinations of ingredients. This cheesy onion bake adds flair to a meal. —Linda Vail, Ballwin, Missouri

  6 medium onions, sliced
  1 cup diced celery
  8 tablespoons butter, *divided*
  1/4 cup all-purpose flour
  1 teaspoon salt
  1/8 teaspoon pepper
1-1/2 cups milk
  1/3 cup grated Parmesan cheese
  1/2 cup chopped pecans

In a large skillet, saute onions and celery in 3 tablespoons butter until tender; drain and set aside. In a saucepan, melt the remaining butter; stir in flour, salt and pepper until smooth. Gradually stir in milk. Bring to a boil; cook and stir for 2 minutes or until thickened. Pour over vegetables; toss to coat.

Pour into an ungreased 2-qt. baking dish. Sprinkle with cheese and pecans. Bake, uncovered, at 350° for 20-25 minutes or until heated through. **Yield:** 6-8 servings.

Spiced Baked Beets

Especially during the fall and winter months, this recipe is a favorite. With its red color, it looks great served at Christmastime. It's nice for taking to potlucks as well. Even people who aren't too fond of beets like this side dish. —Margery Richmond, Lacombe, Alberta

 4 cups shredded peeled beets (about 4 to 5 medium)
 1 medium onion, shredded
 1 medium potato, shredded
 3 tablespoons brown sugar
 3 tablespoons vegetable oil
 2 tablespoons water
 1 tablespoon vinegar
 1/2 teaspoon salt
 1/4 teaspoon pepper
 1/4 teaspoon celery seed
 1/8 to 1/4 teaspoon ground cloves

In a large bowl, combine beets, onion and potato; set aside. In a small bowl, combine brown sugar, oil, water, vinegar and seasonings. Pour over vegetables; toss to coat.

Pour into a greased 1-1/2-qt. baking dish. Cover and bake at 350° for 45 minutes, stirring occasionally. Uncover and bake 15-25 minutes longer or until the vegetables are tender. **Yield:** 8-10 servings.

Whipped Squash

This is an excellent way to serve butternut squash. Its rich flavor and golden harvest color really come through in this smooth vegetable side dish.
—Dorothy Pritchett, Wills Point, Texas

 1 butternut squash (about 2-1/2 pounds), peeled, seeded and cubed
 3 cups water
 3/4 teaspoon salt, optional, *divided*
 2 tablespoons butter
 1 tablespoon brown sugar
 1/8 to 1/4 teaspoon ground nutmeg

In a saucepan over medium heat, bring squash, water and 1/2 teaspoon of salt if desired to a boil. Reduce heat; cover and simmer for 20 minutes or until the squash is tender.

Drain; transfer to a mixing bowl. Add butter, brown sugar, nutmeg and remaining salt if desired; beat until smooth. **Yield:** 6 servings.

Twice-Baked Sweet Potatoes

(Pictured below)

When I prepare these sweet potatoes, I like to serve them with ham. Those two different tastes always team really well. —Miriam Christophel, Battle Creek, Michigan

 6 large sweet potatoes (3-1/2 to 4 pounds)
 1/4 cup orange juice
 6 tablespoons cold butter, *divided*
 1/4 cup all-purpose flour
 1/4 cup packed brown sugar
 1/4 teaspoon ground cinnamon
 1/4 teaspoon ground ginger
 1/8 teaspoon ground mace
 1/4 cup chopped pecans

Pierce potatoes with a fork. Bake at 375° for 40-60 minutes or until tender. Allow potatoes to cool to the touch. Cut them in half lengthwise; carefully scoop out pulp, leaving a 1/4-in. shell. Place pulp in a large bowl. Add orange juice. Melt 3 tablespoons butter; add to pulp and beat until smooth.

Stuff the potato shells; place in an ungreased 15-in. x 10-in. x 1-in. baking pan. In a small bowl, combine flour, brown sugar, cinnamon, ginger and mace. Cut in remaining butter until crumbly. Stir in pecans. Sprinkle over potatoes. Bake at 350° for 20-25 minutes or until golden and heated through. **Yield:** 12 servings.

Holiday Peas and Rice

(Pictured above)

With all the fuss that goes into holiday meals, it's nice to find a side dish like this that's both satisfying and simple. —Patricia Rutherford, Winchester, Illinois

  1/2 cup uncooked long grain rice
  1/8 teaspoon rubbed sage
    2 tablespoons butter
    1 can (14-1/2 ounces) chicken broth
    1 cup fresh *or* frozen peas
    2 tablespoons diced pimientos

In a saucepan, saute rice and sage in butter until rice is lightly browned. Add broth; bring to a boil. Reduce heat; cover and simmer for 20 minutes. Add peas; simmer, uncovered, 10 minutes longer or until heated through, stirring occasionally. Stir in pimientos. **Yield:** 4-6 servings.

Creamy Cabbage

This recipe makes a good side dish for any meal. It's a simple way to spruce up a cabbage dish and has always been happily received at potluck suppers.
      —Alice Lewis, Los Osos, California

    4 cups shredded cabbage
  1/2 cup diced bacon
    1 tablespoon all-purpose flour
  1/2 teaspoon salt
  1/4 teaspoon paprika
  1/8 teaspoon pepper
    1 cup milk
    1 cup soft bread crumbs

In a large saucepan, cook cabbage for 7 minutes in boiling water; drain. In a skillet, cook bacon. Remove bacon and all but

1 tablespoon drippings. Add flour, salt, paprika and pepper to drippings. Gradually add milk; simmer and stir until thickened. Place cabbage in a 1-qt. casserole. Top with sauce. Sprinkle bread crumbs and bacon over the top. Bake at 400° for 15 minutes. **Yield:** 4 servings.

Festive Green Bean Casserole

(Pictured below)

This recipe came from a cookbook my son gave to me over 20 years ago. It's a tasty dish that I make often.
      —June Mullins, Livonia, Missouri

    1 cup chopped sweet red pepper
    1 small onion, finely chopped
    1 tablespoon butter
    1 can (10-3/4 ounces) condensed cream of
      celery soup, undiluted
  1/2 cup milk
    1 teaspoon Worcestershire sauce
  1/8 teaspoon hot pepper sauce
    2 packages (16 ounces *each*) frozen French-style
      green beans, thawed and drained
    1 can (8 ounces) sliced water chestnuts, drained
    1 cup (4 ounces) shredded cheddar cheese

In a skillet, saute the red pepper and onion in butter until tender. Add the soup, milk, Worcestershire sauce and hot pepper sauce; stir until smooth. Stir in the green beans and water chestnuts. Transfer to an ungreased 1-1/2-qt. baking dish. Sprinkle with cheese. Bake, uncovered, at 350° for 15 minutes or until heated through and cheese is melted. **Yield:** 6-8 servings.

Garlicky Green Beans

Crisp-tender green beans are delicious tossed with a garlic butter sauce. With its pretty green color, this fresh dish is an attractive addition to your table.
—Ruth Marie Lyons, Boulder, Colorado

    1 pound fresh green beans
    1/2 cup water
    2 to 3 garlic cloves, minced
    3 tablespoons butter
    1/8 teaspoon salt
Pinch pepper

In a saucepan, bring beans and water to a boil; reduce heat to medium. Cover and cook for 10-15 minutes or until beans are crisp-tender; drain and set aside. In a large skillet, saute garlic in butter until lightly browned, about 1 minute. Add beans, salt and pepper; heat through. **Yield:** 4-6 servings.

Garden Saute

I love to serve this vegetable side dish when we are hosting a dinner party. It's fun, colorful and nicely seasoned with a variety of herbs.
—Nena Williams
Dallas, Texas

    1/4 cup chopped red onion
    1 garlic clove, minced
    1 medium yellow summer squash, sliced
    1 medium zucchini, sliced
    1/2 cup sliced fresh mushrooms
    1 small tomato, cut into wedges
    1/4 cup chopped celery
    1/2 teaspoon lemon juice
    1/4 teaspoon dried rosemary, crushed
    1/4 teaspoon dill weed
    1/4 teaspoon Italian seasoning
    1/8 teaspoon fennel seed
    1/8 teaspoon pepper

In a large skillet coated with nonstick cooking spray, saute onion and garlic until softened. Add remaining ingredients; mix well. Cover and cook over medium heat for 5-7 minutes or until vegetables are tender, stirring occasionally. **Yield:** 6 servings.

Colorful Oven Vegetables

(Pictured above)

As a party planner for a catering company, I often serve this attractive side dish with a steak dinner or at a brunch. Our two grown sons and their families often request these fresh-tasting oven-roasted vegetables, too.
—Grace Ammann, Richfield, Minnesota

    1/3 cup butter
    1/2 teaspoon dried thyme
    1/4 to 1/2 teaspoon salt
    1/4 teaspoon pepper
    3 cups cauliflowerets
    2 cups broccoli florets
    6 medium carrots, julienned
    3 small onions, quartered

Place butter in a shallow 3-qt. baking dish; place in a 400° oven for 5 minutes or until melted. Stir in thyme, salt and pepper. Add the vegetables and toss to coat. Cover and bake for 25-30 minutes or until the vegetables are crisp-tender. **Yield:** 10-12 servings.

   Editor's Note: 2 cups baby carrots may be substituted; cut into julienne strips.

Zesty Corn Custard

My mother handed this recipe down to me—I don't know what else I can say about it except that it's wonderful! —Joni Schaper, Lancaster, California

    2 cups cream-style corn
    2 cups tomato juice
    3 eggs, beaten
    1 cup evaporated milk
    1 cup (4 ounces) shredded cheddar cheese
    1 cup yellow cornmeal
  1/2 cup finely chopped onion
  1/2 cup finely chopped green pepper
    1 teaspoon salt
  1/4 teaspoon pepper
Hot pepper sauce to taste

Combine all ingredients in a large bowl; mix thoroughly. Pour into a greased 13-in. x 9-in. x 2-in. baking dish or 2-1/2-qt. casserole. Set in a shallow pan of hot water. Bake at 350° for 50-55 minutes or until set. **Yield:** 10-12 servings.

Spinach Squares

Even people who don't care for spinach can't pass up these satisfying squares when they're set out. —Patricia Kile, Greentown, Pennsylvania

    2 tablespoons butter, melted, *divided*
    1 cup milk
    3 eggs
    1 cup all-purpose flour
    1 teaspoon baking powder
  3/4 teaspoon salt
  1/2 teaspoon dried oregano
  1/4 teaspoon pepper
  1/4 teaspoon dried basil
  1/4 teaspoon dried thyme
    2 packages (10 ounces *each*) frozen chopped
      spinach, thawed and squeezed dry
    2 cups (8 ounces) shredded cheddar cheese
    2 cups (8 ounces) shredded Monterey Jack cheese
    1 cup chopped onion
Sliced pimientos, optional

Brush the bottom and sides of a 13-in. x 9-in. x 2-in. baking dish with 1 tablespoon butter; set aside. In a mixing bowl, combine remaining butter and the next nine ingredients; mix well.

Stir in the spinach, cheeses and onion. Spread in pan.

Bake, uncovered, at 350° for 30-35 minutes or until a toothpick inserted near the center comes out clean and edges are lightly browned. Cut into squares. Garnish with pimientos if desired. **Yield:** 16-20 side-dish servings or 32 appetizers.

Sweet Potato Bake

(Pictured below)

This is an easy dish to prepare and is a perfect addition to that special holiday meal. — Pam Holloway Marion, Louisiana

    7 large sweet potatoes (about 6 pounds),
      peeled and cubed
  1/4 cup butter
  1/2 cup orange marmalade
  1/4 cup orange juice
  1/4 cup packed brown sugar
    2 teaspoons salt
    1 teaspoon ground ginger
TOPPING:
   12 oatmeal cookies, crumbled
    6 tablespoons butter, softened

Place sweet potatoes in a Dutch oven and cover with water; bring to a boil. Reduce heat; cover and cook just until tender, about 15 minutes. Drain well. Mash potatoes with butter. Add marmalade, orange juice, brown sugar, salt and ginger.

Transfer to a greased 13-in. x 9-in. x 2-in. baking dish. Toss cookie crumbs with butter; sprinkle over the top. Bake, uncovered, at 400° for 20 minutes or until browned. Let stand for 15 minutes before serving. **Yield:** 10-12 servings.

Cranberry Wild Rice Pilaf

This wonderful, moist side dish is perfect for the holidays or anytime a meal requires a special touch. Dried cranberries, currants and almonds add color and texture. —Pat Gardetta, Osage Beach, Missouri

   3/4 cup uncooked wild rice
     3 cups chicken broth
   1/2 cup medium pearl barley
   1/4 cup dried cranberries
   1/4 cup dried currants
     1 tablespoon butter
   1/3 cup sliced almonds, toasted

Rinse and drain rice; place in a saucepan. Add broth and bring to a boil. Reduce heat; cover and simmer for 10 minutes. Remove from the heat; stir in barley, cranberries, currants and butter. Spoon into a greased 1-1/2-qt. baking dish. Cover and bake at 325° for 55 minutes or until liquid is absorbed and rice is tender. Add almonds and fluff with a fork. **Yield:** 6-8 servings.

Deluxe Corn Bread Stuffing

When my husband and I were newlyweds and far from family, we invited some of our friends over for a Thanksgiving feast. I searched for stuffing recipes and combined several to create this pleasing one. —Pamela Rickman, Valdosta, Georgia

     6 cups crumbled corn bread
     2 cups white bread cubes, toasted
     1 cup chopped pecans
   1/4 cup minced fresh parsley
     1 teaspoon dried thyme
   1/2 teaspoon rubbed sage
   1/2 teaspoon salt
   1/2 teaspoon pepper
     1 pound bulk pork sausage
     2 tablespoons butter
     2 large tart apples, diced
     1 cup diced celery
     1 medium onion, finely chopped
1-3/4 to 2-1/4 cups chicken broth

In a large bowl, combine bread, pecans and seasonings; set aside. In a large skillet over medium heat, cook and crumble sausage until no longer pink; remove with a slotted spoon to drain on paper towels. Add butter to drippings; saute apples, celery and onion until tender. Add to bread mixture. Stir in sausage and enough broth to moisten.

Spoon into a greased 3-qt. baking dish; cover and bake at 350° for 45 minutes. Uncover and bake for 10 minutes. Or use to stuff a turkey; bake according to recipe. **Yield:** 10-12 servings (about 11 cups).

Stuffed Baked Potatoes

(Pictured on page 151)

These special potatoes are a hit with my whole family, from the smallest grandchild on up. I prepare them up to a week in advance, wrap them well and freeze. Their flavorful filling goes so nicely with your favorite meat dish —Marge Clark, West Lebanon, Indiana

     3 large baking potatoes (1 pound *each*)
1-1/2 teaspoons vegetable oil, optional
   1/2 cup sliced green onions
   1/2 cup butter, *divided*
   1/2 cup half-and-half cream
   1/2 cup sour cream
     1 teaspoon salt
   1/2 teaspoon white pepper
     1 cup (4 ounces) shredded cheddar cheese
Paprika

Rub potatoes with oil if desired; pierce with a fork. Bake at 400° for 1 hour and 20 minutes or until tender. Allow potatoes to cool to the touch. Cut potatoes in half lengthwise; carefully scoop out pulp, leaving a thin shell. Place pulp in a large bowl.

Saute onions in 1/4 cup butter until tender. Add to potato pulp along with cream, sour cream, salt and pepper. Beat until smooth. Fold in cheese. Stuff potato shells and place in a 13-in. x 9-in. x 2-in. baking pan. Melt remaining butter; drizzle over the potatoes. Sprinkle with paprika. Bake at 350° for 20-30 minutes or until heated through. **Yield:** 6 servings.

Editor's Note: Potatoes may be stuffed ahead of time and refrigerated or frozen. Allow additional time for reheating.

Cherry Almond Mousse Pie, page 232

Dazzling
Desserts

Cranberry Betty

(Pictured below)

For a tart winter dessert, this one is hard to beat. We love the way the sweet apples and brown sugar complement the tangy cranberries. Topped off with the lemon sauce, it's a winner!
—Leona Cullen
Melrose, Massachusetts

    4 cups soft bread crumbs
    6 tablespoons butter, *divided*
    5 cups sliced peeled tart apples (4 to 5 large)
    1 cup packed brown sugar
  3/4 teaspoon ground nutmeg
    2 cups fresh *or* frozen cranberries
LEMON SAUCE:
  1/2 cup sugar
    1 tablespoon cornstarch
Pinch salt
    1 cup water
    1 teaspoon grated lemon peel
    2 tablespoons lemon juice
    2 tablespoons butter

In a skillet, brown the bread crumbs in 3 tablespoons butter. Place half the apples in a greased 8-in. square baking dish. Combine the brown sugar and nutmeg; sprinkle half over apples. Top with half of the bread crumbs. Dot with half of the remaining butter. Place the cranberries on top. Layer with remaining apples, brown sugar mixture, bread crumbs and butter. Cover and bake at 350° for 45 minutes. Uncover and bake 15-20 minutes more or until fruit is tender.

For lemon sauce, combine sugar, cornstarch and salt in a saucepan; add water and lemon peel. Bring to a boil; cook for 2 minutes or until thickened. Remove from the heat; stir in lemon juice and butter until melted. Serve over warm Cranberry Betty. **Yield:** 6-8 servings.

Frozen Mud Pie

(Pictured above)

Here's one of those "looks like you fussed" desserts that is so easy it's become a standard for me. The cookie crust is a snap to make.
—Debbie Terenzini
Lusby, Maryland

1-1/2 cups crushed cream-filled chocolate sandwich
       cookies (about 15)
1-1/2 teaspoons sugar, optional
  1/4 cup butter, melted
    2 pints chocolate chip *or* coffee ice cream,
       softened
  1/4 cup chocolate syrup, *divided*
Additional cream-filled chocolate sandwich cookies,
  optional

In a bowl, combine cookie crumbs and sugar if desired. Stir in butter. Press onto the bottom and up the sides of an ungreased 9-in. pie plate. Refrigerate for 30 minutes.

Spoon 1 pint of ice cream into crust. Drizzle with half of the chocolate syrup; swirl with a knife. Carefully top with remaining ice cream. Drizzle with remaining syrup; swirl with a knife. Cover and freeze until firm. Remove from the freezer 10-15 minutes before serving. Garnish with whole cookies if desired. **Yield:** 8 servings.

Citrus Gingerbread

(Pictured below)

There are lots of orange and pecan trees here in Arizona. This is one of my favorite desserts.
—Margaret Pache, Mesa, Arizona

1/2	cup butter, softened
3/4	cup sugar
1	egg
2	cups all-purpose flour
1	teaspoon baking soda
1	teaspoon ground cinnamon
1/2	teaspoon ground ginger
1/2	teaspoon salt
3/4	cup buttermilk
3	tablespoons molasses
1	cup chopped sectioned oranges (without membrane)
1/2	cup chopped pecans

Confectioners' sugar and orange peel, optional

In a mixing bowl, cream butter and sugar. Add egg. Combine the flour, baking soda, cinnamon, ginger and salt; add to creamed mixture alternately with buttermilk. Stir in molasses. Fold in oranges and pecans. Pour into a greased 9-in. square baking pan.

Bake at 350° for 45-50 minutes or until a toothpick inserted near the center comes out clean. Cool completely. If desired, dust with confectioners' sugar and garnish with the orange peel. **Yield:** 9 servings.

Christmas Rice Pudding

(Pictured above)

My Swedish grandma made this every Christmas Eve and would always put one almond in the rice before serving. Whoever found the almond was supposed to get married next, according to tradition.
—Barbara Garfield, Jamestown, New York

2	cups water
1-3/4	cups uncooked long grain rice
4	cups milk
1-1/2	cups sugar
1/4	cup butter
1	teaspoon salt

Sliced almonds and ground cinnamon, optional

In a saucepan, combine the water and rice. Simmer for 10 minutes; add milk and bring to a boil. Reduce heat and simmer, uncovered, for 60-70 minutes or until rice is tender. Add sugar, butter and salt; mix well. Spoon into small bowls or dessert dishes. Garnish with almonds and sprinkle with cinnamon if desired. **Yield:** 6-8 servings.

Christmas Cheesecake

(Pictured at left)

With a cheery cherry topping and mint green garnish, this is the perfect dessert to top off a holiday dinner.
—Verna Arthur, Perkins, Oklahoma

- 1-1/2 cups graham cracker crumbs (about 24 squares)
- 6 tablespoons butter, melted
- 1 envelope unflavored gelatin
- 1/4 cup cold water
- 1/4 cup milk
- 1 package (8 ounces) cream cheese, softened
- 1/2 cup confectioners' sugar
- 2 teaspoons grated lemon peel
- 1 carton (8 ounces) frozen whipped topping, thawed, *divided*
- 1 can (21 ounces) cherry pie filling

Combine crumbs and butter; press onto the bottom of a greased 9-in. springform pan. Chill 15 minutes. In a saucepan, combine gelatin and water; let stand for 1 minute. Add milk; cook and stir over low heat until gelatin is dissolved.

Beat cream cheese and sugar until light and fluffy. Add gelatin mixture and lemon peel; mix well. Chill until partially set. Fold in 2 cups whipped topping. Pour over crust. Chill until firm, at least 3 hours. Spread pie filling over gelatin layer. Top with remaining whipped topping. **Yield:** 10-12 servings.

Confetti Cream Cake

(Pictured at left)

Luscious layers of cake and creamy filling form this eye-popping dessert. If you're short on time, ready the filling ingredients a day ahead. Then assemble and frost right before serving.
—Jennie Moshier
Fresno, California

- 5 eggs
- 1 teaspoon vanilla extract
- 1 cup sugar
- 1 cup all-purpose flour
- 1/2 teaspoon baking powder
- 1/2 teaspoon salt

FILLING:
- 1 package (8 ounces) cream cheese, softened
- 1 cup sugar, *divided*
- 1 teaspoon vanilla extract

- 1/4 teaspoon ground cinnamon
- 1 cup (8 ounces) sour cream
- 1/2 cup finely chopped walnuts
- 1/2 cup flaked coconut, optional
- 1/3 cup chopped maraschino cherries
- 2 milk chocolate candy bars (1.55 ounces *each*), shaved *or* finely chopped
- 1-1/2 cups heavy whipping cream

In a mixing bowl, beat eggs and vanilla on high until foamy. Add sugar; beat until thick and lemon-colored. Combine flour, baking powder and salt; fold into egg mixture, a third at a time.

Pour into two greased and floured 9-in. round baking pans. Bake at 350° for 25-30 minutes or until cake springs back when lightly touched. Cool for 5 minutes; remove from pans to wire racks to cool completely.

In a mixing bowl, beat cream cheese, 2/3 cup sugar, vanilla and cinnamon until smooth. Stir in sour cream, nuts, coconut and cherries. Fold in chocolate. Beat cream and remaining sugar; set half aside. Fold remaining whipped cream into the cream cheese mixture.

Split each cake into two horizontal layers; spread a fourth of the cream cheese mixture on one layer. Repeat layers. Frost sides with reserved whipped cream. Refrigerate until serving. **Yield:** 10-12 servings.

Lady Lamington Cakes

(Pictured at left)

I learned to turn out these dainty no-bake cakes while living in Australia. Named for the wife of a past governor from "down under," they make a lip-smacking dessert.
—Dee Pufpaff, Raleigh, North Carolina

- 1 package (10-3/4 ounces) frozen pound cake
- 1/3 cup water
- 2 tablespoons butter
- 1/4 cup baking cocoa
- 2-1/2 cups confectioners' sugar
- 4 cups flaked coconut, toasted and chopped

Thaw cake; cut into 3/4-in. slices. Cut each slice into four fingers; set aside. In a microwave-safe bowl or saucepan, heat water and butter until butter is melted. Whisk in cocoa until dissolved. Whisk in sugar to make a thin glaze. Dip cakes into glaze to coat all sides; roll in coconut. Place on waxed paper to dry. Cover and refrigerate. **Yield:** 3 dozen.

Crunchy Baked Apples

(Pictured above)

We live in South Carolina's Piedmont area, which is famous for huge apple orchards. This is one of my family's favorite apple recipes. —Jayne King
Liberty, South Carolina

1/2 cup chopped walnuts
1/4 cup sugar
1/2 teaspoon ground cinnamon
1/4 cup packed brown sugar
1/4 cup raisins
  6 tablespoons butter, melted, *divided*
  4 medium tart apples
  1 lemon, halved
  4 short cinnamon sticks
3/4 cup apple juice

In a blender or food processor, grind walnuts and sugar. Add cinnamon and set aside. Combine the brown sugar, raisins and 2 tablespoons of butter; set aside. Core apples and peel the top two-thirds of each. Rub tops and sides with lemon; squeeze juice into centers. Brush apples with 2 tablespoons butter; press nut mixture evenly over peeled sides.

Place in an ungreased 9-in. square baking dish. Fill apples with raisin mixture. Place a cinnamon stick in each apple; drizzle with remaining butter. Pour apple juice around apples. Bake, uncovered, at 375° for 40-50 minutes or until the apples are tender. Cool apples for 15 minutes before serving. **Yield:** 4 servings.

Cranberry Sherbet

(Pictured below)

Tired of making the same holiday desserts year after year? Try this sweet-tart sherbet. It's a light and refreshing change of pace. —Heather Clement
Indian River, Ontario

  1 package (12 ounces) fresh *or* frozen cranberries
2-3/4 cups water, *divided*
  2 cups sugar
  1 envelope unflavored gelatin
1/2 cup orange juice

In a saucepan, combine cranberries and 2-1/2 cups of water. Bring to a boil; cook gently until all the cranberries have popped, about 10 minutes. Remove from the heat and cool slightly.

Press mixture through a sieve or food mill, reserving juice and discarding skins and seeds. In another saucepan, combine cranberry juice and sugar; cook over medium heat until the sugar dissolves. Remove from the heat and set aside.

Combine gelatin and remaining water; stir until softened. Combine the cranberry mixture, orange juice and gelatin; mix well. Pour into a 2-qt. container; freeze 4-5 hours or until mixture is slushy. Remove from freezer; beat with electric mixer until the sherbet is a bright pink color. Freeze until firm. **Yield:** about 6 cups.

Decadent Fudge Cake

Everyone I serve this to seems to love the rich flavor. Four types of chocolate make it decadent.
—*Anna Hogge, Yorktown, Virginia*

  1   cup butter, softened
1-1/2 cups sugar
  4   eggs
  1   cup buttermilk
 1/2 teaspoon baking soda
2-1/2 cups all-purpose flour
  2   bars (4 ounces *each*) German sweet chocolate, melted
  1   cup chocolate syrup
  2   teaspoons vanilla extract
1-1/4 cups miniature semisweet chocolate chips, *divided*
  4   squares (1 ounce *each*) white baking chocolate, chopped
  2   tablespoons plus 1 teaspoon shortening, *divided*

Cream butter in a large mixing bowl. Gradually mix in sugar. Add eggs, one at a time, beating well after each addition. Combine buttermilk and baking soda; add to creamed mixture alternately with flour, beginning and ending with flour. Add melted chocolate, chocolate syrup and vanilla. Stir in 1 cup miniature chocolate chips. Pour into a greased and floured 10-in. fluted tube pan. Bake at 325° for 1 hour and 15 minutes or until a toothpick comes out clean. Immediately invert cake onto a serving plate; cool completely.

Meanwhile, in a microwave, melt white chocolate and 2 tablespoons shortening; stir until smooth. Cool slightly; drizzle over cake. Melt remaining chips and shortening in a microwave or small saucepan over low heat, stirring until smooth. Remove from the heat; cool slightly. Drizzle over white chocolate. **Yield:** 16-20 servings.

Ambrosia Dessert Bowl

(Pictured above right)

I'm happy to share this wonderful recipe that uses fresh oranges. I've had it a long time. It's nice to treat myself to this light, refreshing fruit bowl. —*Donna Morris Weirsdale, Florida*

 20   large marshmallows
  2   cups heavy whipping cream, *divided*
  2   tablespoons sugar
  2   teaspoons vanilla extract
 1/2 teaspoon almond extract
  1   can (20 ounces) crushed pineapple, well drained
  1   cup flaked coconut
  1   loaf (10-3/4 ounces) frozen pound cake, thawed and cubed (about 4 cups)
  5   to 6 large navel oranges, peeled and sectioned
 1/4 cup slivered almonds, toasted

Place marshmallows and 1/4 cup cream in the top of a double boiler or microwave; heat over boiling water or microwave until the marshmallows are melted and the mixture is smooth. Cool completely.

Meanwhile, whip the remaining cream until thick. Add sugar. Fold into marshmallow mixture. Fold in extracts, pineapple and coconut.

Place half of the pound cake cubes in the bottom of a 2-1/2- to 3-qt. clear glass bowl. Top with half of the orange sections. Top with half of the cream mixture. Repeat layers. Sprinkle with almonds. Chill until serving. **Yield:** 10-12 servings.

Easy Greasing

Save the paper wrapping from sticks of butter and store them in the freezer. When a recipe calls for a greased pan, rub the pan with one of the wrappings.

Peanut Butter Cheese Torte

(Pictured above)

This dessert has long been a favorite with my family. I especially like the fact it requires no baking—and who doesn't like the combination of peanut butter and chocolate? —Ruth Blair, Waukesha, Wisconsin

CRUST:
- 1 cup graham cracker crumbs
- 1/4 cup packed brown sugar
- 1/4 cup butter, melted
- 1/2 cup finely chopped peanuts

FILLING:
- 2 cups creamy peanut butter
- 2 packages (8 ounces *each*) cream cheese, softened
- 2 cups sugar
- 2 tablespoons butter, softened
- 2 teaspoons vanilla extract
- 1-1/2 cups heavy whipping cream, whipped

CHOCOLATE TOPPING:
- 4 ounces semisweet chocolate chips
- 3 tablespoons plus 2 teaspoons hot brewed coffee

Coarsely chopped peanuts, optional

Combine all crust ingredients. Press into the bottom and halfway up the sides of a 10-in. springform pan. Chill. For filling, beat peanut butter, cream cheese, sugar, butter and vanilla in a large mixing bowl on high until smooth, about 2 minutes. Fold in whipped cream. Gently spoon into crust; refrigerate 6 hours or overnight. For topping, melt chocolate with coffee until smooth. Spread over chilled torte. Refrigerate until firm, about 30 minutes. Garnish with chopped peanuts if desired. **Yield:** 14-16 servings.

Maple Biscuit Dessert

(Pictured below)

These biscuits have been made by the women in my family for a long time. We use the maple syrup we boil each sugaring season from the trees on our land.
—Leslie Malter, Waterbury, Vermont

- 2 cups all-purpose flour
- 1 tablespoon baking powder
- 1/2 teaspoon salt
- 1/4 cup shortening
- 3/4 cup milk
- 1-1/2 cups maple syrup

In a bowl, combine flour, baking powder and salt; cut in shortening until mixture resembles coarse crumbs. Add milk; stir just until moistened. Turn onto a lightly floured surface; roll to 1/2-in. thickness. Cut with a 2-in. biscuit cutter.

Pour syrup into an 11-in. x 7-in. x 2-in. baking dish. Place biscuits on top of syrup. Bake at 450° for 12-15 minutes or until biscuits are golden brown. **Yield:** 10-12 servings.

Chocolate Almond Cheesecake

(Pictured above)

My family enjoys a good meal, but we all save room for dessert when this cheesecake is part of the menu. Its rich chocolate flavor is so satisfying when we're craving something sweet and creamy. —Jeri Dobrowski
Beach, North Dakota

- 1-1/4 **cups graham cracker crumbs**
- 1-1/2 **cups sugar,** *divided*
- 1/2 **cup plus 2 tablespoons baking cocoa,** *divided*
- 1/4 **cup butter, melted**
- 2 **packages (8 ounces** *each***) cream cheese, softened**
- 1 **cup (8 ounces) sour cream**
- 3 **eggs**
- 1-1/2 **teaspoons almond extract,** *divided*
- 1 **cup heavy whipping cream**
- 1/4 **cup confectioners' sugar**
- 1/4 **cup sliced almonds, toasted**

Combine crumbs, 1/4 cup sugar, 2 tablespoons cocoa and butter; mix well. Press into the bottom of a 9-in. springform pan; chill. In a mixing bowl, beat the cream cheese, sour cream and remaining sugar until smooth. Add eggs, one at a time, beating well after each addition. Stir in 1 teaspoon of extract and remaining cocoa. Pour into crust.

Bake at 350° for 45-50 minutes or until the center is almost set. Cool completely. Refrigerate at least 8 hours. In a mixing bowl, whip cream until it mounds slightly. Add confectioners' sugar and remaining extract; continue whipping until soft peaks form. Spread evenly over cheesecake. Sprinkle with almonds. Store in refrigerator. **Yield:** 12 servings.

Christmas Special Fruitcake

(Pictured below)

I've made this quick and easy fruitcake many times through the years, giving it to family and friends for Christmas gifts. —Violet Cooper
Port Allegany, Pennsylvania

- 3 **cups coarsely chopped Brazil nuts** *or* **other nuts (walnuts, pecans** *or* **hazelnuts)**
- 1 **pound pitted dates, coarsely chopped**
- 1 **cup halved maraschino cherries**
- 3/4 **cup all-purpose flour**
- 3/4 **cup sugar**
- 1/2 **teaspoon baking powder**
- 1/2 **teaspoon salt**
- 3 **eggs**
- 1 **teaspoon vanilla extract**

In a mixing bowl, combine nuts, dates and cherries. In another bowl, stir together flour, sugar, baking powder and salt; add to nut mixture, stirring until nuts and fruit are well-coated. Beat eggs until foamy; stir in vanilla. Fold into nut mixture. Mix well.

Pour into a greased and waxed paper-lined 9-in. x 5-in. x 3-in. loaf pan. Bake at 300° for 1 hour and 45 minutes. Cool 10 minutes in pan before removing to a wire rack. **Yield:** 24 servings.

Top to bottom: Cranberry
Bundt Cake and Frozen
Pumpkin Dessert

Cranberry Bundt Cake

(Pictured at left)

Cranberry sauce gives this moist cake its pretty swirled look. Serve slices for dessert after dinner.
—*Lucile Cline, Wichita, Kansas*

- 3/4 **cup butter, softened**
- 1-1/2 **cups sugar**
- 3 **eggs**
- 1-1/2 **teaspoons almond extract**
- 3 **cups all-purpose flour**
- 1-1/2 **teaspoons baking powder**
- 1-1/2 **teaspoons baking soda**
- 1/2 **teaspoon salt**
- 1-1/2 **cups (12 ounces) sour cream**
- 1 **can (16 ounces) whole-berry cranberry sauce**
- 1/2 **cup finely chopped pecans**

ICING:
- 3/4 **cup confectioners' sugar**
- 4-1/2 **teaspoons water**
- 1/2 **teaspoon almond extract**

In a large mixing bowl, cream butter and sugar. Add eggs, one at a time, beating well after each addition. Stir in extract. Combine the flour, baking powder, baking soda and salt; add to the creamed mixture alternately with sour cream, beating well after each addition. Spoon a third of the batter into a greased and floured 10-in. fluted tube pan. Top with a third of the cranberry sauce. Repeat layers twice. Sprinkle with pecans.

Bake at 350° for 65-70 minutes or until a toothpick inserted comes out clean. Cool for 10 minutes before removing from pan to a wire rack. Combine icing ingredients until smooth; drizzle over warm cake. **Yield:** 12-16 servings.

Frozen Pumpkin Dessert

(Pictured at left)

This ice cream dessert can be prepared and frozen weeks in advance. I've found it has more mass appeal than traditional pumpkin pie.
—*Susan Bennett Edmond, Oklahoma*

- 1 **can (15 ounces) solid-pack pumpkin**
- 3/4 **cup sugar**
- 1 **teaspoon vanilla extract**
- 1/2 **teaspoon salt**
- 1/4 **teaspoon ground ginger**
- 1/4 **teaspoon ground nutmeg**
- 1/8 **to 1/4 teaspoon ground cloves**
- 2 **quarts vanilla ice cream, softened**
- 1 **cup finely chopped walnuts**

In a large mixing bowl, combine the pumpkin, sugar, vanilla, salt, ginger, nutmeg and cloves. Fold in ice cream. Transfer to a greased 13-in. x 9-in. x 2-in. dish. Sprinkle with walnuts. Cover and freeze overnight. Remove from the freezer 10 minutes before serving. Cut into squares. **Yield:** 16-20 servings.

Cherry-Lemon Icebox Pie

This recipe makes a nice and refreshing finish to a heavy meal. —*Mary Weller, Twin Lake, Michigan*

- 1 **can (14 ounces) sweetened condensed milk**
- 1/2 **cup lemon juice**
- 1/2 **teaspoon vanilla extract**
- 1/2 **teaspoon almond extract**
- 1/2 **cup heavy whipping cream**
- 1 **pastry shell (9 inches), baked**
- 1 **can (21 ounces) cherry pie filling**

In a bowl, combine milk, juice and extracts; stir until thickened, about 2 minutes. Beat cream until stiff; fold into milk mixture. Pour into pastry shell. Refrigerate 10 minutes; top with pie filling. Chill at least 2 hours or overnight. **Yield:** 6-8 servings.

Strawberry Cloud

Serve this in individual dessert cups or parfait glasses to dress up this sweet treat for guests. —*Patricia Kile Greentown, Pennsylvania*

- 1 **package (3 ounces) strawberry-flavored gelatin**
- 1 **package (3 ounces) cook-and-serve vanilla pudding mix**
- 2-1/2 **cups water**
- 1 **carton (8 ounces) frozen whipped topping, thawed**

In a saucepan over medium heat, cook and stir gelatin, pudding mix and water until mixture boils, about 15 minutes. Cool until partially set; fold in whipped topping. Spoon into a bowl or individual dishes or parfait glasses. Chill until ready to serve. **Yield:** 6-8 servings.

Coconut Cream Pie

(Pictured above)

This is my own recipe for a pie that I make often. It's been a family-favorite dessert since the '40s, when I made several of these pies to serve a threshing crew of 21 men! —Vera Moffitt, Oskaloosa, Kansas

```
    3/4  cup sugar
      3  tablespoons all-purpose flour
    1/8  teaspoon salt
      3  cups milk
      3  eggs, beaten
  1-1/2  cups flaked coconut, toasted, divided
      1  tablespoon butter
  1-1/2  teaspoons vanilla extract
      1  pastry shell (9 inches), baked
```

In a medium saucepan, combine the sugar, flour and salt. Stir in milk; cook and stir over medium-high heat until thickened and bubbly. Reduce the heat; cook and stir 2 minutes longer.

Remove from the heat; gradually stir about 1 cup of hot mixture into beaten eggs. Return all to saucepan; cook and stir over medium heat until nearly boiling. Reduce heat; cook and stir about 2 minutes more (do not boil).

Remove from the heat; stir in 1 cup coconut, butter and vanilla. Pour into pie shell; sprinkle with remaining coconut. Chill for several hours before serving. Refrigerate leftovers. **Yield:** 6-8 servings.

Cherry Cream Torte

(Pictured below and on front cover)

When you set this gorgeous dessert on the table, your guests will sing your praises. You're the only one who has to know how simple it is to prepare. —Mary Anne McWhirter
Pearland, Texas

```
      2  packages (3 ounces each) ladyfingers
      2  tablespoons white grape or apple juice
      1  package (8 ounces) cream cheese,
         softened
    2/3  cup sugar
      1  teaspoon almond extract, divided
      2  cups heavy whipping cream, whipped
      1  can (21 ounces) cherry pie filling
```
Toasted sliced almonds, mint leaves and
additional whipped cream

Split ladyfingers lengthwise; brush with juice. Place a layer of ladyfingers around the sides and on the bottom of a lightly greased 9-in. springform pan. In a mixing bowl, beat cream cheese until smooth; add sugar and 1/2 teaspoon extract. Beat on medium for 1 minute. Fold in whipped cream. Spread half over crust.

Arrange remaining ladyfingers in a spoke-like fashion. Spread evenly with the remaining cream cheese mixture. Cover and chill overnight.

Combine the pie filling and remaining extract; spread over the cream cheese layer. Refrigerate for at least 2 hours. To serve, remove sides of pan. Garnish with almonds, mint leaves and whipped cream. **Yield:** 16-18 servings.

Layered Toffee Cake

(Pictured below)

This is a quick and yummy way to dress up a purchased angel food cake. To keep the plate clean while assembling this dessert, cut two half circles of waxed paper to place under the bottom layer and remove them after frosting the cake and sprinkling on the toffee.
—Pat Squire, Alexandria, Virginia

  2 **cups heavy whipping cream**
1/2 **cup caramel *or* butterscotch ice cream topping**
1/2 **teaspoon vanilla extract**
  1 **prepared angel food cake (16 ounces)**
  9 **Heath candy bars (1.4 ounces *each*), chopped**

In a mixing bowl, beat cream just until it begins to thicken. Gradually add ice cream topping and vanilla, beating until soft peaks form.

Cut cake horizontally into three layers. Place the bottom layer on a serving plate; spread with 1 cup cream mixture and sprinkle with 1/2 cup candy bar. Repeat. Place top layer on cake; frost top and sides with remaining cream mixture and sprinkle with the remaining candy bar. Store in the refrigerator. **Yield:** 12-14 servings.

Chocolate Truffle Pie

(Pictured above)

I discovered a fast recipe for a delectable chocolate mousse some years ago and thought it might make a good filling for a pie. The chocolate lovers in our family endorse this scrumptious dessert, saying that it "melts in your mouth!" —Keri Scofield Lawson
Fullerton, California

    2 **cups (12 ounces) semisweet chocolate chips**
1-1/2 **cups heavy whipping cream, *divided***
  1/4 **cup confectioners' sugar**
    1 **tablespoon vanilla extract**
    1 **chocolate cookie crust (8 *or* 9 inches)**
**Whipped cream and chocolate-covered peppermint
  candies, optional**

In a microwave-safe dish, combine the chocolate chips and 1/2 cup of cream; cook on high for 1-2 minutes, stirring every 30 seconds until smooth. Cool to room temperature. Stir in sugar and vanilla; set aside. In a small mixing bowl, beat remaining cream until soft peaks form. Beat in chocolate mixture on high, one-third at a time; mix well. Spoon into crust. Refrigerate for at least 3 hours. Garnish with whipped cream and candies if desired. **Yield:** 8-10 servings.

Fudge Pudding Cake

(Pictured above)

I usually pop this cake in the oven just as we're sitting down to dinner. When we're through eating the main course, the dessert is ready! —Roxanne Bender
Waymart, Pennsylvania

  3/4 **cup sugar**
    1 **tablespoon butter, softened**
  1/2 **cup milk**
    1 **cup all-purpose flour**
    2 **tablespoons baking cocoa**
    1 **teaspoon baking powder**
  1/4 **teaspoon salt**
  1/2 **cup chopped walnuts**
TOPPING:
  1/2 **cup sugar**
  1/2 **cup packed brown sugar**
  1/4 **cup baking cocoa**
 1-1/4 **cups boiling water**
Ice cream, optional

In a mixing bowl, beat sugar, butter and milk. Combine flour, cocoa, baking powder and salt; stir into the sugar mixture. Add walnuts. Pour into a greased 9-in. square baking pan. For topping, combine sugars and cocoa; sprinkle over batter. Pour water over all. Do not stir.

Bake at 350° for 30 minutes. Cool for 10 minutes. Spoon some of the fudge sauce over each serving; top with ice cream if desired. **Yield:** 9 servings.

Layered Dessert

High on our list of long-time favorites, this fluffy, fruity treat continues to hold its own against new dessert recipes I try. —Pat Habiger, Spearville, Kansas

  1 **cup crushed vanilla wafers,** *divided*
  1 **package (3 ounces) cook-and-serve vanilla pudding mix**
  2 **medium ripe bananas,** *divided*
  1 **package (3 ounces) strawberry gelatin**
  1 **cup whipped topping**

Spread half of the crushed wafers in the bottom of a greased 8-in. square pan. Prepare pudding mix according to package directions; spoon hot pudding over crumbs. Slice one banana; place over pudding. Top with remaining crumbs. Chill for 1 hour.

Meanwhile, prepare gelatin according to package directions; chill for 30 minutes or until partially set. Pour over crumbs. Slice remaining banana and place over gelatin. Spread whipped topping over all. Chill for 2 hours. **Yield:** 9 servings.

Fruit-Topped Almond Cream

This recipe makes a refreshing dessert. It's delicious with fresh berries, but it can be made all year using whatever fruit is available. —Donna Friedrich
Fishkill, New York

  1 **package (3.4 ounces) instant French vanilla pudding mix**
 2-1/2 **cups cold milk**
  1 **cup heavy whipping cream**
  1/2 **to 3/4 teaspoon almond extract**
  3 **cups assorted fruit (strawberries, grapes, raspberries, blueberries, mandarin oranges)**

In a large mixing bowl, combine pudding mix and milk. Beat on low speed for 2 minutes; set aside. In a small mixing bowl, beat cream and extract until stiff peaks form. Fold into pudding. Spoon into a shallow 2-qt. serving dish. Chill. Top with fruit just before serving. **Yield:** 8 servings.

Pumpkin Pecan Pie

(Pictured below)

Whenever we have family gatherings during the holidays, this is one of the most-requested desserts. It's a nice variation on traditional pumpkin pie.
— *Linda Frew, Cooper, Texas*

3/4 cup packed brown sugar
1/2 teaspoon ground cinnamon
1/4 teaspoon salt
  1 cup canned pumpkin
  3 eggs, lightly beaten
1/2 cup dark corn syrup
  1 teaspoon vanilla extract
  1 unbaked pastry shell (9 inches)
3/4 cup coarsely chopped pecans
About 20 pecan halves
Whipped cream, optional

In a large mixing bowl, combine brown sugar, cinnamon and salt. Add pumpkin, eggs, corn syrup and vanilla; beat well. Pour into the pastry shell. Sprinkle with chopped pecans. Place pecan halves around the outer edge of filling.

Bake at 425° for 15 minutes. Reduce heat to 350°; bake 25 more minutes or until a knife inserted near the center comes out clean. Cool. Serve with whipped cream if desired. **Yield:** 6-8 servings.

Holiday Pumpkin Pound Cake

(Pictured above)

Instead of traditional pumpkin pie, I bake this scrumptious cake for Thanksgiving. As it bakes, the comforting spicy aroma fills the house.
— *Virginia Loew Leesburg, Florida*

2-1/2 cups sugar
    1 cup vegetable oil
    3 eggs
    3 cups all-purpose flour
    2 teaspoons baking soda
    1 teaspoon ground cinnamon
    1 teaspoon ground nutmeg
  1/2 teaspoon salt
  1/4 teaspoon ground cloves
    1 can (15 ounces) solid-pack pumpkin
Confectioners' sugar

In a mixing bowl, blend sugar and oil. Add eggs, one at a time, beating well after each addition. Combine flour, baking soda, cinnamon, nutmeg, salt and cloves; add to egg mixture alternately with pumpkin. Pour into a greased 12-cup fluted tube pan.

Bake at 350° for 60-65 minutes or until a toothpick inserted near the center comes out clean. Cool for 10 minutes before inverting onto a wire rack. Remove pan; cool completely. Dust with confectioners' sugar. **Yield:** 12-16 servings.

Top to bottom: Gingerbread Trifle,
Gingerbread Men and Gingerbread Cake

Gingerbread Cake

(Pictured at left)

I drizzle an easy orange sauce over homemade ginger-bread for an old-fashioned holiday dessert. Cut just the number of squares needed, so you can use the extra cake to make the two other gingerbread treats on this page. —Shannon Sides, Selma, Alabama

  1/2 **cup butter-flavored shortening**
  1/3 **cup sugar**
    1 **cup molasses**
  3/4 **cup water**
    1 **egg**
2-1/3 **cups all-purpose flour**
    1 **teaspoon baking soda**
    1 **teaspoon ground ginger**
    1 **teaspoon ground cinnamon**
  3/4 **teaspoon salt**
ORANGE SAUCE:
    1 **cup confectioners' sugar**
    2 **tablespoons orange juice**
  1/2 **teaspoon grated orange peel**

In a large mixing bowl, cream shortening and sugar. Add the molasses, water and egg. Combine the flour, baking soda, ginger, cinnamon and salt; add to creamed mixture and beat until combined. Pour into a greased 15-in. x 10-in. x 1-in. baking pan.

Bake at 350° for 18-22 minutes or until a toothpick inserted near the center comes out clean. Cool on a wire rack. In a bowl, combine the sauce ingredients. Serve with cake. **Yield:** 4 servings with sauce plus leftovers.

Gingerbread Men

(Pictured at left)

Cookie cutters work well to form these fun and festive fellows from our Test Kitchen. Kids of all ages will enjoy spreading the cutouts with soft, sweet white chocolate frosting, then giving them character by decorating with colorful store-bought candies.

    1 **piece (10 inches x 7 inches) Gingerbread Cake (recipe above)**
  1/4 **cup butter, softened**
1-1/2 **squares (1-1/2 ounces) white baking chocolate, melted**

  1/2 **cup confectioners' sugar**
Assorted candies

Using a 3-1/2-in. gingerbread man cookie cutter, cut out six men from the gingerbread cake. In a small mixing bowl, combine the butter, chocolate and confectioners' sugar; beat for 2 minutes or until light and fluffy. Frost gingerbread men and decorate with candies as desired. **Yield:** 6 gingerbread men.

Gingerbread Trifle

(Pictured at left)

This tasty dessert was a hit when I served it to our Bible study group. It's a wonderful blend of flavors and a great ending to holiday meals. If you don't have leftover gingerbread, bake some from a boxed mix to assemble this trifle. —Betty Kleberger, Florissant, Missouri

    2 **cups cold milk**
    1 **package (3.4 ounces) instant French vanilla pudding mix**
    7 **cups cubed Gingerbread Cake (recipe at left)**
  3/4 **cup English toffee bits *or* almond brickle chips**
    1 **carton (8 ounces) frozen whipped topping, thawed**
    1 **maraschino cherry**

In a mixing bowl, beat milk and pudding mix on low speed for 2 minutes. In a 2-qt. serving bowl, layer half of the cake cubes and pudding. Sprinkle with 1/2 cup toffee bits. Top with remaining cake and pudding.

Spread whipped topping over the top; sprinkle with remaining toffee bits. Garnish with the cherry. **Yield:** 8-10 servings.

Ginger Facts

Gingerroot is characterized by its strong sweet, yet woodsy smell. It is tan in color with white to creamy-yellow flesh that can be coarse yet stringy.

Ginger was used in ancient times as a food preservative and a remedy for digestive problems. Greeks would eat ginger wrapped in bread to treat digestive problems. Eventually ginger was added to the bread dough creating gingerbread... a treat many around the globe enjoy today!

Baked Cranberry Pudding

(Pictured below)

This is an old-fashioned pudding that's a cranberry lover's delight. Serve warm topped with whipped cream for an elegant look or in bowls with rich cream poured over for a homey touch.
—*Lucy Meyring*
Walden, Colorado

- 1 **cup packed brown sugar**
- 2 **eggs,** *separated*
- 1/2 **cup heavy whipping cream**
- 2 **teaspoons vanilla extract**
- 1 **teaspoon ground cinnamon**
- 1/2 **teaspoon ground nutmeg**
- 1-1/2 **cups all-purpose flour**
- 3 **tablespoons grated orange peel**
- 1 **teaspoon baking powder**
- 1/2 **teaspoon cream of tartar,** *divided*
- 1/8 **teaspoon salt**
- 3 **cups coarsely chopped cranberries**
- 1/4 **cup butter, melted**

TOPPING:
- 1-1/2 **cups sugar**
- 1/2 **cup orange juice**
- 2-1/2 **cups whole cranberries**

Sweetened whipped cream, optional

In a bowl, combine brown sugar and egg yolks. Add whipping cream, vanilla, cinnamon and nutmeg; set aside. In a large bowl, combine flour, orange peel, baking powder, 1/4 teaspoon cream of tartar and salt. Add cranberries and stir to com-

pletely coat. Add brown sugar mixture and butter; mix well. (Batter will be very stiff.) Beat egg whites until foamy. Add remaining cream of tartar; beat until soft peaks form. Fold into batter.

Pour into a greased 9-in. springform pan. Bake at 350° for 45-50 minutes or until a toothpick inserted near center comes out clean.

Meanwhile, for topping, bring sugar and orange juice to a boil in a saucepan. Cook for 3 minutes or until sugar dissolves. Reduce the heat; add the cranberries and simmer 6-8 minutes or until berries pop. Remove from the heat and cover.

When pudding tests done, place springform pan on a jelly roll pan. Spoon warm cranberry sauce evenly over top. Return to the oven for 10 minutes. Cool for 10 minutes before removing sides of springform pan. Cool at least 1 hour or overnight. Before serving, reheat at 350° for 10 minutes. Serve with whipped cream if desired. **Yield:** 8-10 servings.

Chocolate Potato Cake

(Pictured above)

Potatoes are the secret ingredient in this moist, rich chocolate cake with a firm texture. It's wonderful for a special occasion. The white fluffy frosting goes perfectly with the dark chocolate cake.
—*Jill Kinder*
Richlands, Virginia

- 3/4 **cup butter, softened**
- 1-1/2 **cups sugar,** *divided*

4 eggs, *separated*
1 cup hot mashed potatoes (without milk, butter or seasoning)
1-1/2 cups all-purpose flour
1/2 cup baking cocoa
2 teaspoons baking powder
1 teaspoon ground cinnamon
1/2 teaspoon salt
1/2 teaspoon ground nutmeg
1/4 teaspoon ground cloves
1 cup milk
1 teaspoon vanilla extract
1 cup chopped nuts
FLUFFY WHITE FROSTING:
2 egg whites
1-1/2 cups sugar
1/3 cup water
2 teaspoons light corn syrup
1/8 teaspoon salt
1 teaspoon vanilla extract

In a mixing bowl, cream butter and 1 cup sugar. Add egg yolks; beat well. Add potatoes and mix thoroughly. Combine flour, cocoa, baking powder, cinnamon, salt, nutmeg and cloves; add to creamed mixture alternately with milk, beating until smooth. Stir in vanilla and nuts.

In a mixing bowl, beat egg whites until foamy. Gradually add remaining sugar; beat until stiff peaks form. Fold into batter. Pour into a greased and floured 13-in. x 9-in. x 2-in. baking pan. Bake at 350° for 40-45 minutes or until cake tests done. Cool.

Combine first five frosting ingredients in top of a double boiler. Beat with electric mixer for 1 minute. Place over boiling water; beat constantly for 7 minutes, scraping sides of pan occasionally. Remove from heat. Add vanilla; beat 1 minute. Frost cake. **Yield:** 16-20 servings.

Creamy Peach Pie

Sweet peaches are highlighted in this creamy pie. It's wonderful! —*Eva Thiessen, Cecil Lake, British Columbia*

1 package (3 ounces) peach gelatin
2/3 cup boiling water
1 cup vanilla ice cream
1 carton (8 ounces) frozen whipped topping, thawed
1 cup diced peeled fresh peaches
1 deep-dish pastry shell (9 inches), baked
Sliced peaches and mint, optional

In a large bowl, dissolve gelatin in boiling water; stir in ice cream until melted and smooth. Add whipped topping and mix well. Fold in peaches. Pour into pastry shell. Chill until firm, about 3 hours. Garnish with peaches and mint if desired. **Yield:** 6-8 servings.

Fruit 'n' Nut Cherry Pie

(Pictured below)

It's a pleasure to serve this festive ruby-colored pie, which tastes as good as it looks! The filling is an irresistible combination of fruits and nuts.
—*Ruth Andrewson, Leavenworth, Washington*

1 can (21 ounces) cherry pie filling
1 can (20 ounces) crushed pineapple, undrained
3/4 cup sugar
1 tablespoon cornstarch
1 teaspoon red food coloring, optional
4 medium firm bananas, sliced
1/2 cup chopped pecans *or* walnuts
2 pastry shells (9 inches), baked
Whipped cream

In a saucepan, combine pie filling, pineapple, sugar, cornstarch and food coloring if desired; mix well. Bring to a boil over medium heat, stirring constantly. Cook and stir for 2 minutes. Cool. Fold in bananas and nuts. Pour into pie shells. Refrigerate for 2-3 hours. Garnish with whipped cream. Store in the refrigerator. **Yield:** 12-16 servings.

Cranberry Walnut Tart

(Pictured above)

People always tell me how much they like the combination of a tart cranberry taste and the crunchy walnut texture in this dessert. It's great for the holidays.
—Beverly Mix, Missoula, Montana

TART SHELL:
    1 cup all-purpose flour
  1/3 cup sugar
Dash salt
    5 tablespoons cold butter
    1 egg, lightly beaten
  1/2 tablespoon water, optional
FILLING:
  1/2 cup sugar
  1/2 cup light corn syrup
    2 eggs, lightly beaten
    2 tablespoons butter, melted
    1 teaspoon grated orange peel
    1 cup walnut halves
    1 cup fresh *or* frozen cranberries

In a large bowl, combine flour, sugar and salt. Cut in butter until mixture resembles coarse crumbs. Add egg and stir lightly with fork just until mixture forms a ball, adding the water if necessary. Wrap in waxed paper and refrigerate at least 1 hour. Grease a 9-in. fluted tart pan with removable bottom.

Press chilled pastry into the bottom and up the sides of pan. Line pastry shell with foil; fill with pie weights, raw rice or beans to prevent shrinkage. Bake at 375° for 10 minutes. Remove weights and bake another 5 minutes. Cool.

    Meanwhile, for filling, combine sugar, syrup, eggs, butter and peel in a large bowl; set aside. Place walnuts and cranberries in bottom of tart; pour sugar mixture into pan. Bake for 30-35 minutes or until crust is golden, edge of filling is firm and center is almost set. Cool on wire rack. Chill until serving. Store leftovers in the refrigerator. **Yield:** 12 servings.

Frosty Cherry Dessert

This quick-and-easy dessert has saved me when last-minute guests stop by around Christmas. It is cool and fruity, and it tastes wonderful.   *—Diane Hays*
Morris, Minnesota

    2 cans (8 ounces *each*) crushed pineapple, undrained
    1 can (21 ounces) cherry pie filling
    1 can (14 ounces) sweetened condensed milk
    1 carton (8 ounces) frozen whipped topping, optional

In a bowl, combine pineapple, pie filling and milk; fold in the whipped topping. Spread into a 13-in. x 9-in. x 2-in. baking dish that has been sprayed with nonstick cooking spray. Cover and freeze until firm. Garnish with cherries and whipped topping if desired. **Yield:** 12-16 servings.

Golden Lemon Glazed Cheesecake

(Pictured at right)

I've been serving this lemony cheesecake for years as a tasty treat at the open house gatherings we hold at our church during the holiday season.   *—Betty Jacques*
Hemet, California

CRUST:
 2-1/2 cups graham cracker crumbs (30 crackers)
  1/4 cup sugar

      10 tablespoons butter, melted
FILLING:
       3 packages (8 ounces *each*) cream cheese, softened
       3 eggs
  1-1/4 cups sugar
       3 tablespoons lemon juice
       1 teaspoon vanilla extract
       1 tablespoon grated lemon peel
GLAZE:
       1 lemon, sliced paper-thin
       3 cups water, *divided*
       1 cup sugar
       2 tablespoons plus 2 teaspoons cornstarch
   1/3 cup lemon juice

Combine crust ingredients; press onto the bottom and 2 in. up the sides of a 9-in. springform pan. Place pan on a baking sheet. Bake at 350° for 5 minutes. Cool.

In a mixing bowl, beat cream cheese until smooth. Add eggs, one at a time, beating well after each addition. Gradually add sugar, then lemon juice and vanilla. Mix well. Fold in lemon peel; pour into crust. Bake at 350° for 40 minutes. Cool to room temperature; refrigerate until thoroughly chilled, at least 4 hours.

For the glaze, remove any seeds from lemon slices. Reserve 1 slice for garnish; coarsely chop remaining slices. Place in a saucepan with 2 cups water. Bring to a boil; simmer, uncovered, for 15 minutes. Drain, reserving lemon pulp. In a saucepan, combine sugar and cornstarch; stir in remaining water, lemon juice and lemon pulp. Bring to a boil, stirring constantly, and boil 3 minutes. Refrigerate until cool, stirring occasionally. Pour over cheesecake and garnish with reserved lemon slice. Chill. **Yield:** 16 servings.

Pumpkin Sheet Cake
(Pictured above)

The pastor at our church usually cuts his message short on carry-in dinner days when he knows this sheet cake is waiting in the fellowship hall. (I think he prays for leftovers since he gets to take them home!) This moist cake travels well and is also easy to prepare.
—Nancy Baker, Boonville, Missouri

       1 can (16 ounces) solid-pack pumpkin
       2 cups sugar
       1 cup vegetable oil
       4 eggs
       2 cups all-purpose flour
       2 teaspoons baking soda
       1 teaspoon ground cinnamon
   1/2 teaspoon salt
FROSTING:
       5 tablespoons butter, softened
       1 package (3 ounces) cream cheese, softened
       1 teaspoon vanilla extract
  1-3/4 cups confectioners' sugar
       3 to 4 teaspoons milk
Chopped nuts

In a mixing bowl, beat pumpkin, sugar and oil. Add eggs; mix well. Combine flour, baking soda, cinnamon and salt; add to pumpkin mixture and beat until well blended. Pour into a greased 15-in. x 10-in. x 1-in. baking pan. Bake at 350° for 25-30 minutes or until a toothpick comes out clean. Cool.

For frosting, beat the butter, cream cheese and vanilla in a mixing bowl until smooth. Gradually add sugar; mix well. Add enough milk to reach desired spreading consistency. Frost cake. Sprinkle with nuts. **Yield:** 20-24 servings.

Top to bottom: Chocolate Mint Torte and Macadamia Berry Dessert

Chocolate Mint Torte

(Pictured at left)

This frozen treat comes together in a snap. I melt chocolate-covered mint candies and mix them into the creamy filling for refreshing flavor. A cookie-crumb crust and a sprinkling of extra mint candies make it fun any time of the year. —Joni Mehl, Grand Rapids, Michigan

```
27  cream-filled chocolate sandwich cookies, crushed
1/3 cup butter, melted
1/3 cup chocolate-covered mint candies
1/4 cup milk
 1  jar (7 ounces) marshmallow creme
 2  cups heavy whipping cream, whipped
```
Additional whipped cream and chocolate-covered mint candies

In a bowl, combine cookie crumbs and butter. Press onto the bottom and 1-1/2 in. up the sides of a greased 9-in. springform pan. Chill for at least 30 minutes.

In a small saucepan, heat mint candies and milk over low heat until mints are melted; stir until smooth. Cool for 10-15 minutes. Place marshmallow creme in a mixing bowl; gradually beat in mint mixture. Fold in whipped cream. Transfer to prepared crust. Cover and freeze until firm. May be frozen for up to 2 months.

Remove from the freezer about 30 minutes before serving. Remove sides of pan. Garnish with additional whipped cream and candies. **Yield:** 12 servings.

Editor's Note: This recipe was tested with Junior Mints.

Macadamia Berry Dessert

(Pictured at left)

My family and friends love this dessert. The crunchy nut crust and colorful filling make it special enough for guests. During the holidays, I substitute a can of whole-berry cranberry sauce for the raspberries. —Louise Watkins, Sparta, Wisconsin

```
 1  cup crushed vanilla wafers (about 32 wafers)
1/2 cup finely chopped macadamia nuts
1/4 cup butter, melted
 1  can (14 ounces) sweetened condensed milk
 3  tablespoons orange juice
 3  tablespoons lemon juice
```

```
 1  package (10 ounces) frozen sweetened
    raspberries, thawed
 1  carton (8 ounces) frozen whipped topping,
    thawed
```
Fresh raspberries and additional whipped topping, optional

Combine the wafer crumbs, nuts and butter. Press onto the bottom of a greased 9-in. springform pan. Bake at 375° for 8-10 minutes or until golden brown. Cool completely.

In a mixing bowl, beat the milk, orange juice and lemon juice on low speed until well blended. Add raspberries; beat on low until blended. Fold in whipped topping. Pour over the crust. Cover and freeze for 3 hours or until firm. May be frozen for up to 3 months.

Remove from the freezer 15 minutes before serving. Carefully run a knife around edge of pan to loosen. Remove sides of pan. Garnish with raspberries and whipped topping if desired. **Yield:** 12 servings.

Date Nut Log

My mother once served this dessert after a big holiday meal. We all thought it was delicious. —Carla Hodenfield, Mandan, North Dakota

```
2-1/2 cups graham cracker crumbs, (about 40
      squares), divided
5-1/3 cups miniature marshmallows
    8 ounces dates, chopped
    2 cups chopped walnuts
1-1/4 cups heavy whipping cream
```
Whipped cream, optional

In a bowl, combine 2 cups of graham cracker crumbs, marshmallows, dates and walnuts. Stir in whipping cream; mix thoroughly. Shape into a 14-in. x 3-in. log. Roll in remaining crumbs. Wrap tightly in plastic wrap or foil. Refrigerate at least 6 hours or overnight. Slice; garnish with whipped cream if desired. **Yield:** 10-12 servings.

About Dates
- Avoid buying dates that are sticky or have crystallized sugar on the surface.
- Fresh dates should be firm and springy and should have a fresh smell, not sour. Fresh dates should be kept in plastic bags in the refrigerator and will keep for several weeks.
- Dried dates should be firm, but not hard. they will keep for up to a year, refrigerated.

Fall Pear Pie

(Pictured below)

A wide slice of this festive fruity pie is a great end to a delicious meal. The mellow flavor of pears is a refreshing alternative to the more common pies for the holidays. It's nice to serve a dessert that's a little unexpected. —Ken Churches, San Andreas, California

    8 cups thinly sliced peeled pears
  3/4 cup sugar
  1/4 cup quick-cooking tapioca
  1/4 teaspoon ground nutmeg
Pastry for double-crust pie (9 inches)
    1 egg, lightly beaten
  1/4 cup heavy whipping cream, optional

In a large bowl, combine pears, sugar, tapioca and nutmeg. Line a pie plate with bottom pastry; add pear mixture. Roll out remaining pastry to fit top of pie; cut large slits in top. Place over filling; seal and flute edges. Brush with egg.

Bake at 375° for 55-60 minutes or until the pears are tender. Remove to a wire rack. Pour cream through slits if desired. **Yield:** 8 servings.

Quick Coconut Cream Pie

I've found a way to make coconut cream pie without a lot of fuss and still get terrific flavor. Using a convenient purchased crust, instant pudding and frozen whipped topping, I can enjoy an old-time dessert even when time is short. —Betty Claycomb
Alverton, Pennsylvania

    1 package (5.1 ounces) instant vanilla pudding mix
1-1/2 cups cold milk
    1 carton (8 ounces) frozen whipped topping,
       thawed, *divided*
  3/4 to 1 cup flaked coconut, toasted, *divided*
    1 pastry shell, baked *or* graham cracker crust
       (8 *or* 9 inches)

In a mixing bowl, beat pudding and milk on low speed for 2 minutes. Fold in half of the whipped topping and 1/2 to 3/4 cup of coconut. Pour into crust. Spread with remaining whipped topping; sprinkle with remaining coconut. Refrigerate until serving. **Yield:** 6-8 servings.

Apple Walnut Cake

(Pictured at right)

This moist cake is perfect for brunch. It gets its appeal from big chunks of sweet apples, nutty flavor and creamy frosting. —Renae Moncur, Burley, Idaho

  1-2/3 cups sugar
      2 eggs
    1/2 cup vegetable oil
      2 teaspoons vanilla extract
      2 cups all-purpose flour
      2 teaspoons baking soda
  1-1/2 teaspoons ground cinnamon
      1 teaspoon salt
    1/2 teaspoon ground nutmeg
      4 cups chopped unpeeled apples
      1 cup chopped walnuts
FROSTING:
      2 packages (3 ounces *each*) cream cheese, softened
      3 tablespoons butter, softened
      1 teaspoon vanilla extract
  1-1/2 cups confectioners' sugar

In a mixing bowl, beat sugar and eggs. Add oil and vanilla; mix well. Combine flour, baking soda, cinnamon, salt and nutmeg; gradually add to sugar mixture, mixing well. Stir in apples and walnuts. Pour into a greased and floured 13-in. x 9-in. x 2-in. baking pan. Bake at 350° for 50-55 minutes or until cake tests done. Cool on a wire rack.

For frosting, beat cream cheese, butter and vanilla in a mixing bowl. Gradually add confectioners' sugar until the frosting has reached desired spreading consistency. Frost cooled cake. **Yield:** 16-20 servings.

Pumpkin Ice Cream

This ice cream is as simple as opening a can, stirring and freezing. Plus, if you're like me and looking for a good way of using up your homegrown pumpkins, feel free to substitute fresh-picked for canned.
—Linda Young, Longmont, Colorado

      1 cup canned pumpkin
    1/4 teaspoon pumpkin pie spice

      1 quart vanilla ice cream, softened
Gingersnaps, optional

In a medium bowl, mix the pumpkin and pie spice until well blended. Stir in ice cream. Freeze until serving. Garnish with gingersnaps if desired. **Yield:** 4-6 servings.

Poor Man's Pecan Pie

This recipe's easy to make, and most of the ingredients are in everybody's cupboard. And it does really taste like pecan pie. We have it quite often, but it's tradition to have this pie during the holidays.
—Fay Harrington, Seneca, Missouri

      3 eggs
      1 cup sugar
      1 cup old-fashioned oats
    3/4 cup dark corn syrup
    1/2 cup flaked coconut
      2 tablespoons butter, melted
      1 teaspoon vanilla extract
      1 unbaked pastry shell (9 inches)
Whipped topping and toasted coconut, optional

In a bowl, combine the first seven ingredients; mix well. Pour into pastry shell. Bake at 375° for 15 minutes; reduce heat to 350°. Bake for 30-35 minutes or until a toothpick inserted near the center comes out clean. If necessary, cover edges of crust with foil to prevent overbrowning. Cool on a wire rack. Garnish with whipped topping and toasted coconut if desired. **Yield:** 8-10 servings.

Raisin Spice Cake

(Pictured above)

This nutty, golden cake is one of my mom's best. It's a wonderfully different use for pumpkin. It's bound to become a favorite with your family, too.
—Ruby Williams, Bogalusa, Louisiana

- 2 cups all-purpose flour
- 2 cups sugar
- 2 teaspoons pumpkin pie spice
- 2 teaspoons baking powder
- 1 teaspoon baking soda
- 1/2 teaspoon salt
- 4 eggs
- 1 can (16 ounces) solid-pack pumpkin
- 3/4 cup vegetable oil
- 2 cups bran cereal (not flakes)
- 1 cup chopped pecans
- 1 cup raisins
- Confectioners' sugar, optional

Combine flour, sugar, pumpkin pie spice, baking powder, baking soda and salt; set aside. In a large bowl, beat eggs. Add pumpkin and oil; stir in cereal just until moistened. Add dry ingredients and stir just until combined. Fold in pecans and raisins. Pour into a greased 10-in. tube pan. Bake at 350° for

60-65 minutes or until a toothpick inserted near the center comes out clean. Cool in pan for 10 minutes before removing to a wire rack to cool completely. Dust with confectioners' sugar before serving if desired. **Yield:** 12-16 servings.

Black Walnut Pie

(Pictured below)

Black walnuts are abundant here in the Ozarks. My aunt gave me this recipe and I think it's one of the best pies I've ever tasted. It's a pretty addition to any holiday table.
—Helen Holbrook, De Soto, Missouri

- 1 tablespoon plus 1/2 cup sugar, *divided*
- 1 tablespoon all-purpose flour
- 1 unbaked pastry shell (9 inches)
- 1 cup light corn syrup
- 1/2 cup packed brown sugar
- 3 tablespoons butter
- 3 eggs, lightly beaten
- 1 cup chopped black walnuts

Combine 1 tablespoon sugar and flour; sprinkle over bottom of pie shell and set aside. In a medium saucepan, bring corn syrup, brown sugar and remaining sugar just to a boil. Remove from the heat; stir in butter until melted. Let cool for 3 minutes. Gradually stir eggs into hot mixture. Add walnuts and mix well. Pour into pie shell.

Preheat the oven to 350°. Place pie in oven; immediately

reduce heat to 325°. Bake for 55 minutes or until the top is browned. **Yield:** 8 servings.

Editor's Note: Regular walnuts can be substituted for the black walnuts.

Pistachio Pudding Tarts

Any time you want a treat that's green, refreshing and delightful, try these tempting tarts.

—Bettye Linster, Atlanta, Georgia

  1 **cup butter, softened**
  1 **package (8 ounces) cream cheese, softened**
  2 **cups all-purpose flour**
  1 **package (3.4 ounces) instant pistachio pudding mix**
1-3/4 **cups cold milk**

In a mixing bowl, combine butter, cream cheese and flour; mix well. Shape into 48 balls (1 in. each); press onto the bottom and up the sides of ungreased miniature muffin cups.

Bake at 400° for 12-15 minutes or until lightly browned. Cool for 5 minutes; carefully remove from pans to a wire rack to cool completely.

For filling, combine pudding and milk in a mixing bowl; beat on low speed for 2 minutes. Cover; refrigerate for 5 minutes. Spoon into tart shells; serve immediately. **Yield:** 4 dozen.

Pumpkin Cake

(Pictured above right)

A slice into this fun pumpkin-shaped dessert reveals a moist banana cake inside. A tempting nut filling joins two cakes to form the pumpkin. Decorating is easy with orange-tinted frosting.

—Julianne Johnson
Grove City, Minnesota

  2 **packages (18-1/2 ounces** *each***) banana cake mix**
  2 **tablespoons butter**
  2 **tablespoons all-purpose flour**
1/2 **cup half-and-half cream**
1/2 **cup sugar**
  1 **teaspoon vanilla extract**

1/2 **teaspoon salt**
1/2 **cup chopped pecans**
BUTTERCREAM FROSTING:
3/4 **cup butter, softened**
3/4 **cup shortening**
  6 **cups confectioners' sugar**
  1 **teaspoon vanilla extract**
  2 **to 4 tablespoons milk**
Red, yellow and green food coloring
Ice cream cone or banana

Prepare and bake cakes in 12-cup fluted tube pans according to package directions; cool. For filling, melt butter in a saucepan. Stir in flour to form a smooth paste. Gradually add cream and sugar, stirring constantly until thick. Boil 1 minute; remove from heat. Stir in vanilla and salt. Fold in nuts; cool.

Level the bottom of each cake. Spread one cake bottom with filling; put cake bottoms together to form a pumpkin. Set aside. In a mixing bowl, cream butter and shortening. Beat in sugar and vanilla. Add milk until desired consistency is reached. Combine red and yellow food coloring to make orange; tint about three-fourths of the frosting orange. Tint remaining frosting green.

Place a small glass upside down in the center of the cake to support the "stem." Put a dollop of frosting on the glass and top with an ice cream cone or banana. Cut the cone or banana to the correct length; frost with green frosting. Frost cake with orange frosting. **Yield:** 12-16 servings.

In a mixing bowl, cream butter and sugar until fluffy. Beat in egg, sour cream and vanilla. Combine flour, cocoa, coffee, baking powder, baking soda and salt; add to creamed mixture and mix well. Pour into a greased 9-in. round baking pan.

Bake at 350° for 30 minutes or until a toothpick inserted near the center comes out clean. Cool for 10 minutes; remove from pan to a wire rack to cool completely.

For topping, combine chocolate chips, cream, sugar, butter and corn syrup in a saucepan; bring to a boil, stirring constantly. Reduce heat to medium; cook and stir for 7 minutes. Remove from the heat; stir in vanilla. Cool for 10-15 minutes. Beat with a wooden spoon until slightly thickened, about 4-5 minutes. Stir in nuts. Place cake on a serving plate; pour topping over cake. **Yield:** 8-10 servings.

Macadamia Fudge Cake

(Pictured above)

Our daughter and her husband operate a cookie factory in Hawaii. After she sent us a big supply of macadamia nuts, I came up with this cake for special dinners. —Marguerite Gough, Salida, Colorado

- 1/2 cup butter, softened
- 3/4 cup sugar
- 1 egg
- 3/4 cup sour cream
- 1/2 teaspoon vanilla extract
- 1 cup all-purpose flour
- 1/4 cup baking cocoa
- 1-1/2 teaspoons instant coffee granules
- 1/2 teaspoon baking powder
- 1/2 teaspoon baking soda
- 1/4 teaspoon salt

TOPPING:
- 1 cup (6 ounces) semisweet chocolate chips
- 2/3 cup heavy whipping cream
- 1/2 cup sugar
- 2 tablespoons butter
- 2 tablespoons corn syrup
- 1 teaspoon vanilla extract
- 1-1/2 cups coarsely chopped macadamia nuts *or* almonds

Traditional Pumpkin Pie

(Pictured below)

Usually I prepare two different desserts for our holiday dinner, but one of them must be pumpkin pie. My version calls for more eggs than most, making this pie's pumpkin custard filling especially rich-tasting.

If desired, cut the pastry scraps with a 1-in. leaf-shaped cookie cutter; place on an ungreased baking sheet. Bake at 350° for 10-15 minutes or until lightly browned. Place on baked pies. **Yield:** 2 pies (6-8 servings each).

Holiday Meringue Dessert

(Pictured at left)

This recipe's become our traditional dessert for Christmas dinner and seems appropriate for the season since the meringue shells look like mounds of snow. Whatever the topping, it's very festive.
—Catherine Morrison, Newport, Pennsylvania

 1 egg white
1/8 teaspoon cream of tartar
1/8 teaspoon almond extract
Dash salt
 1/3 cup sugar
 2 scoops chocolate ice cream
Chocolate sauce
 2 tablespoons flaked coconut, toasted
Maraschino cherries

Place egg white in a mixing bowl and let stand at room temperature for 30 minutes. Beat until foamy. Add cream of tartar, extract and salt; beat until soft peaks form. Gradually add sugar, 1 tablespoon at a time, beating on high until very stiff peaks form.

Cover a baking sheet with foil or parchment paper. Spoon the egg mixture into two mounds on paper. Using the back of a spoon, build up the edges slightly.

Bake at 300° for 35 minutes. Turn oven off; let shells dry in the oven for at least 1 hour with the door closed. To serve, fill shells with ice cream; top with chocolate sauce, coconut and cherries. **Yield:** 2 servings.

 2 cups all-purpose flour
3/4 teaspoon salt
2/3 cup shortening
 4 to 6 tablespoons cold water
FILLING:
 6 eggs
 1 can (29 ounces) solid-pack pumpkin
 2 cups packed brown sugar
 2 teaspoons ground cinnamon
 1 teaspoon salt
1/2 teaspoon *each* ground cloves, nutmeg and ginger
 2 cups evaporated milk

In a bowl, combine flour and salt; cut in shortening until crumbly. Sprinkle with water, 1 tablespoon at a time, tossing with a fork until dough forms a ball. Divide dough in half.

On a floured surface, roll out each portion to fit a 9-in. pie plate. Place pastry in plates; trim pastry (set scraps aside if leaf cutouts are desired) and flute edges. Set shells aside.

For filling, beat eggs in a mixing bowl. Add pumpkin, sugar, cinnamon, salt, cloves, nutmeg and ginger; beat just until smooth. Gradually stir in milk. Pour into pastry shells.

Bake at 450° for 10 minutes. Reduce heat to 350°; bake 40-45 minutes longer or until a knife inserted near the center comes out clean. Cool on wire racks.

Upper Crust

A cool kitchen will help add to the success of making pastry crusts. In addition, the pie crust ingredients (even the flour) should be cold to produce the best results. And remember that any time you add water to the pie dough, the water should be iced.

Neapolitan Cheesecake

(Pictured below)

This rich, creamy cheesecake is a crowd-pleasing stand-out. It has won first-place ribbons at numerous fairs and is my family's favorite dessert. It's an indulgence sure to produce oohs and aahs when served to guests.
—Sherri Regalbuto, Carp, Ontario

- 1 **cup chocolate wafer crumbs**
- 5 **tablespoons butter, melted, *divided***
- 3 **packages (8 ounces *each*) cream cheese, softened**
- 3/4 **cup sugar**
- 3 **eggs**
- 1 **teaspoon vanilla extract**
- 5 **squares (1 ounce *each*) semisweet chocolate, *divided***
- 2-1/2 **squares (2-1/2 ounces) white baking chocolate, *divided***
- 1/3 **cup mashed sweetened strawberries**
- 2 **teaspoons shortening, *divided***

Combine crumbs and 3 tablespoons of butter; press onto the bottom of an ungreased 9-in. springform pan. Place pan on a baking sheet. Bake at 350° for 8 minutes; cool.

In a mixing bowl, beat cream cheese and sugar until smooth. Beat in eggs, one at a time. Add vanilla. Divide into three portions, about 1-2/3 cups each. Melt 2 squares semi-sweet chocolate; stir into one portion of batter. Melt 2 squares of white chocolate; stir into second portion. Stir strawberries into remaining batter. Spread semisweet mixture evenly over crust. Carefully spread with white chocolate mixture, then strawberry mixture.

Bake at 425° for 10 minutes; reduce heat to 300°. Bake 50-55 minutes or until center is nearly set. Remove from oven; immediately run a knife around edge. Cool; remove from pan.

Melt remaining semisweet chocolate, remaining butter and 1 teaspoon of shortening; cool for 2 minutes. Pour over cake. Melt remaining white chocolate and shortening; drizzle over glaze. Refrigerate leftovers. **Yield:** 12-14 servings.

Gingerbread with Brown Sugar Sauce

(Pictured above)

The aroma of this gingerbread is what I remember most about my grandmother's kitchen. That was decades ago, but whenever I catch a whiff of ginger and cinnamon, I'm back with Grandmother. —*Toni Hamm*
Vandergrift, Pennsylvania

- 6 **tablespoons shortening**
- 1/2 **cup packed brown sugar**
- 1/3 **cup molasses**

1 egg
1-1/2 cups all-purpose flour
1/2 teaspoon baking soda
1/2 teaspoon ground cinnamon
1/2 teaspoon ground ginger
1/8 teaspoon salt
1/2 cup buttermilk
BROWN SUGAR SAUCE:
1 cup packed brown sugar
4-1/2 teaspoons cornstarch
1/2 cup cold water
1-1/2 teaspoons vinegar
1 tablespoon butter
1-1/2 teaspoons vanilla extract

In a mixing bowl, cream shortening, brown sugar, molasses and egg; mix well. Combine flour, baking soda, cinnamon, ginger and salt; add to the molasses mixture alternately with buttermilk. Pour into a greased 9-in. round baking pan.

Bake at 350° for 25-30 minutes or until a toothpick comes out clean. Cool for 10 minutes before removing from pan to a wire rack.

For sauce, combine brown sugar, cornstarch, water and vinegar in a saucepan; stir until smooth. Add butter. Bring to a boil; boil and stir for 2 minutes. Remove from the heat and stir in vanilla. Serve over gingerbread. **Yield:** 6-8 servings.

Chocolate Chip Cookie Dough Cheesecake

(Pictured at right)

I created this recipe to combine two of my all-time favorites—cheesecake for the grown-up in me and chocolate chip cookie dough for the little girl in me.
—Julie Craig, Jackson, Wisconsin

1-3/4 cups crushed chocolate chip cookies *or* chocolate wafer crumbs
1/4 cup sugar
1/3 cup butter, melted
FILLING:
3 packages (8 ounces *each*) cream cheese, softened
1 cup sugar
3 eggs
1 cup (8 ounces) sour cream
1/2 teaspoon vanilla extract

COOKIE DOUGH:
1/4 cup butter, softened
1/4 cup sugar
1/4 cup packed brown sugar
1 tablespoon water
1 teaspoon vanilla extract
1/2 cup all-purpose flour
1-1/2 cups miniature semisweet chocolate chips, *divided*

In a small bowl, combine cookie crumbs and sugar; stir in butter. Press onto the bottom and 1 in. up the sides of a greased 9-in. springform pan; place pan on a baking sheet. Set aside.

In a mixing bowl, beat cream cheese and sugar until smooth. Add eggs; beat on low just until combined. Add sour cream and vanilla; beat just until blended. Pour over crust; set aside.

In another mixing bowl, cream butter and sugars on medium speed for 3 minutes. Add water and vanilla. Gradually add flour. Stir in 1 cup chocolate chips. Drop dough by teaspoonfuls over filling, gently pushing dough below surface (dough should be completely covered by filling).

Bake at 350° for 45-55 minutes or until center is almost set. Cool on a wire rack for 10 minutes. Carefully run a knife around edge of pan to loosen; cool 1 hour longer. Refrigerate overnight; remove sides of pan. Sprinkle with remaining chips. Refrigerate leftovers. **Yield:** 12-14 servings.

*Clockwise from top left: Almond Cranberry Tart,
Cranberry Nut Dessert and Cranberry Ice*

Cranberry Nut Dessert

(Pictured at left)

This wonderful no-crust dessert is loaded with cranberries and nuts. It's a seasonal favorite with my family.
—*Peggy Van Arsdale, Trenton, New Jersey*

        1 **cup all-purpose flour**
        1 **cup sugar**
      1/4 **teaspoon salt**
        2 **cups fresh *or* frozen cranberries**
      1/2 **cup chopped walnuts**
      1/2 **cup butter, melted**
        2 **eggs, beaten**
      1/2 **teaspoon almond extract**
Whipped cream *or* ice cream, optional

In a bowl, combine the flour, sugar and salt. Add cranberries and nuts; toss to coat. Stir in the butter, eggs and extract (mixture will be very thick if using frozen berries). Spread into a greased 9-in. pie plate.

Bake at 350° for 40 minutes or until a toothpick inserted near the center comes out clean. Serve warm with whipped cream or ice cream if desired. **Yield:** 8 servings.

Almond Cranberry Tart

(Pictured at left)

Because it needs to chill, this is a fantastic make-ahead dessert. —*Billie Moss, El Sobrante, California*

  1-1/4 **cups sugar, *divided***
        1 **cup finely chopped toasted slivered almonds**
        1 **cup all-purpose flour**
      1/2 **cup cold butter**
        1 **egg**
        1 **teaspoon vanilla extract**
        1 **envelope unflavored gelatin**
      1/4 **cup water**
        1 **package (12 ounces) fresh *or* frozen cranberries**
      1/2 **cup red currant jelly**
Whipped cream and additional chopped almonds, optional

In a bowl, combine 1/4 cup sugar, almonds and flour. Cut in the butter until crumbly. Beat egg and vanilla; add to flour

mixture and stir until moistened. Cover and chill for 30 minutes.

Coat fingers with flour and press mixture into the bottom and 1-1/2 in. up the sides of a greased 9-in. springform pan. Bake at 350° for 25-30 minutes or until golden brown. Cool.

Meanwhile, soften gelatin in water; set aside. In a saucepan, cook cranberries, jelly and remaining sugar over medium-low heat until berries pop. Remove from the heat; stir in gelatin until dissolved. Cool; pour into crust. Chill for at least 4 hours. Garnish with whipped cream and almonds if desired. **Yield:** 8-10 servings.

Cranberry Ice

(Pictured at left)

Cranberries, lemon and orange meld together to make a refreshing ice that really hits the spot after a heavy holiday meal. —*Eleanor Dunbar, Peoria, Illinois*

        4 **cups fresh *or* frozen cranberries**
        4 **cups cold water, *divided***
        1 **package (3 ounces) lemon gelatin**
        2 **cups boiling water**
        3 **cups sugar**
      1/2 **cup lemon juice**
      1/2 **cup orange juice**

In a saucepan, bring cranberries and 2 cups cold water to a boil. Reduce heat; simmer for 5 minutes. Press through a strainer to remove skins; set juice aside and discard skins.

In a bowl, stir gelatin, boiling water and sugar until dissolved. Add cranberry, lemon and orange juices and remaining cold water. Pour into a 13-in. x 9-in. x 2-in. pan.

Cover and freeze until ice begins to form around the edges of the pan, about 1-1/2 hours; stir. Freeze until mushy, about 30 minutes. Spoon into a freezer container; cover and freeze. **Yield:** 20 servings.

Cranberry Pointers

- You can store cranberries in an airtight plastic bag in the refrigerator for at least 1 month; frozen for up to 1 year.
- Make quick work of chopping cranberries by using a food processor with a metal blade. Use quick on/off pulses until they are chopped.
- Cook cranberries only until they pop; otherwise, they can turn mushy and bitter.

Caramel Fudge Cheesecake

(Pictured below)

It's hard to resist this chocolaty cheesecake with its fudgy crust, crunchy pecans and gooey caramel layer. I combined recipes to create this version, which satisfies my family's chocolate lovers and cheesecake lovers.
—*Brenda Ruse, Truro, Nova Scotia*

- 1 **package fudge brownie mix (8-inch square pan size)**
- 1 **package (14 ounces) caramels**
- 1/4 **cup evaporated milk**
- 1-1/4 **cups coarsely chopped pecans**
- 2 **packages (8 ounces *each*) cream cheese, softened**
- 1/2 **cup sugar**
- 2 **eggs**
- 2 **squares (1 ounce *each*) semisweet chocolate, melted**
- 2 **squares (1 ounce *each*) unsweetened chocolate, melted**

Prepare brownie batter according to the package directions. Spread into a greased 9-in. springform pan. Place pan on a baking sheet. Bake at 350° for 20 minutes. Cool for 10 minutes on a wire rack. Meanwhile, in a microwave-safe bowl, melt

caramels with milk. Pour over brownie crust; sprinkle with pecans.

In a mixing bowl, combine the cream cheese and sugar; mix well. Add eggs, beating on low speed just until combined. Stir in melted chocolate. Pour over pecans.

Bake at 350° for 35-40 minutes or until the center is almost set. Cool on a wire rack for 10 minutes. Run a knife around edge of pan to loosen; cool completely. Chill overnight. Remove sides of pan before serving. Store leftovers in the refrigerator. **Yield:** 12 servings.

Editor's Note: This recipe was tested using Hershey caramels.

Cherry Banana Cream Pie

(Pictured above)

This dessert has a crunchy crust spread with a rich butter layer, topped with a filling flavored with banana, cherries and chocolate. Guests tell me the pie reminds them of a banana split...and then ask for seconds.
—*Denise Elder, Hanover, Ontario*

- 3/4 **cup butter, softened, *divided***
- 2 **cups crushed vanilla wafers (about 60)**
- 3/4 **cup confectioners' sugar**

FILLING:

> 1 cup heavy whipping cream
> 1/4 cup sugar
> 2 tablespoons baking cocoa
> 1 cup chopped walnuts
> 1 large firm banana, thinly sliced
> 1/3 cup halved maraschino cherries

Whipped topping, chocolate curls and additional
  maraschino cherries

Melt 1/2 cup of butter; toss with the wafer crumbs. Press into a 9-in. pie plate. In a small mixing bowl, cream the remaining butter; beat in confectioners' sugar until combined. Spread
over the crust.

In another mixing bowl, beat the cream, sugar and cocoa
until stiff peaks form. Fold in walnuts, banana and maraschino cherries. Spoon into crust.

Cover and refrigerate the pie for 8 hours or overnight.
Garnish with whipped topping, chocolate curls and cherries.
Yield: 6-8 servings.

Heirloom Fruitcake

*When I couldn't find a recipe for fruitcake made with
butter, honey, eggs and cream, I created this one. I like
this cake because it's not as sweet as many traditional
varieties. —Sharon McClatchey, Muskogee, Oklahoma*

> 1/3 cup butter, softened
> 3 tablespoons brown sugar
> 2 eggs
> 3 tablespoons honey
> 1/2 cup all-purpose flour
> 1/2 teaspoon salt
> 1/2 teaspoon baking powder
> 1/8 teaspoon ground allspice
> 1/8 teaspoon ground nutmeg
> 2 tablespoons half-and-half cream
> 1 cup raisins
> 1 cup chopped dates
> 1 package (6 ounces) dried apricots, finely chopped
> 3 cups pecan halves

In a mixing bowl, cream the butter, sugar, eggs and honey. Combine dry ingredients; add to creamed mixture alternately with
cream. Beat in raisins, dates, apricots and pecans. Pack into
two greased and floured 7-3/4-in. x 3-5/8-in. x 2-1/4-in.
loaf pans. Place pans on middle rack of oven; place a shallow pan of hot water on lowest rack.

Bake at 300° for 60-65 minutes or until a toothpick inserted near the center comes out clean. Cool completely in
pan. Loosen edges with a knife and remove from pan. Store
in an airtight container in the refrigerator. **Yield:** 2 loaves.

Apple Date Crisp

(Pictured above)

*My mother loves to make this old-fashioned dessert,
and my father, brother and I love to eat it. Each serving is chock-full of apple slices, crunchy nuts and chewy
dates. It's a satisfying way to end a delicious meal.
—Karin Cousineau, Burlington, North Carolina*

> 8 cups sliced peeled tart apples
> 2 cups chopped dates
> 2/3 cup packed brown sugar
> 1/2 cup all-purpose flour
> 1 teaspoon ground cinnamon
> 1/3 cup cold butter
> 1 cup chopped nuts

Additional apple slices, optional

Combine the apples and dates in an ungreased 13-in. x 9-in.
x 2-in. baking dish. In a small bowl, combine sugar, flour and
cinnamon; cut in butter until crumbly. Add nuts; sprinkle over
apples. Bake at 375° for 35-40 minutes or until apples are
tender. Serve warm. Garnish with apple slices if desired. **Yield:**
6-8 servings.

Creamy Caramel Flan

(Pictured above)

If you're unfamiliar with flan, think of it as a tasty variation on custard. One warning, though—it's very filling. A small slice goes a long way! —Pat Forte
Miami, Florida

3/4 cup sugar
1 package (8 ounces) cream cheese, softened
5 eggs
1 can (14 ounces) sweetened condensed milk
1 can (12 ounces) evaporated milk
1 teaspoon vanilla extract

In a heavy saucepan over medium-low heat, cook and stir sugar until melted and golden, about 15 minutes. Quickly pour into an ungreased 2-qt. round baking or souffle dish, tilting to coat the bottom; let stand for 10 minutes.

In a mixing bowl, beat the cream cheese until smooth. Add eggs, one at a time, beating well after each addition. Add remaining ingredients; mix well. Pour over caramelized sugar. Place the dish in a larger baking pan. Pour boiling water into larger pan to a depth of 1 in.

Bake at 350° for 50-60 minutes or until center is just set (mixture will jiggle). Remove dish from larger pan to a wire rack; cool for 1 hour. Refrigerate overnight. To unmold, run a knife around edges and invert onto a large rimmed serving platter. Cut into wedges or spoon onto dessert plates; spoon sauce over each serving. **Yield:** 8-10 servings.

Cranberry Sauce Cake

(Pictured below)

This moist cake is so easy to make because it's mixed in one bowl. Slice it at the table so everyone can see how beautiful it is. —Marge Clark, West Lebanon, Indiana

3 cups all-purpose flour
1-1/2 cups sugar
1 can (16 ounces) whole-berry cranberry sauce
1 cup mayonnaise
1/3 cup orange juice
1 tablespoon grated orange peel
1 teaspoon baking soda
1 teaspoon salt
1 teaspoon orange extract
1 cup chopped walnuts
ICING:
1 cup confectioners' sugar
1 to 2 tablespoons orange juice

In a mixing bowl, combine flour, sugar, cranberry sauce, mayonnaise, orange juice and peel, baking soda, salt and orange extract; mix well. Fold in walnuts.

Cut waxed or parchment paper to fit the bottom of a 10-in. tube pan. Spray the pan and paper with nonstick cooking spray. Pour batter into paper-lined pan. Bake at 350° for 60-70 minutes or until a toothpick comes out clean. Cool 10 min-

utes in pan before removing to a wire rack. Combine icing ingredients; drizzle over the warm cake. **Yield:** 12-16 servings.

Editor's Note: Reduced-fat or fat-free mayonnaise may not be substituted for regular mayonnaise in this recipe.

Pecan Fudge Pie

This fudgy pie is the perfect showcase for crunchy pecans. It's a special chocolaty twist on traditional pecan pie. Top it with whipped cream, and you won't wait long for compliments!
— *Jacquelyn Smith*
Soperton, Georgia

1-1/4	cups light corn syrup
1/2	cup sugar
1/3	cup baking cocoa
1/3	cup all-purpose flour
3	eggs
3	tablespoons butter, softened
1-1/2	teaspoons vanilla extract
1/4	teaspoon salt
1	cup chopped pecans
1	unbaked pastry shell (9 inches)

Whipped cream, optional

In a large mixing bowl, beat the first eight ingredients until smooth. Stir in nuts; pour into pie shell. Bake at 350° for 55-60 minutes or until set. Cool completely. Garnish with whipped cream if desired. **Yield:** 6-8 servings.

Chocolate and Fruit Trifle

(Pictured above right)

Layers of devil's food cake, a creamy pudding mixture, red berries and green kiwi are perfect for the holidays. I like making it in a clear glass trifle bowl to show off its festive colors. — *Angie Dierikx, State Center, Iowa*

1	package (18-1/4 ounces) devil's food cake mix
1	can (14 ounces) sweetened condensed milk
1	cup cold water
1	package (3.4 ounces) instant vanilla pudding mix
2	cups heavy whipping cream, whipped

2	tablespoons orange juice
2	cups fresh strawberries, chopped
2	cups fresh raspberries
2	kiwifruit, peeled and chopped

Prepare cake batter according to package directions; pour into a greased 15-in. x 10-in. x 1-in. baking pan. Bake at 350° for 20 minutes or until a toothpick inserted near the center comes out clean. Cool completely on a wire rack. Crumble enough cake to measure 8 cups; set aside. (Save remaining cake for another use.)

In a mixing bowl, combine milk and water until smooth. Add pudding mix; beat on low speed for 2 minutes or until slightly thickened. Fold in the whipped cream.

To assemble, spread 2-1/2 cups pudding mixture in a 4-qt. glass bowl. Top with half of the crumbled cake; sprinkle with 1 tablespoon orange juice. Arrange half of the berries and kiwi over cake. Repeat pudding and cake layers; sprinkle with remaining orange juice. Top with remaining pudding mixture. Spoon remaining fruit around edge of bowl. Cover and refrigerate until serving. **Yield:** 12-16 servings.

yolks; return all to pan, stirring constantly. Bring to a gentle boil; cook and stir 2 minutes longer. Remove from heat. Stir in vanilla. Pour into a bowl and cover with waxed paper. Chill 20 minutes.

Meanwhile, cut cake into 3/4-in. slices; spread with jam. Cut each slice into thirds; place with jam side up in a 3-qt. trifle dish or a deep salad bowl.

Cover with berries. Top with custard. Cover and chill overnight. Just before serving, whip cream and sugar until stiff; spread over custard. Garnish with almonds and berries if desired. **Yield:** 10-12 servings.

Snowflake Cake

(Pictured below)

The coconut sprinkled on this old-fashioned fluffy frosting gives the impression of snow inside the house without the cold. It's a beautiful dessert that is a fitting end to a delicious meal.
— *Lynne Peterson*
Salt Lake City, Utah

> 2 **eggs plus 4 egg yolks**
> 1-1/2 **cups sugar**
> 1 **cup milk**
> 1/2 **cup butter**

Raspberry Trifle

(Pictured above)

The first time I served my trifle was for a family dinner. Everyone loved it! I've since found that it also goes over well at potlucks and buffet dinners.
— *Betty Howlett, Elmira, Ontario*

> 1/4 **cup sugar**
> 3 **tablespoons cornstarch**
> 3 **cups milk**
> 4 **egg yolks, beaten**
> 2 **teaspoons vanilla extract**
> 1 **loaf (1 pound) frozen pound cake, thawed**
> 3/4 **cup raspberry jam**
> 3 **cups fresh *or* frozen unsweetened raspberries, thawed and drained**
> 1 **cup heavy whipping cream**
> 2 **tablespoons confectioners' sugar**
> 2 **tablespoons sliced almonds, toasted**

Fresh raspberries, optional

In a saucepan, combine the sugar and cornstarch. Stir in milk until smooth. Cook and stir over medium-high heat until thickened and bubbly. Reduce heat; cook and stir 2 minutes longer. Remove from heat. Stir a small amount of hot filling into egg

2-1/2 cups all-purpose flour
    1 tablespoon baking powder
    1 teaspoon vanilla extract
  1/2 cup chopped nuts, optional
FROSTING:
1-3/4 cups sugar
  1/2 cup water
    4 egg whites
  1/2 teaspoon cream of tartar
    1 teaspoon vanilla extract
    2 cups flaked coconut

In a mixing bowl, beat eggs, yolks and sugar until light and fluffy, about 5 minutes. In a saucepan, heat milk and butter until butter is melted. Combine flour and baking powder; add to egg mixture alternately with milk mixture. Beat until well mixed. Add vanilla. Fold in nuts if desired. Pour into three greased 9-in. round baking pans.

Bake at 350° for 15-18 minutes or until a toothpick inserted near the center comes out clean. Cool in pans 10 minutes before removing to a wire rack to cool completely.

For frosting, in a saucepan, bring sugar and water to a boil. Boil 3-4 minutes or until a candy thermometer reads 242° (firm-ball stage). Meanwhile, beat egg whites and cream of tartar in a mixing bowl until foamy. Slowly pour in hot sugar mixture and continue to beat on high for 6-8 minutes or until stiff peaks form. Add vanilla.

Frost the tops of two cake layers and sprinkle with coconut; stack on a cake plate with plain layer on top. Frost sides and top of cake; sprinkle with coconut. Refrigerate for several hours. **Yield:** 12-16 servings.

Editor's Note: We recommend that you test your candy thermometer before each use by bringing water to a boil; the thermometer should read 212°. Adjust your recipe temperature up or down based on your test.

Chocolate Eclairs

(Pictured above right)

I won the grand prize with this recipe at a "Chocolate Lovers Cook-Off" contest in our town. This is one of my most-requested desserts.   —*Janet Davis*
Murfreesboro, Tennessee

    1 cup water
  1/2 cup butter
    1 cup all-purpose flour
  1/4 teaspoon salt
    4 eggs

FILLING:
2-1/2 cups cold milk
    1 package (5.1 ounces) instant vanilla pudding mix
    1 cup heavy whipping cream
  1/4 cup confectioners' sugar
    1 teaspoon vanilla extract
CHOCOLATE ICING:
    2 squares (1 ounce *each*) semisweet chocolate
    2 tablespoons butter
    1 cup confectioners' sugar
    2 to 3 tablespoons hot water

In a saucepan over medium heat, bring water and butter to a boil. Add flour and salt all at once; stir until a smooth ball forms. Remove from heat. Add eggs, one at a time, beating well after each addition.

With a tablespoon or a pastry bag with a No. 10 or larger tip, spoon or pipe dough into 4-in.-long x 1-1/2-in.-wide strips on a greased baking sheet. Bake at 450° for 15 minutes. Reduce the heat to 325°; bake 20 minutes longer. Cool on a wire rack.

For filling, combine milk and pudding mix; mix according to package directions. In a mixing bowl, beat cream until soft peaks form. Beat in sugar and vanilla; fold into pudding. Fill cooled shells. (Chill remaining pudding for another use.)

For icing, melt chocolate and butter in a saucepan over low heat. Stir in sugar. Add hot water until icing is smooth and reaches desired consistency. Cool slightly. Spread over the eclairs. Chill until serving. **Yield:** 8-9 servings.

Crimson Devonshire Cream

(Pictured above)

Once when my mom was preparing a holiday dinner, she served this lighter dessert. Ever since then, we have all looked forward to this delicious treat.
—*Cindy Cafasso, Barrington, New Hampshire*

- 1 **teaspoon unflavored gelatin**
- 3/4 **cup cold water**
- 1 **cup heavy whipping cream**
- 1/2 **cup sugar**
- 1-1/2 **teaspoons vanilla extract**
- 1 **cup (8 ounces) sour cream**

CRIMSON SAUCE:

- 2-1/4 **cups fresh *or* frozen cranberries, *divided***
- 1-1/3 **cups water**
- 1/4 **cup orange juice**
- 4 **teaspoons grated orange peel**
- 3/4 **cup sugar**

In a saucepan, soften gelatin in water; heat over low until gelatin dissolves. Cool. In a mixing bowl, beat cream, sugar and vanilla until soft peaks form. Combine the gelatin mixture and sour cream; mix well. Gently whisk into the cream mixture.

Pour into small bowls or parfait glasses. Refrigerate until set, about 1 hour.

For sauce, combine 1-1/2 cups cranberries, water, orange juice and peel in a saucepan; bring to a boil. Reduce heat; simmer, uncovered, for 15 minutes. Sieve sauce, discarding

skins. Return sauce to pan; add sugar and remaining cranberries. Cook over medium heat until berries pop, about 8 minutes. Chill. Spoon over each serving. **Yield:** 8 servings.

Pumpkin Chiffon Torte

(Pictured below)

After a sumptuous holiday meal, this light and tasty dessert is perfect. It's a deliciously different way to feature the flavor of pumpkin. —*Lynn Kumm Osmond, Nebraska*

- 1 **cup finely crushed gingersnaps (about 24)**
- 3 **tablespoons butter, melted**
- 2 **envelopes unflavored gelatin**
- 1/2 **cup milk**
- 1/2 **cup sugar**
- 1 **can (15 ounces) solid-pack pumpkin**
- 1/2 **teaspoon salt**
- 1/2 **teaspoon ground cinnamon**
- 1/4 **teaspoon ground ginger**
- 1/4 **teaspoon ground cloves**
- 1 **carton (8 ounces) frozen whipped topping, thawed**

Additional whipped topping, optional

In a small bowl, combine cookie crumbs and butter. Press onto the bottom of a greased 9-in. springform pan; set aside. In a saucepan, combine gelatin and milk; let stand for 5 minutes.

Heat milk mixture to just below boiling; remove from the heat. Stir in sugar until dissolved. Add the pumpkin, salt, cinnamon, ginger and cloves; mix well. Fold in whipped topping. Pour over crust.

Refrigerate until set, about 3 hours. Remove sides of pan just before serving. Garnish with additional whipped topping if desired. **Yield:** 16 servings.

Cranberry Eggnog Cheesecake

The holidays wouldn't be complete without cranberries and eggnog. I use them both in this flavorful and lovely cheesecake. It's a perfect finale for Christmas dinner. —Nancy Zimmerman
Cape May Court House, New Jersey

  1 **cup sugar**
  2 **tablespoons cornstarch**
  1 **cup cranberry juice**
1-1/2 **cups fresh *or* frozen cranberries**
CRUST:
  1 **cup graham cracker crumbs (about 14 squares)**
  3 **tablespoons sugar**
  3 **tablespoons butter, melted**
FILLING:
  4 **packages (8 ounces *each*) cream cheese, softened**
  1 **cup sugar**
  3 **tablespoons all-purpose flour**
  4 **eggs**
  1 **cup eggnog**
  1 **tablespoon vanilla extract**

In a saucepan, combine the first four ingredients; bring to a boil. Reduce heat; cook and stir over medium heat for 2 minutes. Remove from the heat; set aside. In a small bowl, combine cracker crumbs and sugar; stir in butter. Press onto the bottom of a greased 9-in. springform pan. Bake at 325° for 10 minutes. Cool on a wire rack.

In a mixing bowl, beat cream cheese and sugar until smooth. Add flour and beat well. Add eggs; beat on low just until combined. Add eggnog and vanilla; beat just until blended. Pour two-thirds of the filling over crust. Top with half of the cranberry mixture (cover and chill remaining cranberry mixture). Carefully spoon remaining filling on top. Place pan on a baking sheet. Bake at 325° for 60-70 minutes or until center is almost set.

Cool on a wire rack for 10 minutes. Carefully run a knife around edge of pan to loosen; cool 1 hour longer. Refrigerate overnight. Remove sides of pan. Spoon remaining cranberry mixture over cheesecake. **Yield:** 12 servings.

Editor's Note: This recipe was tested with commercially prepared eggnog.

Pecan Tarts
(Pictured above)

The flaky crust combined with a rich center makes these little tarts a satisfying snack to serve and eat. They look so appealing on a pretty platter and make a great dessert when you're entertaining. —Jean Rhodes
Tignall, Georgia

1/2 **cup butter, softened**
  1 **package (3 ounces) cream cheese, softened**
  1 **cup all-purpose flour**
1/4 **teaspoon salt**
FILLING:
  1 **egg**
3/4 **cup packed dark brown sugar**
  1 **tablespoon butter, melted**
  1 **teaspoon vanilla extract**
2/3 **cup chopped pecans**
Maraschino cherry halves, optional

In a mixing bowl, beat butter and cream cheese; blend in flour and salt. Refrigerate for 1 hour. Shape into 1-in. balls; press into the bottom and up the sides of greased miniature muffin cups.

For filling, beat the egg in a small mixing bowl. Add sugar, butter and vanilla; mix well. Stir in pecans. Spoon into shells. Bake at 325° for 25-30 minutes. Cool in pan on a wire rack. Decorate with maraschino cherries if desired. **Yield:** about 20

Pecan Cake Roll

(Pictured below)

When I was still teaching, I'd bring this dessert to share with the other faculty and staff. It'd usually be gone before the school day ever started! —Shirley Awald
Walkerton, Indiana

    4   **eggs,** *separated*
    1   **cup confectioners' sugar**
    2   **cups ground pecans**
    1   **cup heavy whipping cream**
    3   **tablespoons sugar**
    2   **teaspoons baking cocoa**
  1/2   **teaspoon vanilla extract**
Chocolate shavings and additional confectioners' sugar, optional

In a mixing bowl, beat egg yolks and confectioners' sugar until thick, about 5 minutes. In another bowl, beat whites until soft peaks form; fold into yolk mixture. Fold in pecans until well blended (batter will be thin).

Grease a 15-in. x 10-in. x 1-in. baking pan; line with waxed paper and grease and flour the paper. Spread batter into pan.

Bake at 375° for 10-15 minutes or until cake springs back when lightly touched. Turn onto a linen towel dusted with confectioners' sugar. Peel off paper and roll cake up in towel, starting with short end. Cool on wire rack 1 hour.

Meanwhile, beat the cream, sugar, cocoa and vanilla in a mixing bowl until soft peaks form. Carefully unroll cake. Spread filling over cake; roll up again. Refrigerate. If desired, garnish with chocolate shavings and confectioners' sugar. **Yield:** 10-12 servings.

Editor's Note: This cake does not contain flour.

Fluffy Cranberry Cheese Pie

(Pictured above right)

This pie has a light texture and zippy flavor that is festive for the holidays or anytime. And, even though it looks fancy, it's easy to make. —Mary Parkonen
W. Wareham, Massachusetts

CRANBERRY TOPPING:
    1 **package (3 ounces) raspberry gelatin**
 1/3 **cup sugar**
1-1/4 **cups cranberry juice**
    1 **can (8 ounces) jellied cranberry sauce**
FILLING:
    1 **package (3 ounces) cream cheese, softened**
 1/4 **cup sugar**
    1 **tablespoon milk**
    1 **teaspoon vanilla extract**
 1/2 **cup frozen whipped topping**
    1 **pastry shell (9 inches), baked**

In a mixing bowl, combine gelatin and sugar; set aside. In a saucepan, bring cranberry juice to a boil. Remove from the heat and pour over gelatin mixture, stirring to dissolve. Stir in the cranberry sauce. Chill until slightly thickened.

    Meanwhile, in another mixing bowl, beat cream cheese, sugar, milk and vanilla until fluffy. Fold in the whipped topping. Spread evenly into pie shell. Beat cranberry topping until frothy; pour over filling. Chill overnight. **Yield:** 6-8 servings.

Apple Cranberry Tart

(Pictured at right)

People practically inhale this dessert. I modified a recipe years ago to come up with a different way of using cranberries, a favorite fruit of mine.   *—Jo Ann Fisher*
Huntington Beach, California

1-1/3 **cups sugar**
1-1/4 **cups unsweetened apple juice *or* cider, *divided***
    3 **medium tart apples, peeled and cubed**
    1 **package (12 ounces) fresh *or* frozen cranberries**
 1/2 **cup all-purpose flour**
Pastry for single-crust pie (10 inches)
TOPPING:
 1/3 **cup chopped pecans**
 1/3 **cup all-purpose flour**
 1/4 **cup packed brown sugar**
    3 **tablespoons butter, melted**
  12 **pecan halves**

In a saucepan over medium heat, bring sugar and 3/4 cup apple juice to a boil, stirring occasionally. Add apples and cranberries; return to a boil. Reduce heat; simmer, uncovered, until apples are tender and berries pop, about 5-8 minutes. Whisk flour and remaining juice until smooth; stir into cranberry mixture. Bring to a boil; cook and stir for 2 minutes. Cool to room temperature.

    Fit pastry into an 11-in. fluted tart pan with removable bottom, or press onto the bottom and 1 in. up the sides of a 10-in. springform pan. Line pastry with double thickness of heavy-duty foil.

    Bake at 450° for 5 minutes. Remove foil; bake 7-10 minutes or until pastry is nearly done. Cool. Add apple mixture. Combine first four topping ingredients; sprinkle over filling. Arrange pecan halves on top. Bake at 375° for 30-35 minutes or until golden brown. **Yield:** 12 servings.

Chocolate Yum-Yum Cake

(Pictured above)

My grandmother first made this cake, and my mother made it often when I was a little girl. You can frost it or just sprinkle it with a little powdered sugar.
—Dorothy Colli, West Hartford, Connecticut

```
1/2  cup butter
  2  squares (1 ounce each) unsweetened baking
     chocolate
1-1/2  cups water
  1  cup sugar
1/2  cup raisins
1/2  teaspoon ground cinnamon
1/4  teaspoon ground cloves
1-1/2  teaspoons vanilla extract
Pinch salt
1-3/4  cups all-purpose flour
  1  teaspoon baking soda
ICING:
1/2  cup confectioners' sugar
  1  to 2 teaspoons milk
1/4  teaspoon vanilla extract
```

In a large saucepan over low heat, melt butter and chocolate, stirring constantly. Add water, sugar, raisins, cinnamon and cloves; bring to a boil. Boil for 5 minutes, stirring occasionally. Remove from the heat; pour into a mixing bowl and cool for 15 minutes. Add vanilla and salt. Combine flour and baking soda; add to chocolate mixture and mix well. Pour into a greased and floured 8-cup fluted tube pan.

Bake at 350° for 45 minutes or until a toothpick inserted near the center comes out clean. Cool in pan for 10 minutes before removing to a wire rack to cool. Combine icing ingredients; spoon over cooled cake. **Yield:** 8-10 servings.

Editor's Note: An 11-in. x 7-in. x 2-in. baking pan can be used. Bake for 25-30 minutes or until cake tests done.

Walnut Mincemeat Pie

(Pictured below)

As a cold and tasty finishing touch, my husband and I usually put a dip of ice cream on top of this pie. The recipe comes from my mother. Each year, I make it for Christmas and for my sister-in-law's New Year's party.
—Laverne Kamp, Kutztown, Pennsylvania

```
  2  eggs
  1  cup sugar
  2  tablespoons all-purpose flour
1/8  teaspoon salt
```

2 cups prepared mincemeat
1/2 cup chopped walnuts
1/4 cup butter, melted
1 unbaked pastry shell (9 inches)

In a small mixing bowl, lightly beat eggs. Combine sugar, flour and salt; gradually add to eggs. Stir in mincemeat, nuts and butter; pour into pastry shell.

Bake at 400° for 15 minutes. Reduce heat to 325°; bake for 35-40 minutes or until a knife inserted near the center comes out clean. Cool completely. Store in refrigerator. **Yield:** 6-8 servings.

Eggnog Cake

(Pictured at right)

With its moist cake layers, creamy filling and chocolate frosting, this cake appeals to all palates!
—*Edith Disch, Fairview Park, Ohio*

1/2 cup butter, softened
1 cup sugar, *divided*
2 eggs, *separated*
3/4 cup orange juice
1-1/2 teaspoons grated orange peel
1 teaspoon vanilla extract
2 cups sifted cake flour
2 teaspoons baking powder
1/2 teaspoon ground nutmeg
1/4 teaspoon baking soda
1/4 teaspoon salt
EGGNOG FILLING:
5 tablespoons all-purpose flour
1-1/4 cups eggnog
1 cup butter, softened
3/4 cup sugar
1 teaspoon vanilla extract
1/4 teaspoon ground nutmeg
CHOCOLATE ICING:
2 squares (1 ounce *each*) unsweetened baking chocolate, melted
2/3 cup confectioners' sugar
1/4 teaspoon ground cinnamon
1/8 teaspoon ground nutmeg
3 tablespoons butter, softened
2 tablespoons heavy whipping cream
2 to 3 tablespoons hot water

Cream butter and 3/4 cup sugar. Add yolks, one at a time, beating well after each addition. Combine orange juice, peel and vanilla. Combine the next five ingredients; add to creamed mixture alternately with juice mixture, beating well. In another bowl, beat whites until foamy; gradually add remaining sugar, beating until soft peaks form. Fold into batter.

Line two greased 9-in. round baking pans with waxed paper; grease paper. Pour batter into pans. Bake at 350° for 20 minutes or until cake tests done. Cool 5 minutes; remove to wire rack. Peel off paper; cool.

For filling, combine flour and a small amount of eggnog in a pan; stir until smooth. Stir in remaining eggnog; bring to a boil, stirring constantly. Cook and stir 2 minutes. Cool completely. Cream butter and confectioners' sugar; add vanilla and nutmeg. Gradually beat in eggnog mixture.

For frosting, mix chocolate, confectioners' sugar, cinnamon and nutmeg. Beat in butter and cream. Add water until frosting reaches desired consistency. Split cakes in half; spread filling on three layers. Stack with plain layer on top; frost the top. **Yield:** 14 servings.

Editor's Note: This recipe was tested with commercially prepared eggnog.

The Cake Divide

One way to make splitting a cake easier is to stick toothpicks at 1-1/2 in. intervals at the level you want to cut. Let the toothpicks guide you as you use a long, thin (preferably serrated) knife to cut the cake in half.

Cinnamon Apple Dumplings

(Pictured below)

When Mom made pies to feed the crew during wheat harvest, she always had plenty of dough left over, so she treated us kids to these special apple dumplings.
—Marie Hattrup, The Dalles, Oregon

    1 **cup all-purpose flour**
1/4 **teaspoon salt**
1/3 **cup shortening**
    3 **tablespoons ice water**
    2 **medium tart apples**
    3 **tablespoons sugar**
1/2 **teaspoon ground cinnamon**
Half-and-half cream
SAUCE:
1/3 **cup sugar**
    2 **tablespoons red-hot candies *or* 1/4 teaspoon**
       ground cinnamon
1/2 **teaspoon cornstarch**
2/3 **cup water**
    1 **tablespoon butter**
Additional half-and-half cream, optional

In a medium bowl, combine flour and salt. Cut in shortening until mixture resembles coarse crumbs. With a fork, stir in wa-

ter until dough forms a ball. Roll out on a floured surface to a 14-in. x 7-in. rectangle; cut pastry in half.

Peel and core apples; place one on each square of pastry. Combine sugar and cinnamon; spoon into apples. Moisten edges of pastry and gather around apples; pinch and seal.

Place dumplings in an ungreased 9-in. x 5-in. loaf pan or a shallow 1-1/2-qt. baking dish. Brush with cream.

In a small saucepan, combine the first five sauce ingredients; bring to a boil over medium-low heat, stirring frequently. Boil for 3 minutes. Pour between dumplings.

Bake at 400° for 35-45 minutes or until pastry is golden brown and apples are tender. Serve warm with cream if desired. **Yield:** 2 servings.

Coconut Fruitcake

(Pictured above)

A neighbor gave me this recipe when we first moved to this small town, saying it dated back to the 1800s and everybody in the area made it. I soon discovered why when I took a taste…and I'm not a fruitcake fan!
—Lorraine Groh, Ferryville, Wisconsin

    2 **cups all-purpose flour**
    1 **teaspoon baking powder**
    1 **teaspoon salt**
    1 **pound chopped fruitcake mix**
1-1/2 **cups flaked coconut**

1 cup golden raisins
1 cup chopped nuts
1/2 cup butter, softened
1 cup sugar
3 eggs, beaten
1 teaspoon lemon extract
1/2 cup orange juice
Additional candied fruit *or* nuts, optional

In a large bowl, combine flour, baking powder and salt. Add fruitcake mix, coconut, raisins and nuts; mix well.

In a mixing bowl, cream butter and sugar. Add eggs and extract; mix well. Stir in the flour mixture alternately with orange juice. Pack into a greased 10-in. tube pan lined with waxed paper.

Bake at 250° for 2 to 2-1/2 hours or until cake tests done. Cool for 10 minutes. Loosen edges with a sharp knife. Remove from pan to cool completely on a wire rack. Garnish with candied fruit or nuts if desired. **Yield:** 12-16 servings.

Harvest Sweet Potato Pie

My father called this "royal pie," fit for a king with its deliciously different flavor. This is a hand-me-down recipe, a treasure in our family. —Fae Fisher
Callao, Virginia

4 eggs
1 can (12 ounces) evaporated milk
1-1/4 cups sugar
3/4 cup butter, melted
2 teaspoons ground cinnamon
2 teaspoons pumpkin pie spice
1 teaspoon vanilla extract
1 teaspoon lemon extract
1/2 teaspoon salt
1/2 teaspoon ground nutmeg
4 cups mashed cooked sweet potatoes
2 unbaked pastry shells (9 inches)
Whipped cream, optional

In a mixing bowl, combine the first 10 ingredients; mix well. Beat in sweet potatoes. Pour into pastry shells. Bake at 425° for 15 minutes. Reduce heat to 350°; bake 30-35 minutes longer or until a knife inserted near the center comes out clean. Cool completely. Serve with whipped cream if desired. Store in the refrigerator. **Yield:** 12-16 servings.

Old-Fashioned Rice Pudding
(Pictured above)

This comforting dessert is a wonderful end to any meal. As a girl, I waited eagerly for the first heavenly bite. Today, my husband tops his with a scoop of ice cream.
—Sandra Melnychenko, Grandview, Manitoba

4-1/2 cups milk
1/2 cup uncooked long grain rice
1/3 cup sugar
1/2 teaspoon salt, optional
1/2 cup raisins
1 teaspoon vanilla extract
Ground cinnamon, optional

In a saucepan, combine milk, rice, sugar and salt if desired; bring to a boil over medium heat, stirring constantly. Pour into a greased 1-1/2-qt. baking dish. Cover and bake at 325° for 45 minutes, stirring every 15 minutes. Add raisins and vanilla; cover and bake for 15 minutes. Sprinkle with cinnamon if desired. Serve warm or chilled. Store in the refrigerator. **Yield:** about 6 servings.

Black Forest Torte

(Pictured above)

I'm proud to prepare this delectable dessert for family and friends alike. Folks love the chocolate cake layers separated by a dreamy cream filling. —Glatis McNiel
Constantine, Michigan

- 1-1/3 cups all-purpose flour
- 1-3/4 cups sugar
- 1-1/4 teaspoons baking soda
- 1/4 teaspoon baking powder
- 2/3 cup butter
- 4 squares (1 ounce *each*) unsweetened chocolate
- 1-1/4 cups water
- 1 teaspoon vanilla extract
- 3 eggs

CHOCOLATE FILLING:
- 2 bars (4 ounces *each*) German sweet chocolate, *divided*
- 3/4 cup butter
- 1/2 cup chopped pecans

CREAM FILLING:
- 2 cups heavy whipping cream
- 1 tablespoon confectioners' sugar
- 1 teaspoon vanilla extract

In a mixing bowl, combine flour, sugar, baking soda and baking powder. In a saucepan, melt butter and chocolate; cool. Pour chocolate mixture, water and vanilla into flour mixture. Beat on low for 1 minute, then on medium for 2 minutes. Add eggs, one at a time, beating well after each addition. Divide batter among two 9-in. round pans that have been greased, floured and lined with waxed paper. Bake at 350° for 25-30 minutes or until cakes test done. Cool in pans 10 minutes. Remove to a wire rack.

For chocolate filling, melt 1-1/2 bars of German chocolate over low heat. Stir in butter and nuts. Watching closely, cool filling just until it reaches spreading consistency. For cream filling, whip cream with sugar and vanilla until stiff peaks form.

To assemble, slice cooled cake layers in half horizontally. Place one bottom layer on a serving platter; cover with half of the chocolate filling. Top with a second cake layer; spread on half of the cream filling. Repeat layers. Grate remaining German chocolate; sprinkle on the top. Refrigerate until serving. **Yield:** 12-16 servings.

Gingerbread Yule Log

(Pictured below)

Whenever our family gets together for the holidays, this is what I'm asked to bring. I've made it for parties, too, and there have never been any leftovers.
—Bernadette Colvin, Houston, Texas

- 3 eggs, *separated*
- 1/2 cup molasses
- 1 tablespoon butter, melted
- 1/4 cup sugar
- 1 cup all-purpose flour
- 3/4 teaspoon *each* baking powder and baking soda

1/2 teaspoon *each* ground cinnamon, ginger and
  cloves
1/8 teaspoon salt
SPICED CREAM FILLING:
1-1/2 cups heavy whipping cream
1/3 cup confectioners' sugar
  1 teaspoon ground cinnamon
  1 teaspoon vanilla extract
1/4 teaspoon ground cloves
Additional ground cinnamon, optional

In a mixing bowl, beat yolks on high until thickened, about 3 minutes. Beat in molasses and butter. In another bowl, beat whites until foamy; gradually add sugar, beating until soft peaks form. Fold into yolk mixture. Combine dry ingredients; gently fold into egg mixture until well mixed. Spread in a greased and floured waxed paper-lined 15-in. x 10-in. x 1-in. baking pan. Bake at 375° for 9-12 minutes or until cake springs back when lightly touched.

Turn onto a linen towel dusted with confectioners' sugar. Peel off paper and roll cake up in towel, starting with a short side. Cool on a wire rack. Meanwhile, beat the first five filling ingredients in a mixing bowl until soft peaks form. Unroll cake; spread with half the filling. Roll up. Place on serving plate. Spread remaining filling over cake. Sprinkle with cinnamon if desired. **Yield:** 10 servings.

Cook and stir over medium-low heat until mixture is thick enough to coat a metal spoon and reaches 160°, about 15 minutes. Stir in the remaining ingredients. Refrigerate for several hours or overnight. Fill ice cream freezer cylinder two-thirds full; freeze according to manufacturer's instructions. Refrigerate remaining mixture until ready to freeze. Remove ice cream from the freezer 10 minutes before serving. **Yield:** 1 gallon.

German Chocolate Ice Cream

(Pictured above right)

I found this recipe years ago and have taken it to ice cream socials ever since.—Peggy Key, Grant, Alabama

1-1/2 cups sugar
1/4 cup all-purpose flour
1/4 teaspoon ground cinnamon
1/4 teaspoon salt
  4 cups milk
  3 eggs, beaten
  1 quart half-and-half cream
  2 packages (4 ounces *each*) German sweet
    chocolate, melted
  1 cup flaked coconut
  1 cup chopped pecans

In a large heavy saucepan, combine the sugar, flour, cinnamon and salt. Gradually add milk and eggs; stir until smooth.

Pineapple Upside-Down Cake

You need just a few easy ingredients to dress up a boxed mix. It bakes up so moist and pretty, no one will believe it wasn't made from scratch. —Gloria Poyer Hackettstown, New Jersey

  6 canned pineapple slices
  6 maraschino cherries
  1 cup chopped walnuts, divided
  1 package (18-1/4 ounces) white cake mix

Place pineapple slices in a greased and floured 10-in. tube pan. Place a cherry in the center of each slice. Sprinkle half of the walnuts around the pineapple. Prepare cake mix according to package directions; spoon batter over pineapple layer. Sprinkle with remaining nuts.

Bake at 350° for 40-45 minutes or until a toothpick inserted near the center comes out clean. Cool for 10 minutes before inverting onto a wire rack to cool completely. **Yield:** 10 servings.

Strawberry Nut Roll

(Pictured above)

The oldest of seven children, I did a lot of cooking and baking while I was growing up. Desserts like this refreshing rolled shortcake are my favorite. The nutty cake, creamy filling and fresh strawberries make pretty swirled slices. —*Judy Hayes, Peosta, Iowa*

> 6 eggs, *separated*
> 3/4 cup sugar, *divided*
> 1 cup ground walnuts, toasted
> 1/4 cup dry bread crumbs
> 1/4 cup all-purpose flour
> 1/8 teaspoon salt
> Confectioners' sugar
> FILLING:
> 1 pint fresh strawberries
> 1 cup heavy whipping cream
> 2 tablespoons sugar
> 1 teaspoon vanilla extract
> Confectioners' sugar

In a mixing bowl, beat egg whites until soft peaks form. Gradually add 1/4 cup sugar, beating until stiff peaks form. Set aside. In another mixing bowl, beat egg yolks and remaining sugar until thick and lemon-colored. Combine walnuts, bread crumbs, flour and salt; add to yolk mixture. Mix well. Fold in egg white mixture.

Line a greased 15-in. x 10-in. x 1-in. baking pan with waxed paper; grease the paper. Spread batter evenly into pan. Bake at 375° for 15 minutes or until cake springs back when lightly touched. Cool for 5 minutes. Invert cake onto a kitchen towel dusted with confectioners' sugar. Gently peel off waxed paper. Roll up cake in the towel jelly-roll style, starting with a short side. Cool on a wire rack.

Slice six large strawberries in half; set aside for garnish. Thinly slice remaining berries; set aside. In a mixing bowl, beat cream until soft peaks form. Gradually add sugar and vanilla, beating until stiff peaks form. Unroll cake; spread with filling to within 1/2 in. of edges. Top with sliced berries. Roll up again. Place, seam side down, on serving platter. Chill until serving. Dust with confectioners' sugar. Garnish with reserved strawberries. Refrigerate leftovers. **Yield:** 12 servings.

Cherry Almond Mousse Pie

(Pictured on page 183)

Christmas is the perfect time to treat your family and guests to a luscious pie with chocolate, cherries and nuts in a creamy vanilla mousse. It's a sweet yet light dessert. —*Dorothy Pritchett, Wills Point, Texas*

> 1 can (14 ounces) sweetened condensed milk, *divided*
> 1 square (1 ounce) unsweetened chocolate
> 1/2 teaspoon almond extract, *divided*
> 1 pastry shell (9 inches), baked
> 1 jar (10 ounces) maraschino cherries, drained
> 1 package (8 ounces) cream cheese, softened
> 1 cup cold water
> 1 package (3.4 ounces) instant vanilla pudding mix
> 1 cup heavy whipping cream, whipped
> 1/2 cup chopped toasted almonds
> Chocolate curls, optional

In a saucepan over low heat, cook and stir 1/2 cup of milk and chocolate until the chocolate is melted and mixture is thickened, about 4-5 minutes. Stir in 1/4 teaspoon extract. Pour into pastry shell; set aside. Reserve eight whole cherries for garnish. Chop the remaining cherries; set aside.

In a mixing bowl, beat the cream cheese until light. Gradually beat in water and remaining milk. Add pudding mix and remaining extract; mix well. Fold in whipped cream. Stir in chopped cherries and almonds. Pour over the pie. Chill 4 hours or until set. Garnish with whole cherries and chocolate curls if desired. **Yield:** 8-10 servings.

Peppermint Charlotte

My guests always save room for this pretty pink peppermint dessert. You'll know why after just one cool and fluffy bite. —*Lucille Watters, Palmyra, Missouri*

> 2 **envelopes unflavored gelatin**
> 3-1/2 **cups milk**
> 1/2 **cup sugar**
> 1/8 **teaspoon salt**
> 5 **egg yolks, beaten**
> 1/2 **cup finely crushed peppermint candy**
> 8 **drops red food coloring**
> 1-1/2 **cups heavy whipping cream, whipped**
> 12 **ladyfingers, split**

In a saucepan, soften gelatin in milk for 1 minute. Stir in sugar and salt. Cook and stir over medium-low heat for 5 minutes or until gelatin is dissolved. Remove from the heat. Stir a small amount of hot mixture into egg yolks. Return all to the pan. Cook and stir over low heat until the mixture thickens slightly and coats the back of a metal spoon or reaches 160° (do not boil).

Remove from the heat. Add candy and food coloring; stir until candy is dissolved. Refrigerate, stirring occasionally, until mixture begins to thicken, about 30 minutes. Fold in whipped cream. Place ladyfinger halves around a greased 9-in. springform pan. Pour mixture into center of pan. Cover and chill for 4 hours or overnight. Just before serving, run a knife around edge of pan to loosen; remove sides. **Yield:** 10-12 servings.

Mom's Cranberry Pie

My family absolutely loves cranberries, especially in a pie. I've made this recipe for years and it's a must for the holidays. —*Laura Belscher, Buffalo, New York*

> 2 **cups fresh** *or* **frozen cranberries**
> 1 **to 1-1/2 cups sugar**
> 2 **tablespoons all-purpose flour**
> 1 **teaspoon vanilla extract**
> 1/2 **cup water**
> 1 **teaspoon grated orange peel, optional**
> **Pastry for a double-crust pie (9 inches)**

In a large bowl, combine first six ingredients. Pour filling into pie shell and top with a lattice crust. Bake at 350° for 1 hour or until crust is golden brown. Cool. **Yield:** 8 servings.

Pecan Torte

(Pictured below)

This is an old family recipe that uses our Texas pecans. I've made it often for birthdays and family gatherings. My brother-in-law said it was the only cake he's ever eaten in which the cake tastes as good as the frosting! —*Joan Rice, De Soto, Texas*

> 12 **eggs,** *separated*
> 2 **cups sugar**
> 2-1/2 **cups ground pecans**
> 1/2 **cup dry bread crumbs**
> 1/2 **teaspoon vanilla extract**
> **BUTTER CREAM FROSTING:**
> 1 **cup milk**
> 1/4 **cup cornstarch**
> 2 **cups (12 ounces) semisweet chocolate chips**
> 1 **cup butter, softened**
> 2 **cups confectioners' sugar**
> 2 **teaspoons vanilla extract**
> **Whole pecans, optional**

In a mixing bowl, beat egg yolks and sugar until thick and lemon-colored, about 5-6 minutes. Combine pecans and bread crumbs; stir into yolk mixture with vanilla. In another mixing bowl, beat the egg whites until stiff peaks form; fold into batter. Divide evenly among three greased and waxed paper-lined 9-in. round baking pans. Bake at 350° for 25-30 minutes or until cakes test done. Cool for 10 minutes before removing from pans; cool completely on a wire rack.

For frosting, combine milk and cornstarch in a saucepan until well blended. Add chocolate chips. Cook and stir over medium heat until thickened. Cool to room temperature. In a mixing bowl, cream butter and confectioners' sugar. Add vanilla and beat until smooth. Stir in chocolate mixture; beat until fluffy. Spread between cooled cake layers. Frost top and sides. Garnish with pecans if desired. **Yield:** 12-16 servings.

Festive Cranberry Cake

(Pictured below)

This cake, a favorite in my family, makes good use of our cranberry harvest. What's more, since you can prepare it the night before, this recipe is a real time-saver. —Gladys Wilson, Anchorage, Alaska

    3/4 cup butter, softened
    1 cup sugar
    2 eggs
2-1/4 cups all-purpose flour
    1 teaspoon baking powder
    1 teaspoon baking soda
    1 cup buttermilk
    1 cup fresh or frozen cranberries
    1 cup chopped dates
    1 cup chopped pecans
GLAZE:
    1/2 cup orange juice
    1/4 cup sugar
Fresh mint and additional cranberries, optional

In a mixing bowl, cream butter and sugar. Add eggs; beat well. Combine dry ingredients; add to creamed mixture alternately with buttermilk. Stir in cranberries, dates and pecans. Spread in a greased and floured 10-in. tube pan. Bake at 350° for 60-70 minutes or until a toothpick inserted near the center comes out clean. Cool in pan for 10 minutes.

Meanwhile, for glaze, heat orange juice and sugar in a small saucepan until sugar dissolves. Invert cake onto a serving plate. With a toothpick, punch holes in cake. Spoon glaze over cake. Cover and refrigerate for at least 8 hours. Garnish with mint and cranberries if desired. **Yield:** 12-16 servings.

Eggnog Pound Cake

A flavorful blend of eggnog and nutmeg makes this cake a natural holiday favorite. It uses a convenient boxed mix base. —Theresa Koetter, Borden, Indiana

    1 package (18-1/4 ounces) yellow cake mix
    1 cup eggnog
    3 eggs
    1/2 cup butter, softened
    1/2 to 1 teaspoon ground nutmeg
CUSTARD SAUCE:
    1/4 cup sugar
    1 tablespoon cornstarch
    1/4 teaspoon salt
    1 cup milk
    1 egg yolk, lightly beaten
    1 teaspoon butter
    1 teaspoon vanilla extract
    1/2 cup heavy whipping cream, whipped

In a mixing bowl, combine the first five ingredients. Beat on low until moistened, scraping bowl occasionally. Beat on medium for 2 minutes. Pour into a greased and floured 12-cup fluted tube pan. Bake at 350° for 40-45 minutes or until a toothpick inserted near the center comes out clean. Cool in pan for 10 minutes; invert onto a wire rack. Remove from pan; cool completely.

For sauce, combine sugar, cornstarch and salt in a saucepan; gradually stir in milk. Bring to a boil over medium heat; boil for 1-2 minutes, stirring constantly. Blend a small amount into egg yolk. Return all to the pan; mix well. Cook and stir for 2 minutes. Remove from the heat; stir in butter and vanilla. Cool for 15 minutes. Fold in whipped cream. Store in the refrigerator. Serve with the cake. **Yield:** 16-20 servings.

Editor's Note: This recipe was tested with commercially prepared eggnog.

Spiced Chiffon Cake

(Pictured at right)

Whenever any member of the family wants a cake for a special occasion, they request this one. It really is very good! —Vera Woodward, Carmichael, California

2-1/2 cups sugar
    2 cups all-purpose flour
    1 tablespoon baking powder
    1 teaspoon salt
    1 teaspoon ground cinnamon
    1/2 teaspoon ground allspice
    1/2 teaspoon ground cloves
    1/2 teaspoon ground nutmeg
    3/4 cup cold water
    1/2 cup vegetable oil
    7 eggs, *separated*
    1/2 teaspoon cream of tartar
GLAZE:
    2 tablespoons butter
    1 tablespoon all-purpose flour
    1/8 teaspoon salt
    1/4 cup milk
    1/4 cup packed brown sugar
    1/4 teaspoon vanilla extract
    1 cup confectioners' sugar
Chopped walnuts

In a large mixing bowl, combine sugar, flour, baking powder, salt, cinnamon, allspice, cloves and nutmeg. Add water, oil and egg yolks. Beat on low speed just until combined. Increase speed and beat until smooth. Set aside. In a mixing bowl, beat egg whites with cream of tartar until stiff peaks form; fold into batter. Pour into an ungreased 10-in. tube pan. Bake at 325° for 70 minutes or until top springs back when lightly touched. Im-

mediately invert pan; cool completely. Remove from pan.

For glaze, melt butter in a saucepan. Whisk in flour and salt until smooth. Add milk, stirring constantly. Bring to a boil; cook and stir until thick and bubbly. Remove from the heat; beat in brown sugar and vanilla. Add confectioners' sugar; mix until smooth. Drizzle over cake. Sprinkle with nuts. **Yield:** 12 servings.

Caramel Custard

(Pictured at left)

My husband and I have enjoyed this simple dessert many times, especially after a Tex-Mex meal. In fact, I've made it so often I don't even look at the recipe. —Linda McBride, Austin, Texas

1-1/2 cups sugar, *divided*
    6 eggs
    2 teaspoons vanilla extract
    3 cups milk

In a heavy saucepan over low heat, cook and stir 3/4 cup sugar until melted and golden. Pour into eight 6-oz. custard cups, tilting to coat bottom of cup; let stand for 10 minutes. In a large bowl, beat eggs, vanilla, milk and remaining sugar until combined but not foamy. Pour over caramelized sugar.

Place the cups in two 8-in. square baking pans. Pour boiling water in pans to a depth of 1 in. Bake at 350° for 40-45 minutes or until a knife inserted near center comes out clean. Remove from pans to cool on wire racks. To unmold, run a knife around rim of cup and invert onto dessert plate. Serve warm or chilled. **Yield:** 8 servings.

Apricot Fruitcake

My husband didn't care for fruitcake, which I love, until he tasted this one. Apricots add a unique sweetness, while three kinds of nuts add a nice crunch.
— *Clare Brooks, Juneau, Alaska*

>   2 cups *each* coarsely chopped pecans,
>   walnuts and Brazil nuts
>   2 cups golden raisins
>   2 cups *each* coarsely chopped dried apricots
>   and dates
>   1 cup *each* red and green candied cherries, halved
> 1/2 cup honey
> 1/4 cup water
>   1 teaspoon lemon juice
>   1 cup butter, softened
> 1-1/4 cups packed brown sugar
>   4 eggs
>   2 cups all-purpose flour
>   1 teaspoon ground cinnamon
> 1/2 teaspoon salt
> 1/2 teaspoon *each* ground cloves, mace and nutmeg
> 1/4 teaspoon baking soda

In a large bowl, combine the nuts, fruits, honey, water and lemon juice; set aside. In a mixing bowl, cream butter and sugar. Add eggs and mix well. Fold into fruit mixture. Combine dry ingredients; gradually fold into the fruit mixture until evenly coated. Pour into two greased and waxed paper-lined 9-in. x 5-in. x 3-in. loaf pans.

With a shallow pan of water on a lower oven rack, bake at 275° for 2-1/2 hours or until cake tests done. Cover with foil during the last 30 minutes. Cool 10 minutes; remove to wire rack to cool completely. Remove waxed paper and wrap each cake in foil. Place in plastic bags and store in a cool dry place. **Yield:** 2 loaves.

Festive Mint Sundaes

These simple-to-make sundaes get their holiday look from chopped green cherries and their tempting taste from chocolate mint candies that are melted and drizzled on top. — *Carole Martin, Tallahassee, Florida*

>   1 jar (8 ounces) green maraschino cherries,
>   undrained
> Vanilla ice cream
>   18 mint Andes candies

Place cherries with juice in a blender or food processor; cover and chop. Spoon ice cream into bowls; top with cherries. Place six mints in a small heavy-duty resealable plastic bag; microwave just until melted.

Snip a small opening in one corner of bag; squeeze melted chocolate over sundaes. Garnish with remaining mints; serve. **Yield:** 6 servings.

Cranberry Apple Crisp

(Pictured below)

This is a wonderful dessert for fall, when both cranberries and apples are in season. The fruits are quite compatible in flavor and color, and they help make any table look festive and inviting. — *Martha Sue Stroud
Clarksville, Texas*

>   3 cups chopped peeled tart apples
>   2 cups fresh *or* frozen cranberries
>   1 cup sugar
>   3 tablespoons all-purpose flour
> **TOPPING:**
> 1-1/2 cups quick-cooking oats
> 1/2 cup all-purpose flour
> 1/2 cup packed brown sugar
> 1/2 cup butter, melted
> 1/4 cup chopped pecans

Combine apples, cranberries, sugar and flour. Pour into a greased 11-in. x 7-in. x 2-in. baking dish. In a bowl, mix topping ingredients until crumbly; sprinkle over apple mixture. Bake at 350° for 50-55 minutes or until the fruit is tender. **Yield:** 6-8 servings.

Marbled Peppermint Angel Cake

Although it doesn't puff up as much as other angel food cakes during baking, the refreshing minty flavor and festive red swirls raise this version above ordinary desserts! —Kathy Kittell, Lenexa, Kansas

1-1/2 cups egg whites (about 12)
1-1/2 teaspoons cream of tartar
1-1/2 teaspoons vanilla extract
   1 teaspoon peppermint extract
1/4 teaspoon salt
1-1/2 cups sugar, *divided*
   3/4 cup all-purpose flour
   6 drops red food coloring, optional
GLAZE:
   2 cups confectioners' sugar
   1/4 cup milk
   1/4 teaspoon peppermint extract
   6 drops red food coloring, optional
   1/4 cup crushed peppermint candies

In a mixing bowl, beat egg whites, cream of tartar, extracts and salt on high speed. Gradually add 3/4 cup of sugar, beating until stiff peaks form and sugar is dissolved. Combine flour and remaining sugar; gradually fold into the batter, 1/4 cup at a time.

Divide batter in half; tint half with red food coloring. Alternately spoon plain and pink batters into an ungreased 10-in. tube pan. Cut through the batter with a knife to remove air pockets. Bake at 350° for 30-40 minutes or until cake springs back when lightly touched. Immediately invert pan; cool completely. Run a knife around sides of cake and remove from the pan.

For glaze, combine confectioners' sugar, milk, extract and food coloring if desired. Drizzle over cake. Sprinkle with crushed candies. **Yield:** 12-16 servings.

Toffee-Mocha Cream Torte

(Pictured at right)

Instant coffee granules give the moist chocolate cake a mild mocha flavor…while the fluffy whipped cream layers, blended with brown sugar and toffee bits, are deliciously rich. —Lynn Rogers, Richfield, North Carolina

   1 cup butter, softened
   2 cups sugar

   2 eggs
1-1/2 teaspoons vanilla extract
2-2/3 cups all-purpose flour
   3/4 cup baking cocoa
   2 teaspoons baking soda
1/4 teaspoon salt
   1 cup buttermilk
   2 teaspoons instant coffee granules
   1 cup boiling water
TOPPING:
   1/2 teaspoon instant coffee granules
   1 teaspoon hot water
   2 cups heavy whipping cream
   3 tablespoons light brown sugar
   6 Heath candy bars (1.4 ounces *each*), crushed, *divided*

In a mixing bowl, cream butter and sugar. Beat in eggs and vanilla. Combine flour, cocoa, baking soda and salt; add to creamed mixture alternately with buttermilk. Dissolve coffee in water; add to batter. Beat for 2 minutes.

Pour into three greased and floured 9-in. round baking pans. Bake at 350° for 16-20 minutes or until a toothpick inserted near the center comes out clean. Cool for 10 minutes before removing from pans to wire racks to cool completely.

For topping, dissolve coffee in water in a mixing bowl; cool. Add cream and brown sugar. Beat until stiff peaks form. Place bottom cake layer on a serving plate; top with 1-1/3 cups of topping. Sprinkle with 1/2 cup of crushed candy bars. Repeat layers twice. Store in the refrigerator. **Yield:** 12-14 servings.

Walnut Wedges

(Pictured at right)

When you want to serve something light but fancier than cookies, these dainty treats make a beautiful dessert. With a prepared pie crust, they're easy...yet have a special holiday look—the perfect combination for a busy time of year. —Connie Meinke
Neenah, Wisconsin

Pastry for double-crust pie
1 cup finely chopped walnuts
1/3 cup sugar
2 tablespoons honey
1 teaspoon ground cinnamon
1 teaspoon lemon juice
1 to 2 tablespoons milk
1/2 cup semisweet chocolate chips
1 teaspoon shortening

Roll out bottom crust to a 10-1/2-in. circle; place on an ungreased baking sheet. Combine nuts, sugar, honey, cinnamon and lemon juice; spread over crust. Roll out remaining pastry and place over nuts. With fork tines, seal edges together and pierce holes in top. Brush with milk.

Bake at 375° for 15-20 minutes or until lightly browned. Cool for 10 minutes. Cut into 16-20 wedges. Cool completely. In a small saucepan, melt chocolate chips and shortening over low heat; drizzle over wedges. **Yield:** 16-20 servings.

Baked Fudge Pudding

(Pictured at right)

This easy-to-make pudding is a true chocolate lover's delight. I always look forward to that first dishful warm from the oven. You can top it with whipped cream, spoon it over ice cream or enjoy the fudgy flavor all by itself! —Sue Ann Chapman, Tulsa, Oklahoma

2 cups sugar
1/2 cup all-purpose flour
1/2 cup baking cocoa
4 eggs
2 teaspoons vanilla extract
1 cup butter, melted
1 cup chopped pecans
Mint chocolate chip ice cream, whipped cream,
  chopped pecans *and/or* chocolate sauce, optional

In a mixing bowl, combine sugar, flour and cocoa. Add eggs and mix well. Beat in vanilla and butter; stir in pecans. Pour into a greased 8-in. square baking pan. Place in a larger pan filled with 1 in. of hot water. Bake at 300° for 65 minutes or until set. Serve warm or at room temperature; top with ice cream, whipped cream, pecans and/or chocolate sauce if desired. **Yield:** 9 servings.

Paradise Pumpkin Pie

(Pictured at right)

Whenever I take this pie to a holiday party, potluck supper or bake sale, I take along copies of the recipe, too—I'm sure to be asked for it. With the pie's very rich taste, even a sliver is satisfying! —Karen Owen
Rising Sun, Indiana

1 package (8 ounces) cream cheese, softened
1/4 cup sugar
1/2 teaspoon vanilla extract
1 egg
1 unbaked pastry shell (9 inches)
FILLING:
1 can (16 ounces) solid-pack pumpkin
1 cup evaporated milk
2 eggs, beaten
1/4 cup sugar
1/4 cup packed brown sugar
1 teaspoon ground cinnamon
1/4 teaspoon salt
1/4 teaspoon ground nutmeg
TOPPING:
2 tablespoons all-purpose flour
2 tablespoons brown sugar
1 tablespoon butter, softened
1/2 cup chopped pecans

In a mixing bowl, beat cream cheese until smooth. Add sugar and vanilla; mix well. Add egg; beat until smooth. Spread over bottom of pie shell. Chill 30 minutes. In a mixing bowl, beat filling ingredients until smooth. Carefully pour over the cream cheese layer. Cover edge of pie with foil. Bake at 350° for 30 minutes. Remove foil; bake 25 minutes longer.

Meanwhile, mix flour, brown sugar and butter until crumbly; stir in pecans. Sprinkle over pie. Bake 10-15 minutes more or until a knife inserted near the center comes out clean. Cool on a wire rack. Store in the refrigerator. **Yield:** 6-8 servings.

Top to bottom: Eggnog Cake Roll (recipe on page 240), Walnut Wedges, Paradise Pumpkin Pie and Baked Fudge Pudding

Apricot Layer Cake

(Pictured above)

You don't have to tell anyone this tender fruity layer cake starts with a convenient mix. Of course, the cat will be out of the bag once folks request the recipe!
—Molly Knapp, Eureka, Illinois

  1 package (18-1/2 ounces) white cake mix
1-1/4 cups water
  3 egg whites
 1/3 cup vegetable oil
  1 tablespoon grated orange peel
  1 teaspoon orange *or* lemon extract
 2/3 cup apricot preserves
BROWN BUTTER FROSTING:
 1/2 cup butter
3-1/2 to 4 cups confectioners' sugar
 1/3 cup orange juice
 1/4 cup chopped pecans

In a mixing bowl, combine the first six ingredients; beat on low speed for 30 seconds or until moistened. Beat on high for 2 minutes. Pour into two greased and floured 8-in. round baking pans. Bake at 350° for 30-35 minutes or until a toothpick inserted near the center comes out clean. Cool for 10 minutes; remove from pans to a wire rack to cool completely.

Split each layer in half horizontally. Spread the cut side of each bottom layer with 1/3 cup apricot preserves; replace tops and set aside.

For frosting, in a heavy saucepan, cook and stir butter over medium heat for 7-8 minutes or until golden brown. Pour into a mixing bowl; add 3 cups confectioners' sugar and orange

juice. Beat until smooth. Add enough of the remaining sugar to reach spreading consistency. Spread frosting between filled cakes; frost top and sides of cake. Sprinkle with nuts. Store in the refrigerator. **Yield:** 12 servings.

Eggnog Cake Roll

(Pictured on page 239)

This festive dessert is on the menu for lots of special occasions at our house—especially Christmas.
—Lee Herzog, Salt Lake City, Utah

  4 eggs, *separated*
 3/4 cup sugar, *divided*
1-1/2 teaspoons vanilla extract, *divided*
 3/4 cup sifted cake flour
 3/4 teaspoon baking powder
 1/4 teaspoon salt
 1/4 teaspoon ground nutmeg
  4 tablespoons confectioners' sugar, *divided*
  4 teaspoons cornstarch
1-1/2 cups eggnog
  1 can (8 ounces) crushed pineapple, *drained*
 2/3 cup quartered maraschino cherries
 1/4 cup flaked coconut
  1 cup heavy whipping cream
Green food coloring
Additional maraschino cherries, optional

In a large mixing bowl, beat egg yolks until thick and lemon-colored, about 3 minutes. Add 1/2 cup of sugar; beat 2 minutes. Add 1 teaspoon vanilla; mix well. In another mixing bowl, beat egg whites until foamy; gradually add remaining sugar, beating until soft peaks form. Fold into yolk mixture. Combine cake flour, baking powder, salt and nutmeg. Fold into egg mixture until no flour streaks remain. Spread batter evenly in a greased and floured 15-in. x 10-in. x 1-in. baking pan. Bake at 375° for 13-15 minutes or until a toothpick comes out clean.

Turn out onto a linen towel dusted with 2 tablespoons confectioners' sugar. Roll cake up in towel, starting with a short end. Cool on wire rack. Meanwhile, for filling, combine cornstarch and a small amount of eggnog in a saucepan; mix until smooth. Stir in remaining eggnog; bring to a boil, stirring constantly. Cook and stir 2 minutes more. Remove from heat; stir in remaining vanilla. Cool.

Unroll cake; spread with filling. Sprinkle with pineapple, cherries and coconut; roll up again. Whip cream with remaining confectioners' sugar; tint green. Spread over outside of cake roll. Chill for 3-4 hours. **Yield:** 10-12 servings.

Strawberry Schaum Torte

I've served this impressive dessert at baptisms and holidays and enjoy making it for our children and grand-children when they come to visit.
—Geraldine Sauke, Alberta Lea, Minnesota

> 6 egg whites
> 1 teaspoon baking powder
> 1/4 teaspoon salt
> 2 teaspoons vinegar
> 2 teaspoons water
> 2 teaspoons vanilla extract
> 2 cups sugar

FILLING:

> 1 package (3 ounces) strawberry gelatin
> 1/2 cup boiling water
> 1 cup fresh *or* frozen sliced strawberries
> 1 teaspoon lemon juice

Dash salt
1-1/2 cups heavy whipped cream

Place first six ingredients in a large mixing bowl. Beat at high speed. Gradually add sugar; continue beating on high until stiff peaks form. Spread evenly in a greased 13-in. x 9-in. x 2-in. baking pan. Bake at 300° for 45 minutes. Turn off oven and do not open door. Let cool in oven overnight.

For filling, dissolve gelatin in water in a bowl. Stir in strawberries, lemon juice and salt (mixture will thicken quickly). Fold in cream. Spread filling over crust. Refrigerate until serving time. **Yield:** 12 servings.

Old-Fashioned Coconut Pie

(Pictured above)

My husband says it's not good cooking unless it's made from scratch. This is an old-fashioned way of making coconut pie from scratch. *—Barbara Smith Franklin, Georgia*

> 1/4 cup all-purpose flour
> 1 cup sugar

Dash salt

> 2 cups milk
> 3 egg yolks, beaten
> 1-1/2 teaspoons vanilla extract
> 1-1/4 cups flaked coconut, *divided*
> 1 pie shell (9 inches), baked

MERINGUE:

> 3 egg whites
> 6 tablespoons sugar

In a saucepan, combine flour and sugar; add salt, milk and egg yolks. Mix well. Cook over medium heat, stirring constantly, until mixture is thickened and bubbly. Reduce heat; cook and stir 2 minutes more. Remove from the heat; stir in vanilla and 1 cup coconut. Pour hot filling into pie shell.

For meringue, beat egg whites in a mixing bowl until soft peaks form. Gradually beat in sugar until mixture forms stiff glossy peaks and sugar dissolves. Spread meringue over hot filling. Sprinkle with remaining coconut. Bake at 350° for 12-15 minutes or until golden. Cool. Store in the refrigerator. **Yield:** 6-8 servings.

Prebaking a Pastry Shell

Place pastry in the pie plate and flute edges. Line unpricked shell with double thickness of heavy-duty foil.

If desired, fill shell with dried beans, uncooked rice or pie weights. The weight will keep the crust from puffing up, shrinking and slipping down the pie plate during baking.

Bake at 450° for 8 minutes. With oven mitts, carefully remove the foil and beans, rice or weights. Bake 5-6 minutes longer or until light golden brown.

Cool on a wire rack. Let beans or rice cool, then store. They may be reused for pie weights, but they cannot be cooked or used in recipes.

Vanilla Wafer Fruitcake

(Pictured at right)

This was my dear grandmother's recipe. She was a farmer's wife and a very good cook. —Rita Bingham
Edmond, Oklahoma

- **1/2 pound candied cherries**
- **1/2 pound candied pineapple slices**
- **1 pound walnuts, pecans *or* combination of both**
- **1 pound vanilla wafers**
- **1/4 pound raisins**
- **2 eggs**
- **1/2 cup sugar**
- **1/4 teaspoon salt**
- **1 can (5 ounces) evaporated milk**

Reserve four whole cherries, two pineapple slices and 16 pecan or walnut halves. Chop remaining fruit and nuts. Crush vanilla wafers; combine with chopped fruit, nuts and raisins and set aside. In a bowl, beat eggs well. Stir in sugar, salt and milk. Combine wafer/nut mixture with egg mixture.

Pack into a waxed paper-lined angel food cake pan. Decorate top with reserved whole candy and nuts. Bake at 325° for 45 minutes. Let stand 10 minutes. Run a sharp knife around edge; turn cake out of pan, then back over again so decorations are on top. **Yield:** about 40 servings.

Yule Log

(Pictured at right)

It's become a tradition to prepare this Yule Log for holiday gatherings. The filling recipe came from an aunt and the butter cream frosting was my creation.
—Rosie Flanagan, Buchanan, Michigan

- **5 eggs, *separated***
- **2/3 cup sugar**
- **2 tablespoons all-purpose flour**
- **3 tablespoons unsweetened cocoa**

FILLING:
- **2-1/2 tablespoons all-purpose flour**
- **1/2 cup milk**
- **1/2 cup butter, softened**
- **1/2 cup sugar**
- **1/2 teaspoon vanilla extract**
- **1/2 cup chopped walnuts, optional**

MOCHA BUTTER CREAM FROSTING:
- **1 cup butter, softened**
- **1/2 cup confectioners' sugar**
- **1 tablespoon unsweetened cocoa**
- **1 teaspoon strong coffee**

Confectioners' sugar, optional

Chopped nuts, optional

In a large mixing bowl, beat egg yolks at high speed until light and fluffy. Gradually add sugar, beating until mixture is thick and light-colored. Add flour and cocoa, beating on low speed. In another bowl, beat egg whites until soft peaks form; fold into batter. Mix until no streaks of white remain.

Grease a 15-in. x 10-in. x 1-in. pan; line with waxed paper, and grease and flour paper. Spread batter evenly in pan. Bake at 350° for 15 minutes or until cake springs back when touched lightly. Cover with waxed paper and cool completely on wire rack. Remove paper; invert cake onto an 18-in.- long piece of waxed paper dusted with confectioners' sugar. Trim edges from all four sides of cake.

For filling, combine flour and milk in a saucepan. Cook over low heat, stirring until thick. Cool. In a mixing bowl, cream butter, sugar and vanilla. Add flour mixture; beat until fluffy. Fold in walnuts if desired. Spread on cake; roll up jelly-roll style, starting from one short end. For frosting, beat butter until fluffy in a small bowl. Beat in sugar, cocoa and coffee. Spread over cake, using a fork to create a bark-like effect. Sprinkle with confectioners' sugar and nuts if desired. **Yield:** 14-18 servings.

Holiday Pound Cake

(Pictured at right)

This cake is attractive and it tastes good, too. I'm always asked for the recipe.
—Nancy Reichert
Thomasville, Georgia

- **1 cup butter, softened**
- **1 package (8 ounces) cream cheese, softened**
- **1-1/2 cups sugar**
- **4 eggs**
- **1-1/2 teaspoons vanilla extract**
- **2-1/4 cups cake flour**
- **1-1/2 teaspoons baking powder**
- **1/2 teaspoon salt**
- **3/4 cup well-drained maraschino cherries**
- **1 cup chopped pecans, *divided***
- **1-1/2 cups confectioners' sugar**
- **2 to 3 tablespoons milk**

In a large mixing bowl, cream butter, cream cheese and sugar. Add eggs, one at a time, beating well after each addition. Add vanilla. Sift flour together with baking powder and salt; stir into creamed mixture. Fold in cherries and 1/2 cup nuts. Sprinkle remaining nuts into a greased 10-in. fluted tube pan. Pour batter into pan. Bake at 325° for about 70 minutes or until cake tests done. Cool cake in pan 5 minutes on wire rack before removing from pan. Cool thoroughly. Make a glaze with confectioners' sugar and milk; drizzle over cake. **Yield:** 12-16 servings.

Top to bottom: Holiday Pound Cake, Yule Log and Vanilla Wafer Fruitcake

Coconut Cake Supreme

(Pictured above)

I make most cakes from scratch, but during the holiday rush, this recipe that starts with a convenient box mix buys me some time. Most eager eaters don't suspect the shortcut when you dress up the cake with coconut filling and frosting.
                                                    —Betty Claycomb
                                                    Alverton, Pennsylvania

    1 package (18-1/4 ounces) yellow cake mix
    2 cups (16 ounces) sour cream
    2 cups sugar
1-1/2 cups flaked coconut
    1 carton (8 ounces) frozen whipped topping, thawed
Fresh mint and red gumdrops, optional

Prepare and bake cake according to package directions in two 9-in. round baking pans. Cool in pans for 10 minutes before removing to a wire rack to cool completely.

For filling, combine sour cream and sugar; mix well. Stir in coconut (filling will be soft). Set aside 1 cup of filling for frosting.

To assemble, split each cake into two horizontal layers. Place one layer on a serving platter; cover with a third of the filling. Repeat layers. Fold reserved filling into whipped topping; frost cake. Refrigerate for at least 4 hours. Garnish with mint and gumdrops if desired. **Yield:** 10-12 servings.

Chocolate Crepes with Cranberry Sauce

With its unique flavor and festive look, this dessert has become a "must" for Christmas at our house. It's an elegant addition to the dinner table. The cranberry sauce adds nice holiday color drizzled over the chocolate crepes. Any time someone new tries these, I'm asked to share the recipe, which I do cheerfully.
                                          —Lynda Sarkisian, Inman, South Carolina

    1 package (3.4 ounces) instant vanilla pudding mix
2-1/2 cups milk, *divided*
    1 carton (8 ounces) frozen whipped topping, thawed
    2 tablespoons vegetable oil
    3 eggs
1-1/2 teaspoons vanilla extract
    1/4 cup sugar
1-1/2 cups all-purpose flour
    2 tablespoons baking cocoa
    1/8 teaspoon salt
CRANBERRY SAUCE:
1-1/2 cups fresh *or* frozen cranberries
    1 cup cranberry juice
    1/2 cup packed brown sugar
1-1/2 teaspoons cornstarch
    1/2 teaspoon grated orange peel
    1/4 teaspoon ground nutmeg
    1/8 teaspoon salt
    2 tablespoons butter
    1 teaspoon vanilla extract

In a medium bowl, whisk the pudding mix and 1 cup of the milk until smooth. Fold in the whipped topping; cover and chill.

In a blender container, combine oil, eggs, vanilla, sugar, flour, cocoa, salt and remaining milk; process until smooth. Let stand for 20 minutes.

Meanwhile, combine the first seven sauce ingredients in a small saucepan; bring to a boil. Reduce heat and simmer until smooth and thickened, stirring constantly, about 15 minutes. Remove from the heat; stir in the butter and vanilla. Keep warm.

Heat a lightly greased 6-in. skillet over medium heat until hot. Pour 3 tablespoons crepe batter into skillet and swirl quickly so bottom is evenly covered. Cook until top appears dry and bottom is lightly browned; turn and cook 15-20 seconds longer.

Remove and keep warm. Repeat with remaining batter. To serve, fold crepes in quarters; place three on a dessert plate. Top with chilled pudding mixture and warm sauce. **Yield:** 6-8 servings.

Pumpkin Ice Cream Roll

(Pictured below)

This wonderful, light and lovely dessert is our standby at Thanksgiving and Christmas. The subtle taste of pumpkin and the refreshing ice cream make a most delicious after-dinner treat!
—Gayle Lewis
Yucaipa, California

    3/4 cup all-purpose flour
      2 teaspoons pumpkin pie spice
      1 teaspoon baking powder
Dash salt
      3 eggs
      1 cup sugar
    2/3 cup pumpkin
Confectioners' sugar
      1 quart butter pecan ice cream, softened
Whipped cream, optional
Toasted chopped pecans, optional

In a small bowl, combine flour, pumpkin pie spice, baking powder and salt. In a mixing bowl, beat eggs at high speed for 5 minutes or until pale yellow. Gradually beat in sugar. Stir in pumpkin. Fold in dry ingredients.

Line a 15-in. x 10-in. x 1-in. baking pan with greased and floured waxed paper. Pour batter into pan; bake at 375° for 15 minutes. Turn cake out onto a linen towel sprinkled with confec-tioners' sugar. Peel off paper; roll up cake with towel. Cool on a wire rack. Unroll cake onto a baking sheet.

Spread softened ice cream to within 1 in. of edges. Roll up cake again, without the towel. Cover and freeze. To serve, let stand a few minutes at room temperature before slicing. If desired, dust cake with confectioners' sugar and top with the whipped cream and pecans. **Yield:** 10 servings.

Deep-Dish Cherry Pie

My great-aunt in Pennsylvania is a great country cook, and she gave this recipe to me. It's one of my husband's favorites. I like it, too—it's easier than two-crust pies, plus I've used both fresh and frozen cherries with good results. —Lillian Heston, Warren, New Jersey

      6 cups pitted tart red cherries
    3/4 cup sugar
    3/4 cup packed brown sugar
      3 tablespoons cornstarch
      1 teaspoon almond extract
Few drops red food coloring, optional
Dash salt
      3 to 4 tablespoons butter
CRUST:
  1-1/2 cups all purpose flour
      1 tablespoon sugar
    1/2 teaspoon salt
    1/2 teaspoon ground nutmeg
    1/2 cup plus 2 tablespoons shortening
      4 to 5 tablespoons ice water
Milk *or* cream
Additional sugar

In a large mixing bowl, combine cherries, sugars, cornstarch, extract, food coloring and salt. Place in a greased 1-1/2-qt. to 2-qt. casserole. Dot with butter. Set aside.

For crust, combine flour, sugar, salt and nutmeg. Cut in shortening. Add water, a little at a time, until a dough forms. Do not overmix.

Roll out on a floured surface to fit the top of the casserole. Place on top of the cherries, pressing against the sides of the dish. Cut decorative designs or slits in center of crust. Brush with milk or cream and sprinkle with sugar. Bake at 350° for 1 hour or until crust is golden brown. Cool at least 15 minutes before serving. **Yield:** 8-10 servings.

Carrot Cake

(Pictured below)

We have enjoyed this cake for years. Whenever there's a gathering of family and friends, my cake is always requested. —Melanie Habener, Santa Maria, California

3 eggs, beaten
3/4 cup vegetable oil
3/4 cup buttermilk
2 cups sugar
2 teaspoons vanilla extract
2 cups all-purpose flour
2 teaspoons ground cinnamon
2 teaspoons baking soda
1/2 teaspoon salt
1 can (8 ounces) crushed pineapple, undrained
2 cups grated carrots
1 cup raisins
1 cup chopped nuts
1 cup flaked coconut
CREAM CHEESE FROSTING:
1/2 cup butter, softened
1 package (8 ounces) cream cheese, softened
1 teaspoon vanilla extract
1 package (16 ounces) confectioners' sugar
2 tablespoons heavy whipping cream

In a mixing bowl, combine eggs, oil, buttermilk, sugar and vanilla; mix well. Combine flour, cinnamon, baking soda and salt; stir into egg mixture. Stir in pineapple, carrots, raisins, nuts and coconut. Pour into a greased and floured 13-in. x 9-in. x 2-in. baking pan.

Bake at 350° for 50-55 minutes or until cake tests done. Remove to a wire rack to cool. In another mixing bowl, combine all frosting ingredients; beat until creamy. Spread on cooled cake. **Yield:** 12-16 servings.

Pumpkin Trifle

(Pictured above)

One of the nice things about this trifle is the way it uses up leftover cakes that never seem to get eaten! It's convenient, too—it tastes like a traditional pumpkin pie, even though you don't have to make a crust or bake it. —Melody Hurlbut, St. Agatha, Ontario

2 to 3 cups crumbled unfrosted spice cake, muffins *or* gingerbread, *divided*
1 can (15 ounces) solid-pack pumpkin
2-1/2 cups cold milk
4 packages (3.4 ounces *each*) instant butterscotch pudding mix
1 teaspoon ground cinnamon
1/4 teaspoon ground nutmeg
1/4 teaspoon ground ginger
1/4 teaspoon ground allspice
2 cups heavy whipping cream
Maraschino cherries, optional

Set aside 1/4 cup of cake crumbs for topping. Divide remaining crumbs into four portions; sprinkle one portion into a trifle bowl or 3-qt. serving bowl.

In a large mixing bowl, combine pumpkin, milk, pudding mixes and spices; mix until smooth. Spoon half into the serving bowl. Sprinkle with a second portion of crumbs.

Beat cream until stiff; spoon half into bowl. Sprinkle with a third portion of crumbs. Top with the remaining pumpkin mixture, then last portion of crumbs and remaining whipped cream. Sprinkle with the reserved crumbs.

Cover and chill at least 2 hours before serving. Garnish with cherries if desired. **Yield:** 12-15 servings.

Chocolate Raspberry Layer Cake

This recipe pulls together some of my favorite flavors. It's delicious, practically foolproof and looks beautiful. Impress dinner guests with this pretty cake.
— *Robert Ulis, Alexandria, Virginia*

1 package (18-1/4 ounces) yellow cake mix
1 cup (6 ounces) semisweet chocolate chips
2 tablespoons milk
1/2 to 1 teaspoon almond extract
1 carton (8 ounces) frozen whipped topping, thawed
1/3 cup raspberry jam *or* preserves

Bake cake according to package directions, using two greased and floured 9-in. round baking pans. Cool for 10 minutes; remove from pans to wire racks to cool completely. In a microwave or double boiler, melt chocolate chips; stir in milk and extract. Fold in whipped topping.

Place one cake layer on a serving plate. Spread with raspberry jam. Top with second cake layer. Frost top and sides with chocolate topping. Store in the refrigerator. **Yield:** 8-10 servings.

Snowflake Pudding

Flakes of coconut give my pudding its snow-like texture—and plenty of taste besides! The crimson currant-raspberry sauce is delicious and pretty, too.
— *Patricia Stratton, Muskegon, Michigan*

1 envelope unflavored gelatin
1-1/4 cups milk, *divided*
1/2 cup sugar
1/2 teaspoon salt
1 teaspoon vanilla extract
1-1/3 cups flaked coconut, toasted
1 cup heavy whipping cream, whipped
SAUCE:
1 package (10 ounces) frozen sweetened
 raspberries, thawed
1-1/2 teaspoons cornstarch
1/2 cup red currant jelly

In a small bowl, combine gelatin and 1/4 cup milk; let stand for 1 minute. In a saucepan, combine sugar, salt and remaining milk; heat just until sugar is dissolved. Remove from the heat; stir in gelatin mixture and vanilla. Refrigerate until partially set. Fold in coconut and whipped cream. Pour into dessert dishes or small bowls; refrigerate for at least 2 hours.

Meanwhile, strain raspberries to remove seeds. Combine cornstarch, raspberry pulp and currant jelly in a saucepan; stir until smooth. Bring to a boil; boil and stir for 2 minutes. Chill for at least 1 hour. Pour sauce over pudding just before serving. **Yield:** 6 servings.

Buttermilk Pecan Pie

(Pictured below)

This is the treasured "golden oldie" that my grandmother made so often whenever we'd come to visit. Grandma grew her own pecans, and we never tired of cracking them and picking out the meat when we knew we'd be treated to her special pie! — *Mildred Sherrer, Bay City, Texas*

1/2 cup butter
2 cups sugar
5 eggs
2 tablespoons all-purpose flour
2 tablespoons lemon juice
1 teaspoon vanilla extract
1 cup buttermilk
1 cup chopped pecans
1 unbaked pastry shell (10 inches)

In a mixing bowl, cream butter and sugar. Add eggs, one at a time, beating well after each addition. Blend in flour, lemon juice and vanilla. Stir in buttermilk and pecans. Pour into the pie shell. Bake at 325° for 55 minutes or until set. Cool on a wire rack. Store in the refrigerator. **Yield:** 8 servings.

Cranberry Cheesecake

(Pictured at right)

Every year when the cranberries are harvested, my family looks forward to eating this cheesecake.
—Nairda Monroe, Webberville, Michigan

2 cups graham cracker *or* shortbread cookie crumbs
1/3 cup butter, melted
CRANBERRY TOPPING:
  1/3 cup water
  2/3 cup sugar
  2 cups fresh cranberries
  1 teaspoon lemon juice
FILLING:
  4 packages (8 ounces *each*) cream cheese, softened
  1 cup sugar
  5 eggs
  1 tablespoon lemon juice

Combine crumbs and butter; press into the bottom of a 9-in. springform pan. Place pan on a baking sheet. Bake at 300° for 5-8 minutes. Cool. Meanwhile, for topping, combine water and sugar in a saucepan. Bring to a boil over medium heat; boil 1 minute. Stir in berries. Cover; reduce heat. Cook until most berries have popped, about 3 minutes. Add lemon juice. Press through a sieve or food mill; set aside.

For filling, beat cream cheese in a large mixing bowl until light. Gradually beat in sugar. Add eggs, one at a time, beating well after each. Add lemon juice. Pour into crust; spoon 4 tablespoons topping on filling and "marble" with a knife or spatula. Bake at 350° for 45 minutes. Turn oven off; let cake stand in oven 2 hours. Remove from oven; cool. Pour remaining topping on top; refrigerate overnight. **Yield:** 12-16 servings.

Pumpkin Cheesecake

(Pictured at right)

When I was young, we produced several ingredients for this longtime favorite on the farm.
—Evonne Wurmnest, Normal, Illinois

CRUST:
  1 cup graham cracker crumbs
  1 tablespoon sugar
  4 tablespoons butter, melted
FILLING:
  2 packages (8 ounces *each*) cream cheese, softened
  3/4 cup sugar
  1 can (15 ounces) solid-pack pumpkin
1-1/4 teaspoons ground cinnamon
  1/2 teaspoon *each* ground ginger and nutmeg
  1/4 teaspoon salt
  2 eggs
TOPPING:
  2 cups (16 ounces) sour cream
  2 tablespoons sugar
  1 teaspoon vanilla extract
  12 to 16 pecan halves

Combine crust ingredients. Press into bottom of a 9-in. springform pan; chill. For filling, beat cream cheese and sugar in a large mixing bowl until well blended. Beat in pumpkin, spices and salt. Add eggs, one at a time, beating well after each. Pour into crust. Place pan on a baking sheet.

Bake at 350° for 50 minutes. Meanwhile, for topping, combine sour cream, sugar and vanilla. Spread over filling; bake 5 minutes more. Cool on rack; chill overnight. Garnish slices with a pecan. **Yield:** 12-16 servings.

Candy Apple Pie

This is the only apple pie my husband will eat, but that's all right since he makes it as often as I do. It's the sweet treat that usually tops off our holiday meals.
—Cindy Kleweno, Burlington, Colorado

6 cups thinly sliced peeled baking apples
2 tablespoons lime juice
3/4 cup sugar
1/4 cup all-purpose flour
1/2 teaspoon ground cinnamon *or* nutmeg
1/4 teaspoon salt
Pastry for double-crust pie (9 inches)
2 tablespoons butter
TOPPING:
  1/4 cup butter
  1/2 cup packed brown sugar
  2 tablespoons heavy whipping cream
  1/2 cup chopped pecans

In a large bowl, toss apples with lime juice. Combine dry ingredients; add to the apples and toss lightly. Line a 9-in. pie plate with bottom crust and trim even with edge; fill with apple mixture. Dot with butter. Roll out remaining pastry to fit top of pie. Place over filling. Trim, seal and flute edges high; cut slits in pastry. Bake at 400° for 40-45 minutes or until golden brown and apples are tender.

Meanwhile, melt butter in a small saucepan. Stir in brown sugar and cream; bring to a boil, stirring constantly. Remove from the heat; and stir in pecans. Pour over top crust. Bake 3-4 minutes longer or until bubbly. Serve warm. **Yield:** 8 servings.

Top to bottom: Pumpkin Cheesecake and Cranberry Cheesecake

Chocolate Cookie Torte

This recipe has been used many times in our family for get-togethers. It's easy to make and beautiful.
—Irene Bigler, New Cumberland, Pennsylvania

- 1/2 cup butter, softened
- 1 cup sugar
- 1 egg
- 1 egg yolk
- 1/2 teaspoon vanilla extract
- 2 cups all-purpose flour
- 1 teaspoon baking powder
- 1/2 teaspoon salt

Additional sugar

FROSTING:
- 2 cups (12 ounces) semisweet chocolate chips
- 1/2 cup half-and-half cream
- 2 cups heavy whipping cream, whipped
- 2 teaspoons vanilla extract

Chocolate sprinkles

In a mixing bowl, cream butter and sugar. Beat in the egg, yolk and vanilla. Combine flour, baking powder and salt; gradually add to the creamed mixture and mix well. Form into a long log; cut into eight equal pieces. Shape each into a ball; wrap in plastic wrap. Refrigerate for 1 hour.

Roll balls in additional sugar; place between two sheets of waxed paper. Roll each into a 6-in. circle. Remove top sheet of waxed paper; flip the circles onto ungreased baking sheets. Remove waxed paper; prick dough with a fork.

Bake at 350° for 10-12 minutes or until lightly browned. Carefully loosen cookies and cool on paper towels. For frosting, melt chocolate chips with half-and-half in a heavy saucepan, stirring occasionally. Cool. Combine whipped cream and vanilla; fold into chocolate mixture. Layer cookies, spreading 1/4 cup frosting between each layer. Spread remaining frosting over sides and top. Decorate with chocolate sprinkles. Refrigerate overnight. **Yield:** 8-10 servings.

Raspberry Meringue Pie

We have raspberry bushes, so I'm always looking for recipes using this delicious fruit. This is one of our favorites. —Mrs. Anton Sohrwiede, McGraw, New York

- 1 cup all-purpose flour
- 1/3 cup sugar
- 1 teaspoon baking powder
- 1/4 teaspoon salt
- 2 tablespoons cold butter
- 1 egg, beaten
- 2 tablespoons milk

TOPPING:
- 2 egg whites
- 1/2 cup sugar
- 2 cups unsweetened raspberries

In a bowl, combine the flour, sugar, baking powder and salt; cut in butter. Combine egg and milk; stir into flour mixture (dough will be sticky). Press into the bottom and up the sides of a greased 9-in. pie plate; set aside.

In a mixing bowl, beat egg whites on medium speed until soft peaks form. Gradually beat in sugar, 1 tablespoon at a time, until stiff peaks form. Fold in raspberries. Spoon over the crust. Bake at 350° for 30-35 minutes or until browned. Cool on a wire rack. Refrigerate leftovers. **Yield:** 6-8 servings.

Ice Cream Sundae Dessert

When I was growing up, my siblings and I couldn't wait to dig into this tempting ice cream dessert. It's cool and smooth with a ribbon of fudge inside. Now whenever I make it for my family, I think of Mom.
—Anne Heinonen, Howell, Michigan

- 2 cups (12 ounces) semisweet chocolate chips
- 1 can (12 ounces) evaporated milk
- 1/2 teaspoon salt
- 1 package (12 ounces) vanilla wafers, crushed
- 1/2 cup butter, melted
- 2 quarts vanilla ice cream *or* flavor of your choice, softened

In a saucepan over medium heat, melt chocolate chips with milk and salt; cook and stir until thickened, about 25 minutes. Remove from the heat; set aside. Combine wafer crumbs and butter; set aside 1 cup. Press remaining crumbs into a greased 13-in. x 9-in. x 2-in. pan. Chill for 10-15 minutes.

Pour chocolate over the crumbs. Cover and freeze for 20-25 minutes or until firm. Spread the ice cream over chocolate. Sprinkle with reserved crumbs. Freeze at least 2 hours before serving. **Yield:** 12-16 servings.

Four-Nut Brittle, page 285

Sweet Treats

Southern Pralines

(Pictured above)

This recipe is truly Southern, and it's been a family favorite for years. I've packed many a Christmas tin with this candy. —*Bernice Eberhart, Fort Payne, Alabama*

    3 cups packed brown sugar
    1 cup heavy whipping cream
    2 tablespoons corn syrup
  1/4 teaspoon salt
  1/4 cup butter
    2 cups chopped pecans
1-1/4 teaspoons vanilla extract

In a large heavy saucepan over medium heat, bring brown sugar, cream, corn syrup and salt to a boil, stirring constantly. Cook until a candy thermometer reads 234° (soft-ball stage), stirring occasionally. Remove from the heat; add butter (do not stir). Cool until candy thermometer reads 150°, about 35 minutes. Stir in the pecans and vanilla. Stir with a wooden spoon until candy just begins to thicken but is still glossy, about 5-7 minutes. Quickly drop by heaping teaspoonfuls onto waxed paper; spread to form 2-in. patties. Store in an airtight container. **Yield:** 3-4 dozen.

Editor's Note: We recommend that you test your candy thermometer before each use by bringing water to a boil; the thermometer should read 212°. Adjust your recipe temperature up or down based on your test.

Pink Peppermint Cookies

(Pictured below)

The combination of cool peppermint and chocolate makes these treats nearly irresistible. Decorate them with designs such as stars, snowflakes or Christmas trees. —*Renee Schwebach, Dumont, Minnesota*

    1 cup butter, softened, *divided*
  1/2 cup sugar
    1 egg
   10 to 12 drops red food coloring
  3/4 teaspoon peppermint extract
    2 cups all-purpose flour, *divided*
  1/2 teaspoon baking soda
  1/4 teaspoon cream of tartar
  1/4 teaspoon salt
    1 tablespoon chocolate syrup

In a mixing bowl, cream 3/4 cup butter and the sugar. Beat in egg, food coloring and peppermint extract. Combine 1-3/4 cups flour, baking soda, cream of tartar and salt; add to creamed mixture. Shape into a ball. Cover and chill for 1-2 hours.

Meanwhile, in a bowl, combine chocolate syrup and remaining butter and flour; stir until well blended. Spoon into a pastry bag with a small round tip. Shape dough into 3/4-in. balls. Place on ungreased baking sheets; flatten into 1-1/2-in. circles. Pipe chocolate mixture on top of cookies in simple holiday designs. Bake at 375° for 5-7 minutes. Cool on wire racks. **Yield:** 4 dozen.

Spice Cookies with Pumpkin Dip

(Pictured above)

My husband and two kids eat the first dozen of these cookies, warm from the oven, before the next baking pan is even done. A co-worker gave me the recipe for the pumpkin dip, which everyone loves with the cookies.
—Kelly McNeal, Derby, Kansas

1-1/2 cups butter, softened
   2 cups sugar
   2 eggs
 1/2 cup molasses
   4 cups all-purpose flour
   4 teaspoons baking soda
   2 teaspoons ground cinnamon
   1 teaspoon ground ginger
   1 teaspoon ground cloves
   1 teaspoon salt
Additional sugar
PUMPKIN DIP:
   1 package (8 ounces) cream cheese, softened
   2 cups canned pumpkin pie mix

   2 cups confectioners' sugar
 1/2 to 1 teaspoon ground cinnamon
 1/4 to 1/2 teaspoon ground ginger

In a mixing bowl, cream butter and sugar. Add eggs, one at a time, beating well after each addition. Add molasses; mix well. Combine flour, baking soda, cinnamon, ginger, cloves and salt; add to creamed mixture and mix well. Refrigerate overnight.

Shape into 1/2-in. balls; roll in sugar. Place 2 in. apart on ungreased baking sheets. Bake at 375° for 6 minutes or until edges begin to brown. Cool for 2 minutes before removing to a wire rack.

For dip, beat cream cheese in a mixing bowl until smooth. Add pumpkin pie mix; beat well. Add sugar, cinnamon and ginger; beat until smooth. Serve with cookies. Store leftover dip in the refrigerator. **Yield:** about 20 dozen (3 cups dip).

Harvest Sugar Cookies

Rich buttery cookies like these never last long at a party or potluck. I got this recipe from a friend in Texas years ago and have used it many times since. You can cut these cookies into pumpkins or leaves or whatever shape you'd like.   *—Lynn Burgess, Rolla, Missouri*

 3/4 cup butter, softened
   1 cup sugar
   2 eggs
   1 teaspoon vanilla extract
2-3/4 cups all-purpose flour
   1 teaspoon baking powder
 1/2 teaspoon salt
Frosting *or* additional sugar, optional

In a mixing bowl, cream butter and sugar. Add eggs and vanilla; beat until light and fluffy. Combine flour, baking powder and salt; gradually add to creamed mixture and mix well. Refrigerate for 1 hour or until firm.

On a lightly floured surface, roll the dough to 1/4-in. thickness. Cut with cookie cutters of your choice. Using a floured spatula, place cookies on greased baking sheets. Sprinkle with sugar if desired (or frost baked cookies after they have cooled).

Bake at 375° for 8-10 minutes or until lightly browned. Cool on wire racks. **Yield:** 6-7 dozen (2-1/2-inch cookies).

Editor's Note: For a richer color, tint frosting with food coloring paste available at kitchen and cake decorating supply stores.

Clockwise from top right: Cutout Christmas Cookies, Granny's Spice Cookies and Date Swirls

Cutout Christmas Cookies

(Pictured at left)

Ground cinnamon and a hint of ground cloves and ginger give these cutouts great flavor. —Carolyn Moseley
Dayton, Ohio

- 1 cup butter, softened
- 1 cup sugar
- 2 eggs
- 1-1/2 teaspoons vanilla extract
- 3-1/2 cups all-purpose flour
- 1 teaspoon ground cinnamon
- 1/2 teaspoon baking powder
- 1/2 teaspoon salt
- 1/4 teaspoon ground cloves
- 1/4 teaspoon ground nutmeg
- 1 egg white, beaten

Colored decorating sugars

In a mixing bowl, cream butter and sugar. Add eggs and vanilla. Combine flour, cinnamon, baking powder, salt, cloves and nutmeg; gradually add to creamed mixture and mix well. Chill for at least 1 hour. On a lightly floured surface, roll dough, a portion at a time, to 1/8-in. thickness. Cut into desired shapes. Place on ungreased baking sheets.

Bake at 350° for 12-14 minutes or until edges begin to brown. Carefully brush with egg white; sprinkle with colored sugar. Return to the oven for 3-5 minutes or until lightly browned. **Yield:** about 6 dozen (2-inch cookies).

Granny's Spice Cookies

(Pictured at left)

No one can compete with Granny's cooking, but these spice cookies come pretty close! —Valerie Hudson
Mason City, Iowa

- 1 cup butter, softened
- 1-1/2 cups sugar
- 1 egg, lightly beaten
- 2 tablespoons light corn syrup
- 2 tablespoons grated orange peel
- 1 tablespoon cold water
- 3-1/4 cups all-purpose flour
- 2 teaspoons baking soda
- 2 teaspoons ground cinnamon
- 1 teaspoon ground ginger
- 1/2 teaspoon ground cloves

Red-hot candies, nonpareils *and/or* sprinkles

In a mixing bowl, cream butter and sugar. Add egg, corn syrup, orange peel and cold water. Combine flour, baking soda, cinnamon, ginger and cloves; add to creamed mixture and mix well. Chill for at least 1 hour. On a lightly floured surface, roll dough, a portion at a time, to 1/8-in. thickness. Cut into desired shapes. Place on greased baking sheets. Decorate as desired. Bake at 375° for 6-8 minutes or until lightly browned. **Yield:** about 4 dozen (3-inch cookies).

Date Swirls

(Pictured at left)

A ribbon of chopped dates and nuts is swirled into these tasty cookies. —Donna Grace, Clancy, Montana

FILLING:
- 2 cups chopped dates
- 1 cup water
- 1 cup sugar
- 1 cup chopped nuts
- 2 teaspoons lemon juice

DOUGH:
- 1 cup butter
- 1 cup packed brown sugar
- 1 cup sugar
- 3 eggs
- 1 teaspoon lemon extract
- 4 cups all-purpose flour
- 1 teaspoon salt
- 3/4 teaspoon baking soda

In a saucepan, combine filling ingredients. Cook over medium-low heat, stirring constantly, until mixture becomes stiff, about 15-20 minutes. Chill. For dough, cream butter and sugars in a mixing bowl. Add eggs, one at a time, beating well after each addition. Add extract. Combine flour, salt and baking soda; gradually add to creamed mixture and mix well. Chill for at least 1 hour.

On a lightly floured surface, roll out half of the dough to a 12-in. x 9-in. rectangle, about 1/4-in. thick. Spread with half of filling. Roll up, starting with long end. Repeat with remaining dough and filling. Wrap with plastic wrap; chill overnight. Cut rolls into 1/4-in. slices. Place 2 in. apart on greased baking sheets. Bake at 375° for 8-10 minutes or until lightly browned. Cool on wire racks. **Yield:** 4 dozen.

Orange Chocolate Meltaways

(Pictured below)

The combination of chocolate and orange makes these some of the best truffles I've ever had. As holiday gifts, they're showstoppers.
—Lori Kostecki
Wausau, Wisconsin

> 1 package (11-1/2 ounces) milk chocolate chips
> 1 cup (6 ounces) semisweet chocolate chips
> 3/4 cup heavy whipping cream
> 1 teaspoon grated orange peel
> 2-1/2 teaspoons orange extract
> 1-1/2 cups finely chopped toasted pecans

COATING:

> 1 cup (6 ounces) milk chocolate chips
> 2 tablespoons shortening

Place chocolate chips in a mixing bowl; set aside. In a saucepan, bring cream and orange peel to a gentle boil; immediately pour over chips. Let stand for 1 minute; whisk until smooth. Add the extract. Cover and chill for 35 minutes or until mixture begins to thicken. Beat for 10-15 seconds or just until mixture lightens in color (do not overbeat).

Spoon rounded teaspoonfuls onto waxed paper-lined baking sheets. Cover and chill for 5 minutes. Gently shape into balls; roll half in pecans. In a microwave or double boiler, melt

chocolate and shortening; stir until smooth. Dip remaining balls in chocolate. Place on waxed paper to harden. Store in the refrigerator. **Yield:** 6 dozen.

Jewel Nut Bars

(Pictured above)

These colorful bars, with the eye-catching appeal of candied cherries and the crunchy goodness of mixed nuts, are certain to become a holiday standby year after year. I get lots of compliments on the rich, chewy crust and the combination of sweet and salty flavors.
—Joyce Fitt, Listowel, Ontario

> 1-1/4 cups all-purpose flour
> 2/3 cup packed brown sugar, *divided*
> 3/4 cup cold butter
> 1 egg
> 1/2 teaspoon salt
> 1-1/2 cups salted mixed nuts
> 1-1/2 cups halved green and red candied cherries
> 1 cup (6 ounces) semisweet chocolate chips

In a bowl, combine flour and 1/3 cup brown sugar; cut in butter until mixture resembles coarse crumbs. Press into a lightly greased 13-in. x 9-in. x 2-in. baking pan. Bake at 350° for 15 minutes.

Meanwhile, in a mixing bowl, beat egg. Add salt and remaining brown sugar. Stir in the nuts, cherries and chocolate chips. Spoon evenly over crust. Bake at 350° for 20 minutes. Cool on a wire rack. Cut into bars. **Yield:** 3 dozen.

Surprise Meringues

(Pictured below)

These crisp, delicate cookies are light as a feather. Mini chocolate chips and chopped nuts are a delightful and yummy surprise in every bite. This fun cookie is a fitting finale to a big meal. —Gloria Grant
Sterling, Illinois

    3   egg whites
  1/8   teaspoon cream of tartar
  3/4   cup sugar
  1/8   teaspoon salt
    1   teaspoon vanilla extract
    1   cup (6 ounces) miniature semisweet chocolate chips
  1/4   cup chopped pecans *or* walnuts

In a mixing bowl, beat egg whites and cream of tartar until soft peaks form. Gradually add sugar, salt and vanilla, beating until stiff peaks form and sugar is dissolved, about 5-8 minutes. Fold in the chocolate chips and nuts.

Drop by rounded teaspoonfuls onto greased baking sheets. Bake at 300° for 30 minutes or until lightly browned. Cool on baking sheets. Store in an airtight container. **Yield:** 4 dozen.

Candy Bar Fudge

(Pictured above)

I've made this chewy and chocolaty fudge many times. Packed with nuts and caramel, it's like a candy bar. Everyone who tries it loves it. —Lois Zigarac
Rochester Hills, Michigan

  1/2   cup butter
  1/3   cup baking cocoa
  1/4   cup packed brown sugar
  1/4   cup milk
3-1/2   cups confectioners' sugar
    1   teaspoon vanilla extract
   30   caramels
    1   tablespoon water
    2   cups salted peanuts
  1/2   cup semisweet chocolate chips
  1/2   cup milk chocolate chips

In a microwave-safe bowl, combine the butter, cocoa, brown sugar and milk. Microwave on high until mixture boils, about 3 minutes. Stir in confectioners' sugar and vanilla. Pour into a greased 8-in. square baking pan.

In another microwave-safe bowl, heat caramels and water on high for 2 minutes or until melted. Stir in peanuts; spread over chocolate layer. Microwave chocolate chips on high for 1 minute or until melted; spread over caramel layer. Chill until firm. **Yield:** 2-3/4 pounds.

Editor's Note: This recipe was tested in a 700-watt microwave.

Cashew Sandwich Cookies

(Pictured below)

*If your family and friends enjoy rich-tasting confec-
tions, these treats are bound to be a hit at holiday
gatherings! Filled with chocolate and cashews, the sandwich cookies have melt-in-your-mouth appeal.*
—*Melissa Boder, Salem, Virginia*

> 1 cup butter, softened
> 3/4 cup sugar
> 2 egg yolks
> 1/2 cup sour cream
> 1 teaspoon vanilla extract
> 1 teaspoon lemon juice
> 3 cups all-purpose flour

FILLING:

> 2 cups (12 ounces) semisweet chocolate chips
> 1/2 cup butter
> 1 can (10 ounces) salted cashews, finely chopped

Confectioners' sugar, optional

In a mixing bowl, cream butter and sugar. Add egg yolks, sour
cream, vanilla and lemon juice; mix well. Add flour; mix well.
Cover and chill for at least 2 hours or until easy to handle. On
a floured surface, roll out dough to 1/8-in. thickness. Cut with
a 2-in. round cookie cutter. Place 1 in. apart on ungreased baking sheets. Bake at 350° for 11-13 minutes or until edges

are lightly browned. Cool on wire racks.

For filling, melt chocolate chips and butter in a small
saucepan. Remove from the heat; stir in cashews. Spread on
the bottom of half of the cookies; top each with another
cookie. Dust tops with confectioners' sugar if desired. **Yield:**
about 4 dozen.

Chewy Date Nut Bars

(Pictured above)

*You'll need just six ingredients to bake up these chewy
bars chock-full of walnuts and dates.*
—*Linda Hutmacher, Teutopolis, Illinois*

> 1 package (18-1/4 ounces) yellow cake mix
> 3/4 cup packed brown sugar
> 3/4 cup butter, melted
> 2 eggs
> 2 cups chopped dates
> 2 cups chopped walnuts

In a mixing bowl, combine cake mix and brown sugar. Add
butter and eggs; beat on medium speed for 2 minutes. Combine dates and walnuts; stir into batter (the batter will be stiff).
Spread into a greased 13-in. x 9-in. x 2-in. baking pan.

Bake at 350° for 35-45 minutes or until edges are gold-
en brown. Cool on a wire rack for 10 minutes. Run a knife
around sides of pan to loosen; cool completely before cutting. **Yield:** 3 dozen.

Old-Fashioned Gingersnaps

(Pictured below)

I discovered this recipe many years ago, and it's been a favorite among our family and friends since. Who doesn't like cookies during the holidays?
—*Francis Stoops, Stoneboro, Pennsylvania*

3/4 cup butter, softened
1 cup sugar
1 egg
1/4 cup molasses
2 cups all-purpose flour
2 teaspoons baking soda
1/4 teaspoon salt
1 teaspoon ground cinnamon
1 teaspoon ground cloves
1 teaspoon ground ginger
Additional sugar

In a mixing bowl, cream the butter and sugar. Add egg and molasses; beat well. Sift together dry ingredients; gradually add to creamed mixture. Mix well. Chill the dough. Roll into 1-1/4-in. balls and dip into sugar. Place 2 in. apart on ungreased baking sheets. Bake at 375° for about 10 minutes or until set and surface cracks. Cool on wire racks. **Yield:** about 4 dozen.

Dairy State Fudge

(Pictured above)

I grew up on a dairy farm in Wisconsin, so it's only natural I have a lot of recipes that use dairy ingredients. I make this candy nearly every Christmas. You'll find it's hard to eat just one piece. —*Jan Vande Slunt Waupun, Wisconsin*

1 package (8 ounces) cream cheese, softened
2 tablespoons butter
2 pounds white candy coating, broken into small pieces
1 to 1-1/2 cups chopped pecans, walnuts *or* hickory nuts

Line a 9-in. square baking pan with foil; butter the foil and set aside. In a mixing bowl, beat cream cheese until fluffy; set aside.

In the top of a double boiler, melt butter. Add candy coating; heat and stir until melted and smooth. Pour over the cream cheese; beat until smooth and glossy, about 7-10 minutes. Stir in nuts. Pour into prepared pan. Cool. Remove from pan and cut into 1-in. pieces. Store in the refrigerator. **Yield:** 64 pieces.

Chocolate Malted Cookies

(Pictured below)

These cookies are the next best thing to a good old-fashioned malted milk. With malted milk powder, chocolate syrup plus chocolate chips and chunks, these are the best cookies I've ever tasted…and with six kids, I've made a lot of cookies over the years.
—Teri Rasey-Bolf, Cadillac, Michigan

1 cup butter-flavored shortening
1-1/4 cups packed brown sugar
1/2 cup malted milk powder
2 tablespoons chocolate syrup
1 tablespoon vanilla extract
1 egg
2 cups all-purpose flour
1 teaspoon baking soda
1/2 teaspoon salt
1-1/2 cups semisweet chocolate chunks
1 cup (6 ounces) milk chocolate chips

In a mixing bowl, cream shortening and brown sugar. Add malted milk powder, chocolate syrup and vanilla; beat for 2 minutes. Add egg.

Combine flour, baking soda and salt; gradually add to creamed mixture. Stir in chocolate chunks and chips. Shape into 2-in. balls; place 3 in. apart on ungreased baking sheets.

Bake at 375° for 12-14 minutes or until golden brown. Cool for 2 minutes before removing to a wire rack. **Yield:** about 1-1/2 dozen.

Deluxe Chocolate Marshmallow Bars

(Pictured at right)

I'd have to say that I've been asked to share this chocolaty layered bar recipe more than any other in my collection. It's a longtime favorite of our three daughters. I can't count how many times we've all made these!
—Esther Shank, Harrisonburg, Virginia

Rolled Oat Cookies

(Pictured below)

I like to keep some of this dough ready in the freezer since it's so handy to slice, bake and serve at a moment's notice. These wholesome cookies are super with a cup of coffee—in fact, we occasionally grab a few for breakfast when we're in a hurry. —Kathi Peters
Chilliwack, British Columbia

> 1 cup butter
> 1 cup packed brown sugar
> 1/4 cup water
> 1 teaspoon vanilla extract
> 3 cups quick-cooking oats
> 1-1/4 cups all-purpose flour
> 1 teaspoon salt
> 1/4 teaspoon baking soda

In a mixing bowl, cream butter and sugar. Add water and vanilla; mix well. Combine dry ingredients; add to creamed mixture and mix well. Chill for 30 minutes.

Shape into two 1-1/2-in. rolls; wrap tightly in waxed paper. Chill for 2 hours or until firm. Cut into 1/2-in. slices and place 2 in. apart on greased baking sheets.

Bake at 375° for 12 minutes or until lightly browned. Remove to wire racks to cool. **Yield:** about 3-1/2 dozen.

> 3/4 cup butter
> 1-1/2 cups sugar
> 3 eggs
> 1 teaspoon vanilla extract
> 1-1/3 cups all-purpose flour
> 3 tablespoons baking cocoa
> 1/2 teaspoon baking powder
> 1/2 teaspoon salt
> 1/2 cup chopped nuts, optional
> 4 cups miniature marshmallows

TOPPING:
> 1-1/3 cups chocolate chips
> 1 cup peanut butter
> 3 tablespoons butter
> 2 cups crisp rice cereal

In a mixing bowl, cream butter and sugar. Add eggs and vanilla; beat until fluffy. Combine flour, cocoa, baking powder and salt; add to creamed mixture. Stir in nuts if desired. Spread in a greased 15-in. x 10-in. x 1-in. pan.

Bake at 350° for 15-18 minutes. Sprinkle marshmallows evenly over cake; return to oven for 2-3 minutes. Using a knife dipped in water, spread the melted marshmallows evenly over cake. Cool.

For topping, combine chocolate chips, peanut butter and butter in a small saucepan. Cook over low heat, stirring constantly, until melted and well blended. Remove from heat; stir in cereal. Immediately spread over bars. Chill. **Yield:** about 3 dozen.

Buttersweets

(Pictured above)

With cream cheese, cherries and a sweet topping, this recipe turns chocolate chip cookies into something special. These are pretty to look at and taste like a combination of cookie and candy. —LeeAnn McCue
West Springfield, Massachusetts

  1 **tube (18 ounces) refrigerated chocolate chip cookie dough**
  1 **package (3 ounces) cream cheese, softened**
3/4 **cup confectioners' sugar**
1/4 **cup chopped maraschino cherries**
  1 **drop red food coloring, optional**
1/2 **cup semisweet chocolate chips**
  2 **tablespoons butter**

With a sharp knife, cut cookie dough into eight equal slices. Cut each slice into quarters; roll into balls. Place 2 in. apart on ungreased baking sheets. Bake at 375° for 10 minutes or until golden brown. Immediately make a deep impression in the center of each cookie using the back of a small melon baller or small spoon. Cool for 5 minutes; remove to wire racks to cool completely.

Meanwhile, in a mixing bowl, cream the cream cheese and sugar. Pat cherries dry with paper towels. Stir cherries and food coloring if desired into creamed mixture. Place a teaspoonful of filling into the center of each cookie. In a heavy saucepan over low heat, melt chocolate chips and butter, stirring occasionally. Drizzle over cookies. Store in the refrigerator. **Yield:** 32 cookies.

Aunt Rose's Fantastic Butter Toffee

(Pictured below)

I love good old-fashioned home cooking! This toffee comes from the heart. It's been a favorite in my family since I was a little girl! —Rosie Kimberlin
Los Angeles, California

  2 **cups whole unblanched almonds (about 10 ounces)**
 11 **ounces milk chocolate**
  1 **cup butter**
  1 **cup sugar**
  3 **tablespoons water**

Spread almonds in an ungreased baking pan and toast in 350° oven for about 10 minutes, shaking pan occasionally. Cool. Finely grind chocolate in a food processor (do not over-process). Set aside. Coarsely chop almonds in food processor. Sprinkle 1 cup over bottom of a greased 15-in. x 10-in. x 1-in. baking pan. Sprinkle with 1 cup ground chocolate. Set aside.

In a heavy saucepan, combine butter, sugar and water; cook over medium heat, stirring occasionally, until the mixture reaches 290° (soft-crack stage). Very quickly pour over chocolate and nuts. Sprinkle remaining chocolate over toffee; top with remaining nuts. Refrigerate and break into pieces. Store in an airtight container. **Yield:** about 2 pounds.

Editor's Note: We recommend that you test your candy thermometer before each use by bringing water to a boil; the thermometer should read 212°. Adjust your recipe temperature up or down based on your test.

Chocolate Mint Brownies

(Pictured below)

One of the best things about this recipe is the brownies get moister if you leave them in the refrigerator a day or two. The problem at our house is no one can leave them alone for that long! —Helen Baines
Elkton, Maryland

　1　cup all-purpose flour
1/2　cup butter, softened
1/2　teaspoon salt
　4　eggs
　1　teaspoon vanilla extract
　1　can (16 ounces) chocolate syrup
　1　cup sugar
FILLING:
　2　cups confectioners' sugar
1/2　cup butter, softened
　1　tablespoon water
1/2　teaspoon mint extract
　3　drops green food coloring
TOPPING:
　1　package (10 ounces) mint chocolate chips
　9　tablespoons butter

Combine the first seven ingredients in a large mixing bowl; beat at medium speed for 3 minutes. Pour batter into a greased 13-in. x 9-in. x 2-in. baking pan. Bake at 350° for 30 minutes (top of brownies will still appear wet). Cool completely.

Combine filling ingredients in a medium mixing bowl; beat until creamy. Spread over cooled brownies. Refrigerate until set.

For topping, melt chocolate chips and butter over low heat in a small saucepan. Let cool for 30 minutes or until lukewarm, stirring occasionally. Spread over filling. Chill before cutting. Store in the refrigerator. **Yield:** 5-6 dozen.

Mocha Truffles

(Pictured above)

Nothing compares to the melt-in-your-mouth flavor of these truffles…or to the simplicity of the recipe. Whenever I make them for my family or friends, they're quickly devoured. No one has to know how easy they are to prepare! —Stacy Abell, Olathe, Kansas

　2　packages (12 ounces *each*) semisweet chocolate
　　chips
　1　package (8 ounces) cream cheese, softened
　3　tablespoons instant coffee granules
　2　teaspoons water
　1　pound dark chocolate candy coating
White candy coating, optional

In a microwave-safe bowl or double boiler, melt chocolate chips. Add cream cheese, coffee and water; mix well. Refrigerate until firm enough to shape. Shape into 1-in. balls and place on a waxed paper-lined baking sheet. Chill for 1-2 hours or until firm.

Melt dark chocolate coating in microwave-safe bowl or double boiler. Dip balls and place on waxed paper to harden. If desired, melt white coating and drizzle over truffles. **Yield:** about 5-1/2 dozen.

Molasses Creams

(Pictured below)

Making these treats seems to put me in a holiday mood. Maybe it's the soft centers, or perhaps the aroma of ginger and cloves. Whatever the case, a few Molasses Creams and a glass of milk or cup of warm tea always hit the spot! —Virginia Krites, Cridersville, Ohio

1-1/2 cups butter, softened
   2 cups sugar
   2 eggs, lightly beaten
 1/2 cup molasses
   4 cups all-purpose flour
   2 teaspoons baking soda
   1 teaspoon ground cinnamon
 3/4 teaspoon ground ginger
 1/2 teaspoon ground cloves
FROSTING:
   3 tablespoons butter, softened
1-1/2 cups confectioners' sugar
   1 tablespoon vanilla extract
   1 to 2 tablespoons milk

In a large mixing bowl, cream butter and sugar. Add eggs and molasses; mix thoroughly. Combine dry ingredients; gradually add to creamed mixture. Shape into 1-in. balls. Place on ungreased baking sheets (do not flatten).

    Bake at 350° for 10-12 minutes or until done (centers will be slightly soft). In a small mixing bowl, beat butter, sugar, vanilla and enough milk until creamy. Frost cookies while warm. **Yield:** about 8 dozen.

Easy Microwave Caramels

(Pictured above)

I usually make an extra batch of these caramels and freeze them for company or last-minute gift-giving. After only about 20 quick seconds in the microwave, the frozen caramel is soft enough to cut, wrap and pack into a candy jar. —Darleen Worm
Fond du Lac, Wisconsin

   1 cup butter
2-1/3 cups packed brown sugar
   1 cup light corn syrup
   1 can (14 ounces) sweetened condensed milk
 1/8 teaspoon salt
   1 teaspoon vanilla extract
 1/2 cup chopped walnuts, optional

In 2-qt. microwave-safe pitcher, combine butter, sugar, syrup, milk and salt. Microwave on high 3 to 4 minutes, stirring once after about 2 minutes. When butter is melted, stir well. Microwave on high for about 14 minutes or until mixture reaches 245° (firm-ball stage). No stirring is needed. Remove from microwave; stir in vanilla and walnuts.

    Allow to stand for 10 minutes, stirring several times. Pour

into greased 13-in. x 9-in. x 2-in. pan (smaller 11-in. x 7-in. x 2-in. pan yields thicker candy as shown in photo). Refrigerate until cool. Invert the pan. Carefully tap out whole block of candy; cut into squares. Wrap in waxed paper and store in the refrigerator or freezer. **Yield:** about 2-3/4 pounds.

Editor's Note: This recipe was tested in a 700-watt microwave oven. We recommend that you test your candy thermometer before each use by bringing water to a boil; the thermometer should read 212°. Adjust your recipe temperature up or down based on your test.

Coconut Washboards

(Pictured below)

These are my husband's favorite cookies, so I've made them a lot during the many years we've been married.
—Tommie Sue Shaw, McAlester, Oklahoma

- 1/2 **cup butter, softened**
- 1/2 **cup shortening**
- 2 **cups packed brown sugar**
- 2 **eggs**
- 1/4 **cup water**
- 1 **teaspoon vanilla extract**
- 4 **cups all-purpose flour**
- 1-1/2 **teaspoons baking powder**
- 1/2 **teaspoon baking soda**
- 1/4 **teaspoon salt**
- 1 **cup flaked coconut**

In a mixing bowl, cream butter, shortening and sugar for 2 minutes or until fluffy. Add eggs; mix well. Gradually add water

and vanilla; mix well. Combine flour, baking powder, baking soda and salt; add to the creamed mixture. Fold in coconut. Cover and refrigerate for 2-4 hours.

Shape into 1-in. balls. Place 2 in. apart on greased baking sheets; flatten with fingers into 2-1/2-in. x 1-in. oblong shapes. Press lengthwise with a floured fork. Bake at 400° for 8-10 minutes or until lightly browned. Cool 2 minutes before removing to a wire rack. **Yield:** about 9 dozen.

Maple Butterscotch Brownies

(Pictured above)

Generally, I'll make a double recipe of these brownies— they go so fast no matter where I take them!
—Grace Vonhold, Rochester, New York

- 1-1/2 **cups packed brown sugar**
- 1/2 **cup butter, melted**
- 1-1/2 **teaspoons maple flavoring**
- 2 **eggs**
- 1-1/2 **cups all-purpose flour**
- 1 **teaspoon baking powder**
- 1 **cup chopped walnuts**

Confectioners' sugar, optional

In a bowl, combine brown sugar, butter and maple flavoring. Beat in the eggs, one at a time. Combine flour and baking powder; add to egg mixture. Stir in walnuts. Pour into a greased 9-in. square baking pan. Bake at 350° for 30 minutes or until brownies test done. Cool. Dust with confectioners' sugar if desired. **Yield:** 16 brownies.

Holiday Hideaways

(Pictured above)

People eagerly anticipate these tasty cookies as part of our "season's eatings" each year. The surprise cherry center surrounded by a fluffy cookie makes this treat especially fun.
—*Marianne Blazowich*
Jeannette, Pennsylvania

      3/4 **cup sugar**
      2/3 **cup butter-flavored shortening**
        1 **egg**
        1 **tablespoon milk**
        1 **teaspoon vanilla extract**
    1-3/4 **cups all-purpose flour**
        1 **teaspoon baking powder**
      1/2 **teaspoon baking soda**
      1/2 **teaspoon salt**
        2 **jars (10 ounces *each*) maraschino cherries, well drained**
       10 **ounces white candy coating, *divided***
        4 **tablespoons butter-flavored shortening, *divided***
        8 **ounces dark chocolate candy coating**
Finely chopped pecans

In a mixing bowl, cream sugar and shortening. Add egg, milk and vanilla. Combine dry ingredients; gradually add to the creamed mixture and mix well. Form 2 teaspoonfuls of dough into a ball. Flatten ball and place a cherry in the center; roll dough around cherry. Repeat with remaining dough and cherries. Place balls 2 in. apart on ungreased baking sheets.

Bake at 350° for 10-12 minutes or until set and the edges are lightly browned. Cool 1 minute before removing to wire racks to cool completely. Grate 2 oz. white candy coating; set aside. Melt remaining white coating with 2 tablespoons shortening; melt dark coating with remaining shortening. Dip half the cookies into white coating; place on waxed paper. Sprinkle with pecans. Dip the remaining cookies in dark coating; place on waxed paper. Sprinkle with grated white coating. Store in a covered container in the refrigerator. **Yield:** about 4-1/2 dozen.

Sour Cream Drops

(Pictured below)

My mother is an excellent baker, and this is her recipe. Whether Mom makes these cookies or I do, they always disappear. —*Tracy Betzler, Reston, Virginia*

      1/4 **cup shortening**
      3/4 **cup sugar**
        1 **egg**
      1/2 **cup sour cream**
      1/2 **teaspoon vanilla extract**
    1-1/3 **cups all-purpose flour**
      1/4 **teaspoon baking soda**
      1/4 **teaspoon baking powder**
      1/4 **teaspoon salt**
BURNT SUGAR FROSTING:
        2 **tablespoons butter**
      1/2 **cup confectioners' sugar**

1   cup finely chopped dried apricots
1/4 cup sliced almonds
1/4 cup flaked coconut

In a saucepan, melt chocolate and butter over low heat, stirring constantly until all of the chocolate is melted. Remove from the heat; stir in brown sugar, eggs and vanilla until blended. Set aside.

In a bowl, combine flour, baking powder and salt. Stir in chocolate mixture. Combine apricots, almonds and coconut; stir half into batter. Pour into a greased 9-in. square baking pan. Sprinkle remaining apricot mixture on top. Bake at 350° for 25 minutes or until golden brown. Cool. **Yield:** about 2 dozen.

Pinwheel Cookies

These pretty pinwheel cookies have tempting swirly layers of orange and chocolate. I really mess up my kitchen whenever I bake a batch, but the smiles on the faces of family and friends enjoying them makes it all worthwhile. —Paulette Morgan, Moorhead, Minnesota

1   cup butter, softened
1   package (3 ounces) cream cheese, softened
1   cup sugar
1   egg
1   tablespoon grated orange peel
1   teaspoon vanilla extract
3-1/2 cups all-purpose flour
1   teaspoon salt
FILLING:
1   cup (6 ounces) semisweet chocolate chips
1   package (3 ounces) cream cheese, softened
1/2 cup confectioners' sugar
1/4 cup orange juice

In a mixing bowl, cream the butter, cream cheese and sugar. Add egg, orange peel and vanilla; mix well. Combine flour and salt; add to the creamed mixture and mix well. Cover and chill for 4 hours or until firm.

Meanwhile, combine all filling ingredients in a small saucepan. Cook and stir over low heat until smooth; set aside to cool. On a floured surface, divide dough in half; roll each half into a 12-in. x 10-in. rectangle. Spread with filling. Carefully roll up into a tight jelly roll and wrap in waxed paper. Chill overnight.

Remove waxed paper; cut rolls into 1/4-in. slices. Place on ungreased baking sheets. Bake at 375° for 8-10 minutes or until lightly browned. Remove to wire racks to cool. **Yield:** about 8 dozen.

1/4 teaspoon vanilla extract
3   to 4 teaspoons hot water

In a mixing bowl, cream shortening and sugar. Add egg, sour cream and vanilla. Combine dry ingredients; add to the creamed mixture. Chill for at least 1 hour. Drop by tablespoonfuls 2 in. apart onto greased baking sheets.

Bake at 425° for 7-8 minutes or until lightly browned. Remove to wire racks to cool. For frosting, melt butter in a small saucepan until golden brown; stir in the sugar, vanilla and enough water to achieve a spreading consistency. Frost cooled cookies. **Yield:** about 2-1/2 dozen.

Apricot Angel Brownies

(Pictured above)

To tell the truth, I'm not a "chocoholic." I enjoy fruit desserts and custards more than anything. So my brownies have neither milk nor dark chocolate—but still satisfy every sweet tooth. —Tamara Sellman Barrington, Illinois

2   bars (2 ounces *each*) white baking chocolate
1/3 cup butter
1/2 cup packed brown sugar
2   eggs, beaten
1/4 teaspoon vanilla extract
3/4 cup all-purpose flour
1/2 teaspoon baking powder
1/4 teaspoon salt

Peanut Butter Sandwich Cookies

(Pictured above)

All my days seem to be busy ones, so when I find time to bake a treat, I like it to be special. The creamy filling gives traditional peanut butter cookies a new twist.
—Debbie Kokes, Tabor, South Dakota

    1   cup butter-flavored shortening
    1   cup creamy peanut butter
    1   cup sugar
    1   cup packed brown sugar
    1   teaspoon vanilla extract
    3   eggs
    3   cups all-purpose flour
    2   teaspoons baking soda
  1/4   teaspoon salt
FILLING:
  1/2   cup creamy peanut butter
    3   cups confectioners' sugar
    1   teaspoon vanilla extract
    5   to 6 tablespoons milk

In a mixing bowl, cream the shortening, peanut butter and sugars. Add vanilla. Add eggs, one at a time, beating well after each addition. Combine flour, baking soda and salt; add to creamed mixture. Shape into 1-in. balls; place 2 in. apart on ungreased baking sheets. Flatten to 3/8-in. thickness with a fork.

Bake at 375° for 7-8 minutes or until golden. Cool on wire racks. In a mixing bowl, beat filling ingredients until smooth. Spread on the bottom of half of the cookies and top each with another cookie. **Yield:** about 4 dozen.

Mounds Balls

(Pictured below)

I make these bite-size treats as gifts for friends and receive many thank-you notes in return. The mailman doesn't mind delivering them, though. He gets a box of candy, too!
—Kathy Dorman, Snover, Michigan

  1/2   pound butter, softened
    1   pound confectioners' sugar
    1   pound flaked coconut
    1   cup chopped walnuts
  1/2   cup sweetened condensed milk
    1   teaspoon vanilla extract
CHOCOLATE COATING:
    2   cups (12 ounces) semisweet chocolate chips
    4   squares (1 ounce *each*) unsweetened chocolate
2-inch x 1-inch x 1/2-inch piece paraffin wax
Round wooden toothpicks
Styrofoam sheets

In mixing bowl, cream butter and sugar. Add coconut, walnuts, milk and vanilla; stir until blended. Chill until slightly firm;

shape into walnut-sized balls. Insert a toothpick in each ball. Place balls on sheets; freeze.

In the top of a double boiler over simmering water, melt chocolate and wax. Keep warm over hot water. Using picks as handles, dip frozen balls into chocolate mixture; stick picks upright into waxed paper-covered Styrofoam sheet. Chill until firm. Remove toothpicks and package candy in individual paper liners. (Candy may be frozen.) **Yield:** about 7 dozen.

Double-Decker Brownies

(Pictured at right)

With two taste-tempting layers and savory frosting, no one will be able to eat just one of these brownies!
—Heather Hooker, Belmont, Ontario

CHOCOLATE LAYER:
- 2 eggs, lightly beaten
- 1 cup sugar
- 3/4 cup all-purpose flour
- 1/2 cup chopped walnuts
- Pinch salt
- 1/2 cup butter, melted
- 1/4 cup baking cocoa

BUTTERSCOTCH LAYER:
- 1/2 cup butter, softened
- 1-1/2 cups packed brown sugar
- 2 eggs
- 2 teaspoons vanilla extract
- 1-1/2 cups all-purpose flour
- 1/2 cup chopped walnuts
- 1/4 teaspoon salt

FROSTING:
- 1/2 cup packed brown sugar
- 1/4 cup butter
- 3 tablespoons milk
- 1-1/2 cups confectioners' sugar, sifted
- 1/3 cup semisweet chocolate chips
- 1/3 cup butterscotch chips
- 1 tablespoon shortening

In a bowl, combine eggs, sugar, flour, walnuts and salt. In another bowl, stir butter and cocoa until smooth; add to egg mixture and blend well with a wooden spoon. Pour into a greased 13-in. x 9-in. x 2-in. baking pan; set aside.

For butterscotch layer, cream butter and brown sugar in a mixing bowl. Beat in eggs and vanilla. Stir in flour, walnuts and salt. Spoon over the chocolate layer. Bake at 350° for 30-35 minutes or until brownies begin to pull away from sides of pan; cool.

For frosting, combine brown sugar, butter and milk in a small saucepan; bring to a boil and boil for 2 minutes. Remove from the heat; stir in confectioners' sugar until smooth. Quickly spread over brownies. In a small saucepan over low heat, melt chocolate chips, butterscotch chips and shortening, stirring frequently. Drizzle over frosting. **Yield:** 3 dozen.

Turtle Pretzels

Sweet and crunchy, these tasty treats will be gobbled up in no time!
—Barbara Loudenslager
O'Fallon, Missouri

- 1 package (14 ounces) caramels
- 1 tablespoon water
- 1 package (10 ounces) pretzel rods
- 8 ounces German sweet chocolate *or* semisweet chocolate
- 2 teaspoons shortening
- 1 cup finely chopped pecans

In a double boiler, melt caramels in water. Dip half of each pretzel into the hot caramel. Place on a greased sheet of foil to cool. In a saucepan, melt chocolate and shortening over low heat. Dip caramel-coated end of pretzels into the chocolate; sprinkle with nuts. Return to foil. **Yield:** about 2-1/2 dozen.

Pumpkin Bars

(Pictured below)

What could be more appropriate for a Thanksgiving treat than these deliciously moist bars? Actually, they're a hit with my family any time of the year.
—*Brenda Keller, Andalusia, Alabama*

    4 **eggs**
1-2/3 **cups sugar**
    1 **cup vegetable oil**
    1 **can (15 ounces) solid-pack pumpkin**
    2 **cups all-purpose flour**
    2 **teaspoons ground cinnamon**
    2 **teaspoons baking powder**
    1 **teaspoon baking soda**
    1 **teaspoon salt**
ICING:
    1 **package (3 ounces) cream cheese, softened**
    2 **cups confectioners' sugar**
1/4 **cup butter, softened**
    1 **teaspoon vanilla extract**
    1 **to 2 tablespoons milk**

In a mixing bowl, beat eggs, sugar, oil and pumpkin. Combine flour, cinnamon, baking powder, baking soda and salt; gradually add to pumpkin mixture and mix well. Pour into an ungreased 15-in. x 10-in. x 1-in. baking pan. Bake at 350° for 25-30 minutes. Cool completely.

For icing, beat cream cheese, sugar, butter and vanilla in a small mixing bowl. Add enough of the milk to achieve desired spreading consistency. Spread over bars. **Yield:** 2 dozen.

Spiced Almond Cookies

(Pictured above)

These cookies are my all-time favorite. The recipe has won ribbons at fairs and applause from family and guests alike. —*Wanda Daily, Milwaukie, Oregon*

    1 **cup butter, softened**
1/2 **cup shortening**
    1 **cup sugar**
    1 **cup packed brown sugar**
    2 **eggs**
    4 **cups all-purpose flour**
    2 **teaspoons ground cinnamon**
    1 **teaspoon baking soda**
    1 **teaspoon salt**
    1 **teaspoon ground cloves**
    1 **teaspoon ground allspice**
    1 **cup slivered almonds**

In a mixing bowl, cream butter, shortening and sugars until light and fluffy. Add eggs and beat well. Combine dry ingredients; stir into creamed mixture along with nuts.

Shape into three 9-in. x 1-1/2-in. rolls; wrap each roll in waxed paper. Refrigerate for 2-3 days for spices to blend. Cut into 1/4 in. slices and place 2 in. apart on ungreased baking sheets. Bake at 350° for 12-14 minutes or until set. Remove to wire racks to cool. **Yield:** 7 dozen.

Sweet Peanut Treats

(Pictured below)

We sold tempting bars almost like these at the refreshment stand at a Minnesota state park where I worked in the '70s, and they were a favorite of employees and visitors alike. Now I make this recipe when I want to serve a special treat. —Phyllis Smith
Olympia, Washington

- **2 cups semisweet chocolate chips**
- **2 cups butterscotch chips**
- **1 jar (18 ounces) creamy peanut butter**
- **1 cup butter**
- **1 can (5 ounces) evaporated milk**
- **1/4 cup cook-and-serve vanilla pudding mix**
- **1 package (2 pounds) confectioners' sugar**
- **1 pound salted peanuts**

In the top of a double boiler over simmering water, melt chocolate chips, butterscotch chips and peanut butter; stir until smooth. Spread half into a greased 15-in. x 10-in. x 1-in. baking pan. Chill until firm.

Meanwhile, in a saucepan, bring butter, milk and pudding mix to a boil. Cook and stir for 2 minutes. Remove from the heat; add confectioners' sugar and beat until smooth. Spread over chocolate mixture in pan. Stir peanuts into remaining chocolate mixture; mix well. Carefully spread over pudding layer. Refrigerate. Cut into 1-in. squares. **Yield:** 10 dozen.

Chocolate Truffle Cookies

(Pictured above)

I experimented with a chocolate cookie recipe until I was satisfied with the results. I entered these cookies at our county fair and won a blue ribbon. If you love chocolate, I'm sure you'll like these cookies.
—Sharon Miller, Thousand Oaks, California

- **1-1/4 cups butter, softened**
- **2-1/4 cups confectioners' sugar**
- **1/3 cup baking cocoa**
- **1/4 cup sour cream**
- **1 tablespoon vanilla extract**
- **2-1/4 cups all-purpose flour**
- **2 cups (12 ounces) semisweet chocolate chips**
- **1/4 cup chocolate sprinkles**

In a large mixing bowl, cream butter, sugar and cocoa until light and fluffy. Beat in sour cream and vanilla. Add flour; mix well. Stir in chocolate chips. Refrigerate for 1 hour.

Shape into 1-in. balls; dip in chocolate sprinkles. Place, sprinkled side up, 2 in. apart on ungreased baking sheets.

Bake at 325° for 10 minutes or until set. Cool for 5 minutes before removing to wire racks to cool completely. **Yield:** about 5-1/2 dozen.

Get Soft

If your stored cookies get too crisp for your liking, put them in a plastic bag with a piece of bread. The next day you'll have soft cookies again.

Top to bottom: Celestial Bars,
Chocolate Reindeer and
Italian Horn Cookies

Celestial Bars

(Pictured at left)

My aunt gave me the recipe for these wonderfully nutty bars. They feature a marbled base, fluffy icing and pretty chocolate glaze. —Maribeth Gregg, Cable, Ohio

- 1/2 cup butter, softened
- 2 cups packed brown sugar
- 1 teaspoon vanilla extract
- 1/2 teaspoon almond extract
- 3 eggs
- 2 cups all-purpose flour
- 1/2 teaspoon salt
- 1-1/2 cups chopped pecans
- 2 squares (1 ounce *each*) unsweetened chocolate, melted

ICING:
- 1/2 cup butter, softened
- 3 cups confectioners' sugar
- 3 to 4 tablespoons milk
- 1 teaspoon vanilla extract

GLAZE:
- 1/2 cup semisweet chocolate chips
- 2 teaspoons shortening

In a mixing bowl, cream butter and brown sugar. Add extracts. Add eggs, one at a time, beating well after each addition. Combine flour and salt; add to creamed mixture and mix well. Stir in pecans. Divide batter in half; stir chocolate into one portion. Alternately spoon plain and chocolate batters into a greased 13-in. x 9-in. x 2-in. baking pan. Swirl with a knife (the batter will be thick).

Bake at 350° for 16-20 minutes or until a toothpick comes out clean. Cool completely. For icing, cream butter and confectioners' sugar in a mixing bowl. Add milk and vanilla; mix until smooth. Spread over bars. For glaze, melt chocolate chips and shortening in a microwave or double boiler. Drizzle over bars. Let stand until chocolate is completely set before cutting. **Yield:** 4 dozen.

Chocolate Reindeer

(Pictured at left)

These cute cutout reindeer really fly off the plate! The subtle chocolate color and taste make them a nice alternative to plain vanilla sugar cookies.
—Lisa Rupple, Keenesburg, Colorado

- 1 cup butter, softened
- 1 cup sugar
- 1/2 cup packed brown sugar
- 1 egg
- 1 teaspoon vanilla extract
- 2-3/4 cups all-purpose flour
- 1/2 cup baking cocoa
- 1 teaspoon baking soda
- 44 red-hot candies

ICING (optional):
- 1-1/2 cups confectioners' sugar
- 2 to 3 tablespoons milk

In a mixing bowl, cream butter and sugars until fluffy. Beat in egg and vanilla. Combine flour, cocoa and baking soda; add to creamed mixture and mix well. Cover and refrigerate for at least 2 hours. On a lightly floured surface, roll dough to 1/8-in. thickness. Cut with a reindeer-shaped cookie cutter. Place on greased baking sheets.

Bake at 375° for 8-9 minutes. Immediately press a red-hot candy onto each nose. Cool for 2-3 minutes; remove from pans to wire racks. If desired, combine confectioners' sugar and milk until smooth. Cut a small hole in the corner of a heavy-duty resealable plastic bag; fill with icing. Pipe around edges of cookies and add a dot for eye. **Yield:** about 3-1/2 dozen.

Italian Horn Cookies

(Pictured at left)

My family has been making these delicate fruit-filled Christmas cookies for generations. —Gloria Siddiqui
Houston, Texas

- 1 cup cold butter
- 4 cups all-purpose flour
- 2 cups vanilla ice cream, softened
- 1 can (12-1/2 ounces) cherry filling

Sugar

In a large bowl, cut butter into flour until mixture resembles coarse crumbs. Stir in ice cream. Divide into four portions. Cover and refrigerate for 2 hours.

On a lightly floured surface, roll each portion to 1/8-in. thickness. With a fluted pastry cutter, cut into 2-in. squares. Place about 1/2 teaspoon filling in the center of each square. Overlap two opposite corners of dough over the filling and seal. Sprinkle lightly with sugar. Place on ungreased baking sheets.

Bake at 350° for 10-12 minutes or until bottoms are light brown. Cool on wire racks. **Yield:** about 5 dozen.

German Chocolate Brownies

(Pictured below)

As a young girl, I was always in search of something new to make. That's how I came across these brownies. I carry them to family dinners over the holidays, but they're great anytime!
—Karen Grimes
Stephens City, Virginia

 1/2 cup butter
   1 package (4 ounces) German sweet chocolate, broken into squares
 1/2 cup sugar
   1 teaspoon vanilla extract
   2 eggs, lightly beaten
   1 cup all-purpose flour
 1/2 teaspoon baking powder
 1/4 teaspoon salt
TOPPING:
   2 tablespoons butter, melted
 1/2 cup packed brown sugar
   1 cup flaked coconut
 1/2 cup chopped pecans
   2 tablespoons corn syrup
   2 tablespoons milk

In a saucepan, melt butter and chocolate, stirring until smooth. Cool slightly. Add sugar and vanilla; mix. Beat in the eggs. Mix in flour, baking powder and salt. Pour into a greased 9-in. square baking pan.

Bake at 350° for 18-22 minutes or until a toothpick comes out clean. For topping, combine butter and brown sugar in a bowl. Add coconut, pecans, corn syrup and milk; mix well. Drop by teaspoonfuls onto warm brownies; spread evenly. Broil several inches from the heat for 2-4 minutes or until top is browned and bubbly. **Yield:** 16 brownies.

After-School Gingersnaps

These cookies were always my favorite after-school treat. I could hardly wait to get home for my snack of gingersnaps and a tall glass of milk. Whenever I make these wonderful cookies, I recall the warmth of home filled with the spicy aroma of ginger! —Alice Thomas
Phoenix, Maryland

 3/4 cup butter, softened
 1/2 cup sugar
 1/2 cup packed brown sugar
 1/4 cup dark molasses
   1 egg, beaten
 2-1/4 cups all-purpose flour
   2 to 3 teaspoons ground cinnamon
   2 to 3 teaspoons ground ginger
 1-1/2 teaspoons baking soda
 1/4 teaspoon salt

In a mixing bowl, cream butter and sugars. Add molasses and egg. Combine flour, cinnamon, ginger, baking soda and salt; add to creamed mixture and mix well. Cover and refrigerate for 1 hour.

Roll out the dough on a lightly floured surface to 1/8-in. thickness. Cut into desired shapes with a 2-1/2-in. cookie cutter. Place on ungreased baking sheets.

Bake at 375° for 5-6 minutes or until set (do not overbake). Remove to wire racks to cool. **Yield:** about 6 dozen.

Chocolate Peanut Butter Pizza

(Pictured above right)

This is probably the most unusual "pizza" you'll ever see! It's a great dessert for kids, although adults snap

it up, too. Everyone loves the chewy crust and the great flavor. —Bernice Arnett, Marshfield, Missouri

- 1/2 **cup shortening**
- 1/2 **cup peanut butter**
- 1/2 **cup packed brown sugar**
- 1/2 **cup sugar**
- 2 **eggs, lightly beaten**
- 1/2 **teaspoon vanilla extract**
- 1-1/2 **cups all-purpose flour**
- 2 **cups miniature marshmallows**
- 1 **cup (6 ounces) semisweet chocolate chips**

In a mixing bowl, cream shortening, peanut butter and sugars. Beat in eggs and vanilla. Stir in flour and mix well. Pat into a greased 12-in. pizza pan.

Bake at 375° for 12 minutes. Sprinkle with the marshmallows and chocolate chips. Return to the oven for 4-6 minutes or until lightly browned. **Yield:** 16-20 servings.

Mom's Soft Raisin Cookies

(Pictured at right)

With four sons in service during World War II, my mother sent these favorite cookies as a taste from home to "her boys" in different parts of the world. These days, many of my grandchildren are enjoying them just as much as we did in the past.* —Pearl Cochenour Williamsport, Ohio

- 2 **cups raisins**
- 1 **cup water**
- 1 **cup shortening**
- 1-3/4 **cups sugar**
- 2 **eggs**
- 1 **teaspoon vanilla extract**
- 3-1/2 **cups all-purpose flour**
- 1 **teaspoon baking powder**
- 1 **teaspoon baking soda**
- 1 **teaspoon salt**
- 1/2 **teaspoon ground cinnamon**
- 1/2 **teaspoon ground nutmeg**
- 1/2 **cup chopped walnuts**

Combine raisins and water in a small saucepan; bring to a boil. Cook for 3 minutes; remove from the heat and let cool (do not drain). In a mixing bowl, cream shortening and sugar. Add eggs and vanilla.

Combine dry ingredients; gradually add to creamed mixture and mix well. Stir in nuts and raisins. Drop by teaspoonfuls 2 in. apart on greased baking sheets. Bake at 350° for 12-14 minutes. **Yield:** about 6 dozen.

Black Forest Brownies

(Pictured above)

Although I enjoy sweets, other recipes have failed me (I'm a beginning baker). But not this one! It's easy, and the ingredients are always on hand. —Toni Reeves
Medicine Hat, Alberta

- 1-1/3 cups all-purpose flour
- 1 teaspoon baking powder
- 1/2 teaspoon salt
- 1 cup butter
- 1 cup baking cocoa
- 4 eggs, beaten
- 2 cups sugar
- 1-1/2 teaspoons vanilla extract
- 1 teaspoon almond extract
- 1 cup chopped maraschino cherries
- 1/2 cup chopped nuts

ICING:
- 1/4 cup butter, softened
- 1 teaspoon vanilla extract
- 2 cups confectioners' sugar
- 6 tablespoons baking cocoa
- 1/4 cup milk
- 1/4 cup chopped nuts

Combine flour, baking powder and salt; set aside. In a large saucepan, melt butter. Remove from the heat and stir in cocoa until smooth. Blend in eggs, sugar and extracts. Stir in flour mixture, cherries and nuts. Pour into a greased 13-in. x 9-in. x 2-in. baking pan.

Bake at 350° for 35 minutes or until a toothpick comes out clean. For icing, blend butter, vanilla, sugar, cocoa and milk until smooth; spread over hot brownies. Sprinkle with nuts. Cool. **Yield:** 3 dozen.

Chewy Pecan Cookies

(Pictured below)

Oatmeal cookies were always my son's favorite when he was small. I wanted to send him some recently, but I couldn't find the recipe. So I got out the ingredients and made my own. My family thought they were the best I've ever made! —Janice Jackson
Haleyville, Alabama

- 1 cup butter, softened
- 1 cup sugar
- 3/4 cup packed brown sugar
- 3 eggs
- 1/4 cup milk
- 1 teaspoon vanilla extract
- 2-1/4 cups all-purpose flour
- 1 tablespoon ground cinnamon
- 1 teaspoon baking soda
- 1 teaspoon salt
- 1 teaspoon pumpkin pie *or* apple pie spice
- 2 cups quick-cooking oats
- 2 cups raisins
- 1-1/2 cups chopped pecans

In a large mixing bowl, cream butter and sugars. Add eggs, milk and vanilla; mix well. Combine next five ingredients; gradually add to creamed mixture. Stir in oats, raisins and nuts; mix well. Drop by tablespoonfuls onto greased baking sheets.

Bake at 350° for 10-12 minutes or until light golden brown. Remove to wire racks to cool. **Yield:** 5-6 dozen.

Mocha Cherry Cookies

(Pictured above)

Flecked with cherries and glistening with sugar, these dainty cookies always go over big. They're rich and tender with a pleasant chocolate-coffee flavor.
—Diane Molbert, Emerald Park, Saskatchewan

    1 **cup butter, softened**
  1/2 **cup sugar**
    1 **teaspoon vanilla extract**
    1 **teaspoon instant coffee granules**
    1 **teaspoon hot water**
  1/4 **cup baking cocoa**
    2 **cups all-purpose flour**
  1/2 **cup chopped maraschino cherries**
  1/2 **cup chopped walnuts**
Additional sugar
Melted semisweet chocolate, optional

In a mixing bowl, cream butter and sugar until fluffy. Add vanilla. Dissolve coffee granules in water; add to creamed mixture with cocoa. Add flour and mix well. Stir in cherries and walnuts. Shape into 1-1/4-in. balls; roll in sugar. Place on ungreased baking sheets.

Bake at 325° for 20-22 minutes. Cool on wire racks. Drizzle with chocolate if desired. **Yield:** about 3 dozen.

Chocolate-Tipped Butter Cookies

(Pictured above)

My husband and I enjoy these buttery cookies so much that we have a difficult time not hiding them from guests! They're a great holiday treat.
—Thara Baker-Alley, Columbia, Missouri

    1 **cup plus 3 tablespoons butter, softened,**
      divided
  1/2 **cup confectioners' sugar**
    2 **cups all-purpose flour**
    1 **teaspoon vanilla extract**
    1 **cup (6 ounces) semisweet chocolate chips**
  1/2 **cup finely chopped pecans *or* walnuts**

In a mixing bowl, cream 1 cup butter and sugar. Add flour and vanilla; mix well. Cover and refrigerate for 1 hour. Shape 1/4 cupfuls of dough into 1/2-in.-thick logs. Cut logs into 2-1/2-in. pieces; place on ungreased baking sheets.

Bake at 350° for 12-14 minutes or until lightly browned. Cool on wire racks. In a microwave or double boiler, melt chocolate and remaining butter. Dip one end of each cookie into chocolate and then into nuts; place on waxed paper until chocolate is set. **Yield:** about 5 dozen.

Chocolate Walnut Squares

(Pictured above)

Rich and satisfying, these bars create a symphony of flavors with every bite. The nutty crust, exquisite chocolate layer and creamy frosting make this treat one of my personal favorites. —Anne Heinonen
Howell, Michigan

    1 **cup butter, softened**
    2 **cups sugar**
    4 **eggs**
    1 **tablespoon vanilla extract**
    2 **cups all-purpose flour**
1/2 **teaspoon salt**
    2 **cups chopped walnuts**
    2 **squares (1 ounce *each*) unsweetened chocolate, melted**

FROSTING:

    5 **tablespoons all-purpose flour**
    1 **cup milk**
    1 **cup butter, softened**
    1 **cup confectioners' sugar**
    2 **teaspoons vanilla extract**

In a mixing bowl, cream butter and sugar. Beat in eggs and vanilla. Add flour and salt; mix well. Fold in walnuts. Spread half of the batter into a greased 13-in. x 9-in. x 2-in. baking pan. Add chocolate to the remaining batter; mix well. Carefully spread over batter in pan.

Bake at 350° for 30-35 minutes or until a toothpick comes out with moist crumbs. Cool completely. For frosting, mix flour and milk in a saucepan until smooth. Cook and stir over medium heat until a thick paste forms, about 10 minutes. Cool completely. In a mixing bowl, cream butter and confectioners' sugar. Add vanilla and mix well. Gradually add the milk mixture; beat for 5 minutes. Frost cake. Store in the refrigerator. **Yield:** 20-24 servings.

Washboard Cookies

(Pictured below)

These cookies were the treat we would enjoy when we traveled on family shopping trips to Ft. Worth many years ago. By the time we got to Ft. Worth, they were all gone! —John Cas Roulston, Stephenville, Texas

1/2 **cup butter, softened**
    1 **cup packed dark brown sugar**
    1 **egg**
    1 **tablespoon hot water**
    1 **teaspoon vanilla extract**
1/2 **teaspoon baking soda**
1-3/4 **cups all-purpose flour**
Sugar

In a mixing bowl, cream the butter, brown sugar and egg. Add water and vanilla to creamed mixture. Combine baking soda and flour; add to mixture and mix well. Shape into walnut-sized balls. Place on greased baking sheets; flatten with a fork that

has been dipped in water. Sprinkle with sugar. Bake at 325° for 15-20 minutes or until edges begin to brown. Cool on waxed paper. **Yield:** 3-1/2 dozen.

Chocolate Peanut Butter Brownies

(Pictured above)

I sent these brownies to my sons at college. They hid a few from their roommates just so there would be some left! —Patsy Burgin, Lebanon, Indiana

        1/2 **cup butter**
          2 **squares (1 ounce *each*) unsweetened chocolate**
          2 **eggs**
          1 **cup sugar**
        1/2 **cup all-purpose flour**
FILLING:
        1/2 **cup creamy peanut butter**
        1/4 **cup butter, softened**
      1-1/2 **cups confectioners' sugar**
          2 **to 3 tablespoons half-and-half cream *or* milk**
GLAZE:
          1 **square (1 ounce) semisweet baking chocolate**
          1 **tablespoon butter**

In a small saucepan, melt butter and chocolate over low heat; set aside. In a mixing bowl, beat eggs and sugar until light and lemon-colored. Add flour and melted chocolate; stir well. Pour into a greased 9-in. square baking pan. Bake at 350° for 25 minutes or until a toothpick comes out with moist crumbs. Cool.

For filling, beat peanut butter, butter and confectioners' sugar in a mixing bowl. Stir in cream until mixture reaches desired spreading consistency. Spread over cooled brownies. Cover; refrigerate until firm. For glaze, melt chocolate and butter in a saucepan, stirring until smooth. Drizzle over filling. Refrigerate before cutting. Store in refrigerator. **Yield:** about 5 dozen.

Coated Cookie Drops

(Pictured below)

It's a good thing these no-bake drops are simple because I like to serve them throughout the year. Their moist, cake-like center and sweet coating satisfy the chocolate lover in everyone. I'm asked for the recipe time and time again. —Amanda Reid, Oakville, Iowa

          1 **package (20 ounces) chocolate cream-filled sandwich cookies**
          1 **package (8 ounces) cream cheese, softened**
        15 **ounces white candy coating**
        12 **ounces chocolate candy coating**
Red *and/or* green candy coating, optional

Place the cookies in a blender or food processor; cover and process until finely crushed. In a small mixing bowl, beat cream cheese and crushed cookies until blended. Roll into 3/4-in. balls. Cover and refrigerate for at least 1 hour.

In a small saucepan over low heat, melt white candy coating, stirring until smooth; dip half of the balls to completely coat. Melt chocolate candy coating and dip remaining balls. Place on waxed paper until hardened.

Drizzle white candies with remaining chocolate coating and chocolate candies with remaining white coating. Or melt red or green coating and drizzle over balls. Store in the refrigerator. **Yield:** about 7-1/2 dozen.

Top to bottom: Popcorn Almond Brittle (recipe on page 282), Napoleon Cremes, Truffle Cups and Holiday Wreath

Napoleon Cremes

(Pictured at left)

For the annual Christmas open house we host, I set out a buffet with lots of food and candies like these lovely layered treats. They're so creamy…and with a green pistachio layer of pudding peeking out, they're very merry. —Gloria Jesswein, Niles, Michigan

   1 cup butter, softened, *divided*
1/4 cup sugar
1/4 cup baking cocoa
   1 teaspoon vanilla extract
   1 egg, lightly beaten
   2 cups finely crushed graham cracker crumbs (about 32 squares)
   1 cup flaked coconut
   3 tablespoons milk
   1 package (3.4 ounces) instant pistachio *or* lemon pudding mix
   2 cups confectioners' sugar
TOPPING:
   1 cup (6 ounces) semisweet chocolate chips
   3 tablespoons butter

In a double boiler or microwave, combine 1/2 cup butter, sugar, cocoa and vanilla; cook and stir until butter is melted. Add egg; cook and stir until mixture thickens, about 5 minutes. Stir in crumbs and coconut. Press into a greased 9-in. square baking pan.

In a mixing bowl, cream the remaining butter. Add the milk, pudding mix and confectioners' sugar; beat until fluffy. Spread over crust. Refrigerate until firm, 1-1/2 to 2 hours. Melt the chocolate chips and butter; cool. Spread over the pudding layer. Refrigerate. Cut into bars. **Yield:** 4 dozen.

Truffle Cups

(Pictured at left)

When I serve this elegant confection for the holidays, it never fails to draw compliments. Delightfully tempting, the cups are a fun fluffy variation on traditional truffles. They are truly delectable! —Katie Dowler, Birch Tree, Missouri

   1 package (11-1/2 ounces) milk chocolate chips
   2 tablespoons shortening

   1 pound white candy coating, cut into 1/2-inch pieces
1/2 cup heavy whipping cream

In a double boiler or microwave, melt chips and shortening. Stir until smooth; cool for 5 minutes. With a narrow pastry brush, "paint" the chocolate mixture on the inside of 1-in. foil candy cups. Place on a tray and refrigerate the cups until firm, about 45 minutes.

Remove about 12 cups at a time from the refrigerator; remove and discard foil cups. Return chocolate cups to the refrigerator.

For filling, melt confectionery coating and cream; stir until smooth. Transfer to a mixing bowl; cover and refrigerate for 30 minutes or until mixture begins to thicken. Beat filling for 1-2 minutes or until light and fluffy. Use a pastry star tube or spoon to fill the chocolate cups. Store in the refrigerator. **Yield:** 5 dozen.

Holiday Wreath

(Pictured at left)

My mom gave me this recipe. I look forward to crafting and sharing the wreath every Christmas. It's crisp and chewy as well as a real eye-catcher on the table. —Denise Glisson, Kingshill, U.S. Virgin Islands

 30 large marshmallows
1/2 cup butter
   1 tablespoon vanilla extract
 20 to 22 drops green food coloring
3-1/2 cups cornflakes
Red-hot candies
Red shoestring licorice and one red Dot candy, optional

In a heavy saucepan, combine marshmallows, butter, vanilla and food coloring; cook and stir over low heat until smooth. Remove from the heat; add cornflakes and mix well.

Drop by spoonfuls onto greased foil, forming a 9-in. wreath. Decorate with red-hot candies. If desired, form a bow with the licorice and place on wreath; add Dot on top of the bow. **Yield:** 10-12 servings.

Kitchen Hints

While cooking, place a recipe card between the prongs of a fork and put the fork upside down in an empty glass. This holds the card at the right angle to read and also keeps it away from spatters and spills.

Wyoming Whopper Cookies

(Pictured below)

I came up with this recipe while trying to match a commercial cookie that was good, but too crumbly to travel with. —Jamie Hirsch, Powell, Wyoming

- 2/3 **cup butter**
- 1-1/2 **cups chunky-style peanut butter**
- 1-1/4 **cups packed brown sugar**
- 3/4 **cup sugar**
- 3 **eggs, beaten**
- 6 **cups old-fashioned oats**
- 2 **cups (12 ounces) semisweet chocolate chips**
- 1-1/2 **cups raisins**
- 2 **teaspoons baking soda**

In a large saucepan, melt butter over low heat. Blend in peanut butter, sugars and eggs; mix until smooth. Add oats, chocolate chips, raisins and baking soda (dough will be sticky). Drop on greased baking sheets with a No. 20 ice cream scoop or large spoon. Flatten slightly. Bake at 350° for about 15 minutes. Remove to wire racks to cool. **Yield:** 2 dozen.

Editor's Note: This recipe was prepared using Jif brand peanut butter. If another brand is used, add several tablespoons water to mixture.

Popcorn Almond Brittle

(Pictured on page 280)

With popcorn, almonds and candied cherries tossed together in a sweet crisp coating, this is a festive favorite we enjoy every year. —Ruth Peterson, Jenison, Michigan

- 6 **cups popped popcorn**
- 1 **cup slivered almonds**
- 1/2 **cup *each* red and green candied cherries, chopped**
- 1-1/2 **cups sugar**
- 1/2 **cup corn syrup**
- 1/2 **cup water**
- 1/2 **teaspoon salt**
- 2 **tablespoons butter**
- 1 **teaspoon vanilla extract**

In a greased 13-in. x 9-in. x 2-in. baking pan, combine popcorn, almonds and cherries. Bake at 350° for 10 minutes. Turn oven off and keep mixture warm in the oven. Meanwhile, in a large heavy saucepan, combine the sugar, corn syrup, water and salt; cook and stir over low heat until sugar is dissolved.

Cook over medium heat, without stirring, until a candy thermometer reads 305°-310° (hard-crack stage). Remove from the heat; stir in butter and vanilla. Immediately pour over popcorn mixture; toss gently. Spread onto a greased baking sheet. When cool, break into small pieces. **Yield:** about 1-1/2 pounds.

Editor's Note: We recommend testing your candy thermometer before each use by bringing water to a boil; the temperature should be 212°. Adjust your recipe temperature up or down based on your test.

Chocolate Mint Wafers

(Pictured above right)

These cookies remind me of after-dinner mints. With my husband and our two children munching on these chocolaty treats, a batch never stays around long.
—Annette Esau, Durham, Ontario

- 2/3 **cup butter, softened**
- 1/2 **cup sugar**
- 1/2 **cup packed brown sugar**
- 1/4 **cup milk**
- 1 **egg**

2 cups all-purpose flour
3/4 cup baking cocoa
1 teaspoon baking powder
1/2 teaspoon baking soda
1/4 teaspoon salt
FILLING:
2-3/4 cups confectioners' sugar
1/4 cup half-and-half cream
1/4 teaspoon peppermint extract
1/4 teaspoon salt
Green food coloring

In a mixing bowl, cream butter and sugars. Add milk and egg; mix well. Combine dry ingredients; gradually add to creamed mixture and mix well. Cover and chill 2 hours or until firm. Roll chilled dough on a floured surface to 1/8-in. thickness. Cut with a 1-1/2-in. cookie cutter and place 1 in. apart on greased baking sheets.

Bake at 375° for 5-6 minutes or until edges are lightly browned. Remove to wire racks to cool completely. Combine filling ingredients; spread on half of the cookies and top with another cookie. **Yield:** about 7-1/2 dozen.

Chocolate Buttermilk Squares

(Pictured at right)

Every time I take a pan of these squares to a potluck, it comes back clean! At home, they disappear as fast as I make them. —Clarice Baker, Stromsburg, Nebraska

1 cup water
1 cup butter
1/4 cup baking cocoa
2 cups sugar
2 cups all-purpose flour
1/2 teaspoon salt
1/2 cup buttermilk
1 teaspoon baking soda
2 eggs, beaten
1 teaspoon vanilla extract
3 to 4 drops red food coloring, optional
FROSTING:
1/2 cup butter
1/4 cup baking cocoa
1/4 cup buttermilk
1 pound confectioners' sugar
1 teaspoon vanilla extract
Dash salt
3/4 cup chopped almonds, optional

In a saucepan, bring water, butter and cocoa to a boil. Cool. Meanwhile, in a large mixing bowl, combine the sugar, flour and salt. Pour cocoa mixture over dry ingredients; mix well. Combine buttermilk and baking soda; add to cocoa mixture along with eggs, vanilla and food coloring if desired. Mix until well blended. Pour into a greased and floured 15-in. x 10-in. x 1-in. baking pan. Bake at 350° for 20 minutes.

For frosting, melt butter; add cocoa and buttermilk. Stir in sugar, vanilla and salt. Spread over warm cake; top with nuts if desired. **Yield:** 15 servings.

Fudge-Topped Brownies

(Pictured above)

If you love brownies and fudge, why not combine the two? Mix up a pan of these exquisite brownies for any holiday or special gathering…or just when you want to treat yourself to the ultimate chocolate dessert.
—*Judy Olson, Whitecourt, Alberta*

      1 cup butter
      4 squares (1 ounce *each*) unsweetened chocolate
      2 cups sugar
      2 teaspoons vanilla extract
      4 eggs
1-1/2 cups all-purpose flour
      1 teaspoon baking powder
  1/2 teaspoon salt
      1 cup chopped walnuts
TOPPING:
4-1/2 cups sugar
      1 can (12 ounces) evaporated milk
  1/2 cup butter
      1 package (12 ounces) semisweet chocolate chips
      1 package (11-1/2 ounces) milk chocolate chips
      1 jar (7 ounces) marshmallow creme
      2 teaspoons vanilla extract
      2 cups chopped walnuts

In a saucepan over low heat, melt butter and chocolate. Remove from heat. Blend in sugar and vanilla. Beat in eggs. Combine flour, baking powder and salt; add to chocolate mixture. Stir in nuts. Pour into a greased 13-in. x 9-in. x 2-in. bak-

ing pan. Bake at 350° for 25-30 minutes or until top springs back when lightly touched.

In a heavy saucepan, combine sugar, milk and butter; bring to a boil over medium heat. Reduce heat; simmer 5 minutes, stirring constantly. Remove from heat. Stir in the chips, creme and vanilla; beat until smooth. Add nuts.

Spread over warm brownies. Freeze until firm. Cut into 1-in. squares. Store in the refrigerator. **Yield:** about 10 dozen.

Maple Peanut Delights

(Pictured below)

This wonderful candy recipe makes a big batch—enough to fill several Christmas gift boxes and still have treats left for my husband, Albert, and our grandchildren. One of our daughters-in-law shared the recipe a few years ago.　　　　—*Katie Stutzman, Goshen, Indiana*

      1 package (8 ounces) cream cheese, softened
  1/2 cup butter, softened
      6 cups confectioners' sugar
      1 teaspoon maple flavoring
      2 pounds dark chocolate candy coating
      1 cup chopped peanuts

In a mixing bowl, beat cream cheese, butter, confectioners' sugar and flavoring until smooth. Cover and refrigerate for 1 hour. Shape into 1-in. balls.

In a microwave or heavy saucepan, melt candy coating, stirring often. Dip balls in coating; sprinkle with peanuts. Place on waxed paper-lined baking sheets. Refrigerate. **Yield:** about 8 dozen.

Four-Nut Brittle

(Pictured on page 251)

We delight in being hospitable—it's the true mark of a country home...even if it is in the city. This recipe is one I created myself. I enjoy various kinds of nuts and wanted a candy that has a different crunch in every bite.
—Kelly-Ann Gibbons, Prince George, British Columbia

    2 cups sugar
    1 cup light corn syrup
    1/2 cup water
    1/2 cup salted peanuts
    1/2 cup *each* coarsely chopped almonds, pecans and
        walnuts
    1/4 cup butter
    2 teaspoons baking soda
1-1/2 teaspoons vanilla extract

Butter the sides of a large heavy saucepan. Add sugar, corn syrup and water; bring to a boil, stirring constantly. Cook and stir over medium-low heat until a candy thermometer reads 238° (soft-ball stage). Stir in nuts and butter. Cook over medium heat to 300° (hard-crack stage).

Remove from the heat; vigorously stir in baking soda and vanilla until blended. Quickly pour onto two greased baking sheets, spreading as thinly as possible with a metal spatula. Cool completely; break into pieces. Store in an airtight container with waxed paper between layers. **Yield:** 1-3/4 pounds.

Editor's Note: We recommend that you test your candy thermometer before each use by bringing water to a boil; the thermometer should read 212°. Adjust your recipe temperature up or down based on your test.

Anise Hard Candy

I like to wrap pieces of this candy in plastic wrap to share with friends.   —Bea Aubry, Dubuque, Iowa

    2 cups sugar
    1 cup light corn syrup
    1 cup water
    2 teaspoons anise extract *or* 1 teaspoon anise oil
    6 to 9 drops red food coloring

In large heavy saucepan, combine sugar, corn syrup and water. Bring to a boil over medium heat, stirring occasionally. Cover and cook for 3 minutes or until sugar is dissolved. Uncover;

cook on medium-high heat, without stirring, until a candy thermometer reads 300° (hard-crack stage). Remove from heat; stir in extract and food coloring (keep face away from mixture as the aroma will be very strong).

Pour into a buttered 13-in. x 9-in. x 2-in. pan. When cooled slightly but not hardened, cut into 1-in. squares. Cool completely. Store in an airtight container. **Yield:** about 8-1/2 dozen.

White Christmas Candy

(Pictured above)

During the holiday season years ago, my husband brought this wonderful candy home from work. The co-worker who'd shared it graciously included the recipe...and I've been making it ever since.
—Carol Hammond, Helena, Alabama

    2 pounds white candy coating, cut into small chunks
    1/2 pound crushed candy canes *or* crushed peppermint
        candies

Melt candy coating over medium-low heat, stirring until smooth. Stir in peppermint candy. Spread on waxed paper-lined baking sheets; refrigerate for 8-10 minutes. Break into small pieces; store in airtight containers. **Yield:** 2-1/2 pounds.

Gingerbread Cookies With Buttercream Icing

(Pictured below right)

These holiday-spiced cookies are the first ones I make in December. The recipe came from my mother-in-law. If you like, tint the buttery icing a cheery pink or green.
—*Ann Scherzer, Anacortes, Washington*

   2/3 cup shortening
     1 cup sugar
     1 egg
   1/4 cup molasses
     2 cups all-purpose flour
     1 teaspoon baking soda
     1 teaspoon salt
     1 teaspoon *each* ground cinnamon, cloves and ginger
ICING:
     3 cups confectioners' sugar
   1/3 cup butter, softened
     1 teaspoon vanilla extract
   1/4 teaspoon lemon extract
   1/4 teaspoon butter flavoring
     3 to 4 tablespoons milk

In a mixing bowl, cream shortening and sugar. Beat in egg and molasses. Combine flour, baking soda, salt and spices; gradually add to the creamed mixture and mix well. Refrigerate for 2 hours or overnight. On a lightly floured surface, roll dough to 1/4-in. thickness. Cut into desired shapes. Place on ungreased baking sheets.

Bake at 350° for 8-10 minutes or until edges begin to brown. Cool on a wire rack. For icing, beat sugar, butter and flavorings in a mixing bowl. Gradually stir in milk until smooth and thick. Frost cookies. **Yield:** about 3-1/2 dozen (2-1/2-inch cookies).

Quick Toffee Bars

These buttery, beautiful, quick bars are my all-time favorite...and a fast way to fill the cookie jar when company's coming!
—*Jeanette Wubbena, Standish, Michigan*

    12 graham crackers, broken into quarters
     1 cup butter
   1/2 cup sugar
     1 cup chopped nuts
     1 cup (6 ounces) semisweet chocolate chips

Line a 15-in. x 10-in. x 1-in. jelly roll pan with waxed paper and grease the paper. Arrange graham crackers in pan and set aside. In a saucepan, melt butter and sugar over medium heat; let boil gently for 3 minutes. Spread evenly over graham crackers. Sprinkle nuts on top. Bake at 325° for 10 minutes. Cool.

Meanwhile, melt chocolate chips; spread over bars and allow to cool again. After chocolate is set, pan can be turned over so waxed paper can be peeled off. Bars can be frozen. **Yield:** 4 dozen.

Penuche

My mom used to make this brown sugar fudge every year during the holidays, both for our family and to give as gifts. It has such wonderful old-fashioned flavor. We still savor the tradition.
—*Rosemarie Anderson, Great Valley, New York*

     2 cups packed brown sugar
     1 cup sugar
     1 cup half-and-half cream
     2 tablespoons light corn syrup
     1 teaspoon lemon juice
Pinch salt
     2 tablespoons butter
     1 teaspoon vanilla extract
   1/2 cup chopped pecans

In a large heavy saucepan, combine sugars, cream, corn syrup, lemon juice and salt. Bring to a boil over medium heat, stirring occasionally. Cook, without stirring, until a candy ther-

mometer reads 238° (soft-ball stage). Hold at soft-ball stage for 5-6 minutes. Remove from the heat. Add butter; do not stir. Cool to 110°. Stir in vanilla; beat vigorously by hand until mixture is very thick and slightly lighter in color, about 20 minutes. Quickly stir in pecans, then pour into a greased 8-in. square pan. Cool. Cut into 1-in. squares. **Yield:** 1-3/4 pounds.

Creamy Caramels

(Pictured above)

I discovered this recipe in a local newspaper several years ago and have made these soft buttery caramels ever since. Everyone asks for the recipe once they have a taste. —*Marcie Wolfe, Williamsburg, Virginia*

    1 cup sugar
    1 cup dark corn syrup
    1 cup butter
    1 can (14 ounces) sweetened condensed milk
    1 teaspoon vanilla extract

Line an 8-in. square pan with foil and butter the foil; set aside. Combine sugar, corn syrup and butter in a 3-qt. saucepan. Bring to a boil over medium heat, stirring constantly. Boil slowly for 4 minutes without stirring.

Remove from the heat and stir in milk. Reduce heat to medium-low and cook until candy thermometer reads 238° (soft-ball stage), stirring constantly. Remove from the heat and stir in vanilla. Pour into prepared pan. Cool. Remove from pan and cut into 1-in. squares. Wrap individually in waxed paper; twist ends. **Yield:** 64 pieces.

Editor's Note: It is recommended that you test your candy thermometer before each use. Bring water to a boil; the thermometer should read 212°. Adjust your recipe temperature up and down based on your test.

Mountain Cookies

(Pictured below)

I've been making these deliciously different cookies for over 10 years. My kids especially like the creamy coconut filling. Wherever I take these cookies, people ask for the recipe. You'll be hard-pressed to eat just one!
—*Jeanne Adams, Richmond, Vermont*

    1 cup butter, softened
    1 cup confectioners' sugar
    2 teaspoons vanilla extract
    2 cups all-purpose flour
  1/2 teaspoon salt
FILLING:
    1 package (3 ounces) cream cheese, softened
    1 cup confectioners' sugar
    2 tablespoons all-purpose flour
    1 teaspoon vanilla extract
  1/2 cup finely chopped pecans
  1/2 cup flaked coconut
TOPPING:
  1/2 cup semisweet chocolate chips
    2 tablespoons butter
    2 tablespoons water
  1/2 cup confectioners' sugar

In a mixing bowl, cream butter, sugar and vanilla. Combine flour and salt; gradually add to the creamed mixture and mix well. Shape into 1-in. balls; place 2 in. apart on ungreased baking sheets. Make a deep indentation in the center of each cookie. Bake at 350° for 10-12 minutes or until the edges just start to brown. Remove to wire racks to cool completely.

For the filling, beat cream cheese, sugar, flour and vanilla in a mixing bowl. Add pecans and coconut; mix well. Spoon 1/2 teaspoon into each cookie. For topping, heat chocolate chips, butter and water in a small saucepan until melted. Stir in sugar. Drizzle over cookies. **Yield:** 4 dozen.

EQUIVALENT MEASURES

3 teaspoons	= 1 tablespoon	**16 tablespoons**	= 1 cup
4 tablespoons	= 1/4 cup	**2 cups**	= 1 pint
5-1/3 tablespoons	= 1/3 cup	**4 cups**	= 1 quart
8 tablespoons	= 1/2 cup	**4 quarts**	= 1 gallon

FOOD EQUIVALENTS

Grains

Macaroni	1 cup (3-1/2 ounces) uncooked	= 2-1/2 cups cooked
Noodles, Medium	3 cups (4 ounces) uncooked	= 4 cups cooked
Popcorn	1/3 to 1/2 cup unpopped	= 8 cups popped
Rice, Long Grain	1 cup uncooked	= 3 cups cooked
Rice, Quick-Cooking	1 cup uncooked	= 2 cups cooked
Spaghetti	8 ounces uncooked	= 4 cups cooked

Crumbs

Bread	1 slice	= 3/4 cup soft crumbs, 1/4 cup fine dry crumbs
Graham Crackers	7 squares	= 1/2 cup finely crushed
Buttery Round Crackers	12 crackers	= 1/2 cup finely crushed
Saltine Crackers	14 crackers	= 1/2 cup finely crushed

Fruits

Bananas	1 medium	= 1/3 cup mashed
Lemons	1 medium	= 3 tablespoons juice, 2 teaspoons grated peel
Limes	1 medium	= 2 tablespoons juice, 1-1/2 teaspoons grated peel
Oranges	1 medium	= 1/4 to 1/3 cup juice, 4 teaspoons grated peel

Vegetables

Cabbage	1 head	= 5 cups shredded	**Green Pepper**	1 large	= 1 cup chopped
Carrots	1 pound	= 3 cups shredded	**Mushrooms**	1/2 pound	= 3 cups sliced
Celery	1 rib	= 1/2 cup chopped	**Onions**	1 medium	= 1/2 cup chopped
Corn	1 ear fresh	= 2/3 cup kernels	**Potatoes**	3 medium	= 2 cups cubed

Nuts

Almonds	1 pound	= 3 cups chopped	**Pecan Halves**	1 pound	= 4-1/2 cups chopped
Ground Nuts	3-3/4 ounces	= 1 cup	**Walnuts**	1 pound	= 3-3/4 cups chopped

EASY SUBSTITUTIONS

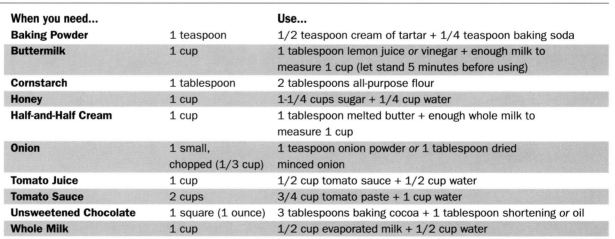

When you need...		Use...
Baking Powder	1 teaspoon	1/2 teaspoon cream of tartar + 1/4 teaspoon baking soda
Buttermilk	1 cup	1 tablespoon lemon juice *or* vinegar + enough milk to measure 1 cup (let stand 5 minutes before using)
Cornstarch	1 tablespoon	2 tablespoons all-purpose flour
Honey	1 cup	1-1/4 cups sugar + 1/4 cup water
Half-and-Half Cream	1 cup	1 tablespoon melted butter + enough whole milk to measure 1 cup
Onion	1 small, chopped (1/3 cup)	1 teaspoon onion powder *or* 1 tablespoon dried minced onion
Tomato Juice	1 cup	1/2 cup tomato sauce + 1/2 cup water
Tomato Sauce	2 cups	3/4 cup tomato paste + 1 cup water
Unsweetened Chocolate	1 square (1 ounce)	3 tablespoons baking cocoa + 1 tablespoon shortening *or* oil
Whole Milk	1 cup	1/2 cup evaporated milk + 1/2 cup water

General Recipe Index

This handy index lists every recipe by food category, major ingredient and/or cooking method, so you can easily locate recipes to suit your needs.

Alphabetical Index

This handy index lists every recipe in alphabetical order so you can easily find your favorites.